INNOVATIONS
The Comprehensive Infant Curriculum

Dedication

To my parents, my first and best teachers.

—Kay

To Mom and Dad, the smartest people I know.

Thanks for being my first and best teachers.

Love and appreciation,

—Linda

INNOVATIONS

The Comprehensive Infant CURRICULUM

A complete, interactive curriculum for infants from birth to 18 months

Illustrations: Joan Waites
Webs: K. Whelan Dery
Photographs: Kay Albrecht,
Nancy Alexander, and
CLEO Photography

Kay Albrecht / Linda G. Miller

Reprinted February 2015

Bulk Purchase

Gryphon House books are available at special discount when purchased in bulk for special premiums and sales promotions as well as for fund-raising use. Special editions or book excerpts also can be created to specification. For details, contact the Director of Marketing at the address on this page.

Library of Congress Cataloging-in-Publication Data

Albrecht, Kay M.
    Innovations : the Comprehensive... / Kay Albrecht, Linda G. Miller...
        p. cm.
    Includes bibliographical references and index
    ISBN 978-0-87659-213-7
    1. Infants--Development. 2. Infants--Care. 3. Infant psycology.
    4. Learning, Psychology of. I. Miller, Linda G. II. Title

HQ774.A634 2000
305.232—dc21   00-044277

Disclaimer

The publisher and the authors cannot be held responsible for injury, mishap, or damages incurred during the use of or because of the activities in this book. The authors recommend appropriate and reasonable supervision at all times based on the age and capability of each child.

Permission is granted to photocopy all forms and postcards for personal use or to hand out to parents.

ACKNOWLEDGMENTS

The road to completion of any book is certainly a long and winding one! Along the way, a number of people have profoundly influenced the direction of our work and our writing. We would like to acknowledge a few of them here.

No one has influenced our work as much as Magda Gerber, who gave us a benchmark for respectful teaching. Her eloquence in reminding teachers and parents about the importance of mutual respect forms the foundation of our ideas about infant curriculum.

Much of the work of figuring out infant development and curriculum as it is conceptualized here came from experiences at HeartsHome Early Learning Center. The school's cofounders Lynne Meservey, Jackie Legg, and Kay Albrecht, had a vision of providing high quality care and early childhood education to very young students before it was clear how to do so. Their work was important as a starting place for this book. But it was the teachers, particularly Carla Gwinn, Brenda Kerr, Melinda Rauch, Cheryl Peterson, and Martha Ward, who brought the vision to life. It is the inspiration of these and other HeartsHome teachers you see on the pages of this book. And, it is the parents of the school (particularly Julie Hempel, who guided us to true partnerships with parents; Chris Caprioli, who taught us to validate and appreciate the incredible competence of the HeartsHome teachers each and every day; and Ruth Johnson, who carries on the collaboration between teachers and parents today) who helped us along the winding road. Finally, we acknowledge the children whose growth and development led to discoveries about curriculum and whose success in elementary school proves that developmental education is great preparation for lifelong learning. Their experiences come to life on the pages and in the pictures of this book.

Linda Miller gratefully acknowledges the contributions of John Walden and Richard Brogdon for challenging her intellect, as well as helping formulate both her philosophy of education and very broad definition of curriculum. Appreciation also goes to the educators of the Catholic Schools, Archdiocese of Mobile, particularly, Tom Doyle, Gwen Byrd, and Sr. Martha Belke, for "adopting" a young Protestant and teaching her both to teach well and to love it.

Kay Albrecht thanks Ruth Highberger, whose introduction to the thrill of children's development, created the fork in the road that began the journey down this path. And Pam Wilder, who helped flesh out the concept of primary teaching in the real world of the classroom, long before there was any written information about how to do so.

Lastly, we gratefully acknowledge our families, who nurtured us, loved us, supported us, fed us, and picked up the slack for us while we wound our way down this road.

Table of Contents

Introduction 13

Chapter 1—Getting Started
Developmental Tasks 18
Innovations in Observation/Assessment 18
   Seeing Children as Unique 19
   Insuring Developmentally Appropriate Practice 19
   Using Observation and Assessment Strategies 21
   Giving Feedback to Parents about Developmental
      Growth 21
Innovations in Child Development 22
Innovations in Interactive Experiences 22
Innovations in Teaching 23
Innovations in Parent Partnerships 23
Innovations in Environments 23
Possibilities Plans 24
   Webs 24
   Activities and Experiences 24
   Concepts Learned 28
   Resources 29

Chapter 2—Separating from Parents
Introduction 31
Innovations in Observation/Assessment 32
   Observation/Assessment Instrument 32
Innovations in Child Development 34
   Principles of Developmental Theory 34
Innovations in Interactive Experiences 35
Innovations in Teaching 37
   Infant Temperament 37
   A Family Is a Family 38
   Gradual Enrollment 39
   Using Individualized Scheduling to Make the Day
      Go Smoothly 40
   Maximizing Interactions during Basic Care and
      Routines 41
   Coping with Crying 42
   Guidance and Discipline 44
      What Is Guidance and Discipline with
         Infants? 44
            Distraction 44
            Redirection 45
      Teacher Competencies to Support Separating
         from Parents 46
      Resources for Teachers 47
Innovations in Parent Partnerships 47
   School- or Teacher-initiated Possibilities 47
   Parent Participation Possibilities 48
   Parent Postcards 48
      Create a Separation and Reunion Ritual 49
      Arrival and Departure Routines ARE
         Transitions 50

Call If Your Plans Change 50
Develop a Backup Plan 51
Thumb and Finger Sucking 51
Always Say Goodbye 52
Pacifiers 53
Security Items 54
Resources for Parents 55
Innovations in Environments 55
   Creating a Warm, Inviting, Home-Like Setting 55
   Creation of Different Spaces within the
      Classroom 56
   Activities and Experiences vs. Centers 57

Possibilities Plan: Me! 59
Web 59
Me! Planning Pages 60
Dramatic Possibilities 62
Sensory/Art Possibilities 63
Curiosity Possibilities 64
Literacy Possibilities 65
Music Possibilities 68
Movement Possibilities 69
Outdoor Possibilities 70
Project Possibilities 71
Parent Participation Possibilities 72
   Parent Postcards 72
      Helping Your Baby Develop a Positive Sense
         of Self 72
      Every Child Is Unique 73
Concepts Learned in Me! 74
Resources 74
   Prop Boxes 74
   Picture File/Vocabulary 75
   Books 75
   Rhymes/Fingerplays 75
   Music/Songs 75
   Toys and Materials 76

Possibilities Plan: Mommies and Daddies 77
Web 77
Mommies and Daddies Planning Pages 78
Dramatic Possibilities 80
Sensory/Art Possibilities 82
Curiosity Possibilities 83
Literacy Possibilities 84
Music Possibilities 85
Movement Possibilities 86
Outdoor Possibilities 88
Project Possibilities 88
Parent Participation Possibilities 89
   Parent Postcards 90
      You Are Your Child's Best Teacher 90
      Including Children in Routines 91
Concepts Learned in Mommies and Daddies 92
Resources 92
   Prop Boxes 92

Picture File/Vocabulary 93
Books
Rhymes/Fingerplays 93
Music/Songs 93
Toys and Materials 94

Chapter 3—Connecting with School and Teacher

Introduction 95
Innovations in Observation/Assessment 96
    Observation/Assessment Instrument 96
Innovations in Child Development 98
    Development of Attachment 98
    Stages of Attachment 98
    Object Permanence 100
Innovations in Interactive Experiences 101
Innovations in Teaching 102
    Primary Teaching 102
        Components of Primary Teaching 104
    Continuity of Care 104
    Facilitating Adjustment and Attachment 105
    Validating What Moms and Dads Know 106
    Creating Memories and Recording
        Development 107
    Guidance and Discipline 107
        Ignoring as a Guidance Strategy 107
    Teacher Competencies to Support Connecting
        with School and Teacher 108
    Resources for Teachers 108
Innovations in Parent Partnerships 108
    School- or Teacher-initiated Possibilities 108
    Parent Participation Possibilities 109
    Parent Postcards 110
        Just How Long Will Adjustment Take? 110
        Facilitating Adjustment
        Attachment Behavior, Stage 1—Indiscriminate
            Attachment: What Parents Can Do 111
        We Are Now Partners 112
        Creating Partnerships—Two-way
            Communication 114
        Help! My Child Got Bitten!—Understanding
            Exploratory Biting 115
        What Can Teachers Do to Prevent Investigative/
            Exploratory Biting? 116
        What Can Parents Do to Prevent Investigative/
            Exploratory Biting? 117
    Resources for Parents 118
Innovations in Environments 118
    Multiple Sources of Stimulation 118
        Increasing and Decreasing Stimulation 119
        Oral Stimulation 119
        Mirrors 119
    Activities and Experiences vs. Centers 120
Possibilities Plan: Inside and Outside 121
    Web 121

Inside and Outside Planning Pages 122
Dramatic Possibilities 124
Sensory/Art Possibilities 125
Curiosity Possibilities 127
Literacy Possibilities 129
Music Possibilities 131
Movement Possibilities 132
Outdoor Possibilities 133
Project Possibilities 134
Parent Participation Possibilities 135
    Parent Postcards 136
        Controlling Transition Stress 136-7
        Car Seat Safety 138
Concepts Learned in Inside and Outside 139
Resources 139
    Prop Boxes 139
    Picture File/Vocabulary 140
    Books 140
    Rhymes/Fingerplays 140
    Music/Songs 140
    Toys and Materials 141
Possibilities Plan: Open and Close 143
Web 143
Open and Close Planning Pages 144
Dramatic Possibilities 146
Sensory/Art Possibilities 147
Curiosity Possibilities 148
Literacy Possibilities 150
Music Possibilities 151
Movement Possibilities 153
Outdoor Possibilities 154
Project Possibilities 154
Parent Participation Possibilities 155
    Parent Postcards 156
        Process Is the Goal 156
        Object Permanence 157
Concepts Learned in Open and Close 158
Resources 158
    Prop Boxes 158
    Picture File/Vocabulary 159
    Books 159
    Rhymes/Fingerplays 159
    Music/Songs 159
    Toys and Materials 160

Chapter 4—Relating to Self and Others

Introduction 161
Innovations in Observation/Assessment 162
    Observation/Assessment Instrument 162
Innovations in Child Development 164
    Social Development 164
    Play 164
    Piaget and Play 164
    Parten and Play 165

Vygotsky and Play   165
Innovations in Interactive Experiences   166
Innovations in Teaching   167
  Stage 2—Discriminate Attachment: What Teachers
    Can Do   167
  Encouraging Prosocial Behavior   168
  Making Toys and Finding Materials   168
  Guidance and Discipline   171
    Teaching Social Problem-Solving   171
      Patterning and Modeling with Infants   171
      Calling for Help   171
      Trading   172
      Taking Turns   172
      Walking Away   172
      Plan-making   173
    Handling Biting in the Classroom   173
      Prevention   174
      Anticipation   174
      Substitution   175
      Supervising and Shadowing Biters   175
      Responding to Biting   175
  Teacher Competencies to Support Babies Relating
    to School and Teacher   176
  Resources for Teachers
Innovations in Parent Partnerships   177
  School- or Teacher-initiated Possibilities   177
  Parent Postcards
    Attachment Stage 2—Discriminate Attachment:
      What Can Parents Do?   179
    What to Expect Socially from Your Baby   180
    Appropriate Expectations for Infants with
      Friends   181
    Action/Reaction Biting: Help! My Child Got
      Bitten, Again!   182
    What Can Teachers Do to Prevent Action/
      Reaction Biting?   183
    What Can Parents Do to Prevent Action/
      Reaction Biting?   184
    Learning Social Problem-Solving Step One:
      Calling for Help   185
  Resources for Parents   186
Innovations in Environments   186
  The Role of Play Props and Play Cues in
    Stimulating Play   186
  Guidance and Discipline   187
    Room Arrangement as a Guidance Strategy   187
  Activities and Experiences vs. Centers   188
Possibilities Plan: Big and Little   **189**
  Web   189
  Big and Little Planning Pages   190
  Dramatic Possibilities   192
  Sensory/Art Possibilities   193
  Curiosity Possibilities   195
  Literacy Possibilities   197
  Music Possibilities   199
  Movement Possibilities   200

  Outdoor Possibilities   201
  Project Possibilities   202
  Parent Participation Possibilities   203
    Parent Postcards   203
      Do Children Learn While They Play?   203
      Transmitting Values to Children   204
  Concepts Learned in Big and Little   204
  Resources   205
    Prop Boxes   205
    Picture File/Vocabulary   205
    Books   205
    Rhymes/Fingerplays   205
    Music/Songs   205
    Toys and Materials   206
Possibilities Plan: Cars, Trucks, and Trains   207
  Web   207
  Cars, Trucks, and Trains Planning Pages   208
  Dramatic Possibilities   210
  Sensory/Art Possibilities   211
  Curiosity Possibilities   212
  Literacy Possibilities   213
  Music Possibilities   215
  Movement Possibilities   216
  Outdoor Possibilities   216
  Project Possibilities   217
  Parent Participation Possibilities   218
    Parent Postcards   219
      Drive-time Activities   219
      Gender Role Stereotytping   220
      Preparing for Time Away from Your
        Child   221
  Concepts Learned in Cars, Trucks, and Trains   222
  Resources   222
    Prop Boxes   222
    Picture File/Vocabulary   222
    Books   223
    Rhymes/Fingerplays   223
    Music/Songs   223
    Toys and Materials   224

Chapter 5—Communicating with Parents, Teachers, and Friends

Introduction   225
Innovations in Observation/Assessment   226
  Observation/Assessment Instrument   227
Innovations in Child Development   228
  Brain Growth and Development   228
  Language Development   229
    Expressive and Receptive Language   231
  Intellectual Development   231
  Piaget's Sensori-motor Stages of Cognitive
    Development   232
Innovations in Interactive Experiences   233
Innovations in Teaching   234
  What Does Brain-based Care and Early Education

Look Like? 234
Stimulating Developmental Growth 235
Early Identification of Developmental
 Challenges 236
Techniques for Stimulating Language
 Development 237
What Does Attachment Have to Do with
 Intellectual and Language Development? 238
Separation Anxiety: What Teachers Can Do? 238
Simplifying Piaget 239
Multiple Intelligences 240
Books for Babies 242
Teacher Competencies to Support Communicating
with Parents, Teachers, and Friends 243
Resources for Teachers 243
Innovations in Parent Partnerships 244
School- or Teacher-initiated Possibilities 244
 Picture Book Exchange 244
 Trash as Treasure 244
 Coupon Exchange 244
 Visiting Reader 244
Parent Postcards 244
 What Is Developmentally Appropriate Care and
 Early Education for Infants?—The Role of the
 Teacher 245
 What Is Developmentally Appropriate Care and
 Early Education for Infants?—The Role of
 Curriculum (Activities and Experiences) 247
 Using Found and Discarded Items for Toys 248
 Good Books for Babies 249
 Attachment Stage 3—Separation Anxiety: What
 Can Parents Do? 250
 How Babies Learn 251
 The Amazing Infant Brain 252
 Supporting Brain Development at Home 253
 Appropriate Expectations for Learning Academic
 Skills 254
 Teaching Your Child to Read 255
 Teaching Your Child to Write 256
Resources for Parents 257
Innovations in Environments 257
Creating a Classroom that Values Multiple
 Intelligence 257
Activities and Experiences vs. Centers 258
Possibilities Plan: Storybook Classics 259
Web 259
Storybook Classics Planning Pages 260
Dramatic Possibilities 262
Sensory/Art Possibilities 263
Curiosity Possibilities 265
Literacy Possibilities 267
Music Possibilities 269
Movement Possibilities 270
Outdoor Possibilities 272
Project Possibilities 273
Parent Participation Possibilities 273

Parent Postcard 275
 Tips for Reading to Your Infant 275
Concepts Learned in Storybook Classics 276
Resources 276
 Prop Boxes 276
 Picture File/Vocabulary 277
 Books 277
 Rhymes/Fingerplays 277
 Music/Songs 277
 Toys and Materials 278
Possibilities Plan: Sounds 279
Web 279
Sounds Planning Pages 280
Dramatic Possibilities 282
Sensory/Art Possibilities 283
Curiosity Possibilities 284
Literacy Possibilities 286
Music Possibilities 287
Movement Possibilities 290
Outdoor Possibilities 292
Project Possibilities 293
Parent Participation Possibilities 293
 Parent Postcards 294
 Watch Those Ears! 294
 Sound Opportunities 295
Concepts Learned in Sounds 296
Resources 296
 Prop Boxes 296
 Picture File/Vocabulary 296
 Books 297
 Rhymes/Fingerplays 297
 Music/Songs 298
 Toys and Materials 298

Chapter 6—Moving Around
Introduction 299
Innovations in Observation/Assessment 300
 Observation/Assessment Instrument 300
Innovations in Child Development 301
 Physical Development 301
 Table of Physical Development Milestones 302
 Infant Nutrition 302
 What Do Infants Really Need to Eat? 302
 24 Hour Food Guide 303
 Breastfeeding Issues 303
 Formula-feeding Issues 304
 Infant Health 305
 Health Policies 305
 Illness and the Very Young Child 305
 Infant Safety 307
 Get a Choke Tube and Use It! 307
Innovations in Interactive Experiences 307
Innovations in Teaching 308
 Encouraging Independence and Autonomy 308
 Nutrition 309
 Introducing Solid Foods 309

Health   310
  Handwashing and Diapering Procedure   310
  Daily Health Conversations   311
  Making Determinations about Sending Children
    Home   312
Safety   314
  Bottle Safety at School   314
Guidance and Discipline   315
  Natural and Logical Consequences   315
  Setting Appropriate Limits   315
Teacher Competencies to Support Babies Learning
  to Move   318
Resources for Teachers   318
Innovativons in Parent Partnerships   319
  School- or Teacher-initiated Possibilities   319
  Parent Participation   319
  Parent Postcards   319
    Appropriate Expectations for Self-Control   320
    Natural and Logical Consequences   321
    Setting Appropriate Limits   322
    Coping with Ear Infections   324
  Resources for Parents   325
Innovations in Environments   325
  Environmental Sanitation   325
  Bringing Indoor Materials Outside   325
  Activities and Experiences vs. Centers   326

Possibilities Plan: Competent Me   327
  Web   327
  Competent Me Planning Pages   328
  Dramatic Possibilities   330
  Sensory/Art Possibilities   331
  Curiosity Possibilities   332
  Literacy Possibilities   334
  Music Possibilities   335
  Movement Possibilities   336
  Outdoor Possibilities   338
  Project Possibilities   339
  Parent Participation Possibilities   340
    Parent Postcards   341
      Encouraging Independence and
        Autonomy   341
      Continuing to Support Independence and
        Autonomy   342
  Concepts Learned in Competent Me   343
  Resources   343
    Prop Boxes   343
    Picture File/Vocabulary   344
    Books   344
    Rhymes/Fingerplays   344
    Music/Songs   344
    Toys and Materials   345

**Possibilities Plan: Windows, Walls, Doors,
and Hallways   347**
  Web   347
  Windows, Walls, Doors, and Hallways Planning
    Pages   348

Dramatic Possibilities   350
Sensory/Art Possibilities   352
Curiosity Possibilities   353
Literacy Possibilities   354
Music Possibilities   355
Movement Possibilities   356
Outdoor Possibilities   358
Project Possibilities   359
Parent Participation Possibilities   360
  Parent Postcards   361
    Childproofing Your Home   361
Concepts Learned in Doors, Walls, Windows, and
  Hallways   362
Resources   362
  Prop Boxes   362
  Picture File/Vocabulary   363
  Books   363
  Rhymes/Fingerplays   363
  Music/Songs   363
  Toys and Materials   364

Chapter 7—Expressing Feelings with Parents, Teachers, and Friends

Introduction   365
Innovations in Observation/Assessment   366
  Observation/Assessment Instrument   366
Innovations in Child Development   367
  Emotional Development   367
Innovations in Interactive Experiences   369
Innovations in Teaching   370
  Stimulating Emotional Development   370
  Floor Time as a Practice   372
  Beyond Products: Supporting Emerging Creativity
    in Young Children   373
  Guidance and Discipline   374
    Managing Normal Aggression in Very Young
      Children   374
  Conferencing with Parents of Infants   375
    Communicating with Parents of Infants Is
      Different   375
    Conferences are Parent Education   376
    Reconceptualizing Conferencing   377
    Formal Conferences with Written
      Documentation   377
    Informal Conferences with Written
      Documentation   378
    Formal Oral Conferences   379
    Informal Oral Conferences   380
    Preventing Child Abuse and Neglect   381
  Teacher Competencies to Support Infants
    Expressing Feelings with Parents, Teachers, and
    Friends   382
  Resources for Teachers   383
Innovations in Parent Partnerships   383
  School- or Teacher-Initiated Activities   383

Parent Postcards   384
  Managing Normal Aggression in Very Young
    Children   384
Resources for Parents   386
Innovations in Environments   386
  Windows and Natural Light   386
  Not Too Much Stuff   386
  Activities and Experiences vs. Centers   387
Possibilities Plan: Senses   389
Web   389
Senses Planning Pages   390
Dramatic Possibilities   392
Sensory/Art Possibilities   394
Curiosity Possibilities   395
Literacy Possibilities   397
Music Possibilities   399
Movement Possibilities   401
Outdoor Possibilities   402
Project Possibilities   402
Parent Participation Possibilities   403
  Parent Postcards   404
      Cooking with Kids   404
Concepts Learned in Senses   405
Resources   405
  Prop Boxes   405
  Picture File/Vocabulary   406
  Books   406

Rhymes/Fingerplays   406
Music/Songs   406
Toys and Materials   407
**Possibilities Plan: Bubbles, Mud, and
  Puddles   409**
Web   409
Bubbles, Mud, and Puddles Planning Pages   410
Dramatic Possibilities   412
Sensory/Art Possibilities   412
Curiosity Possibilities   414
Literacy Possibilities   415
Music Possibilities   417
Movement Possibilities   419
Outdoor Possibilities   420
Project Possibilities   421
Parent Participation Possibilities   421
  Parent Postcards   423
      When Your Child's Teacher Leaves   423
      When Your Child's Day Is Lengthened   424
Concepts Learned in Bubbles, Puddles, and
  Mud   424
Resources   425
  Prop Boxes   425
  Picture File/Vocabulary   425
  Books   425
  Rhymes/Fingerplays   425
  Music/Songs   425
  Toys and Materials   426

Appendix   427

Index   475

Introduction

As "old" educators who have been around the education block more than a few times, we have long searched for curriculum to meet the incredibly broad span of needs for teachers, parents, and the children who benefit from their efforts. Too often we have received books that have been called "curriculum," but aren't. Some "curriculum" books provide activities or ideas and expect the teacher to determine the appropriate developmental skills. Others approach skill acquisition as the result of didactic teaching. Some educators equate "curriculum" with just the content that is included, as if all children need are facts to grow and learn.

All of these approaches to "curriculum" are, in our view, far too narrow. At the very least, curriculum for young children must include teacher observation, assessment, training, and responsivity; parent participation, education, and an appreciation of parents as primary educators; integration of environment, toys, materials, health and safety, and room arrangement; grounding in historical and emerging knowledge of child growth and development; and a sensitivity to the infant's experiences, interactions, reactions, cues, interests, including an understanding of the infant's temperament.

The focus of curriculum, we feel, must be squarely on the child and include all of the elements mentioned thus far. ***This curriculum advocates thinking about and planning for everything that can, by the nature of the setting (school vs. home), contribute to child development and the teacher's relationship with the child and the family.*** We think this is a paradigm shift, a way to move the discussion of curriculum out of the narrow range that leads to evaluating children's potential solely by standardized testing toward a more comprehensive approach that embraces many different ways of knowing and learning. However, the need for teachers to have something that is easy to use regardless of background is essential.

Innovations: The Comprehensive Infant Curriculum meets the needs of teachers by providing everything to implement what we feel is "real" curriculum. The diagram on the next page illustrates what we believe is the purpose of curriculum.

Everything involved in the curriculum works together to benefit the child. Observation and assessment come first, so nothing happens to the child before the teacher learns through observation where the child is developmentally. Our view of curriculum is comprehensive—encompassing all aspects of growing and learning. It embraces the inter-relationship among teacher's planning, the child's interest and response, child development, the child's family context and culture, and the reactions and interactions of the adults and other children.

The last aspect of curriculum we embrace is the open-ended nature of the process. When activities or experiences are presented to very young children, we never know what they are going to do with the experience! This divergence is desirable, and we have included it in two ways. One is by the use of curriculum webs related to each Possibilities Plan, reinforcing once again that we cannot predict where a child's interest might take us. Thus, we need to be prepared to consider alternatives so that we can recognize them when they emerge (an idea our colleagues at Reggio Emilia also embrace). The other is the focus on the child's response as a cue to

what to do next or where to go next. This is the dance between teacher and child—the gentle interplay that occurs over and over again during the day. Following children's interests is at the heart of emergent infant curriculum and is central to our view of curriculum with infants.

It is our wish that **Innovations: The Comprehensive Infant Curriculum** insures that infants will be supported in learning, that teachers will understand and embrace educating infants in a comprehensive way, and that parents and teachers will work cooperatively to make sure it all comes together.

Developmental Tasks

Observations and Assessment

Child Development

Interactive Experiences

Teaching

Parent Participation and

Involvement

Environment

Activities and Experiences

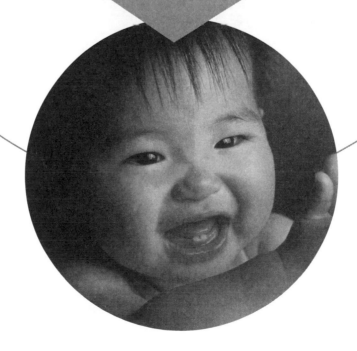

CHAPTER 1
Getting Started

Innovations: The Comprehensive Infant Curriculum is designed for teachers of children ages birth through 18 months. For the purposes of this curriculum, infancy lasts until 18 months, even though children are becoming mobile before this age. In this chapter, Getting Started, you will prepare to use this book by exploring each component of the curriculum.

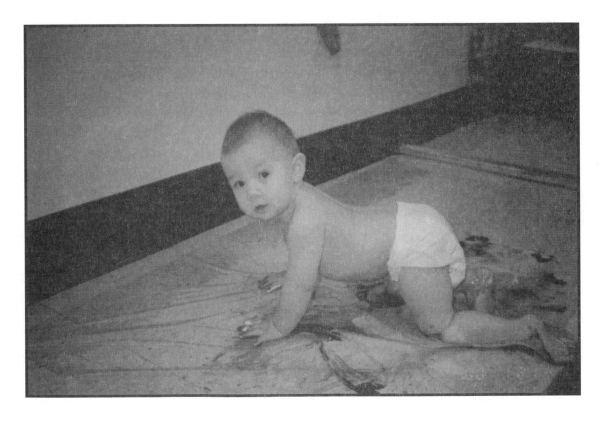

DEVELOPMENTAL TASKS

Chapters 2-7 each identify a major developmental challenge children experience as they learn and grow. Most curriculum models focus on the sequence of emerging development. This curriculum, however, focuses on how development is encouraged, facilitated, and stimulated. It is interactional, viewing development as the complex interplay between the child and his world.

A child's temperament, the quality of the interactions with adults (such as parents, family members, and teachers), interactions with the environment, and interactions with friends are major components of this curriculum. The intent of *Innovations: The Comprehensive Infant Curriculum* is to identify the major interactional tasks in infancy and construct a developmentally appropriate approach to dealing with each task though interactions, experiences, and activities.

The tasks are loosely sequential—that is, a teacher of infants could start with Chapter 2, Separating from Parents, when the child enrolls at school or at the beginning of the school year, and continue to Chapter 3, Connecting with School and Teacher, then to Chapter 4, Relating to Self and Others, and so on. Or, teachers can begin by observing children to match emerging tasks with each child's current developmental experience.

The developmental tasks of this curriculum are Separating from Parents (Chapter 2); Connecting with School and Teacher (Chapter 3); Relating to Self and Others (Chapter 4); Communicating with Parents, Teachers, and Friends (Chapter 5); Moving Around (Chapter 6); and Expressing Feelings with Parents, Teachers, and Friends (Chapter 7).

INNOVATIONS IN OBSERVATION/ASSESSMENT

The National Association for the Education of Young Children, in its position statement on standardized testing, states that "nonstandardized assessments such as systematic observation, anecdotal records, and local and nationally developed checklists play a vital role in planning and implementing instruction and placement of children" (NAEYC, 1988). This curriculum relies on nonstandardized assessment techniques including systematic observation, anecdotal notes, and a normative checklist to accomplish a number of different goals. The first goal is to help the teachers and parents see the children as individuals who have unique skill repertoires. The second goal is to insure developmentally appropriate practice. The third goal is to guide curriculum development that is sensitive to children's emerging skills, but does not frustrate or over-stimulate.

Seeing Children as Unique

Comparison of children begins to occur early in infant programs. Parents, who visit the classroom upon arrival and departure, get to know the children in the group and notice the developmental changes in children. Teachers, who have watched a number of children grow and develop, sometimes compare children across time. Parents, who are watching their own child grow up in a group, often compare their child's development with the development of other children in the group. Using nonstandardized assessment techniques, particularly developmental observation, notes, and assessments, helps parents and teachers see their children as individuals. When used as an integrated part of a high-quality program, developmental assessments show progress in relation to each child's personal skill repertoire rather than comparing children to each other.

The results of systematic observation, anecdotal notes, and developmental assessments provide a common ground between parents and teachers. As they watch skills emerge, it is logical to talk about new skills and how changes give further insight into the child's individuality. Discussion of developmental maturation also serves as a marvelous parent education tool. As parents see their child grow and develop, they come to understand the sporadic nature of development as well as to see ways to enhance further development during time with their children. The developmental approach focuses parents' attention on the things children **can** do, instead of the things they cannot. This focus on successful activities and accomplishments enhances the child's self-esteem (Curry & Johnson, 1990).

An unexpected benefit of using assessment techniques like these can occur. When parents have frequent opportunities to recognize the developmental progress children are making and discuss that progress with their child's teacher, they place a higher value on what goes on during the school day. Frequent communication about emerging and developing skills also serves to alleviate parental guilt and validate the parents' decision on the choice of schools.

Insuring Developmentally Appropriate Practice

Developmentally appropriate practice guides us to modify programs to fit children rather than requiring children to fit programs. The foundation of developmentally appropriate practice is

- Knowledge of where each individual child is on the developmental continuum in each area of development, and
- Understanding of the individuality of each child's development (Bredekamp & Copple, 1997; Bredekamp, 1987).

Developmental assessments guide teachers to gather this information in a truly non-invasive fashion—by careful observation of children involved in daily activities.

This approach also helps to organize teacher behavior. Working with very young children requires that teachers take pleasure in the changes they see as children grow and develop. But, there are times when the sheer demands of the classroom can seem overwhelming. Developmental assessment techniques continually orient teachers' behavior toward certain goals and allow teachers to see progress as they merge routines (such as diapering and feeding children) with stimulation (such as reading books, playing with interesting objects, interacting with caregivers). Success becomes the focus of teachers' interactions with children. Because teachers are carefully observing emerging skills, they can give children repeated experiences with success— doing things the child does well again and again. Success leads to enthusiasm toward new attempts and has a positive impact on the child's emerging sense of self.

This approach offers another benefit. Developmental assessment tools serve as passive training tools for new or less experienced teachers to gain confidence and skill in talking to parents about how children grow and learn. Using developmental assessments helps teachers learn patterns of development, provides a common vocabulary, and builds skills in exchanging that information with parents.

Children in full-day programs have to "live" in their school settings (Greenman, 1988). Because this is the case, stimulation activities must be balanced across the important dimensions of **activity** (quiet or active), **location** (indoor or outdoor), and **initiator** (child-initiated or adult-initiated) (Bredekamp, 1997; National Academy of Early Childhood Programs, 1991). Knowledge of where each child is on the developmental continuum helps teachers keep a good balance among these important dimensions. Using observation and assessment techniques helps teachers match program and stimulation needs to the developmental level of each child—preventing frustration and insuring challenge.

Assessment requires that teachers observe children and use their observations to guide their interactions and the activities and experiences that they plan for children. Most of the indicators on the assessment instruments emerge from child development theory or principles of development and learning during the early years. Skills on the continuum are categorized as 0-6 months, 6-12 months, and 12-18 months. These ages are meant to serve as guides because overlap exists throughout the continuum. In other words, a 12-month-old could still be working on some 6-

12 month skills while having already perfected some 12-18 month skills. Teachers must remember this important developmental reality.

Using Observation and Assessment Strategies

Parent reports of children's development form the first source of anecdotal data collected by teachers. This information is gathered during the enrollment process and sets the stage for the regular exchange of developmental information between parents and teachers.

Teacher observations and anecdotal notes are the next source of information about the child. As teachers go about the day, they observe the child and make anecdotal notes. These notes and observations become the foundation of curriculum planning.

Assessment identifies which skills children have and what children are doing. Assessments are used to identify where a child is developmentally so that teachers can document, validate, and celebrate skills.

Assessments are designed to help teachers observe the different areas of development and follow changes. They are not designed to compare one child to another but instead to identify each child's repertoire of skills. The results of a teacher's observations of the children in his group are then used to plan developmentally appropriate educational activities and experiences.

Infants are very easy to assess. They grow and change quickly through maturation as well as through developmental stimulation. For this reason, tools for collecting information (including checklists, note paper, and pens) need to be kept handy so that teachers can easily record data about children's emerging skills and identify the next skill to begin challenging.

Giving Feedback to Parents about Developmental Growth

There are many ways to share developmental information with parents. Suggestions are included for a daily or weekly technique using written notes (see Communications Sheet in the Appendix on page 430), quarterly or semi-annual sharing that takes place in parent-teacher conferences, conversations that take place during parent participation activities, posting developmental banners, sharing via documentations of children's work, and many other methods. Look in the Innovations in Parent Partnerships and the Possibilities Plans sections of the curriculum for more information.

All the developmental tasks are combined into a complete assessment instrument contained in the Appendix on pages 435-440. This can be used cumulatively to document individual children's movement through these developmental tasks.

INNOVATIONS IN CHILD DEVELOPMENT

Understanding child development theory and research is an important aspect of curriculum. This section explains the underlying theory or child development principles, best practices, or content knowledge leading to specific developmental tasks. It also provides a framework for specific activities that come later. Included in this section are topics such as separation anxiety, primary teaching, literacy development, infant personalities, and social development theories. Teachers can discover the *"what"* in the developmental tasks and the activity sections, but this section on child development provides the *"why."*

INNOVATIONS IN INTERACTIVE EXPERIENCES

Children's experiences at school have so much to do with the way they grow and develop. If they experience school as negative, frustrating, or insensitive, they will view the learning process as overwhelming and insurmountable. If, on the other hand, their experiences are supportive, nurturing, and positive, human development has an almost perfect plan for growing and learning. In fact, during the first three years, development unfolds naturally for most children.

This curriculum advocates thinking about and planning for everything that can, by the nature of the setting (school vs. home), contribute to a child's development and the teacher's relationship with the child and the family. Further, it grounds planning in a developmental, interactive, theoretical framework. Finally, it views all children's experiences, not just formal experiences, as crucial. Children are always learning, and it is the teacher's job to support that learning in whatever forms it may take.

Listed in Innovations in Interactive Experiences are the types of experiences that teachers must observe, plan, support, and provide. Many opportunities to capitalize on children's experiences as they happen occur during the school day. Because they are so important, these experiences should appear on curriculum plans as a validation of these crucial, often spontaneous experiences.

INNOVATIONS IN TEACHING

This section discusses important topics related to the developmental task that are important for teachers to know. Topics covered in the Parent Postcards in the Innovations in Parent Partnerships section are discussed from the teacher's point of view. Expansions include the teacher's role in supporting parents as they learn more about parenting.

Teacher Competencies provides a list of behaviors teachers can use to evaluate themselves in the classroom. Use these skills lists to evaluate your own skill level or to have a mentor or supervisor assess your teaching competence.

Resources for Teachers contains additional suggested reading for teachers. (Complete bibliographic information for references and resources is located in the Appendix on page 469-474.)

INNOVATIONS IN PARENT PARTNERSHIPS

This section gives examples of school-initiated possibilities (such as collecting materials to be made into toys for the classroom) and examples of parent participation possibilities (such as an invitation to parents to come to a parent meeting). In addition, Innovations in Parent Partnerships includes Parent Postcards, which can be shared with parents as they show an interest in the topic of the postcard, at appropriate times during the enrollment cycle, or as developmental issues arise with individual children. A sample chronological dissemination schedule is included in the Appendix on pages 441-444.

INNOVATIONS IN ENVIRONMENTS

Most early childhood educators think of interest or learning centers as an essential part of any classroom setting. Yet, environments for infants are different because they cannot choose to go to different areas until they are mobile. For this reason, teachers must bring the activities and experiences to the child, or they must assist the child in going to where the activities are. A wide range of activities and experiences must be available to infants, but the environments are different.

POSSIBILITIES PLANS

Each of the six developmental tasks contains related curriculum activity plans, called Possibilities Plans. These plans give teachers a way to structure their activities and experiences with children and give parents opportunities to support teacher activities and learn songs, poems, and rhymes that babies are experiencing in the classroom. Plans can be used in total, or activities and experiences can be selected and pulled out to use as appropriate with children in your group. In addition, Possibilities Plans are designed to be expanded—keeping your planning and implementation of curriculum fresh and new.

Webs

Webs show how this quality curriculum encourages open-ended planning. Because *Innovations: The Comprehensive Infant Curriculum* is interactional, teachers adjust their plans according to how babies respond to the experiences. For example, the teacher's plan may focus on "face," but children's interests may change the teacher's plan to focus on "eyes." Webbing opens up the possibilities for interactions, experiences, and activities with babies.

Planning pages help teachers with curriculum planning follow the web. Use these pages to plan for the individual and group needs of infants. Included are lists of possibilities, books, rhymes, fingerplays, music, and appropriate prop boxes.

Activities and Experiences

Each plan is accompanied by numerous activities, called Possibilities, so teachers can plan quality experiences for children in the classroom. Age ranges listed after each activity provide guidelines for ages that children can benefit from the different activities. The same age ranges presented in the developmental tasks are used in the activities. Remember that these ages are just estimates—your knowledge of where your children are on the assessment continuum will help you find activities that match.

This book does not use the traditional idea of interest areas because infants are not yet able to choose to go to different areas of the room. After all, many of them are not yet mobile—much less walking. It is the teacher's responsibility to bring the activity to the infant or carry the infant to the activity.

New situations are interesting to infants, especially when they are in a secure environment where they feel confident to try new things. Teachers often interact both with the baby and with the new toy or situation (called triangulation). In this way the baby finds interest in the novelty, while feeling the security of having a teacher near.

Activities are included in the following categories:

Dramatic Possibilities—Infants are delighted by dolls and stuffed animals. Provide a variety of simple, soft dolls representing a variety of ethnicities. Everything should be durable and washable, without eyes or parts that can come off with persistent handling. Beyond dolls, babies need props like the ones they see in the real world, especially things associated with Mom or Dad (purses, hats, bracelets, toy key rings). The teacher's role includes supplying play cues, participating with children as they play, and labeling what infants do as they take on different roles. Activities contribute to babies' vocabulary development and to their comprehension of the real world.

Sensory/Art Possibilities—Sensory, water, and floating playthings are a mainstay of an infant program. Water is soothing; water toys stimulate play; and the splashing and slapping of water produce interesting reactions. Small wading pools make good dividers of activity space and make cleanup easier because spills are contained. Use smaller tubs with only one or two inches of water inside. Change the water and disinfect the container before another child uses it. The teacher's role includes very close supervision. This is an activity brought out and put away by the teacher who gauges when a child has had enough and is ready to get warm and dry and go on to another activity.

Art activities for young children are really sensory in nature. Very young children (unlike adults) don't care about how an art activity turns out. They are experiencing the moment—enjoying the feel of the finger paint, the smell of the crayons, the texture of the paper.

Curiosity Possibilities—Young children are curious about the world in which they live. They want to find out what is in it and how everything works. They enjoy exploring new things in the environment, and rattles are often favorite toys. An assortment of rattles is a delightful means of interacting with young babies. They love to use long, round, skinny, hard, squeezable, noisy, or musical rattles. They can look, chew, bang, shake, and listen as they enjoy the rattles. The teacher's role is to present various rattles to the child, rattle the toy, and then allow the baby to take over. A toy suspension bar is extremely useful for hanging reaching and grasping rattles over infants while they lay on their backs or in bouncy seats.

Repetition of movement and activity is vitally important for brain development, and rattles are perfect toys to stimulate repeated actions. Repetition helps babies "wire" their brains and strengthens neural pathways that are just developing. Lots of time with these first action/reaction toys that are easily gripped, mouthed, and kicked is clearly a good use of time.

Another type of curiosity or problem-solving experience for young children includes opportunities for reaching and grasping. This will foster independent play and a variety of motor skills such as pulling, batting, and swinging arms and legs. Include materials such as mobiles, cradle gyms, objects suspended on strings, and playthings attached to the wall. The teacher's role is predominantly one of preparation. The teacher models grasping and reaching behavior and positions non-mobile children within reach of the arranged materials.

Focal points at different ages.

Newborns' distance vision is blurred. The focal point is eight to ten inches from the face. After the age of one, vision is as good as normal adult vision.

The next type of problem-solving experiences for young children involve experimenting with interesting materials, both old favorites and new ones. Easy manipulatives and small square blocks are also good. Plastic jars with tops to undo, simple sorting, surprise toys such as a jack-in-the-box, and busy boxes with a variety of things to turn and push are all interesting. The role of the teacher is to interact with the children and provide plenty of invitations to play.

The last type of problem-solving experiences for infants involves mirrors. An important part of the infant environment is strategically placed non-breakable mirrors. At children's eye level, they are used to catch a view of a teacher who may be busy with another child, discover oneself, look at other children, and observe the surrounding environment. Teachers at Reggio Emilia view the child's own image as one of the most interesting images children explore during the first three years (Edwards, Forman, and Gandini, 1998).

Literacy Possibilities—Story and picture books provide images for babies to view without having to be directly involved in play with others. Provide access to sturdy, inexpensive, replaceable books, including cloth books, board books, and plastic books. Display them to the right or the left of the child's shoulders to stimulate gazing and focusing skills.

Give children the opportunity to experiment with and learn about books on their own, actively interacting with them. For infants, that may simply mean mouthing and chewing on books. These early experiences with books as sources of interesting images and stimulation form the foundation of literacy. Later, when babies grow up, teachers can help children learn about the care and maintenance of books.

Teachers should read to babies every day. Make reading books a priority with babies, one at a time or in pairs and trios. Additional literacy opportunities exist with rhymes and fingerplays. The rhyme and repetition in language are important for literacy development. Include many opportunities during the day to involve babies in this kind of interaction.

Music Possibilities—Music is a natural, enjoyable part of the environment for young children. Provide a variety of music (through singing, as well as tapes or CDs) at different times during the day. Avoid playing background music (babies cannot filter out noise as easily as adults can). Background music will result in escalating the noise level as the day continues. Instead, use music to accomplish specific things: transitions, calming for quiet time, and changing the pace of the day when the atmosphere becomes too energetic or not energetic enough. Music is wonderful while children are involved in sensory activities and even when they are playing outside. Recent research suggests that classical music supports brain development and may enhance future math skills.

Movement Possibilities—Babies always need a clean, padded area where they can be placed to stretch, wiggle, turn over, push up, and rest. A gym mat

with a washable cover works well. Padded stools or hassocks are excellent for babies to use to pull to a stand and to cruise along the edges. The teacher's role is interactive. Particularly with emerging skills, teachers should help infants practice skills, yet be near enough to provide support and prevent serious spills and tumbles.

Outdoor Possibilities—Outdoor time is an important part of the day for very young children. The fresh air is a nice change from the closed environment of the classroom. In addition, activities that are moved from the inside to the outside take on a new meaning. The sounds of the neighborhood, the way light changes because of clouds or shade, the feel of the breeze—all add to the richness of the outdoor experience. Outdoor experiences also provide a change of pace and variety for the teacher. Outdoors, the teacher's role is interactive, inviting children to learn as they explore.

Project Possibilities—Projects are repeated activities or experiences that stretch over a period of time—instead of activities that take place in a short amount of time in one day. Projects are important because they provide continuity of experience, as well as an opportunity to practice, perfect, and enjoy experiences again and again. Unlike projects with preschoolers, which often focus on content knowledge and how children interpret this knowledge, projects with infants almost always focus on experiences.

Parent Participation Possibilities—Parents are their child's first and most important teachers. For this reason their participation in their child's school experience is crucial. Parent participation suggestions are listed here, many that are related to the Possibilities Plan. More Parent Postcards are included in the Possibilities Plan sections. These Postcards support the plan and are natural extensions of the activities and experiences that teachers are providing for infants in the classroom.

Concepts Learned

What are infants learning from our choices of activities and experiences? Teachers often see the range and depth of children's learning in the classroom, but parents may fail to see children's playful activities as learning. Concepts Learned addresses this reality. It includes a list of concepts that infants are likely learning because of the planned environment, planned interactions, and planned experiences. Concepts Learned are included in the Resource section of each Possibilities Plan. (Full-page versions that are suitable for copying for parents are included for all Possibilities Plans on pages 452-463.)

The list of Concepts Learned includes content knowledge as well as process knowledge. Content knowledge includes discrete facts or concepts. Process knowledge is "how-to" knowledge learned through practice. Full-page versions of these lists are in the Appendix on pages 452-463. Post them in the classroom for parents to read, send the list home to parents, or use them during parent conferences.

Resources

The Resources section that accompanies each plan provides additional sources for help in planning. Because the classroom environment is an important part of a child's curriculum, suggested prop box materials, fingerplays, books, songs, and toys and materials important for each Possibilities Plan are included.

There is a Picture File/Vocabulary section for each plan. Babies are building cognitive images of the things they are experiencing. Using pictures helps give children a variety of different images. It also adds information to the images that they have already experienced. Collect pictures from a variety of sources, including magazines, calendars, and so on. Look for pictures that show one image clearly. Laminate them or cover with clear contact paper to extend their life, and store them in file folders or boxes. Use these pictures to provide stimulation of cognitive images. Teachers can also use photographs and pictures as support for emerging literacy skills by pointing and naming images in the pictures.

Purchased items are traditional equipment and supplies necessary for supporting the activities in the plan. A list of gathered items that are important for supporting each plan is also included. Although these materials are generally free or inexpensive, it does take time to collect them. Enlist the help of parents in gathering items for use in the classroom.

CHAPTER 2

Separating from Parents

INTRODUCTION

Separating is a crucial developmental task of the first three years of life. Birth itself is the first separation experience an infant has—separating from the warm, protective uterine environment of the mother's body to experience the world outside.

After this first experience, separating becomes a regular and frequent occurrence for infants: separating from the breast or bottle when feeding time is over, separating from Mom when holding time is over, separating from warm clothing to take a bath, separating from a familiar position to be moved around, and so on. Separating continues as infants learn to separate from favorite people, from home, and from favorite things such as toys or security items.

Separating is also the first step in the long process of becoming an autonomous, independent person. Children's success in moving through the developmental task of separating has lifelong implications. When children have positive and supported experiences with separation, they learn to trust the human world in which they live. If instead, they have frustrating and unresponsive experiences with separating, they will learn to mistrust this new world (Erickson, 1963). Basic trust in the world as a responsive, caring place creates a sense of security upon which development can unfold.

INNOVATIONS IN OBSERVATION/ASSESSMENT

Observation/Assessment Instrument

The assessment instrument on the next page is not just a skills checklist. Instead it is designed to guide the teacher's observation of children's development through major interactive tasks of infancy. The assessment's focus is on what IS happening, not just what should happen or what will happen. Use this assessment to lead to developmentally appropriate practice.

	0-6 months	**6-12 months**		**12-18 months**
S1	a. Little or no experience with separating from Mom and Dad; accepts sensitive care from substitute.	b. Some experience with separating from Mom and Dad; prefers familiar caregiver, but accepts sensitive care from substitute.	c. More experience with separating from Mom and Dad; resists separating; shows distress upon separation, and takes time to adjust.	d. Experienced with separating from Mom and Dad; resists initial separation, but adjusts after only a few moments.
S2	a. Startled by new sounds, smells, and people.	b. Orients toward new or interesting stimuli.		c. Seeks new and interesting stimuli.
S3	a. Accepts transitions without notice.	b. Reacts with discomfort during the transition.	c. Resists transition preparation as well as the transition.	d. Anticipates transitions when preparation activities begin. If preparation is to a preferred, familiar activity, transition is accepted.
S4	a. Displays indiscriminate attachment; will accept sensitive care from most familiar adults; exhibits preference for Mom, Dad, or familiar caregiver if present.	b. Displays discriminate attachment; will still accept care from sensitive caregivers, but prefers care from Mom, Dad, or familiar caregivers.		c. Separation anxiety emerges; resists approaches by unfamiliar adults and resists separation from Mom, Dad, and familiar caregivers. Cries, clings, calls for parents when they leave the child's view.
S5	a. Unpredictable daily schedule.	b. Patterns in daily schedule emerge around eating and sleeping.		c. Daily schedule is predictable. Eating and sleeping patterns are relatively stable and predictable.
S6	a. Feeds from breast or bottle.	b. Begins to take baby food from a spoon; begins to sip from a cup.		c. Drinks from bottle and/or cup; eats finger foods.
S7	a. Plays with objects within visual field; bats at objects with hands and feet.	b. Manipulates, mouths, and plays with objects; likes action/reaction toys. Plays with objects then drops them to move on to new objects. May return to objects again and again.		c. Plays with favorite things again and again. Likes to dump out objects and play with them on the floor. Considers all objects and toys in the environment personal play choices, even when being played with by others.

INNOVATIONS IN CHILD DEVELOPMENT

Principles of Developmental Theory

Which of the following diagrams do you think best represents the way infants develop?

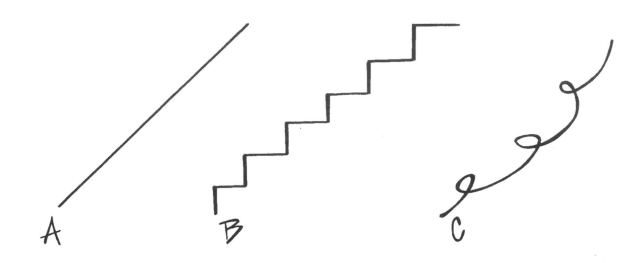

The answer is C. Development is a continuous though uneven cycle—a cycle of ever-increasing skills and abilities where each period of growth is preceded by a brief, sometimes turbulent regression. This development is guided by three underlying principles that help explain the amazing changes that take place during infancy.

The first principle is that growth follows a universal and predictable sequence. Milestones of development can be observed and used to track children's progress along the growth continuums. The predictability of development can be seen in each area of development—physical, social/emotional, and intellectual (which includes cognitive and language development). For example, in the physical area, development proceeds from sitting to crawling to pulling to a stand to walking. Every child follows this same typical pattern of development.

The second principle of development is that each child has an individual pattern and timing of growth. Although the sequence is predictable, each child's individual progress through the sequence is subject to variation. For example, one child may pull to a stand and walk at 7 or 8 months while another may do so at 12-13 months.

The sporadic and uneven nature of development is a part of the principle. Developmental growth seems to come in spurts. A child might work on physical development until she can pull to a stand and walk and then move on to language development or cognitive skill acquisition. Or, a child might make no observable developmental progress at all for a few weeks and then all of a sudden make major strides, seemingly all at once. It is this component of development that illustrates the uniqueness of each child.

The third principle is that development proceeds from the simple to the complex or from the general to the specific. Simple skills must be acquired before more complex ones can be attempted. For example, children always eat first with their fingers before attempting to use a spoon or fork. Controlling fingers is a simpler task than controlling an extension of the fingers, in this case, the fork.

INNOVATIONS IN INTERACTIVE EXPERIENCES

Children's experiences at school have so much to do with the way they will grow and develop. If they experience school as negative, frustrating, or insensitive, they will view the learning process as overwhelming and insurmountable. If, on the other hand, their experiences are supportive, nurturing, and positive, human development has an almost perfect plan for growing and learning. In fact, during the first three years, development unfolds naturally for most children.

This curriculum advocates thinking about and planning for everything that can, by the nature of the setting (school vs. home), contribute to children's development and the teacher's relationship with children and their families.

Many teachers view the activities they plan as the most important part of their job. Although these tasks are important, remember that infants are experiencing all the time—not just when teachers are providing direct stimulation. What is outside the realm of structured activities in the classroom (for example, a child who takes longer to prepare to transition to another place, a child who naps longer or shorter than expected, a child who is suddenly fascinated with an earthworm) is all curriculum. Children are always learning, and it is the teacher's job to support that learning in whatever forms it may take.

Life's minutiae build to create experiences. Infant teachers must be attuned to these everyday, yet important, experiences. They are truly the foundation upon which crucial skills and abilities grow. Think about the following list of experiences, and make sure that the classroom reflects many of them.

☐ Prepare children for transitions. Until they have a great deal more experience with change, infants will struggle each time there is a transition. Talk to infants about what is going to happen to them next and tell them what is happening as it happens (or unfolds).

☐ Leave a written record. Leave a written record for the teacher who is covering breaks or at the end of the day. This can take the form of a Communication Sheet (see Appendix pages 428-429) or a spiral notebook with notes about what the child might need next.

☐ Watch the tone of your voice and your non-verbal cues during interactions. Match what you say with the way you say it and what you do with the way you do it.

☐ Support children as they experience new stimuli. When new things are happening in the school environment, infants need support in taking in the new stimuli. Sometimes this support is preparatory—like warning a baby that the fire alarm is going to go off in a minute and make a loud noise, or reminding children that you are going to pick them up from a comfortable position to move them to the stroller for a ride.

☐ Use routines as a pleasant time for interaction and learning. Take time with diapering, feeding, and playing together. These intimate moments require connections and warm interactions.

☐ Provide support physically as well as visually as new things are experienced. Regardless of temperament, children benefit from being close to someone whom they trust while new experiences are being offered.

Look at the assessment instrument for separating on page 435. At the left side, almost all of the milestones are grounded in the baby's reaction to new experiences—with separation, stimuli, and schedule. As children age, they develop more skills and abilities, just because of experience.

As you complete curriculum planning for the children in your classroom, remember to plan for these types of interactive experiences. Put them on your planning form (pages 450-451). Use the Communication Sheet (pages 428-429) to let parents know that these experiences occurred.

Take the time to be with the infants in your classroom—really be with them. Make every interaction matter, both to you and the baby. When teachers invest in quality time with infants, all kinds of benefits result. Babies are easier to soothe, cues are easier to read, and infants can tolerate more challenge and frustration. Remember, every experience matters!

INNOVATIONS IN TEACHING

Infant Temperament

Regardless of the imprint of biology, environment, parents, and culture, every child is born with a personality—a temperament that guides and influences her approach to the world. Genetically determined at conception, an infant's temperament will manifest itself immediately in a variety of character traits (Chess & Thomas, 1987).

Nine character traits were identified to gauge a child's temperament and to help determine the most effective method of caring for each child:

1) activity level;
2) regularity of biological rhythms, including sleeping, eating, and elimination;
3) approach/withdrawal tendencies;
4) mood;
5) intensity of reaction;
6) adaptability;
7) sensitivity to light, touch, taste, sound, and sights;
8) distractibility, and
9) persistence.

Each of these traits varies along a continuum. Children's points on the continuum can be observed and identified. Liebermann combined the characteristics of temperament into three groups and described them as flexible, fearful, or feisty (California State Department of Education, 1990).

The Flexible Child—The traits of flexible children include regular biological rhythms, adaptability to change and new situations, low intensity, low sensitivity, and positive mood. In school, flexible children are easily recognizable but can be overlooked because they do not demand attention. It is important to the development of flexible children that the teacher devotes attention to them even though such attention is not demanded.

The Fearful Child—Fearful children avoid new situations and are slow to warm to new people and experiences. Their cautious ways mean that teachers must go slowly with them, allowing them to observe a new activity or situation before approaching it. Teachers may also need to introduce children to new stimuli and only gradually withdraw as caution gives way to interest and enjoyment.

The Feisty Child—Feisty children are very active, intense and easily distracted, sensitive, moody, and have irregular rhythms. Feisty children run rather than walk, push the limits, and respond impulsively to intense emotions. Well-planned transitions are very important to feisty children, who will resist being rushed. Feisty children need opportunities for active play, as well as a chance to experience quiet play when the mood strikes.

Temperamental issues must be taken into account along with developmental issues when forming groups, developing curriculum, and establishing routines. Such traits can be considered in planning activities, experiences, and schedules.

A Family Is a Family

One of a teacher's most important roles in the first three years of a child's life is exposing the child to images and ideas about her family and culture of origin. Today, families come in all different sizes and configurations. Some families are traditional nuclear families with a mom, a dad, and children while other families might have two moms or dads, only a mom, only a dad, grandparents who are parenting, or large extended families that share child-rearing responsibilities. And families come from a wide variety of different cultures.

Teachers have a marvelous opportunity to support and validate the family and culture of every child and to begin the process of helping children understand similarities and differences, which are a natural part of the human experience. This support and validation begin with the child's family and culture—in whatever forms they may take. Photos of family members, remembrances such as clothing or gifts that are special, and warm, positive interactions between teachers and family members are excellent examples of ways to validate children's families.

Be sure to use images of families and cultures that are representative of all of the children's experiences. Pictures and photographs should depict the types of families that are represented in your group as well as those that are not. Also, be sensitive to the issues of family structure and cultural differences when you plan events that include parents. For example, make sure non-custodial parents are included in parent conferences, even if the teacher must conduct two conferences because the parents are not willing to conference together. Invite extended family to social events if they share in the child rearing, and send written information to an out-of-town or traveling parent who is not able to visit the school as regularly.

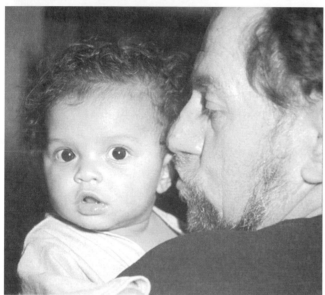

A family is a family. Make sure your classroom supports and validates all the families that are represented, and broadens the view to include other family structures and cultures. Infants who are exposed to inclusive, multicultural environments and experiences have a better chance of growing up with a view of the world as inclusive and multicultural.

Gradual Enrollment

One of the best ways to facilitate a child's adjustment to any new early childhood experience is to encourage the parents and the child to participate with the teacher in a gradual enrollment process. Young children have little experience with change and need time to adjust to new settings. Parents need to understand how new environments work and how teachers will handle the dynamic tasks of caregiving and early education. Gradual enrollment gives children, teachers, and parents time. Although there is no single correct way to do the gradual enrollment, most often it looks like the process outlined on the next page

Ideally, gradual enrollment would take place over a week or so with the parent and child staying one to two hours the first day and working up to a full day. Many parents will be able to arrange this much time for transition. Those who can't should be encouraged to spend at least two days. This gives the child experience with the new environment before being left in the new setting.

Although most schools do not require gradual enrollment, it is one of the most important components of the parent/school connection. It helps both parties understand what to expect.

The Gradual Enrollment Process

1. The parents or a person familiar to the child brings her to school.
2. The child's things are put away in a labeled cubbie.
3. The parent sits on the floor with the child or moves about the room, allowing the child to play in the environment or watch the teachers, parents, and other children.
4. The child's teacher is near during this time but is not in a hurry to interact with the child. The teacher uses this time to observe the child and the parents in action as she or he continues to care for other children and follow the day's routine.
5. As the parent and child settle in, the parent can talk with the teacher as she or he moves about the room caring for other children. As this happens, the teacher's voice will become familiar to the child.
6. When the child needs feeding, diapering, or a nap, the parent proceeds with routine care. The teacher watches and observes.
7. Gradually, during subsequent visits or as the day progresses, the parent and the teacher reverse roles, with the parent becoming the observer and the teacher interacting directly with the child.

When parents are desperate to begin school immediately and cannot participate in the gradual enrollment process, they have more difficulty adjusting to the school, complain more often, and drop out at a higher rate. Parents who are unsuccessful in modifying their expectations, and who don't have the time to work cooperatively with the teacher to make sure the child's adjustment is well planned and implemented, will have more complaints and misunderstandings.

Don't skip gradual enrollment—it is the firm foundation upon which a mutual relationship between the parents and the teacher is built. It also gives infants the time they need to adjust to new places, people, and stimulation.

Using Individualized Scheduling to Make the Day Go Smoothly

Individual scheduling is an important curriculum component for high-quality infant programs. Each child needs to follow her own schedule. That means that one or two children might eat every four hours while another eats every three hours. The same is true for sleeping and elimination. Individual scheduling means letting the child's natural biological rhythms and temperament determine schedule rather than super-imposing a common schedule on all children.

Hidden in this situation is a marvelous tool for infant teachers. Imagine having three or four babies who get hungry at the very same moment—or worse still, who need to be rocked to sleep at the same time. When teachers allow children to determine their own schedules, they are freed from this type of demand. Caregivers are still feeding, changing, and putting children to sleep, but instead of doing it all at once, they are doing it intermittently all day long.

The result is less stress for children waiting to have their needs met and less pressure on teachers to meet multiple needs at once. To follow individual schedules, it is necessary to find out what the child's regular schedule is. Sometimes infant schedules are not very predictable. Even when this is the case, patterns emerge that teachers and parents can use to plan the day. Look for these patterns if the child's schedule isn't predictable.

Maximizing Interactions During Basic Care and Routines

Once the commitment is made to allow children to follow their own schedules, it is then easy to combine one-on-one interaction with routine activities. Time spent diapering, feeding, and putting children to sleep is also used to stimulate and encourage social/emotional, physical, and intellectual (language and cognitive) growth.

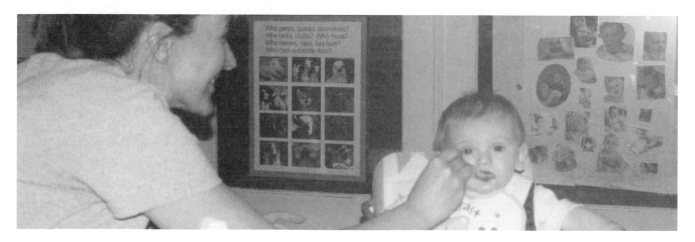

Reciprocity—the give and take of interactions—is virtually guaranteed during routine care. It is really difficult to feed a baby unless the baby opens her mouth; hard to change a diaper on a wiggly baby until you get her attention. Because reciprocal interactions are so important to the development of happy, healthy children, teachers who use routines to insure a healthy dose of reciprocal exchanges are making the most of the time spent on routine care by "ping-ponging"—getting a response and responding to children (Gordon, 1970). Maximizing routine experiences allows children to blossom and teachers to find time for one-on-one interchanges (Gerber, 1998, 1979).

Coping with Crying

Crying infants present a constant dilemma to their teachers. If they respond promptly to crying, many teachers feel they would spend all of their time responding to crying children with little time left for fostering developmental growth. A good understanding of the consequences of letting children cry without prompt adult response will help each infant teacher approach crying children in the most helpful way.

Children cry for a variety of reasons. Sometimes the cause is simple discomfort like a wet diaper or an empty stomach. Sometimes infants cry because they are too hot or too cold. Pain, particularly pain caused by intestinal upsets, can result in lots of crying. Teachers also know that some cries seem to have no identifiable cause. Dealing with crying that has no apparent cause can often be the most difficult situation to handle.

The issue of responding to crying children is complicated by a fairly prevalent view that too much responsiveness may result in spoiled children. Are children spoiled when teachers respond promptly to their cries? Do children who get this kind of attention cry more or less? Research into this area has provided concrete support that children who are held, cuddled, rocked, and so on when they are distressed, cry less frequently (Bell & Ainsworth, 1972). They also cry for shorter periods of time if response to crying is prompt (Korner & Thoman, 1972). No research has documented that children need to cry a little while before being picked up or that responding promptly to crying increases crying.

And, research has provided us with an additional benefit of timely response to crying. Infants often respond to holding by looking around and scanning the environment. When they are in this alert state, babies are more likely to accept transition to another activity or being put down (Korner & Thoman, 1972).

When children's needs are met quickly when they cry, they learn to trust the world around them and the adults who care for them (Erickson, 1963; Jones, 1992). If they learn that they must cry loudly and persistently to get their needs met, they may well use crying behaviors instead of developing other coping strategies or self-management skills.

How can infant teachers respond to crying? Obviously, if the teacher is free to do so, the best cure for crying is to pick up the infant, and hold, cuddle, soothe, and love her. Each prompt response will increase the likelihood that the child will come to trust her caregiver and learn other self-soothing skills.

But what if the teacher is not free to respond promptly? In school settings, it is not unusual for more than one child to cry and need attention at once. Try some of the following strategies if a crying child cannot be responded to immediately.

Move near the child. If she is in a crib, the sight of your face and soothing sounds from your voice may help. Comment on the situation and the reason you cannot help the baby at once. You might say something like "I'm almost finished giving Melanie her bottle. As soon as I'm finished, I'll pick you up." Avoid comments like "You're all right." No crying child is all right. Crying infants are trying to communicate, even if the adults are unsure of the message.

If the child is mobile, move near her and sit down on the floor so the child can get close to you. Sometimes an elbow, knee, arm, or leg can provide the needed touch to calm a crying child even if you cannot pick her up. Again, use your voice to calm and soothe by talking quietly to the child or singing a favorite tune.

Use a security item or favorite toy. Often a security item or favorite toy helps children calm themselves when you are unable to do so in person. There is no reason to limit access to these items unless you find yourself substituting them for adult attention. When you begin to look for a child's favorite toy or blanket, ask yourself if you can respond in person rather than presenting the substitute. If the answer is yes, then do it! No substitute is as good as the real thing.

Get information from the parents. An excellent prevention idea for coping with crying is to get information about what works from parents. Children often develop self-soothing behaviors at home that teachers can remind children to use at school.

Relax. Sometimes teachers themselves contribute to the crying cycle. Teachers can tense up and send messages about stress to babies through voice tone and muscle tension. Every infant teacher should be armed with some relaxation ideas that work. Try slow, deep breaths, visualizing the baby when she was happy and content, or systematic muscle relaxation to help you break the cycle and get the crying under control.

Infants cry to communicate. Promptly responding to crying and developing effective coping strategies to use when prompt response is not possible will lower the frequency and duration of crying, increasing the chances that children in infant programs will quickly gain confidence that the adults who care for them will meet their needs.

Guidance and Discipline

What Is Guidance and Discipline with Infants?

Guidance refers to what teachers do before a problem is present. Discipline is what teachers do after a problem is present. Guidance techniques are preventive in nature; they guide children to maintain self-control without actual intervention by the teacher. Although self-control begins to emerge during the early childhood years, children under the age of three still depend on adults to help them maintain control, particularly in situations in which other children are present.

Distraction

The younger the child is, the fewer times she should be expected to comply with verbal requests. For example, infants will frequently pick up food with their hands. Constant verbal reminders to "use your spoon" fail because we are expecting the child to change her behavior to suit the situation.

A better strategy is to hand the child a spoon. This encourages the child to use a spoon and increases the chance that she might do so by putting the spoon into her hand. It modifies a situation to fit the child's developmental stage.

This guidance technique is called distraction. Distraction involves changing the child's focus from an activity that is unacceptable to one that is acceptable without directly confronting the inappropriate behavior. Distraction works very well with children under the age of three. Use distraction when there is no danger to the child. Distraction also can be used to prevent the escalation of a minor problem into a major one.

Redirection

Redirection is preventive discipline strategy requiring that teachers be particularly good observers of children. Redirection involves anticipating problems and intervening before they occur. The following are examples of redirection:

- Exchanging an inappropriate toy or activity (like eating dirt on the playground) for an appropriate one (like picking up rattles to shake),
- Quietly singing a song to redirect a child's focus from a separation event to what is going on in the classroom, or
- Putting something in a baby's hand when that baby is fingering another child's hair (to prevent pulling hair).

Redirection only works when alert teachers get to a situation before it erupts into a full-scale problem. Once children need more intervention, the opportunity to redirect is lost.

Teacher Competencies to Support Separating from Parents

Sometimes	Usually	Always	
☐	☐	☐	Looks up, acknowledges, and greets children and parents as they arrive in the classroom.
☐	☐	☐	Facilitates child's entry into the classroom and separation from parents as they leave.
☐	☐	☐	Accepts and respects each child as she is. Indicates this respect by talking about what is going to happen and waiting for indications of wants or needs before responding.
☐	☐	☐	Shows an awareness of each child's temperament and level of development.
☐	☐	☐	Responds quickly to children who need attention.
☐	☐	☐	Allows children to follow their own schedules; changes with the children as schedules fluctuate.
☐	☐	☐	Is an alert observer of each child in the classroom.
☐	☐	☐	Uses routines of eating, resting, and diapering as opportunities to maximize reciprocal interactions.
☐	☐	☐	Monitors children's general comfort and health (for example, warmth, dryness, noses wiped, wet clothes changed, and so on).
☐	☐	☐	Invests in quality time with infants throughout the day during both routines and stimulation activities.
☐	☐	☐	Uses floor time to build relationships with children.
☐	☐	☐	Maintains a positive, pleasant attitude toward parents; thinks in terms of creating a partnership to support the child.
☐	☐	☐	Communicates regularly with parents about the child's experience at school; uses a variety of techniques to keep communication flowing freely.
☐	☐	☐	Plans, implements, and evaluates regular parent participation experiences, parent/teacher conferences, and parent education experiences.
☐	☐	☐	Supports children's developing awareness by talking about families, displaying families' photographs, and celebrating accomplishments.
☐	☐	☐	Uses books, pictures, and stories to help children identify with events that occur in the world of the family and the school.

Resources for Teachers

Blecher-Sass, H. (1997). **Good-byes can build trust.** Young Children, 52(7), 12-15.

California Department of Education. (1990). **Flexible, fearful, or fiesty: The different temperaments of infants and toddlers {videotape}.** Sacramento, CA.

Gerber, M. & A. Johnson. (1997). **Your self-confident baby.** New York: Wiley.

Greenspan, S. & Greenspan, N.T. (1989). **The essential partnership.** New York: Penguin Books.

Miller, Karen. (2001). **Ages and stages.** Glen Burnie, MD: TelShare Publishing.

Neugebauer, B. (1992). **Alike and different: Exploring our humanity with children.** Washington, DC: National Association for the Education of Young Children (NAEYC).

Teaching Tolerance Project. (1997). **Starting small: Teaching tolerance in preschool and the early grades.** Montgomery, AL: Southern Poverty Law Center.

Stonehouse, A. (1995). **How does it feel?: Child care from a parent's perspective.** Redmond, WA: Exchange Press.

INNOVATIONS IN PARENT PARTNERSHIPS

School- or Teacher-initiated Possibilities

Pre-enrollment Visit

Plan a pre-enrollment visit for the parents and child to see the classroom and get a glimpse of what the day will be like.

Family Interview

Interview the family and let them interview you. Talk about the school's teaching philosophy and ask the family about their parenting style. Discuss the family's expectations for the child's school experience.

Separation and Reunion Ritual

Establish a separation and reunion routine that both the parents and the teacher will use every day. Write it down so everyone will know what the plan is. (See the Parent Postcard "Creating a Separation and Reunion Ritual" on page 49.)

Parent/Child Photographs

Photograph the parent(s) and child together in the classroom and put this photograph in the crib or on the wall for the child to see.

Parent Participation Possibilities

Gradual Enrollment

Conduct a gradual enrollment where new families gradually increase the amount of time they spend in school—first with Mom's or Dad's support and then for increasing amounts of time without Mom or Dad.

Parent Postcards

Share Parent Postcards with parents as they indicate an interest, at appropriate times during the enrollment cycle, or as developmental issues arise. (See pages 441-444 in the Appendix for a sample dissemination schedule.) Copy postcards. Cut if necessary. Address to parent(s) and place on Communication Sheet, mail to the family, or hand out personally.

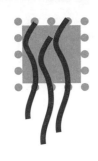

TO

Create a Separation and Reunion Ritual

The way the day begins and ends for your child is so important. It sets the tone for the day and supports the task of learning to separate and reunite. What can you do to make these important times of the day work for you and your child? Establishing a predictable way to separate and reunite with your child helps children feel comfortable in the transition process. It also prevents children from using arrival and departure times as an opportunity to manipulate parents and teachers.

Come into the room, talk a minute with your child's teacher, and put your baby's things away. Next, help your child begin to settle in by offering him or her a toy to play with or a book to look at. Don't rush the separation process. It may take your child as long as 15 minutes or so to get ready for you to leave. When you are ready to leave, tell the teacher, kiss and hug your child, say goodbye and that you'll be back, and leave, smiling and waving all the while.

Do the same upon your return. Instead of rushing off to gather your child's belongings to go home, cherish the reuniting process. Pick up your child, hug and kiss him or her, and then spend a few minutes getting reconnected. Don't be surprised if your child ignores you for a minute or two. He or she may have just figured out that you have been somewhere else all day and may take a few minutes to get over being mad about that! Sit down and watch what he or she is doing, and follow his or her lead about when to try to reunite again.

Predictable beginnings and ends of the day are important to you and to your child. Separations and reunions are easier for adults because we are more experienced in negotiating them. Children, particularly very young children, need lots of help from you to make separations and reunions a pleasant part of their school experience.

Arrival and Departure Routines ARE Transitions

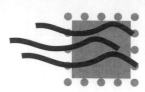

Everything in a child's life is a transition, so expect arrival and departure times to be transitions. Some transitions are handled better than others. Most parents realize that arrival and departure times can't be abrupt and quick—transitions take time. In general, children, even very young children, resist being rushed or hurried. Parents have all been in the situation where they are running late. The harder you push, the slower and more resistant your child becomes! Knowing this is the case, plan arrival and departure routines to accept this inevitable reality.

TO _____

_____

_____

Call If Your Plans Change

Let your child's teacher know if your routine is going to change in any way and for what period of time. Sometimes teachers can offset children's real discomfort about changes in schedule by preparing the child for the change. Even very young children know the sequence of which parent comes in first, then next, then next, and so on. If you let your teacher know, your teacher can help your child accept the increased time at the school without going into the "waiting" mode too soon.

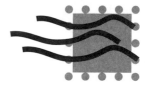

TO _____

_____

_____

Develop a Backup Plan

Develop backup strategies before you need them and practice these routines, too. It's going to happen—a flat tire, a car accident, a last-minute work demand that can't be postponed, more traffic than you have ever seen, the downpour that floods every street leading to the school. Plan now for these situations so that you have a backup if you cannot be predictable in your departure routine. And, don't forget to discuss the plan with your child's teacher. Practice it once or twice before it is needed. Then everyone will know how to handle it if the plan is put into effect.

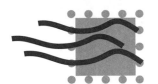

TO _____

_____

_____

Thumb and Finger Sucking

Most pediatricians and child development experts view thumb or finger sucking as an extension of the strong rooting and sucking reflexes with which a child is born. They consider it a normal part of early development. You may disagree. Concerns about thumb or finger sucking causing the mouth or palate to disfigure and issues about lifelong bad habits are common.

Most children give up finger or thumb sucking on their own as they learn other self-soothing and self-comforting behaviors. Don't worry too much about future problems right now. When the time is right, you and your child's teacher can work together to address this concern.

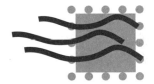

TO _____

_____

_____

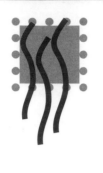

TO _____

Always Say Goodbye

Leaving your child may be as hard for you as it is for him or her. It might seem that leaving without saying goodbye could save you and your infant from suffering through another separation. In fact, the opposite is true.

During the first three years of life, children learn that the world in which they live is a predictable and responsive place to be, or that it isn't. They learn this important lesson from their caregivers. Parents and teachers who provide sensitive, responsive, and predictable care teach children to trust them.

You can help your child learn that although you may leave him or her, you will never disappear without a goodbye kiss and hug and a promise to return. At first, your child may not care too much when you leave. But as your child grows, so will his or her resistance to being separated from you. If you always say goodbye now, when it doesn't matter quite as much, when it does matter a lot, he or she will remember the separation routine you have used over time and find it comforting. And, your child will learn that you mean what you say—that you will come back, just like you said you would.

TO

Follow these hints for safe pacifier use:

- Use only a commercial pacifier, never a home-made one.

- Clean new pacifiers before use according to the manufacturer's directions. Then, clean the pacifier frequently and always after it is dropped on the floor or ground, particularly when your baby is very young. Pacifiers wear out when they are used often. Test the pacifier to make sure the bulb is intact and free of tears. Replace a pacifier as soon as it becomes sticky or shows other signs of wear.

Pacifiers

As new parents, you may wonder whether to give a pacifier to your baby. Some people are strongly in favor of pacifiers. Others insist, just as strongly, that they be avoided. How, then, do you decide? The best way is to watch your baby's behavior to see whether to introduce a pacifier or not. Babies are born with a strong sucking instinct that enables them to nurse or suck a bottle. Sucking that isn't a part of feeding is completely normal behavior for a baby. It usually has the same calming effect on the baby as nursing or taking a bottle. Some babies seem able to satisfy their sucking urge during feeding. Other babies seem to want to suck constantly and will suck on anything that they can get in or near their mouths. If your baby wants to continue to suck after a feeding or sucks on his or her fingers or blanket, you may want to try a pacifier.

Pacifiers come in different sizes and shapes and must meet stringent safety standards set by the U.S. Product Safety Commission. They must be strong so they won't come apart in small pieces and must have a mouth shield large and strong enough to prevent the pacifier from being drawn into the baby's mouth.

Your newborn may reject a pacifier at first. This is primarily because the technique of sucking on the pacifier is slightly different from nursing or taking a bottle. So, the baby has to practice a little to get used to a pacifier. At first, it will get thrust out of the mouth as the baby tries to use a breast-feeding or bottle feeding kind of suck. Don't give up. Your baby might get used to the pacifier after a little more experience. Don't force it, though. Offer the pacifier, but accept your baby's response if he or she rejects it. You may want to try a different kind of pacifier if your baby doesn't like the first one you try. Sometimes the type makes a difference. If your baby does become accustomed to a pacifier, you will want to keep several on hand in case one gets lost.

As your baby grows older, the sucking reflex will disappear. But, your older infant may still use the pacifier for calming down after losing control or to relax enough to fall asleep.

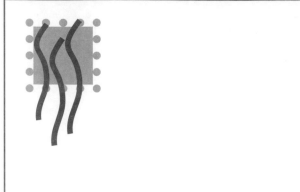

TO
_____
_____

Security Items

As you get to know your baby, there will be many decisions you have to make. Many of these decisions seem so difficult when you are faced with them but can be considered rather directly. One important issue that you might face as new parents is what to do about transitional or security items. Babies often develop attachments to transitional objects such as blankets, stuffed animals, soft, silky fabric, or favorite pieces of clothing such as hats or burp cloths. For some, the item is transitory and changing as long as it is something from home. For others, the intensity of the attachment requires parents to make sure the security object is always nearby.

Like thumb or finger sucking, using transitional items are a normal part of learning to separate and reunite. They can also be an excellent coping mechanism for self-quieting and soothing. In fact, children who have security items often cope better with unfamiliar situations than children who don't have transitional objects.

You might be concerned about when attachment to a security item might become a problem. Look at three issues when deciding about transitional objects—1) the **duration,** 2) the **intensity** of the attachment, and **3)** the **distress** caused by separation from the security item. For example, teenagers rarely carry around transitional objects from early childhood but may, quite normally, keep them in a safe place in their rooms. Children who are traumatized if they misplace their transitional objects as they near the end of the early childhood period (**which actually lasts until age 8**) may be indicating the need for help to solve an underlying problem.

Take a look around school. Children of all ages and particularly very young children use a wide variety of coping mechanisms to manage separation from parents—the most important people in their lives. Your child's teacher will view this as a natural part of growing up and offer the strategies your child has learned at home as a support for encouraging adjustment and maturation.

Resources for Parents

Add these helpful books to your parent library or post this list on your parent bulletin board.

Bailey, Becky. (1998). *10 principles of positive discipline.* Oviedo, FL: Loving Guidance.

Bailey, Becky. (1997). *I love you rituals.* Oviedo, FL: Loving Guidance.

Brazelton, T. B. (1992). *Touchpoints: The essential reference.* Reading, MA: Addison Wesley.

Eisenberg, A. (1996). *What to expect in the first year.* New York: Workman.

Leach, P. (1997) *Your baby and child: From birth to five.* New York: Knopf.

Miller, K. (2000). *Ages and stages.* Glen Burnie, MD: TelShare.

INNOVATIONS IN ENVIRONMENTS

Creating a Warm, Inviting, Home-Like Setting

The transition from home and parents to school often is a difficult one for babies because the two environments are so very different. Imagine going from a closed, soft, dimly lighted place with familiar smells to an open, sanitized, brightly lighted one with unfamiliar scents. No wonder the first week or more can be so difficult!

Create a sense of calm. Creating an inviting environment begins with the use of carpets, curtains, blankets, and pillows to absorb sounds and keep them from bouncing off hard surfaces. Use soft classical music to communicate a sense of calm during the baby's introduction to the classroom.

Include soft elements in the room. Soft elements help make the environment more home-like. Cuddle toys like stuffed animals and terrycloth dolls give babies items to hug and use to comfort themselves. Carpet on the floor or a quilt used during floor time also adds softness.

Create a place for babies' things. This gives children a feeling of security and helps avoid lost articles. A cubbie and a set of hooks provide a place for the diaper bag, diapers, extra clothing, security items from home, art projects, and

notes between home and school. Photographs may be kept in the cubbie or covered with clear contact paper and placed low on the wall or in the infant's crib.

Establish a predictable environment. Infants need a predictable environment with novel and interesting features. A comfortable, calm pace throughout the day is an important part of a predictable environment. Babies' needs are anticipated, so they do not have to wait. Major elements in the classroom, like cribs, low storage units, chairs, food preparation area, and changing area, stay the same. Novel and interesting features include color, texture, sensory experiences, and different toys. Novelty also can be accomplished through mirrors, art projects hanging on the walls, mobiles, activity bars and boxes, appropriate music, and sensory experiences, like smell jars, flour activities, paints, and texture experiences.

Creation of Different Spaces within the Classroom

Because the individual needs of infants vary over the period of the day or even weeks/months, different spaces are needed to meet these different needs. Create places to be alone, places to be with friends, and places to be with teacher.

Creating places to be alone is especially important in the very stimulating environments in which young children find themselves. **Teachers can create these spaces without sacrificing visual supervision of all children.** By breaking up large open spaces, teachers can create smaller, more intimate settings. Children will pursue activities of interest for relatively long periods of time if they are not interrupted. The smaller spaces help keep interruptions to a minimum. Low carts, large soft blocks, toy bars, and activity areas can help create the places to play without interruption.

Creating places to be with friends is important as children are developing a multi-sensory interest in the world around them. Spectator sports are very popular in infant classrooms—watching what other babies are doing, watching what adults are doing, listening to sounds and noises, sensing changes in smells in the classroom, and touching friends who are nearby. Provide enough space to squirm and roll around, perhaps even scoot or crawl while playing.

Infants who are not mobile have little to say about where they are in the environment. Teachers are responsible for providing changes in scenery, position, and stimulation. Examples of changes in scenery include:

1) moving the child from a soft blanket on the floor to a baby bouncer that moves when the baby's arms and legs are wiggled;
2) moving baby from the blanket on the floor to the arms of the teacher so the baby can look around and orient to a part of the classroom that wasn't visible from her back; and
3) laying babies side by side so they can see each other when they turn their heads from side to side, discovering their friends, and so on.

Changes in position help infants use new muscles as well as see new things. Babies enjoy moving from back to stomach or stomach to back. They love being able to sit in an Exer-saucer to scan the environment or watch the activity of the classroom. They also love bouncing in the Johnny Jumper, practicing weight-bearing positions, and balancing with support.

Infants also love changes in stimulation sources. Bouncing in warm water or on bubble wrap provides very different experiences. Bouncing while you watch your friends is very different from bouncing while your teacher counts your bounces and applauds your strong leg muscles.

Creating places to be with teacher allows the kind of intimate communication and face-to-face contact that Gerber and Johnson (1997) and Greenspan (1989) term "falling in love with baby." Such intimacy helps create a feeling of security. Diapering and eating experiences allow the teacher and baby to enjoy one-on-one time. Create places that allow babies to have precious time alone with their teacher. Intimacy like this creates strong bonds between the teacher and the child and is valuable, brain-stimulating curriculum!

Activities and Experiences vs. Centers

Most early childhood educators think of interest or learning centers as an essential part of any classroom setting. Yet, environments for infants are different because they cannot choose to go to different areas until they are mobile. For this reason, teachers must bring the activities and experiences to the child, or they must assist the child in going to where the activities are. A wide range of activities and experiences must be available to infants. In each of the following two plans, *Me!* and *Mommies and Daddies*, activities and experiences are presented in the following areas:

- Dramatic Possibilities
- Sensory/Art Possibilities
- Curiosity Possibilities
- Literacy Possibilities
- Music Possibilities
- Movement Possibilities
- Outdoor Possibilities
- Project Possibilities
- Parent Participation Possibilities

WEB

Me!

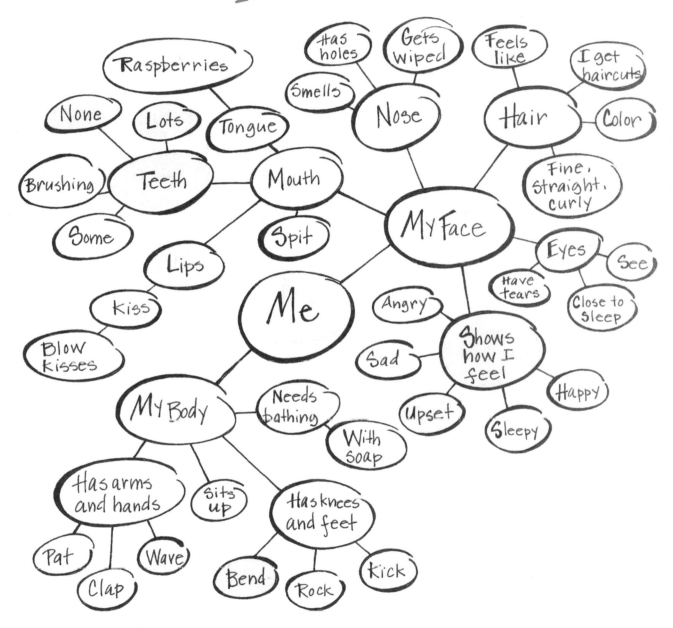

Note: Using the technique of webbing, teachers can follow the leads that children give them, as well as have an unlimited source of options. Always use the webs as a jumping-off point. The possibilities are endless!

PLANNING PAGES

Plan Possibilities

Dramatic

Wrist Rattles 62
Bathing Baby 62
Taking Things Off 62
Night! Night! 63

Sensory/Art

Flour Pat 63
Drawing 63
Foot Painting 64

Curiosity

Peek-a-boo 64
Mirror Play 64
Smelling Game 65

Literacy

Parent Picture Book 65
Eye Winker, Tom Tinker 66
All About You 66
On the Day I Was Born 66
Your Bellybutton 66
Max's Bath 67
Pots and Pans 67
Clap Your Hands 67
Me! Books 67

Music

Johnny Works with One
    Hammer, One Hammer 68
Are You Sleeping? 68

Movement

Johnny Jumper 69
Exer-saucer 69

Outdoor

View from a Blanket 70
Stroll with Baby Dolls 70
Outside Doll Baths 70

Project

Finger Paint Collage 71
Repeated Foot Painting 71

Parent Participation

Parent Picture Book 72
Supporting Possibilities 72
Parent Postcards
    Helping Your Baby Develop a
        Positive Sense of Self 72
    Every Child Is Unique! 73

Me!

Concepts Learned in Me! 74

Prop Boxes

Things that Go on My Head! . . .74
Things that Go on My Feet! . . .74
Things that Go on My Hands! . .74

Picture File/Vocabulary 75

Books

Baby at Home by Monica Wellington
Baby Faces by Margaret Miller
Baby Goes Shopping by Monica Wellington
Baby in a Buggy by Monica Wellington
Baby in a Car by Monica Wellington
Clap Your Hands by Lorinda B. Cauley 67
Contemplating Your Bellybutton by Jun Nanao 66
*Eyes, Nose, Fingers, Toes: A First Book
    All About You* by Judy Hindley 66
From Head to Toe by Eric Carle
I See by Rachel Isadora
I Touch by Rachel Isadora
Max's Bath by Rosemary Wells 67
Max's Bedtime by Rosemary Wells
More, More, More Said the Baby by Vera Williams
My Home by Bill Thomas and Brian Miller
On the Day I Was Born by Debbi Chocolate 66
Peek a Boo by Janet Ahlberg
Pots and Pans by Patricia Hubbell .67
What Do Babies Do? by Debby Slier

Rhymes/Fingerplays

"Eye Winker, Tom Tinker" . .66

Music/Songs

"Are You Sleeping?" 68
"Johnny Works with One
    Hammer" 68

Toys and Materials 76

Wrist Rattles

0-6 months

Materials
Rattles

Use wrist or ankle rattles to show action-reaction to young infants. Gently shake the baby's rattle and then pause to see if she wants to do the same.

Bathing Baby

6-18 months

Materials
Washable dolls or tub toys
Shallow plastic tub
Washcloth and towel
Small (very small!) amount of water
Clean, empty containers of bath products

Teacher Talk
"You're washing the baby, Shauna. Splat! Splat! The water splatters!" Talk with children about what they are doing.

Provide dolls or toys and a shallow plastic tub, so children can play. A washcloth, a towel, and a small amount of water all will add realism to the play. Empty containers of baby lotion, shampoo, and baby powder (all with securely glued tops) are appropriate enrichments.

Taking Things Off

6-18 months

Materials
Prop boxes or baskets
Things to go in them (see Prop box suggestions on page 74)

Teacher Talk
Name the items as the children pick them up and talk about them as infants choose them and play with them.

Young children love taking things off. They learn this long before learning to put things on. Provide items in prop boxes like Things that Go on My Head, Things that Go on My Feet, and Things that Go on My Hands, so infants can enjoy practicing taking things off. Record new skills on the Communication Sheet (pages 429-430), such as "takes off hat," "takes off sock," as you observe the infants.

Night! Night!
6-18 months

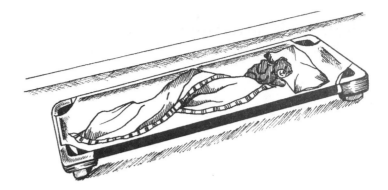

Materials
Low cot
Pillow
Blanket
Cuddle toy(s)
Soft music

Teacher Talk
When a baby puts her head on the pillow, say, "Night, night!" and pat her back.

Preparing for sleep is a familiar routine for very young children. Provide a low cot that infants can easily get into and out of, as well as a pillow, blanket, and cuddle toy(s). Provide soft sleepy music in the area. Join in the play.

SENSORY/ART POSSIBILITIES

Flour Pat
0-6 months

Materials
Shallow plastic tub
Flour

Teacher Talk
Talk about how soft the flour is on baby's skin.

Put a thin layer of flour in the bottom of the tub. Place baby's hand in the tub. Supervise closely.

Drawing
6-18 months

Materials
Large pieces of paper
Large crayons
Masking tape

Early art experiences for infants are actually sensory experiences. Use washable, safe materials for all activities. Provide very large pieces of paper that completely cover a low table or a section of the floor. Wrap masking tape around crayons, so they won't break easily.

The Use of Food in Classroom Activities
Some early childhood educators object to the use of real food materials in activities for children, either because of their sensitivity to the issue of hunger in the world or because they are concerned that children will be confused by food that is not meant to be eaten. Food included in this curriculum is used because it works beautifully as a manipulative activity and it is an extremely inexpensive source of sensory stimulation. Educators with objections can find substitutes for the materials listed. Alternatives are sometimes included in the activities.

Foot Painting

6-18 months

Materials

Large piece of paper	Tape
Paint	Soap and water or hose
Towels	

Tape a large section of paper to the floor or the sidewalk outside. Put globs of paint on the paper near the baby's feet and see what happens. Infants can sit next to the paint globs, lie on their tummies at the edge of the paper, or scoot and crawl over to paint. Help and support children who can stand or walk to step in the paint and then onto a clean portion of the paper. Cleanup will be easy with damp paper towels or with a hose outside. Repeat the process for children over time, selecting a time when each baby is rested, fed, and ready to play. Date the footprints, and write notes about children's actions and reactions to the experience. Take photos to share with parents. Plan to have a towel ready for drying off and clothes ready for redressing.

CURIOSITY POSSIBILITIES

Peek-a-boo

0-6 months

Materials
None needed

Play a game of peek-a-boo. Observe baby's reaction to determine whether or not to continue.

Mirror Play

6-18 months

Materials
Unbreakable large or small mirrors

Teacher Talk
Talk with children about what they are seeing.

Young children find their images to be the most interesting things to observe. Provide many types of mirrors for children to explore. Very large mirrors mounted on the wall give children opportunities to look at objects and adults in different areas in the room. Plastic hand-held mirrors, as well as mirrors in busy boxes and activity centers will allow children to explore their own features. Make a note when the child discovers her own image in the mirror.

? —— Smelling Game

6-18 months

Materials

Food and flower scents	Plastic jars with lids
Cotton balls	Non-toxic glue

Teacher Talk

"That is the vanilla. I see your nose wrinkle."

Provide familiar and new scents for children to explore in the classroom. Punch holes in the lids of plastic jars. Place cotton balls with scents, such as vanilla, peppermint, or flowers, on them in the different jars. Secure the lids with glue. Talk with children as they explore the different smells. Take turns—you smell the scent, then let the baby smell. If appropriate given the age and abilities of your children, create a smelling game. Ask them to find specific smells.

LITERACY POSSIBILITIES

Parent Picture Book

0-6 months

Materials

Camera	Cardboard
Glue or tape	Hole punch
Yarn or string	

Teacher Talk

"Tara, your mommy will be back this afternoon. See your mommy's smile in this picture."

Take photographs of parents as they drop off or pick up children. Attach the photographs to pieces of cardboard. Punch holes in one side of the cardboard. Tie with yarn or string to secure the pages. Use the book to initiate talk about parents during the day. Remind each child that Mommy or Daddy will return. Stand the books to the right or left of a baby's shoulder so she can look from side to side. Or, put the book flat on the floor and lay the baby nearby on her stomach.

___ # Eye Winker, Tom Tinker

0-12 months

Materials
None needed

Repeat the following rhyme with infants as they explore their facial features in the mirror or as you sit with a baby in your lap, gazing at her face.

> *Eye Winker, Tom Tinker*
> Eye winker,
> Tom tinker
> Nose smeller,
> Mouth eater
> Chin chopper,
> Gully, gully, gully!

 ___ # All About You

0-18 months

Materials
Eyes, Nose, Finger, Toes: A First Book All About You by Judy Hindley

Read the book to each baby or to two or three babies at a time. Look for skills like pointing to pictures, saying sounds or words, and turning pages. Note observations in baby's Anecdotal Records (see page 428) and put on the Communication Sheet (see page 429-430).

 ___ # On the Day I Was Born

0-18 months

Materials
On the Day I Was Born by Debbi Chocolate

Young children love to hear about when they were born. Read the book to each baby or to one or two babies at a time.

 ___ # Your Bellybutton

0-18 months

Materials
Contemplating Your Bellybutton by Jun Nanao

Bellybuttons are a favorite subject for young children. Talk about bellybuttons. Touch the baby's bellybutton gently and note her reaction. Use a version of peek-a-boo with the infant's bellybutton to orient the baby to where the bellybutton is.

——— **Max's Bath**

0-18 months

Materials
Max's Bath by Rosemary Wells

Read this book as children play Bathing Baby (page 62). Younger children will enjoy the rhythm of the words; older infants will enjoy the story.

 ——— **Pots and Pans**

0-18 months

Materials
Pots and Pans by Patricia Hubbell

Read this book while babies play with pots and pans. Repeat phrases from this book when babies clang or bang the pots.

 ——— **Clap Your Hands**

0-18 months

Materials
Clap Your Hands by Lorinda B. Cauley

Read this book while you demonstrate the actions.

 ——— **Me! Books**

0-18 months

Materials
Books about babies, such as
 Baby at Home by Monica Wellington
 Baby Faces by Margaret Miller
 Baby Goes Shopping by Monica Wellington
 Baby in a Buggy by Monica Wellington
 Baby in a Car by Monica Wellington
 From Head to Toe by Eric Carle
 I See by Rachel Isadora
 I Touch by Rachel Isadora
 Max's Bedtime by Rosemary Wells
 More, More, More Said the Baby by Vera Williams
 My Home by Bill Thomas and Brian Miller
 Peek a Boo by Janet Ahlberg
 What Do Babies Do? by Debby Slier

Babies love books about babies. Read one of these books at appropriate times. Add to Books Read list (see Appendix page 431).

Johnny Works with One Hammer, One Hammer

0-18 months

Materials
None needed

Use a hand-over-hand approach to help the baby join in the song. Watch for signs of enjoyment such as bouncing or moving to the sounds of the music. Emphasize the motions as you sing or chant.

> *Johnny Works with One Hammer*
> Johnny works with one hammer, (move one hand)
> One hammer, one hammer.
> Johnny works with one hammer.
> Then he works with two.
>
> Johnny works with two hammers, (move two hands)
> Two hammers, two hammers.
> Johnny works with two hammers.
> Then he works with three.
>
> Johnny works with three hammers, (move two hands and one foot)
> Three hammers, three hammers.
> Johnny works with three hammers.
> Then he works with four.
>
> Johnny works with four hammers, (move two hands and two feet)
> Four hammers, four hammers.
> Johnny works with four hammers.
> Then he works with five.
>
> Johnny works with five hammers, (move two hands, two feet, and head)
> Five hammers, five hammers.
> Johnny works with five hammers.
> Then he goes to sleep!

Are You Sleeping?

0-18 months

Materials
None needed

Sing this song when children are playing Night! Night! (page 63). Talk with parents about the songs and rhymes you use with children during the day. Make a copy of the words to send home to parents.

Are You Sleeping?
> Are you sleeping,
> Are you sleeping,
> Brother John, Brother John?
> Morning bells are ringing,
> Morning bells are ringing,
> Ding, ding, dong!
> Ding, ding, dong!

MOVEMENT POSSIBILITIES

 ## Johnny Jumper

6-12 months

Materials
Johnny Jumper

Teacher Talk
Talk about what the infant is doing. "You are bouncing in the Johnny Jumper. Up and down, Marissa."

Over a period of time give each child an opportunity to bounce in the Johnny Jumper to strengthen leg muscles. Position a mirror nearby on the wall, so the child can watch herself jump. **Note:** Children should be in the Johnny Jumper no longer than 10 to 15 minutes. Remove a child immediately if she objects or loses interest in bouncing.

 ## Exer-saucer

6-12 months

Materials
Exer-saucer

Walkers are inappropriate for infants. They are unsafe, limit the child's movements, and do nothing to help the child learn to walk. An Exer-saucer is an appropriate alternative because it allows the child to sit comfortably and put the entire foot flat on the floor when attempting to bear weight. It also provides a space for playing with objects like rattles or a busy box. Sit nearby babies when they are in equipment like this so they can see your face and you can share their experiences. Watch for signs of fatigue, and be sensitive to cues indicating that the baby wants to get out. Limit the child's time in the Exer-saucer to no longer than 10 to 15 minutes and remove her immediately if she objects or loses interest. **Note:** Restriction of motor movement by too much holding, bouncers, and walker can cause motor delays. Babies need lots of unrestricted floor time to practice and perfect motor skills.

OUTDOOR POSSIBILITIES

View from a Blanket
0-6 months

Materials
Blanket

Teacher Talk
"You are stretching your legs, Thomas. Alan is stretching his legs, too."

Spread a blanket on the grass and place a baby (or babies) on it. Talk about the babies' hands, eyes, legs, and so on as they move.

Stroll with Baby Dolls
6-18 months

Materials
Baby dolls
Stroller(s)

Teacher Talk
"The bird is sitting on the branch." "I see a big truck!" "Look, a squirrel!"

Take infants and baby dolls outside for a walk in the stroller. Talk about what you are seeing outdoors.

Outside Doll Baths
6-18 months

Materials
Washable dolls
Shallow plastic tubs
Water
Washcloths and other props

Bring dolls and shallow plastic tubs outside for baby bath time. Describe the dolls' features, including bellybuttons, arms, legs, eyes, and so on. Don't forget washcloths and other props to expand the older infants' play.

Finger Paint Collage

6-18 months

Materials
Large piece of paper
Finger paint
Markers
Camera

Create a collage by using a large piece of paper and letting children finger paint over a span of several days or several weeks. Use different colors of paint and date each color as it is added. Write your observations of children's experiences on the collage. Take photographs of each step in the process. Hang the collage and surround it with the photographs and comments. Send duplicate photos home with parents.

Repeated Foot Painting

6-18 months

Materials
Large piece of paper
Finger paint
Markers
Clear contact paper

Teacher Talk
"You made a green footprint! John made a blue one. We had fun making footprints." Talk with babies about the artwork.

Repeat the foot painting activity (page 64) over time using different colors. Date and label each set of prints. Take photos of the process. Hang the painting and photographs at eye level. Cover with clear contact paper.

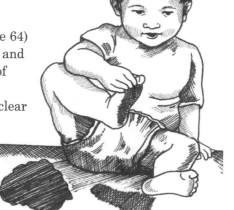

Parent Picture Book

In addition to the pictures taken of parents and children during drop-off and pick-up times, invite parents to provide their own favorite pictures to add to the Parent Picture Book (page 65). Talk to parents about how the pictures are used during the day to keep the connection between the child's family and the school.

Supporting Possibilities

A number of different items are needed for this Possibilities Plan. Ask parents to collect empty plastic jars with lids; empty containers of baby powder, baby lotion, and shampoo; and items that children put on their head, feet, or hands. Let parents know how the items will be used.

Parent Postcards

Parent Postcards in this section are designed to share with parents during the Possibilities Plan. The topics are natural extensions of the activities and experiences that you are planning and implementing for the infants in the classroom. Use the Postcards to connect parents to their children's learning.

Helping Your Baby Develop a Positive Sense of Self

A common myth during infancy is that children who cry should not be picked up immediately. Many parents fear that they will "spoil" their child. But child development researchers tell us it is impossible to "spoil" a very young child by promptly responding to crying. In fact, when a baby's cries are answered quickly, the baby actually cries less often because he or she comes to understand that the communication attempts have been heard and that someone will respond.

Security and confidence result from the loving framework of routines. When the parents respond promptly to baby's cries, the baby learns that the world is a responsive and predictable place to be. The baby cries, an adult responds, and milk is offered as the baby is cuddled in the adult's arms. Through many of these experiences, your baby will develop a positive sense, not only about the world, but also about himself or herself as well.

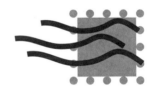

TO _____
_____
_____

TO

Principles of Development

1. Growth follows a universal and predictable sequence.

2. Development proceeds from the simple to the complex or from the general to the specific.

3. Children gain control of their bodies from the top down and from the center out.

4. Each child has an individual pattern and timing of growth—each child is unique.

Every Child Is Unique!

From the first experience of counting baby's fingers and toes, parents are concerned that their child is normal—is like other children at the same age and stage of development. Parents worry. It's your job! A discussion of the general principles of how children develop will help you enjoy your baby's emerging skills.

The first general principle is that growth follows a universal and predictable sequence. These milestones of development are observable. The predictability of development can be seen in each area of development: physical, social/emotional, and intellectual, which includes cognitive and language. For example, physical development proceeds from sitting to crawling, to pulling to a stand, to walking. Each step is predictable and can be observed

The second principle is that development proceeds from the simple to the complex or from the general to the specific. Your baby acquires simple skills before more complex ones can be attempted. For example, children always eat first with their fingers before attempting to use a spoon or fork.

The third principle is that children gain control of their bodies from the top down and from the center out. Both of these trends are affected by children's unique pace through the developmental sequence, the unevenness of development in general, and the opportunities available for experience and practice of emerging skills. For example, babies can control their heads and arms before their feet and hands.

The fourth and most important principle is that each child has an individual pattern and timing of growth—each child is unique. Although the sequence is predictable, each child's individual progress through the sequence is subject to variation. For example, one child may pull to a stand and walk at 7 or 8 months, while another may do so at 12 or 13 months. Both children are normal. It is normal for progress through the sequence to vary.

Revel in your child's unique skill repertoire. Resist the temptation to compare too much, because no one else's child is just like yours!

Concepts Learned in Me!

Concepts Learned

I can do things with my hands and my feet!

Some babies have teeth; some don't.

I can smell with my nose.

I can see with my eyes.

I can taste with my mouth.

I can take things off (socks, shoes, hats)!

I can put things on (hats, sunglasses)!

I can go to sleep.

I can eat.

I have a bellybutton!

I can see myself in the mirror.

I can bounce with my legs in the Johnny Jumper.

I can make things rattle.

I can bathe my baby doll.

I can put my baby to sleep.

I can paint with my hands and my feet.

I can play peek-a-boo!

I can stroll in a stroller.

I can eat with a spoon!

Resources

Prop Boxes

Things that Go on My Head!
- Bows
- Scarves
- Sunglasses

Things that Go on My Feet!
- Boots
- Heels
- Sandals
- Socks
- Tennis Shoes

Things that Go on My Hands!
- Bangle Bracelets
- Gloves
- Mittens
- Wrist Rattles

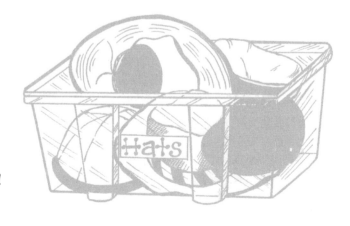

Picture File/Vocabulary

Babies inside
Babies with different
   facial expressions
Bodies
Eyes
Faces
Feet

Babies outside
Hands
Mouth
Nose

Books

Baby at Home by Monica Wellington
Baby Faces by Margaret Miller
Baby Goes Shopping by Monica Wellington
Baby in a Buggy by Monica Wellington
Baby in a Car by Monica Wellington
Clap Your Hands by Lorinda B. Cauley (page 67)
Contemplating Your Bellybutton by Jun Nanao (page 66)
Eyes, Nose, Fingers, Toes: A First Book All About You
   by Judy Hindley (page 66)
From Head to Toe by Eric Carle
I See by Rachel Isadora
I Touch by Rachel Isadora
Max's Bath by Rosemary Wells (page 67)
Max's Bedtime by Rosemary Wells
More, More, More Said the Baby by Vera Williams
My Home by Bill Thomas and Brian Miller
On the Day I Was Born by Debbi Chocolate (page 66)
Peek a Boo by Janet Ahlberg
Pots and Pans by Patricia Hubbell(page 67)
What Do Babies Do? by Debby Slier

Rhymes/Fingerplays

"Eye Winker, Tom Tinker" (page 66)

Music/Songs

"Are You Sleeping?" (page 68)
"Johnny Works with One Hammer" (page 68)

Toys and Materials

The following purchased items are important for this Possibilities Plan of Me!:

Books about babies

Photo albums

Exer-saucer

Rattles

Finger paint and tempera paint

Shallow tub

Hand-held mirrors

Washable dolls

Johnny Jumper

Wrist rattles

Large wall mirrors

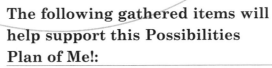

The following gathered items will help support this Possibilities Plan of Me!:

Cuddle toys

Empty bath items (lotion, shampoo, soap, powder)

Prop box items (page 74)

Sleep items (pillow, sheet, blanket)

Mommies and Daddies

WEB

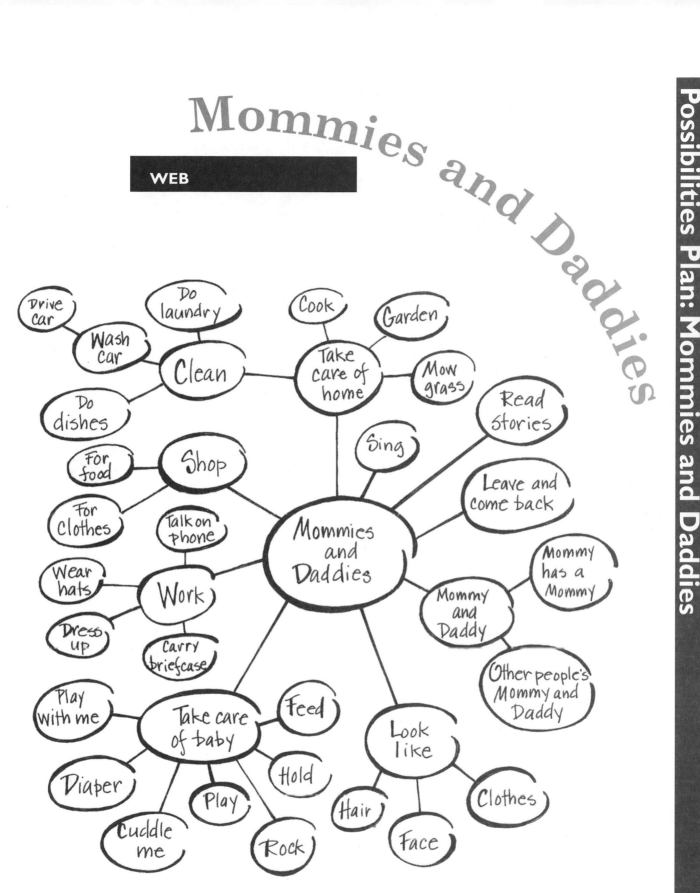

Note: Using the technique of webbing, teachers can follow the leads that children give them, as well as have an unlimited source of options. Always use the webs as a jumping-off point. The possibilities are endless!

Dramatic

Hammer Rattle 80
Gardening 80
Cooking 80
Cleaning 81
Building 81
Camping 81

Sensory/Art

Toes in Flour 82
Fingers in Flour 82
Floating Fish 82

Curiosity

Phone Rattle 83
Telephone Play 83
Food Boxes and Cans 83
Toy Key Rattles 83

Literacy

You Go Away 84
Daddy, Daddy, Be There 84
Are You My Mother? 84
Mommy and Daddy Books 84

Music

Wrist and Ankle Rattles 85
I Went to the Store 85
Commercial Noisemakers 85
Food Container Rattles 86

Movement

Pat-a-cake 86
Mud Digging 86
Lids with Pots and Pans 87
Packing a Picnic Basket 87
Dump and Load Shopping Cart 87

Outdoor

Bouncy Seat Barefoot 88
Texture Walk 88
Outside Dramatic Play 88

Project

"Parents at Work" Picture Album 88

Parent Participation

"Parents at Work" Pictures 89
Supporting Possibilities 89
Parent Postcards
You Are Your Child's Best Teacher . . .90
Including Children in Routines 91

Mommies and Daddies

Concepts Learned in Mommies and Daddies 92

Prop Boxes

Gardening 92
Cooking 92
Cleaning 93
Building 93
Camping 93
Mommy's or Daddy's Work 93

Picture File/Vocabulary 93

Books

Are You My Mother?/
  Eres Tu Mi Mama? by
  P.D. Eastman 84
Daddy Makes the Best Spaghetti
  by Anna Grossnickle Hines 85
Daddy, Daddy, Be There by
  Candy D. Boyd 84
Family by Helen Oxenbury
Just Like Daddy by Frank Asch
What Daddies Do Best/ What Mommies Do Best
  by Laura Numeroff. 85
You Go Away by Dorothy Corey 84

Rhymes/Fingerplays

"Pat-a-cake" 86

Music/Songs

Commercial Noisemakers 85
Food Container Rattles 86
"I Went to the Store" 85

Toys and Materials 94

Hammer Rattle

0-6 months

Materials
Hammer rattle(s) or any rattle

Give young infants a hammer rattle (or any rattle) to hold.
Show baby what happens when she shakes the hammer
rattle.

Gardening

6-18 months

Materials
Gardening items (see Prop Box suggestions
 on page 92)
Shallow plastic tubs
Dirt or sand
Plastic shovels
Gardening catalogs and magazines

Provide gardening items, so children can play in the dirt. Shallow plastic tubs or an
infant sensory table with dirt or sand in it will provide a place for children to
touch, dig, and scoop. Put plastic shovels in each sensory tub. Gardening
catalogs and gardening magazines add page-turning experiences and offer
opportunities to expand vocabulary. **Note:** Expect children to put sensory
materials in their mouths. Remind them to touch with their hands, and to
leave the dirt in the containers. Guide them to do this by giving them
shovels to dig. Remind children that they can play if they keep the materials
out of their mouths. Remove children who are unable to do so with support and
supervision, and bring them to another activity.

Cooking

6-18 months

Materials
Kitchen items (see Prop Box suggestions on page 92)
Food boxes
Cookbooks

Teacher Talk
Narrate children's actions. "Pots have lids. Yes Jojo, you can make noise with the pot
and lid."

Add realistic kitchen items, such as pots, pans, plastic bowls, cans, cardboard food boxes, and cookbooks to the classroom. Look for skills such as taking off lids, putting lids on pots, and matching the right lid to the right pot. **Safety note:** Do not add spoons. Infants will put the spoons into their mouths and the handles may damage the soft palette of the mouth.

 # Cleaning
6-18 months

Materials
Cleaning props that are dry and clean (see suggestion on page 93)

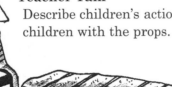

Teacher Talk
Describe children's actions as you play alongside children with the props.

Provide materials for cleaning the way mommies and daddies do. Be certain that all chemicals have been completely cleaned from the containers. Spray bottles with water, cloths, hand brooms, hand mops, hand towels, and soap containers will all add to the children's play.

 # Building
6-18 months

Materials
Plastic hammers, pliers, measuring tape, etc.
See Prop Box suggestions on page 93

Toy construction items such as plastic hammers, pliers, and measuring tape (short in length) make building fun. Also add construction hats, blocks, and trucks that can be pushed or pulled.

 # Camping
6-18 months

Materials
Tent or large sheet
Sleeping bag or blanket
Flashlight(s) or cook set
See Prop Box suggestions on page 93

Children love doing things their parents do. Camping is especially fun with the addition of a tent and a couple of sleeping bags or a sheet and blanket. Also add flashlights and items used for cooking outside, like camp cook sets. Make sure all items are safe for infants.

SENSORY/ART POSSIBILITIES

Toes in Flour
0-6 months

Materials
Shallow plastic tub
Flour

Teacher Talk
Describe how the flour feels as the child wiggles her toes. "The flour feels soft under your feet, Jacque. You wiggled your toes!"

Put a small amount of flour in a shallow plastic tub under a child in a bouncy seat or jumper.

Fingers in Flour
6-18 months

Materials
Wading pool
Flour

Allow children to explore a small amount of flour in a wading pool with you very close by watching, commenting, and supervising for safety. Describe children's actions as you observe their curiosity, smiles, wiggles, and bounces. Record your observations on the Communication Sheet (pages 429-430). Share your observations with parents.

Floating Fish
6-18 months

Materials
Plastic fish that float
Shallow plastic tub

Teacher Talk
Talk about the feel of the water and how the fish float on the water.

Strip infants to their diapers. Provide plastic fish that float in a plastic tub for each baby to explore. Pat the fish and the water to show babies what might happen.

Phone Rattle
0-6 months

Materials
Phone rattle

Give young babies a phone rattle to hold as you support children exploring their environment. Give the rattle a shake to show baby how it works. Observe to see she responds. Record response on Communication Sheet (pages 429-430).

Telephone Play
6-18 months

Materials
Pretend and/or real telephone (without cords)

Teacher Talk
"Hello. Hello, John. You are talking on the phone." Use children's names as you talk with them on the phone.

Both pretend and real telephones (without cords) are great curiosity items for young children. They encourage verbalization and interaction.

Food Boxes and Cans
6-18 months

Materials
Empty boxes and cans
Small items

Provide empty boxes and cans for children to explore. Put small items such as animals and small vehicles into the food boxes and cans. Be certain that all items are safe and do not present choke hazards. Replace surprises often for children to rediscover. Record search-and-find skills, for example, looking where toys were the last time or searching for hidden objects.

Toy Key Rattles
6-18 months

Materials
Toy key rattles

Young children are fascinated by their parents' keys. Provide a variety of toy key rattles for children to explore. When you leave to go outside, offer keys to children to hold on to "just like Mommy does when she comes and goes from school."

LITERACY POSSIBILITIES

You Go Away
0-18 months

Materials
You Go Away by Dorothy Corey

Teacher Talk
"Mommies and daddies leave in the morning, but they come back in the afternoon. Let's read the *You Go Away* book to remember that mommies and daddies come back."

Read this delightful book to describe how parents may leave, but they always come back. Younger infants will like being read to, and older infants will relate to the experiences described in the book. Read this book as parents leave to support recovery from separating.

Daddy, Daddy Be There
0-18 months

Materials
Daddy, Daddy, Be There by Candy D. Boyd

Young children love to hear about their parents. Read the book and talk with children about daddies.

Are You My Mother?
0-18 months

Materials
Are You My Mother?/Eres Tu Mi Mama? by P. D. Eastman

Read the book and describe how children look similar to their parents. Repeat familiar lines often.

Mommy and Daddy Books
0-18 months

Materials
Books about mommies and daddies, such as

Daddy Makes the Best Spaghetti by Anna Grossnickle Hines
Daddy, Daddy, Be There by Candy D. Boyd
Family by Helen Oxenbury
Just Like Daddy by Frank Asch
What Daddies Do Best / What Mommies Do Best by Laura
   Numeroff

Read any of the above books to one baby or two or three babies at appropriate times. Add to the Books Read list (see Appendix page 431).

MUSIC POSSIBILITIES

Wrist and Ankle Rattles
0-6 months

Materials
Wrist and ankle rattles

When older babies are making noise with noisemakers, give younger babies rattles to shake.

I Went to the Store
0-12 months

Materials
Record, tape, or CD of Hap Palmer's "I Went to the Store"

Sing this Hap Palmer song that talks about typical activities in a child's life. Enjoy "I Went to the Store" with infants who are lying on a blanket, sitting in bouncers, or cruising around the room.

Commercial Noisemakers
6-18 months

Materials
Commercial noisemakers

Children will enjoy the action of the noisemakers. Examine materials carefully for safety.

Food Container Rattles

6-18 months

Materials
Empty cardboard food containers
Items to put into the boxes
Tape

Teacher Talk
"That box makes a soft sound. That one makes a loud sound!"

Use empty cardboard food containers to make rattles. Place items (too large to pass through a choke tube) inside the boxes. Tape them securely.

MOVEMENT POSSIBILITIES

Pat-a-cake

0-6 months

Materials
None needed

Teacher Talk
"You playing pat-a-cake, Chelsea. It is fun."

Play pat-a-cake with young babies.

Pat-a-cake
Pat-a-cake, pat-a-cake, baker's man,
Bake me cake as fast as you can.
Pat it and roll it and mark it with "B."
Put it in the oven for baby and me.

Mud Digging

6-18 months

Materials
Shallow plastic tubs
Mud
Plastic shovels
See Gardening Prop Box suggestions on page 92

Teacher Talk
"Not for your mouth, Lacey. Use the shovel to dig." Talk about what each child is doing.

Give each child an opportunity to play and strengthen arm muscles by digging in shallow plastic tubs filled with mud. Always be near and attentive. Remind children to keep the mud in the sand and water table or tub.

Lids with Pots and Pans
6-18 months

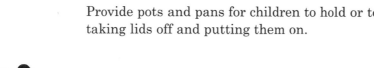

Materials
Unbreakable pots and pans
See the Cooking Prop Box suggestions on page 92

Provide pots and pans for children to hold or to use to practice taking lids off and putting them on.

Packing a Picnic Basket
6-18 months

Materials
Basket
Items for the basket
See the Camping Prop Box suggestions on page 93

Provide a basket and items that might go on a picnic. Children can pack and unpack the basket. Repack the basket often for repetitive unpacking.

Dump and Load Shopping Cart
6-18 months

Materials
Toy shopping cart
Food containers
Paper bag

Provide a toy shopping cart, so children can dump it out and load it up again. Store food containers in a paper bag to transfer to the cart and then back to the bag. Model the process and describe your actions as you model.

Bouncy Seat Barefoot
0-6 months

Materials
Bouncy seat

Position young babies in bouncy seats. Take off their shoes and socks so they can feel the grass as they bounce.

Texture Walk
6-18 months

Materials
None needed

Take infants on a texture walk outside (dirt, grass, sand, bark, mulch). Talk about the different textures as children see or gently help the baby touch the textures with her hand.

Outside Dramatic Play
6-18 months

Materials
Gardening or camping props (see pages 92 and 93)

Some dramatic play opportunities work especially well outside. Try both gardening and camping as outdoor dramatic play experiences.

"Parents at Work" Picture Album
6-18 months

Materials
Photographs
Paper
Glue or tape
Hole punch
Yarn or string

Create a "Parents at Work" picture album with photographs that parents provide. Use the book to talk about what parents do while children are at school. Add to the picture album during the Possibilities Plan by supplementing parent photographs with magazine pictures and advertisements of adults doing similar work. Point to pictures and talk with infants about what their parents do.

PARENT PARTICIPATION POSSIBILITIES

"Parents at Work" Pictures

Ask parents to provide pictures of them at work. Also, ask them to provide professional magazines or advertisements that show adults doing similar work. Talk to parents about how the pictures are used during the day to make the connection between the child's parents and school.

Supporting Possibilities

A number of different items are needed for use in this Possibilities Plan. Ask parents to collect empty food containers, empty cleaning containers, camping items, and picnic items. Let parents know how the items will be used. Check all items for safety.

Parent Postcards

Parent Postcards in this section are designed to share with parents during the Possibilities Plan. The topics are natural extensions of the activities and experiences that you are planning and implementing for the infants in the classroom. Use the Postcards to connect parents to their children's learning.

TO _____

You Are Your Child's Best Teacher

The biggest influence in a child's life is his or her parents. Teachers and extended family and friends are important, but the child's parents are his or her first and most important teachers. Parents have a profound influence on what children learn, what children feel, and how children react to the world around them.

How can parents best fill their role as teachers? Get involved with your child's school. More than any other factor, parent involvement influences children's success. Parents can start early with being present in their child's school during functions and conferences. Also, very simple involvement such as collecting items for the classroom is important because it shows support for the school and the complex work teachers do.

Another way to fill the "teacher role" is to read to your child each day. This will help your child become a reader. Finally, become partners with your child's teacher. Talk about concerns or issues before little concerns become big problems. Ask for reference material and share the ideas you find with your child's teacher. When the parent-teacher relationship works, the teacher-child relationship works, too. It is worth the effort!

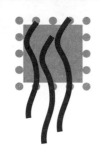

TO

Including Children in Routines

Because of the many changes in society, young children have become more and more isolated. To reverse this negative trend, parents can include their children in common routines throughout the day. Even drive time can be a reconnecting experience for young children. While driving try some of the following activities:

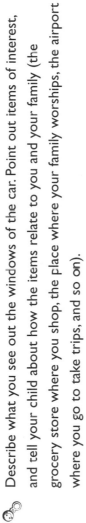

- Describe what you see out the windows of the car. Point out items of interest, and tell your child about how the items relate to you and your family (the grocery store where you shop, the place where your family worships, the airport where you go to take trips, and so on).

- Sing songs or recite rhymes that your child is hearing at school. Reinforce what your child is experiencing at school through these interactions.

- Talk about activities that have occurred in your day as well as your child's day. Help your child transition by also talking about what you both will be doing in the evening.

- Include your child in other routines such as cooking and cleaning. Your child will enjoy being near you and observing the activity. Take all opportunities to interact with your child. Talk, talk, talk, and your child will learn, learn, learn.

You might wonder whether talking to non-verbal infants makes any sense! Children learn language by hearing it used by others and from having success in communicating with others. They may not understand the words you are using when they are very young, but they will understand the tone of your voice, the rhythm of the words you use, and your enthusiasm. All these things lead your baby to an interest in talking to you when he or she is ready!

Concepts Learned

Concepts Learned in Mommies and Daddies

Mommies and daddies come back.

A child has a mommy and a daddy.

Mommies and daddies are special.

Mommies and daddies do different things.

Families love babies and help them.

Mommies and daddies garden, cook, clean, work, and camp out.

Textures feel different.

I can pretend.

Mommies and daddies have car keys.

Pots and pans have lids.

Picnic baskets are full of stuff!

Things float.

I can shake a rattle.

I can dig in the dirt.

I can turn the pages in a book.

I can clean.

I can use the telephone.

I can empty and fill the picnic basket.

Resources

Prop Boxes

Gardening
 Gardening tools   Seed containers
 Gardening gloves   Sun hats
 Plastic tubs   Sunglasses

Cooking
 Dish cloths
 Dish towels   Pots
 Empty food containers   Recipe cards
 Pans   Kitchen utensils

Cleaning
    Clean rags   Small mop
    Empty cleaning containers   Towels
    Hand broom

Building
    Blocks   Measuring tape
    Construction hats   Small trucks
    Construction toys

Camping
    Camp cook kit   Sheet
    Picnic basket   Sleeping bags
    Picnic items   Toy binoculars

Mommy's or Daddy's Work
    Office materials or materials that are used in the work of children's parents

Picture File/Vocabulary

Babies
Daddies
Mommies
Mommies and daddies at home, on the phone, doing chores, doing leisure
activities, playing with baby

Books

Are You My Mother?/Eres Tu Mi Mama? by P.D. Eastman (page 84)
Daddy Makes the Best Spaghetti by Anna Grossnickle Hines (page 85)
Daddy, Daddy, Be There by Candy D. Boyd (page 84)
Family by Helen Oxenbury
Just Like Daddy by Frank Asch
What Daddies Do Best/ What Mommies Do Best by Laura Numeroff (page 85)
You Go Away by Dorothy Corey (page 84)

Rhymes/Fingerplays

"Pat-a-cake" (page 86)

Music/Songs

Commercial Noisemakers (page 85)
Food Container Rattles (page 86)
"I Went to the Store" (page 85)
Wrist and Ankle Rattles (page 85)

Toys and Materials

The following purchased items are important for this Possibilities Plan:

Books about Mommies and Daddies
    Bouncer seat
        Floating plastic fish
        Johnny Jumper
            Noisemakers
            Toy construction items
            Toy key rattles

The following gathered items will help support this Possibilities Plan:

Cleaning containers
Flour
Food containers for rattles
Gardening catalogs and magazines
Picnic basket and items
Pots and pans with lids
Prop box items
Telephones with cords and/or antennae
  removed

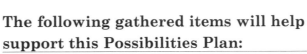

CHAPTER 3

Connecting with School and Teacher

INTRODUCTION

The complement of separating from the comfort and familiarity of home is connecting to the novel and unfamiliar context of school. At many ages and stages during the first three years, it is the experience of connecting that bridges these two worlds.

Connecting is a process, just like separating. It can begin with curiosity, confusion, interest, or wariness. And, connecting takes time.

Emerging knowledge about best practices points to key dimensions that must be part of infant care and education. The dimensions are sensitive responsiveness, positive communication, and age- and stage-appropriate activities and experiences.

Innovations: The Comprehensive Infant Curriculum facilitates all three of these dimensions. By observing first, teachers can sensitively respond to baby's cues. By getting to know each baby individually through observation and assessment and parent participation, teachers foster positive communication. And by selecting a wide variety of possibilities for interaction and experiences, teachers assure the age and stage appropriateness of their curriculum plans.

The infant's connection to school is facilitated by both caring, involved parents and motivated, knowledgeable teachers. This connection is affected by the infant's personal characteristics (Honig, 1982), by the structural components of the program, such as ratio of adults to children or group size, and by dynamic components, such as sensitive responsiveness by caregiver, positive communication between home and school, and appropriate activities (McMullen, 1999). Because so many variables can impact the connection between home and school, all need attention from teachers and parents. This chapter focuses on beginning and strengthening the connecting process.

INNOVATIONS IN OBSERVATION/ ASSESSMENT

Observation/Assessment Instrument

The assessment instrument on the next page is not just a skills checklist. Instead it is designed to guide the teacher's observation of children's development through major interactional tasks of infancy. The assessment's focus is on what IS happening, not just what should happen or what will happen. Use this assessment to lead to developmentally appropriate practice.

Infant (0-18 months) Assessment

Task: Connecting with School and Teacher

	0-6 months		6-12 months	12-18 months
C1	a. Does not resist separating from parents.		b. Resists separating from parents; resists comfort from primary teacher.	c. Resists separating from parents; accepts comfort from primary teacher.
C2	a. Accepts transition from parent to teacher.		b. Maintains physical proximity to primary teacher during separation.	c. Seeks primary teacher's support in separating.
C3	a. Comforts after a period of distress.		b. Comforts quickly after being picked up.	c. Comforts when needs or wants are acknowledged by caregiver.
C4	a. Is unaware of friends in classroom.		b. Visually notices friends in classroom.	c. Gets excited about seeing friends; seeks physical proximity.
C5	a. Uses parents and teacher physically to support exploration of the environment; explores objects placed nearby parents and teachers.		b. Uses parents and teacher visually to support exploration of the environment; manipulates objects found in environment.	c. Explores the environment independently; responds to play cues presented by adults.
C6	a. Focuses on face-to-face interaction.	b. Tracks moving object up and down and right to left.	c. Watches people, objects, and activities in immediate environment.	d. Initiates interactions with people, toys, and the environment.
C7	a. Objects exist only when in view.	b. Objects perceived as having separate existence.	c. Looks where objects were last seen after they disappear.	d. Follows visual displacement of objects.
C8	a. Thinks object disappears when it moves out of view.	b. Looks where object was last seen after it disappears.	c. Follows object as it disappears.	d. Searches for hidden object if the disappearance was observed. 10304_AUT Collected.zip10304_AUT Collected.zip

INNOVATIONS IN CHILD DEVELOPMENT

Nothing matters as much as the first relationships between children and adults. Teachers of infants must understand the profound effect of attachment in the path of a child's life and work diligently to support positive steps toward this key emotional milestone.

Development of Attachment

The moment of birth marks the end of an interdependent, physical connection between mother and child. This connection nurtured the baby, providing everything necessary for growth and development. As this first attachment ends, a second, equally important connection begins. This next connection provides what babies need to survive and thrive in the human world.

Supporting the development of secure, reciprocal attachments between mothers and their infants is a crucial part of the teacher's role. Nothing a teacher does will have more long-term impact on the child, the mother, the family, and the child's success in life. Supporting these emerging human relationships requires that teachers understand attachment theory and the implications for children's experiences in school.

Stages of Attachment

The First Stage (Indiscriminate Attachment)—Ages birth to about 5 or 6 months. Very young children move through four stages of attachment during the first three years of life (Bell & Ainsworth, 1972). The first stage is called indiscriminate attachment. During this stage, there is less difference in the way babies respond to adults. As long as they are fed when hungry and held when uncomfortable, infants allow a caring adult to meet their needs.

Infants during this stage are particularly sensitive and responsive to their mothers. This sensitivity begins during pregnancy as the baby is exposed to the mother's biological rhythms and the sound of her voice. As a result, the baby is born with a familiarity with the mother that is enhanced by new connections from sight, smell, and touch. So, mothers typically are able to calm and soothe their newborns more easily than others are. This preference for the mother continues as the attachment process unfolds.

The Second Stage (Discriminate Attachment)—Ages 5 months to about 11 or 12 months. This stage is called discriminate attachment. Soon babies begin to smile, babble, coo, and respond more quickly to the mother and other familiar adults. During this stage, infants show a definite preference for interaction and comforting from a familiar person—usually the child's mother and father or other frequent caregiver. During this stage, babies are learning that their needs will be met by a caring adult and that they can trust the world to be a responsive place.

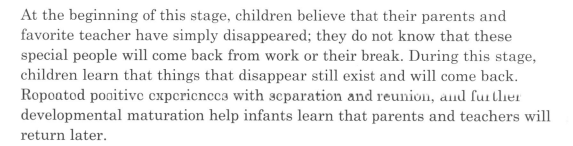

The Third Stage (Separation Anxiety)—Ages 11 or 12 months to about 17 or 18 months. This stage is called separation anxiety. During the third stage of attachment, children begin to show clearly defined preferences for mothers and fathers and the most familiar caregiver. Friendliness toward unfamiliar adults goes away. Children in this stage of development will resist care or attention from unfamiliar adults. They move close to their parents or most frequent caregiver when new people enter the room and cry when their parents and most frequent caregiver leave.

At the beginning of this stage, children believe that their parents and favorite teacher have simply disappeared; they do not know that these special people will come back from work or their break. During this stage, children learn that things that disappear still exist and will come back. Repeated positive experiences with separation and reunion, and further developmental maturation help infants learn that parents and teachers will return later.

The Fourth Stage (Stranger Anxiety)—About 17 or 18 months to 24-25 months. This stage is called stranger anxiety. During the fourth stage of attachment, fear of strange or unknown adults is present. The cautious behavior of stage three infants is replaced with clinging, crying, and fearful responses to strangers and to separation. A child will resist any overture by unfamiliar adults and show great distress when his parent or teacher leaves.

At the end of the fourth stage of attachment, children are usually ready to venture out into the wider social world. But progress through the stages isn't guaranteed. Children's experience at each stage of attachment affects their progress through the next stage and their subsequent emotional development.

Why does attachment matter? Children who have secure attachments are more likely to become self-reliant toddlers and have a positive sense of self

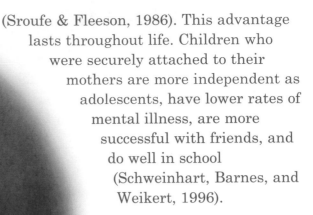

(Sroufe & Fleeson, 1986). This advantage lasts throughout life. Children who were securely attached to their mothers are more independent as adolescents, have lower rates of mental illness, are more successful with friends, and do well in school (Schweinhart, Barnes, and Weikert, 1996).

Attachments are relationships that develop from interactions (Howes & Hamilton, 1992; Shore, 1997). Facilitating attachment means taking the time to develop relationships with infants and their parents. The result will be an attachment to the primary teacher that is remarkably similar to the baby's attachment to the mother— and almost as important for the baby's future development.

Object Permanence

An important concept related to attachment, and to intellectual and physical development, is object permanence. When babies begin to learn that objects hidden from their view still exist, a major reorganization in thought and emotion occurs. They realize that Mom and Dad didn't just disappear. These important people were there the whole time, just not with them!

Object permanence illustrates how development is interconnected. It is really an intellectual skill related to thinking, but its onset initiates a major change in emotional development as infants realize that their parents are actually leaving them behind. Then, increasing physical skills of scooting, crawling, pulling to a stand, and walking create a sense of autonomy that enables children who are still anxious when their parents leave to try physically to close the emotional distance using motor movements.

So, object permanence is a key behavior that signals a host of developmental changes in infants and indicates that development is proceeding.

INNOVATIONS IN INTERACTIVE EXPERIENCES

Knowing about child development theory and best practices helps teachers plan experiences that are developmentally appropriate for children. However, life's minutiae build to create experiences. Infant teachers must be attuned to these everyday, yet important, experiences. They are truly the foundation upon which crucial skills and abilities grow. Think about the following list of experiences and make sure that the classroom reflects many of them. You might also want to use this list as you make notes on the Communication Sheet (pages 429-430) when you are sharing the types of experiences the child had during the day.

- ☐ Provide timely, sensitive responses to bio-behavioral cues.
- ☐ Anticipate infants' needs.
- ☐ Provide affectionate, caring responses to meet needs.
- ☐ Create safe, nurturing, home-like environments.
- ☐ Provide sensitive, individualized responses to routines such as eating, going to sleep, and diapering.
- ☐ Model the behaviors you want infants to use.
- ☐ Provide gentle guidance.
- ☐ Allow and encourage uninterrupted, multi-sensory play.
- ☐ Provide for active exploration of the environment.
- ☐ Help babies wait a moment before getting their needs met; give babies time to indicate preferred responses before acting.
- ☐ Provide reciprocal verbal and nonverbal communications.
- ☐ Provide open-ended experiences that can be initiated by infants as well as by adults.
- ☐ Keep ratios low and group sizes small.
- ☐ Provide stable, consistent teachers who commit to babies over time.

INNOVATIONS IN TEACHING

Primary Teaching

Child development and early childhood literature is full of references to primary teaching as a strategy for facilitating the development of infants during the first three years of life (Greenman & Stonehouse, 1996; Lally, 1995; Raikes, 1993; Reisenberg, 1995). Primary caregiving usually focuses on the development of an intimate, sensitive, and reciprocal relationship between an infant and his most frequent caregiver. This curriculum views primary teaching as a more comprehensive construct—one that offers schools the opportunity to develop close ties between parents, teachers, children, and school.

Powell (1998) supports this program approach where schools work more inclusively with children and parents rather than constructing a separate parent involvement component. When primary teaching is viewed this way, it creates a true partnership with families that places families at the center of the relationship, not on the periphery.

Primary teaching typically involves assigning each baby to a special person to get to know at school. The primary teacher then spends her or his time gathering information and knowledge about the baby's family, culture, unique temperament style, cues, schedule, and personality, so this teacher can be responsive and appropriate in her or his relationships with the child and the family.

There are three components of primary teaching. The first component is the relationship between the parents and the school. Because parents are the most significant people in an infant's life, the relationship between the teacher and the parent is also paramount (Lally, 1995). Seeing each other as partners is an essential component of early education. The parent/teacher/school relationship needs to have the same importance and to develop the same amount of trust as the teacher's relationship with the child.

The second component of primary teaching is the responsive relationship between the baby and teacher. This relationship is based on careful observation of each child's individuality and on "a sense of personal and emotional involvement that is mutual" (Leavitt, 1994). Many researchers—Brazelton (1992), Erickson (1963), Gerber (1997), Honig (1989), Howes, Phillips, & Whitebrook (1992), Shore (1997)—have characterized the interactive relationship between caregivers and babies as crucial. Babies need to know that the human world in which they live is a caring one that is responsive to their bio-behavioral needs.

The concept of reciprocity and mutual trust includes much more than just stimulating interactions (Gerber & Johnson, 1997; Kovach & Da Ros, 1998; McMullen, 1999). Characteristics are:

- interacting, rather than reacting to babies;
- working to read and interpret verbal and nonverbal cues;
- anticipating needs and wants;
- responding quickly and affectionately;
- waiting for cues from the child that he is ready for some action to take place;
- including the child's individuality and temperament in decisions about cue interpretation;
- including the child in the process of caregiving;
- sensitivity to over- or under-stimulation from the environment and the people (and other children) in it; and
- individualizing the schedule or pace of the day.

When infant classrooms reflect these characteristics, trust between infants and teachers naturally emerges (Gerber and Johnson, 1997; Howes & Hamilton, 1992).

Each child is unique. Primary teachers take the time to learn each child's unique qualities to foster positive communication. Teachers gather substantive information about the child from the parents and from observations of the child with his parents at school. This information gives the teacher a running start toward understanding each child's individuality, so the teacher's interactive style can match the baby's emotional and social needs.

The teacher-child relationship is based on mutual personal involvement between the baby and the teacher that is reciprocal in nature. Reciprocity refers to the careful give and take of interactions between the child and the teacher and their mutual interdependence. Gordon (1970) calls this the "ping-ponging" of interactions—the child coos; the adult comments on the vocalization; the child coos longer and louder; the adult smiles and again comments.

This conceptualization of the infant and adult in an interactive and interdependent relationship is confirmed by many experts (Brazelton, 1992; McMullen, 1999). It isn't just the adult's response to the infant that makes the infant respond or connect. The infant is as active a participant as the adult, engaging in continued or modified interaction by his vocalizations and nonverbal responses.

The third component of primary teaching is the balance between routine, interaction, stimulation, and time alone. An unfortunate legacy of the early education movement is the mistaken idea that children need to have constant stimulation. In reality, children need balance in this area. Babies need sensitive responses to routines; warm, caring, intimate interactions with a primary teacher (Honig, 1989); stimulation from the environment; toys, adults, and children in the environment; and, most important, uninterrupted time alone to integrate the experience (Gerber & Johnson, 1997; Greenman & Stonehouse, 1996; Kovach & Da Ros, 1998).

Components of Primary Teaching

1. Mutual relationships between parent and teacher
2. Mutual teacher-child relationships
3. Balance among routines, interactions, stimulation, and time alone

Relationships between teachers and children are not formed overnight; they develop over time. The process of becoming familiar, learning each other's interactive styles, developing a joyful interest in each other's worlds, and learning to understand each other's communication style takes time (Fein, Gariboldi, & Boni, 1993). Primary teaching leads children and their teachers to form such relationships by taking time with each step of the process and by not requiring the child or the teacher to be in a relationship "all at once."

Continuity of Care

Continuity of care is an extension of primary teaching that works to keep all of the components of relationships intact. The teacher stays the same, the peers stay the same, and the context stays the same. It is worth the effort to maintain as many of these components as possible during the first three years.

Because it takes time to develop close, reciprocal relationships, teachers and children need long periods of time together. Continuity of care involves keeping all components of the child's experience continuous—the teacher, the other children in the group, and the context of the child's experience. Frequent moves of children to new classrooms with new teachers disrupt the relationship-building process, forcing everyone (child, parent, and teacher) to start over.

Philosophically and experientially, primary teaching extends the length of time a teacher and her or his small group of children stay together in the same place. Changing any of the components of continuity should be done with great caution. Groups can stay together for at least 18 months and may stay together for up to 3 years. The extended time together allows children to form strong ties to their primary teacher and to begin to form additional secondary relationships with other adults and children in the classroom. This much time allows parents and teachers to get to know and understand each other's needs, expectations, and talents (Edwards, Gandini, and Forman 1998).

When children need changes in their environments, primary teachers make those changes in the familiar setting of the classroom instead of requiring children to move to a new location to have their needs met. Or, children move with their assigned teacher and a group of friends to a new classroom, changing only one of the components of continuous care at a time.

Facilitating Adjustment and Attachment

Researchers have expressed concerns about the development of emotional attachment of infants to their mothers when children begin school during infancy. As this debate continues, a quiet crisis is developing: There is an expanding demand for early education services that exceeds availability (Carnegie Task Force, 1994).

What can teachers do to facilitate attachment of children to their parents and then to their teachers? First, assign a primary teacher to every child—that special person at school who will work sensitively to match responses to cues and communication both between child and teacher and between teacher and parents.

Second, work hard to individualize responses to the baby's cues. Congruence between the infant's nonverbal cues and quick responsiveness will reassure the infant and support the emerging relationship (Kovach & Da Ros, 1998).

Third, invest in observation. Good teachers build an understanding of the infants in their group by being good observers. Observation informs practice and serves as the foundation for matching stimulation activities to emerging development. This goodness of fit is crucial for maximizing the infant's potential.

Fourth, clearly differentiate the teacher's role from the parent's role. Boundaries between infant teachers and the families they serve are often blurred. Both seem to do the same thing during different times of the day. But the roles are not the same. Teachers need to differentiate carefully the teaching role. Teachers listen to, suggest solutions, raise issues, point out alternatives, and provide resources to parents. These are appropriate roles for teachers and schools, for that matter. Directing child rearing or insisting on specific expectations (for example, requiring the parent to take away the bottle on the first birthday) are examples of inappropriate roles for teachers. Think about the following questions to help choose appropriate boundaries.

- Who should be the first person to share the emergence of a new skill or change in growth? Parent or teacher?
- Who should decide when it is time to start solid food? Parent or teacher?
- Who should suggest strategies for helping babies sleep through the night? Parents or teachers?
- Who should be responsible for replacing disposable diapers or formula when the supply at school is depleted? Parent or teacher?

There are many other questions to ask, and there is no absolute right answer to any of these questions. Situations will vary, and teachers need to be aware of carefully differentiating between the parenting role and the teaching role. Success in creating these boundaries will help facilitate the child's adjustment by clarifying both the teacher's and the family's unique roles.

Why does facilitating adjustment matter? These types of experiences can have significance for children for the rest of their lives. Secure attachments to significant adults (including teachers) can compensate for early deprivation and stressful experiences caused by poverty, unskilled parenting, abuse, or neglect (Schweinhart & Weikart, 1996).

Developmental Tasks

Observations and Assessment

Child Development

Interactive Experiences

Teaching

Parent Participation and Involvement

Environment

Activities and Experiences

Validating What Moms and Dads Know

Many parents feel insecure in their roles as their child's first and most important teachers. Some parents try to read everything possible on child rearing and development to try to overcome their feelings of uncertainty and inadequacy. Teachers can help parents by validating what parents know about their child and supporting their parental roles.

Teachers and parents have different views. Parents view the school world through their child's experience; teachers view the school world through the eyes of the group. Further, teachers often disagree with how parents are handling parenting issues because home strategies or techniques differ from those used at school. Teachers who disagree with parents may find it difficult to validate parents.

Despite the fact that infants may spend more waking time in the company of their teacher, parents still have a more profound effect on infants than any other factor. So, when parents want to know what they can do to help their children, embrace their interest and encourage them to stay involved in their child's school, to read to their child each day, and to enjoy being the most influential people in their child's life.

Creating Memories and Recording Development

As you begin this close relationship with the children in your group, you will want to begin a portfolio for each child. Portfolios have several purposes, the most important of which is keeping the focus of curriculum, activities, and experiences on the individual child.

Start by deciding on a format for your portfolios. You may want to use a loose-leaf notebook with pockets in the sides, a packing crate with file folders, or file folders in a magazine holder. During each Possibilities Plan, include things like photographs, lists of books read by the teacher to the child (see page 431), Communication Sheets (see pages 429-430), Anecdotal Observations (see page 428), and work samples.

Collection is just the first stage. You will want to analyze and reflect on your contributions to each portfolio and use the contents to help you get a better view of the child's developmental age and stage, interests, and preferences and to understand the families with which you are working.

Guidance and Discipline

Ignoring as a Guidance Strategy

Ignoring inappropriate behavior is a discipline strategy that teachers often forget to use. The school day can be long, and some children exhibit behaviors that are irritating but not dangerous or really problematic.

For example, infants often dump the contents of manipulative toy containers on the floor or tabletops. An observant teacher uses these experiences to model putting things back in the container and to encourage the baby to help.

To determine if ignoring is an appropriate strategy, ask yourself, "Is this a behavior I can live with in my classroom?" If the answer is yes, try ignoring the behavior. It goes without saying that behavior that hurts other children or destroys the environment or materials cannot be ignored.

Exploratory Biting

Exploratory biting is discussed in a Parent Postcard in this developmental task. The appropriate information for teachers is included in Chapter 4, pages 173-175.

Teacher Competencies to Support Connecting with School and Teacher

Sometimes	Usually	Always	
☐	☐	☐	Greets each child and his parents upon arrival at school.
☐	☐	☐	Has affectionate, appropriate physical contact with infants.
☐	☐	☐	Moves to children to talk rather than calling from a distance.
☐	☐	☐	Understands how to use voice as a teaching tool by speaking slowly and varying intonation and pitch, and exaggerating vocal transitions.
☐	☐	☐	Accepts cultural differences in children without judgment.
☐	☐	☐	Is alert to signs of fatigue, hunger, and frustration.
☐	☐	☐	Monitors children's general comfort; for example, warmth, dryness, dripping noses, wet chins and chests, and so on.
☐	☐	☐	Listens carefully to infant cries; makes decisions quickly and appropriately; does not allow infants to cry without visual, verbal, and physical responses.
☐	☐	☐	Recognizes that adult mood and facial expressions will be seen and felt by infants and will affect children's experiences and development.
☐	☐	☐	Records accurate information about unusual occurrences, accidents, or changes in children's behavior.

Resources for Teachers

National Center for Clinical Infant Programs. (1992). *Heart Start: The emotional foundations of school readiness.* Washington, DC: Zero to Three, the National Center for Clinical Infant Programs.

Shore, R. (1997). *Rethinking the brain: New insights into early development.* New York: Families and Work.

INNOVATIONS IN PARENT PARTNERSHIPS

School- or Teacher-initiated Possibilities

Share Biography

Share a biography and a photo with each family. In your biography, describe your philosophy of early education. Put a magnetic strip on the back of each photo and laminate it or cover it with contact paper, so the family can mount it on the refrigerator for the baby to see.

Mid-Day Reunion

Plan a mid-day parent reunion, particularly for newly enrolled children. Parents may read a book or spend time interacting with their child inside or outside. When it is time to leave, encourage parents to use the same separation and reunion routine that they used in the morning and will use again in the afternoon.

Disposable Camera

Ask parents to send a disposable camera to keep in their child's cubbie. The pictures you take with this camera will allow parents to experience the rich activities their infants enjoy while they are away.

Comfort from Home

Ask parents to leave a part of themselves at school! Infants benefit from having a comfort item that reminds them of their parents, like a throw pillow, a nightgown, or just a handkerchief with a little of Mom's perfume or Dad's aftershave on it. Other ideas include Mom's or Dad's pillowcase (stripped right off the pillow in the morning before leaving), a T-shirt, or a soft hand towel.

Visit Log

Keep a visit log in the child's file. Log each visit the parents make to the school. Use the log as an entry in the child's portfolio. Share the log with parents at parent conference time to help them see their connection (or lack of it) to school.

Parent Participation Possibilities

Meet Parents Tea

Plan a Meet Parents Tea, so parents of infants in your classroom can socialize and get to know each other. Parents whose children are experiencing similar stages of development can be a great resource and comfort for each other.

Parent Postcards

Share Parent Postcards as parents indicate an interest, at appropriate times during the enrollment cycle, or as developmental issues arise. (See page 441 in the Appendix for a sample dissemination schedule.) Copy postcards. Cut if necessary. Address to parent(s) and place on Communication Sheet or hand out personally.

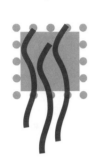

TO

Just How Long Will Adjustment Take?

Many parents view the first few days of a child's school experience as an indication of how things will be when the child completes the adjustment process. Unfortunately, for infants, the initial experience is just the beginning. It is common for infants who are just beginning school to take months to complete adjusting. In general, though, most children are well on their way in about six weeks. What should parents expect as the adjustment process unfolds?

For 1- to 3-month-olds, the initial visit to school may be exciting and interesting or overwhelming. Good school environments are home-like and comfortable but are also more stimulating than the home environments. Depending on the baby's temperament, the response could be interest and curiosity or anxiety and over-stimulation. Babies at this age may initially resist routines such as sleeping and eating, or may shut down and sleep during the entire experience.

For 3- to 9-month-olds, the new and novel environment will probably be engaging, particularly if Mom or Dad is around facilitating the experience. The most common reaction to the adjustment process is to be so interested in the new environment that routines such as sleeping and eating are interrupted. Don't panic if this occurs. A typical schedule will return as the novelty wears off. Expect this part of adjustment to take as much as two weeks.

Infants who start school when they are 11 to 12 or 14 to 17 months old seem to need the longest adjustment period. Separation and stranger anxiety, perfectly normal stages of emotional development, increase the infant's reluctance toward new experiences and the baby's need to have Mom or Dad close. Children who are at this age or stage may need up to six weeks to complete the transition to school.

Starting school after 16 or 17 months is usually met with enthusiasm or concern, depending on the infant's temperament, stage of attachment, and experience with new environments. The good news about this age is that infants are easy to distract after Mom or Dad leaves.

Facilitating Adjustment

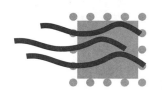

What can parents do to facilitate adjustment? First of all, be patient with the process. It will take a while for your child to adjust. This is normal and should be expected. Stay in close touch with your child's teacher. Good communication helps both you and your baby succeed in adjusting. Talk about your concerns and ask your child's teacher to tell you how she or he is helping your child adjust. Begin the transition process with shorter days. Shorter days in the new environment with new people will be easier for your baby to handle.

Most children make the transition to school in six weeks, but each baby is different. Taking time during the transition process to help your baby adjust will pay off for both of you!

TO
_____
_____
_____

Attachment Behavior, Stage 1—Indiscriminate Attachment: What Parents Can Do

The moment of birth marks the end of an interdependent, physical connection between mother and child. This connection nurtured the baby, providing everything necessary for growth and development. As this first attachment ends, a second, equally important connection begins. This next connection provides what babies need to survive and thrive in the human world. From birth until about 5 or 6 months, your baby will be in the first stage of attaching to his or her significant caregivers—You!

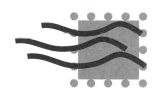

Stage 1 is called indiscriminate attachment and lasts from birth to approximately 5 to 6 months. Stage 1 babies respond to most caring adults, if the babies' needs are met promptly. Crying normally persists for a moment even after babies get a response as their neurological system registers this change.

In Stage 1 of attachment, respond quickly to your baby's cry. Begin to differentiate what cries mean, so you can modify your response to the needs of your baby.

TO
_____
_____
_____

Hold and cuddle your baby. Play with his or her fingers and toes. Talk and sing to your baby while diapering, nursing, and caring for him or her.

Plan a special time each day for "falling in love" with your baby all over again. In a quiet moment gaze into your baby's eyes and really connect. Talk to your baby and listen intently. He or she will be responding to you and looking forward to these special times.

TO _____

We Are Now Partners

Partnerships are special. Although no one is more important to your child than you—his or her parents—starting school means that someone else is sharing the job of providing care and early education to your infant.

Everyone says that involvement in the school will improve the quality of the child's experience. What does involvement mean? And how do you get involved with an already full schedule facing you every day?

Part of being involved is exchanging information with your child's teacher at the beginning or end of the day. Reading and completing the Communication Sheet will take care of this. Another part is looking around the room on a regular basis to see what your child's teacher has prepared to share with you concerning your child's experiences. Look for lesson plans, photographs, developmental banners, and work samples.

There are many more ways to be involved in your child's life at school. Here is a list of ways other parents have involved themselves in school. Look through it and find out which ways might fit your schedule and available time or your particular talents and experiences. Check off the ones that you might like to try and put them in your monthly plan.

☐ Drop by to read a story to your child and others in the group.

☐ Save cereal boxes, orange juice containers, plastic peanut butter jars, boxes with lids, margarine tubs, yogurt containers, paper towel rolls, oatmeal boxes, old magazines, and so on. Keep a paper sack at home to collect these items and bring them in to your child's teacher to convert into teacher-made toys.

TO

We Are Now Partners (continued)

☐ Schedule and attend conferences requested by your child's teacher. Conferences are held regularly and are an excellent time for you to get to know your child's teacher better as you discuss your child's developmental progress.

☐ Read the parent handbook, newsletters, and other written information shared with you by the school or your child's teacher. When the school or teacher takes the time to write something down for you, it is important for you to read it and know about it.

☐ Share family traditions with your child's classroom. Cultural celebrations and special family traditions make your family unique. Sharing these experiences with other children and your child's teachers adds a very special quality to your child's experience and validates his or her uniqueness.

☐ Share your family with us. Bring in pictures of your child's experiences to school.

☐ Encourage visits to school by grandparents, relatives, and friends of your family. Come by for an extra visit when you have time. And don't forget to share your unique expertise. Leisure activities, work-related activities, and your talents are potential resources to enrich the curriculum.

☐ Attend special events planned by your child's teachers. Get-acquainted teas, toy swaps, book exchanges, potluck dinners, happy hour visits, and so on are all planned to involve you and your family.

These are just a few of the ways you can be involved. Remember, we are now partners. Talk to your child's teacher about other ways for you to get involved in your child's education.

TO
_____
_____
_____

Creating Partnerships—Two-way Communication

As parents, you have the greatest influence in your child's life. You also play a major part in determining how satisfied and happy your child is at school. Babies can be sensitive to nonverbal cues. Whether you are relaxed and comfortable or anxious and uncomfortable, your baby will know. Sometimes, school can be a source of anxiety for parents, particularly in the beginning. Almost every difficulty faced at school can be worked through using positive, two-way communication.

Using the written communication system is an important part of this communication. All parents are asked to fill out a daily Communication Sheet. The purpose of this sheet is to create a written, two-way communication system between you and the school.

Teachers need to keep lots of information ready to provide what your baby needs. Information can be lost easily if parents and teachers depend just on their memories and their verbal interactions. Using a written system helps everyone keep up with information that needs to be exchanged and documents the progress of communicating.

Important information about your child's time at home that might be helpful to the teacher includes how long the baby slept, when he or she last ate, information about elimination, and any special instructions for the teacher. This information is so important. Make sure every family member who may take your child to school in the morning recognizes this. It creates a platform from which the teacher is able to anticipate and correctly interpret your child's needs.

Likewise, parents need to know information about what happens each day at school. Your child's activities (eating, sleeping, diaper changes, and so on) will be recorded. Teachers also will record developmental notes and observations.

Use the Communication Sheet to help you get a feel for how the day with your baby went. When you enter the classroom, reunite with your child, read the Communication Sheet, and then ask the teacher any questions you may have.

Parents will have many other types of opportunities for communicating with their child's teacher (conferences, phone calls, notes). Whenever you have a concern, talk with your child's teacher. Don't wait until your concern escalates. Your child's well-being is everyone's concern. The better the communication is between home and school and between school and home, the better the opportunity is for you and your child to feel comfortable with and enjoy his or her school experience.

TO

Help! My Child Got Bitten!—
Understanding Exploratory Biting

All parents dread the time when the teacher tells them their child has been bitten at school. The parent feels helpless for not being there to protect the child from the biter. And parents may wonder why the teacher couldn't or didn't prevent it.

Why does biting seem to occur among children at school? The simple answer to this question, according to noted psychologists Louise Ilg and Florence Ames, is that children bite because they lack language and social skills. They say biting is a developmental phenomenon—it happens at predictable times for predictable reasons tied to children's ages and stages.

For children between early infancy and about 14 or 15 months, biting is often part of the investigation and exploration that defines babies' play. They are curious about things that get put into their mouths. They want to see how things taste and feel. They are interested in exploring everything with their mouths.

Children are also teething during this period. When gums are sore and ache, chewing on something relieves the pressure and feels good! Very rarely at this stage is biting purposeful or intentional.

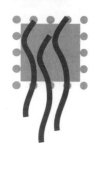

TO

What Can Teachers Do to Prevent Investigative/Exploratory Biting?

Regardless of why the child is biting, teachers have a variety of ways to prevent it. Most of their efforts go into close supervision, careful room arrangements that spread children out in the classroom, and, most important, getting to know your baby's needs and temperament very well. Even with all of these efforts, biting may still occur. What will teachers do when your baby is bitten?

The very first thing your baby's teacher will do is respond quickly and comfort the child who was bitten by holding, cuddling, and helping him or her get over the physical and emotional pain of biting. Then, she will isolate the biter for a short period of time to withdraw attention from the baby who did the biting. And she or he will share the information about the biting incident with you by telling you what happened, when it happened, and how she or he handled the situation, either by telephone or in person at the end of the day.

The teacher won't be sharing with you who did the biting. Information about who the biter isn't helpful because it is the teacher who must handle the situation. As much as you would like to help your baby, you must depend on the teacher to prevent biting at school regardless of who is biting.

What you can count on is accurate information about the situation and what is being done about it. In fact, you should receive a written report. Ask your child's teacher to tell you how she or he handles biting and what she or he is doing to prevent it in your baby's classroom. Your child's teacher is your source of information on what will keep biting from becoming a negative situation for you or your baby. But, if you are not completely convinced, talk to your school director. She or he will be able to connect you to parents of older children who are through the investigative/exploratory biting stage and lived to tell about it!

TO

What Can Parents Do to Prevent Investigative/Exploratory Biting?

The first thing you can do is always respond quickly when your child is hurt. Quick responses help children build a sense of trust that their world is a safe place to be.

Then, never let your child bite you without getting a negative reaction. Tell your baby that you don't like it when he or she hurts you. Remind your child that you always touch him or her softly. Then put your baby down and walk away for a minute or two to communicate that biting won't get your attention—in fact, it will make it disappear.

Plan to work closely with your baby's teacher if biting is occurring at home or in your baby's classroom. Teachers are open to talking and working with you to make sure biting does not become a problem for a particular child. And, expect biting to come and go. It is a developmental phenomenon that will be replaced by more mature skills as your baby grows and learns.

Remember these important points:

- Respond quickly when another child or sibling hurts your child.

- Biting is a developmental phenomenon that comes and goes.

- All children bite occasionally at various ages and stages.

- Your baby's teacher will comfort hurt babies quickly, hugging and cuddling them until they are calm.

- Expect your teacher to talk to you about biting incidents. Expect to see a written report.

- Be your child's first teacher about biting—don't let him or her bite you without getting a negative reaction from you.

- Biting disappears and is replaced by more mature skills as your baby grows.

- Parents of older children can be a resource to help in understanding biting.

- Who did the biting is not as important as the teacher's plan for handling it.

- Talk to your baby's teacher if you have any concerns about any of your baby's behaviors.

Resources for Parents

Add these helpful books to your parent library or post this list on your parent bulletin board.

Greeenspan, S. & Greenspan, N.T. 1989. *First feelings: Milestones in the emotional development of your baby.* New York: Penguin.

Silberg, J. (1999). *125 Brain games for babies.* Beltsville, MD: Gryphon House

Silberg, J. (1993). *Games to play with babies.* Beltsville, MD: Gryphon House.

INNOVATIONS IN ENVIRONMENTS

Multiple Sources of Stimulation

Very young children are constantly exploring the environment through their senses. Carefully plan the classroom to take maximum advantage of the child's natural desire to explore and learn. The environment must first be physically safe, so infants are free, not only to explore, but also to interact with adults and other infants. The environment must be emotionally supportive, so infants have the confidence to try new things. The environment must be cognitively challenging, where children become involved with objects and activities that interest them (Gerber & Johnson, 1997).

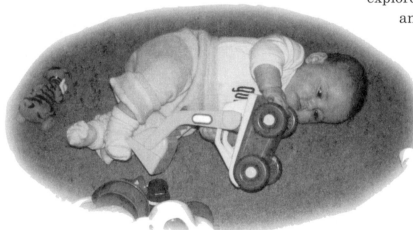

Consider multiple sources of stimulation. Various interesting textures in the environment provide tactile stimulation as the infant is exploring. Hard and smooth surfaces are already present through furnishings in the classroom. Different types of fabric will present an endless variety of textures (satin, cotton, corduroy, tapestry, burlap). Consider contrasts such as hard-soft, rough-smooth, and cool-warm.

A variety of scents also will add variety to the child's environment. Non-toxic lavender, peppermint, and lemon scents can be placed on individual toys or can saturate cotton balls placed in plastic jars with holes punched in the tops for use as smell jars. These scents make a nice addition to the baby powder, baby lotion, and other usual smells in the infant room.

Increasing and Decreasing Stimulation

Teachers in infant environments must be able to increase and decrease the level of activity and stimulation. Lowering the level of light, or raising it, or providing incandescent as well as florescent and full spectrum lighting are examples of ways to change stimulation levels. Adding quiet music or removing all background noise and replacing it with sounds of nature are others. Check your classroom to see which of these dimensions are under your control and can be managed as needed.

Oral Stimulation

Children actively explore their environment in a number of different ways. One important way is by mouthing everything they come in contact with or put in their hands. Offer variety by changing chew toys or anything else that babies enjoy mouthing. Rattles, because of their different shapes, offer an infinite variety of items for chewing. Disinfect items that babies put in their mouths by washing them and rinsing in a bleach-and-water solution of ¼ cup bleach to 1 gallon of water. Regular sanitation after each use with bleach water helps prevent children from sharing colds or other contagious conditions.

Mirrors

In the infant environment, unbreakable mirrors are an incredible source of interest and interaction. More than any other image, babies are drawn to the images of their own faces (Edwards, Gandini & Foreman, 1998; Shore, 1997). For infants, the perfect interactive experience involves discovering and exploring their faces in the mirror.

Not only do mirrors attract the child's attention, but also they allow them visually to orient themselves to others within the classroom. With large mirrors, infants can keep their visual connection with teachers and other children even if they are out of physical reach of them.

Place small unbreakable mirrors in boxes and containers with which young children play. Imagine the delight when an infant looks in a box and sees his own face! Small mirrors with adhesive on the backs can be placed throughout the room, so infants can discover their own image again and again. Mirrors underneath tables, on low shelves, on the walls at various heights, on doors and windowsills, and in cribs will provide stimulating discoveries.

Place larger mirrors over the diaper-changing table, on walls where infants can see themselves eating, and in other areas of the room where children can see their entire images. If possible, cover one entire wall with a mirrored surface. This will brighten the classroom, as well as help infants keep an eye on their teacher.

Activities and Experiences vs. Centers

Most early childhood educators think of interest or learning centers as an essential part of any classroom setting. Yet, environments for infants are different because they cannot choose to go to different areas until they are mobile. For this reason, teachers must bring the activities and experiences to the child, or they must assist the child in going to where the activities are. A wide range of activities and experiences must be available to infants. In each of the following two Possibilities Plans, *Inside and Outside* and *Open and Close*, activities and experiences are presented in the following areas:

- Dramatic Possibilities
- Sensory/Art Possibilities
- Curiosity Possibilities
- Literacy Possibilities
- Music Possibilities
- Movement Possibilities
- Outdoor Possibilities
- Project Possibilities
- Parent Participation Possibilities

WEB

Inside and Outside

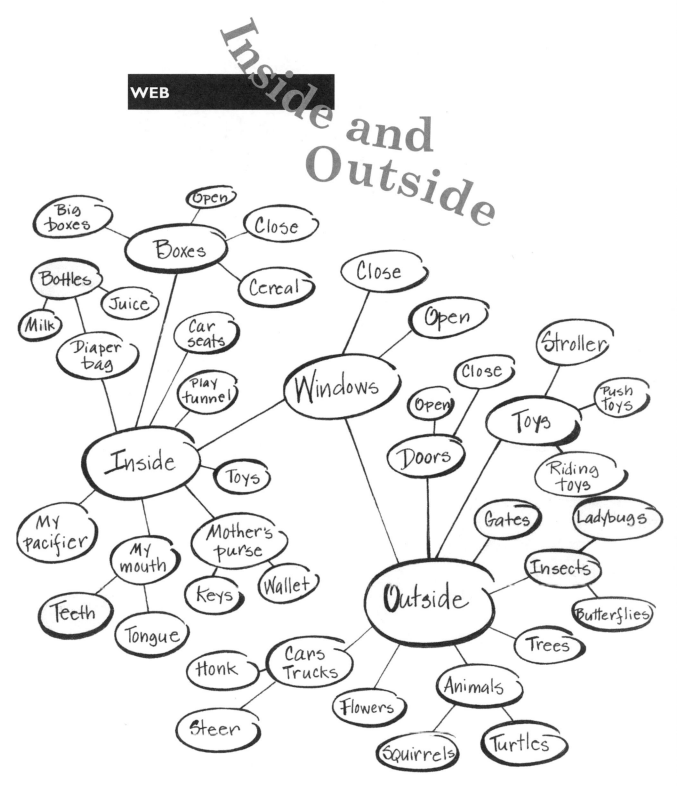

Note: Using the technique of webbing, teachers can follow the leads that children give them, as well as have an unlimited source of options. Always use the webs as a jumping-off point. The possibilities are endless!

PLANNING PAGES

Plan Possibilities

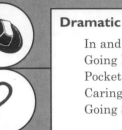

Dramatic

In and Out 124
Going Bye-bye 124
Pocket Clothes 124
Caring for Baby 125
Going Shopping 125

Sensory/Art

Bouncy Seat with Warm Water 125
Warm Water 126
Cool Water 126
Outside Water 126

Curiosity

Ankle Rattles 127
One-piece Puzzles 127
Inside and Outside Purses and
   Briefcases 127
Slide Boxes 128
What's Inside? 128

Outdoor

Play Gym 133
Spray Bottles 133
Box Time 133

Project

Inside Mobiles 134
Outside Mobiles 134
Books Read List 135

Parent Participation

Car Seats 135
Supporting Possibilities 135
Parent Postcards
   Controlling Transition Stress . 136
   Car Seat Safety 138

Literacy

Will I Have a Friend? 129
Goodnight, Moon 129
Picture File Book 129
Inside and Outside Books 130
I See the Moon 130
This Is My Turtle 130
Open, Shut Them 131

Music

Go In and Out the Window 131
Hokey, Pokey 132

Movement

Hands and Knees and Feet
   Inside and Outside 132
Tunnel 133

Inside and Outside

Concepts Learned in

Inside and Outside . . . 139

Prop Boxes

Shopping 139
In and Out 140

Picture File/Vocabulary . . 140

Books

Goodnight Moon by Margaret Wise Brown 129
Inside, Outside, Upside Down by Stan
   and Jan Berenstain 130
Outside Inside by Carolyn Crimi 130
Will I Have a Friend? by Miriam Cohen 129

Rhymes/Fingerplays

"I See the Moon" 130
"Open, Shut Them" 131
"This Is My Turtle" 130

Music/Songs

"Go In and Out the Window" 131
"Hokey Pokey" 132

Toys and Materials 141

 ## In and Out

0-6 months

Materials
None needed

Teacher Talk
Talk with babies describing the actions of the other children. "Matlin, I see you watching Joey. He is playing with the keys. Joey is putting the keys in his mouth."

Position younger babies near where other children are playing.

Going Bye-bye

6-12 months

Materials
Toy keys, jackets, purses, car seats, etc.

Provide items associated with going bye-bye (toy keys, jackets, purses, hats, and car seats). Infants will love to take off clothing and other items. They learn this long before learning to put things on. Name the items and talk about them as infants choose them and play with them. Observe and record your observations as children demonstrate skills such as taking off clothes, putting items in purses or bags, and waving bye-bye.

Pocket Clothes

6-12 months

Materials
Simple clothes with pockets
Rattles

Teacher Talk
Talk about "in" and "out" as pockets are used. "Now it's in the pocket, now it's out!"

Provide simple clothes with pockets. Clothes for older children, not for babies or adults, will work best. Use a variety of different rattles for putting in the pockets and taking out of the pockets. Because aprons are easy to put on and take off, wear one with lots of pockets and a rattle in the pocket.

Caring for Baby

12-18 months

Materials
Diaper bag
Items to go in the diaper bag

The diaper bag is a familiar item for young children. Provide items for taking out and putting in the bag. Include dolls, stuffed animals, diapers, empty baby powder and baby lotion containers, small blankets, and baby toys.

Going Shopping

12 -18 months

Materials
Purses or wallets
Shopping basket
Other props related to shopping
See Shopping Prop Box suggestions on page 139

Teacher Talk
Describe what infants are doing. "Tommie, you have the shopping list for our shopping trip." "That is a cereal box."

Provide items that infants will associate with shopping such as purses or wallets, a shopping basket, and a shopping list. Also, include items that children can put in a shopping cart such as empty food boxes stuffed with paper and taped shut.

SENSORY/ART POSSIBILITIES

Bouncy Seat with Warm Water

0-6 months

Materials
Bouncy seats
Shallow plastic tub(s)
Warm water

Position younger babies in bouncy seats. Take off their shoes and socks. Place a shallow tub with warm water under the seats in such a way that babies can explore the feel of the water with their feet.

Warm Water

6-18 months

Materials
Shallow plastic tubs

Warm water
Wading pool, optional

Toys

Teacher Talk
Talk about bath time as babies play.

For babies who can sit up, provide warm water in shallow tubs for infants to pat and explore. Placing the tubs inside a wading pool will help make cleanup easy. Add toys that float to increase variety. Begin this activity as an individual one and gradually include additional children as infants' experience with water play increases. **Safety note:** As with any activity involving water, supervise closely.

Cool Water

6-18 months

Materials
Shallow plastic tub(s)   Cool water
Towel   Dry clothes

As a variation of the warm water activity, try using water that is cool. Do not include ice cubes because they are a choke hazard. Talk about cool water. Have a towel and clothes ready for drying off and getting dressed. Take the lead from infants. They will let you know when they are ready to end the activity and dry off to begin a new activity. Take photographs and write comments about how children react to the activity. Post where parents can see the photographs or read about how children responded.

Outside Water

6-18 months

Materials
Shallow plastic tubs   Warm and cool water

Teacher Talk
Narrate children's actions. "You placed your hands in the water." "I see your fingers wiggle."

Both the warm and cool water experiences will take on a new dimension outside. Use the words inside and outside as the children play.

? —— Ankle Rattles

0-6 months

Materials
Rattles

Babies will enjoy wearing ankle rattles and hearing the sounds they produce. After placing the rattle on the infant's ankle, give the rattle a gentle shake to demonstrate what happens.

? —— One-piece Puzzles

6-12 months

Materials
Colored construction paper
Cardboard
Glue
Scissors or art knife
Clear contact paper
Elastic pull

Teacher Talk
Talk with infants about what they are doing. "You grabbed the puzzle piece."

Create one-piece puzzles for infants. Glue a solid color paper onto a piece of cardboard. Cut a simple shape from the center of the cardboard. (This is very easy to do using an art knife, but not in the classroom, of course.) Be certain that the inside piece fits easily into the outside piece. Cover with clear contact paper. Add an elastic hand pull to the puzzle piece for younger infants to grab and remove the puzzle piece. Check the puzzles for safety daily to be sure the elastic hand pull does not come loose. Observe the way each child moves the puzzle pieces and record your observations.

? —— Inside and Outside Purses and Briefcases

6- 18 months

Materials
Purses and briefcases
Items to put in them

Teacher Talk
"Ryan, you are going bye-bye with your purse."

Provide interesting items for babies to take out and put in purses and briefcases. Plastic bottles with colored water and glitter with tops glued on securely will be popular. Familiar items like diapers and toy key rattles are also interesting.

? _____ Slide Boxes
6-18 months

Materials
Slide boxes
Items to put inside them

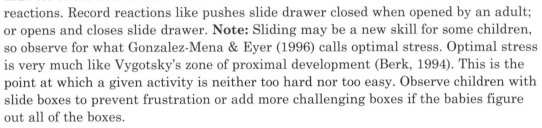

Young children love to explore slide boxes because of the surprise of what may be inside. They also enjoy figuring out the process of opening and closing the drawers of the box. Observe each child's reactions. Record reactions like pushes slide drawer closed when opened by an adult; or opens and closes slide drawer. **Note:** Sliding may be a new skill for some children, so observe for what Gonzalez-Mena & Eyer (1996) calls optimal stress. Optimal stress is very much like Vygotsky's zone of proximal development (Berk, 1994). This is the point at which a given activity is neither too hard nor too easy. Observe children with slide boxes to prevent frustration or add more challenging boxes if the babies figure out all of the boxes.

? _____ What's Inside?
6-18 months

Materials
Formula cans, coffee cans, or oatmeal boxes
Objects to put inside

Teacher Talk
"You poured out the can to see what was inside. Yes, the blocks were hidden inside."

Use formula cans, coffee cans, or oatmeal boxes with objects inside. Smooth edges completely. Objects inside must be too large to fit in the choke tube.

Will I Have a Friend?

0-18 months

Materials
Will I Have a Friend? by Miriam Cohen

Read this book, and then talk about being inside, going to school, and having friends. Record your observations of how each child responds to books (visually attends to the pages, moves to the rhythm of the language, turns pages, points to pictures, makes sounds and words, and indicates to the teacher to read the book again). Communicate your observations to parents using the Communication Sheet (page 430). Add this book to the Books Read list (see page 431) in your classroom.

Goodnight, Moon

0-18 months

Materials
Goodnight Moon by Margaret Wise Brown

Use this book to talk about the moon outside. Point to objects in the book and label them for children. Add this book to the Books Read list (see page 431 in the Appendix).

Picture File Book

0-18 months

Materials
Resealable gallon freezer bags
Items familiar to babies

Teacher Talk
"That is a purse. Does it look like your mommy's purse? I see the handles on the top."

Create this book by using resealable gallon freezer bags or sheet protectors. Choose pictures of items that are familiar to babies and that are related to inside and outside (purses, diaper bags, houses, sky, clouds). Put pictures back to back and seal inside the bags. Join the bags together with metal rings or short lengths of yarn. Use the book to explore vocabulary. **Safety alert:** Watch for chew damage and discard or replace bags.

_____ # Inside and Outside Books

0-18 months

Materials
Books about inside and outside things, such as *Outside Inside* by Carolyn Crimi or
    Inside, Outside, Upside Down by Stan and Jan Berenstain
Magazine
Paper
Glue or tape
Resealable plastic bags

Read books about inside and outside things with children, such as the Berenstain
Bears book *Inside, Outside, Upside Down.* Make concept books for inside and outside
using magazine pictures.

 _____ # I See the Moon

0-18 months

Materials
Paper
Scissors
Tape

Tape a moon shape to the window and point
to it as you say the rhyme below. Post the
words to rhymes on the parent
communication board or give copies to
parents, so they can use them at home or
during drive time.

> *I See the Moon*
>   I see the moon.
>   The moon sees me.
>   God bless the moon,
>   And God bless me.

 _____ # This Is My Turtle

0-18 months

Materials
Toy or stuffed turtles, optional

Teacher Talk
Talk about turtles and how they can pull their arms, legs, tail, and head inside their
shells.

Use this fingerplay as you emphasize the motions. Provide turtles, toy or stuffed, for
infants to hold.

This Is My Turtle
> This is my turtle
> He lives in a shell.
> He likes his home very well.
> He pokes his head out
> When he wants to eat.
> And he pulls it back in
> When he wants to sleep.

Open, Shut Them
6-18 months

Materials
None needed

Enjoy this old classic as you spend one-on-one time with baby.

Open, Shut Them
> Open, shut them, open, shut them, (open and shut baby's hands)
> Give a little clap. (clap baby's hands)
> Open, shut them, open, shut them, (open and shut baby's hands)
> Put them in your lap. (put baby's hand in his lap)

MUSIC POSSIBILITIES

Go In and Out the Window
0-18 months

Materials
None needed

This song is perfect to use in conjunction with inside and outside possibilities. Watch for children responding to the sounds of the music with smiles, bounces, or arm movements. Repeat it often during this plan. Share the words with parents to use at home or during drive time.

Go In and Out the Window
> Go in and out the window,
> Go in and out the window,
> Go in and out the window,
> As we have gone before.

Hokey, Pokey

0-18 months

Materials
None needed

Children enjoy the rhythm and action of this song. They are entertained as the teacher actually does the actions or gently helps the baby do the movements with her using a hand-over-hand approach. Emphasize in and out as you sing the song.

Hokey Pokey
You put your right hand in,
You put your right hand out,
You put your right hand in,
And you shake it all about.
Then you do the hokey pokey,
And you turn yourself around,
That's what it's all about!

You put your left hand in…
You put your right foot in…
You put your left foot in…
You put your right elbow in…
You put your left elbow in…
You put your backside in…
You put your head in…
You put your whole self in…

MOVEMENT POSSIBILITIES

Hands, Knees, and Feet Inside and Outside
0-18 months

Materials
Hand and knee or foot shapes cut from construction paper
Tape

Teacher Talk
Talk about following the hand and knee prints or footsteps to the outside. "We are following the footsteps to the outside." "Step, step, step. Out the door we go." "Reach, crawl, hand, knee."

Secure hand and knee and/or foot shapes to the floor leading to the outside door. Point as you follow the symbols. Also, secure shapes to the sidewalk outside.

Tunnel
6-18 months

Materials
Commercial tunnel or large cardboard box

Teacher Talk
Talk about what each child is doing. "You are crawling into the tunnel. In you go, Martin. I'll wait for you on the other end."

Give each child an opportunity to scoot, crawl, or walk through a tunnel. Use a commercial tunnel or make one using a box from which the staples have been removed. Be certain the tunnel is stationary as children go through.

OUTDOOR POSSIBILITIES

Play Gym
0-6 months

Materials
Play gym
Mat or quilt

Bring a play gym outside. Put the play gym on a mat or quilt in the shade. Moving activities or equipment outside will add novelty.

Spray Bottles
0-18 months

Materials
Spray bottles

Use spray bottles to stimulate baby's senses. Fill with cool water in warm weather and warm water in cooler weather. Spray a hand, a foot, or the surface underneath a hand or foot. Let older infants figure out how the squirt bottle works to squirt the ground, the trees, or the sidewalk.

Box Time
12-18 months

Materials
Large boxes
Sandpaper

Teacher Talk

Talk about the outdoors. "The boxes are on the grass. "You are looking in the box. Do you want to crawl into the box? In you go."

Collect large boxes and check carefully for rough edges. Smooth any rough edges with sandpaper. Remove all staples and reinforce with tape. Take infants and boxes outside.

PROJECT POSSIBILITIES

Inside Mobiles

0-12 months

Materials
Photographs of the children
Markers
Clear contact paper
Fishing line
Coat hanger or small dowels

Teacher Talk
Talk about the photographs as you interact with baby. "I see Samantha." "I see Judith."

Create a mobile for inside the classroom using photographs of children involved in inside activities. Write your observations of children's experiences on the backs of photographs for parents to read and for babies to see print at work. Cover the photographs with clear contact paper and attach to lengths of high-strength monofilament fishing line. Attach the line to a coat hanger or small dowels. Add to the mobile periodically until all infants are pictured. Hang the mobile inside a window or over the diaper changing area. **Note:** Be sure the mobiles are beyond the reach of all children in the classroom.

Outside Mobiles

0-12 months

Materials
Photographs of the children   Markers
Clear contact paper   Fishing line
Coat hanger or small dowels

Teacher Talk
"See the pictures, Dixie Gene. They are outside. I see them blowing in the wind."

Repeat the process described for inside mobiles, but hang the mobile outside the window. Date and label photographs. Talk with babies about the pictures outside and how they move in the wind. Streamers will make the movement more noticeable.

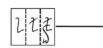

Books Read List

0-18 months

Materials
Books
Paper and pen

Reading to very young babies is a good idea. Not only is it an intimate one-to-one experience, but it also introduces children to language, visual representations with meaning, and vocabulary. To document the importance of reading for children, keep a list of the books that have been read to the children in the classroom. Keep the list handy on a bulletin board or clipboard, so it can be amended as new books are read. Make sure to date each entry and note which children were included in the reading activity. This project can take on even more meaning if the teacher makes notes about reactions to the book or identifies which children liked which book the best. It can also serve as a wonderful resource for parents who may wonder which books to buy or check out of the public library for reading at home.

Take the list to parent meetings and add a copy to the infants' portfolios. Reading to children is the most powerful early literacy activity. This is an excellent way for teachers to help parents see that even babies are learning the precursor skills to reading, including tracking from left to right and from top to bottom, turning pages, pointing to pictures and words, reading context clues, reading pictures, and so on. See page 431 in the Appendix for a sample Books Read list.

PARENT PARTICIPATION POSSIBILITIES

Car Seats

Ask parents to leave their car seats in the classroom for a day. Car seats provide an interesting opportunity for gross motor development (climbing in and out), as well as for dramatic play.

Supporting Possibilities

A number of different common household discards are needed for use in this Possibilities Plan. Ask parents to collect empty plastic jars with lids; empty containers of baby powder, baby lotion, and shampoo; purses; clean, used diaper bags; and small coats. Let parents know how the items will be used in the plan; for example, empty baby shampoo bottles with lids glued and taped will be used for filling and dumping activities.

Parent Postcards

Parent Postcards in this section are designed to share with parents during the Possibilities Plan. The topics are natural extensions of the activities and experiences that you are planning and implementing for the infants in the classroom. Use the postcards to connect parents to their children's learning.

TO
_____
_____

Controlling Transition Stress

Periods of activity and quiet are a natural part of an infant's day. As infants get older, their need for quiet times decreases, but they still require many variations in pace across the day. Young children who are in settings where the activity level and noise level remains high throughout the day may become over-stimulated or experience stress.

When children experience stress, particularly emotional stress, things in the body change. Heart rates increase and body temperatures soar or drop, depending on the emotion. Babies need opportunities to experience optimal levels of arousal—that is, where there is a comfortable balance between being revved up and being calmed down.

The most hectic parts of the school day are arrival and departure times. When parents are dropping off infants in the morning, separating from parents and connecting to school and teacher ARE the activities. Don't expect to see finger paint and water play activities going on during these naturally hectic times! If these activities were added during these already stressful times, children and parents would be overwhelmed.

What can parents do to help make transitions less hectic? The first and most important thing is to speak in a quiet voice. In your excitement to reunite with your baby, you may raise the ambient noise level by calling across the room or talking too loudly to your child.

The second thing you can do is reunite with your child first. Save reading the Communication Sheet or talking to the teacher for later. Even infants who have had very few crying episodes during the school day may begin to cry when their parents re-enter the classroom. These cries mean, "Hey, it's my turn!"

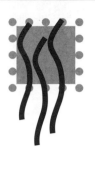

TO _____
   _____
   _____

Controlling Transition Stress (continued)

The third thing you can do is read the Communication Sheet before you ask your child's teacher about the day. Teachers record details about the day on the Communication Sheet. The chart may answer all of your questions without having to talk with the teacher. Remember, babies who are not going home yet will still need attention during your departure.

The fourth thing you can do is ask the teacher questions when she or he is able to answer them. If the teacher is holding a screaming baby or changing a dirty diaper, gather your things together and wait a moment until she or he can give you her or his undivided attention. If it seems like there will never be a quiet time, write your question or comment down, so you won't forget to talk about it later.

Separation experiences are the last interaction you and your child will have every morning until after school. Reuniting experiences are the first interaction you will have after being apart. These experiences form a special bond between you and your baby. It is worth the effort to make them as positive as possible.

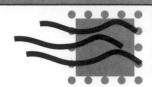

Car Seat Safety

In recent years parents have learned more and more about car seat safety. Most parents understand that infants must be secured in an approved car seat that is installed properly in the correct position.

All young children should be in the back seat. Although airbags can be lifesavers for adults in front seats, they present a great danger for young children.

Hospitals now require that babies leave the hospital in an approved car seat in the back seat of the car. Remember, follow the manufacturer's guidelines concerning the child's weight, age, position in the car, and method of buckling in the seat. Although you might be tempted to buy a car seat at a yard sale, the guidelines that accompany the car seat are crucial. A more recent model may be the best decision.

TO _____

_____

_____

Concepts Learned in Inside and Outside

Concepts Learned

I can put things inside other things.

Keys go inside a purse or pocket.

Things change when I go outside.

Things change when I go inside.

My body fits inside things and outside things.

Cars and trucks have inside and outside.

Insides are different from outsides (boxes, food jars, and bottles).

I can go bye-bye.

I can go shopping.

Water can be warm or cool.

The sky is outside.

I can squeeze a squirt bottle.

My body makes prints.

I can climb in my car seat.

Briefcases have things inside.

Purses have things inside.

Boxes open and close.

I can kick my feet and make noise with ankle rattles.

I can do puzzles.

I can take tops off.

Resources

Prop Boxes

Shopping

   Food boxes

   Hats

   Jackets

   Paper bags

   Purses

   Scarves

   Shopping list

   Toy keys

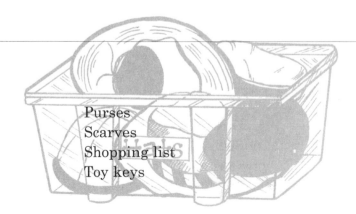

In and Out

Boxes	Oatmeal boxes
Cans	Shoes
Clothes with pockets	Socks

Picture File/Vocabulary

Babies	Diapers
Babies inside	Inside house
Babies outside	Moon
Bottles	Outside house
Bugs	Parents
Butterflies	Purses
Car seats	Stars
Clouds	Stores
Curtains	Windows

Books

Goodnight Moon by Margaret Wise Brown (page 129)

Inside, Outside, Upside Down by Stan and JanBerenstain

Outside Inside by Carolyn Crimi

Will I Have a Friend? by Miriam Cohen (page 129)

Rhymes/Fingerplays

"I See the Moon" (page 130)

"Open, Shut Them" (page 131)

"This Is My Turtle" (page 130)

Music/Songs

"Go In and Out the Window" (page 131)

"Hokey Pokey" (page 132)

 Toys and Materials

The following purchased items are important for this Possibilities Plan:

Activity gym

Books about inside and outside

Clear contact paper or laminating film

Dolls

Rattles

Shallow tubs

Stuffed animals

Toy or stuffed turtles

The following gathered items will help support this Possibilities Plan:

Blanket

Car seats

Empty baby items (lotion, powder)

Sheet

Toy turtles

Toys that float

Prop box items

WEB

Open and Close

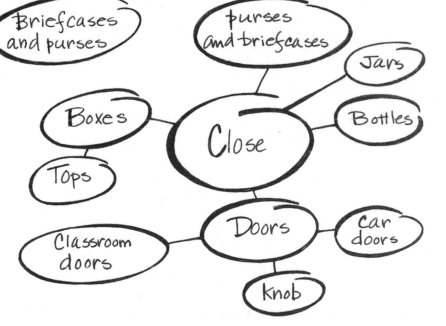

Note: Using the technique of webbing, teachers can follow the leads that children give them, as well as have an unlimited source of ideas. Always use the webs as a jumping-off point. The possibilities are endless!

Plan Possibilities

Dramatic

Open and Close Baby Play 146
Going on a Picnic 146
Going Places 146

Sensory/Art

Baby's First Book 147
Gelatin Gigglers 148

Curiosity

Hand Hiding 148
Jack-in-the-Box 148
Pop-up Pals 149
Mirror with Curtain 149
Boo! Boxes .149
Socks and Cans 150

Literacy

Happy Birthday, Moon 150
Goodnight Moon 150
Open and Close Books 150

Music

Good Morning to You 151
If You're Happy and You Know It . . .151
A Tisket, a Tasket 152
Where Is Thumbkin? 152

Movement

Reaching and Grasping Rattles 153
Open and Close Box 153
Shoeboxes 153

Outdoor

Open/Close Eyes, Hands, Mouth 154
Open/Close Door 154

Project

Open/Close Picture Book 154
Open/Close Flap 155

Parent Participation

Supporting Possibilities 155
Baby Picnic 155
Parent Postcards
Process Is the Goal 156
Object Permanence 157

Open and Close

Books

Arthur's Eyes by Marc T. Brown
Arthur's Nose by Marc T. Brown
Bright Eyes, Brown Skin by Cheryl Willis Hudson
Close Your Eyes by Jean Marzollo
Eyes, Nose, Ears and Toes by Jane Conteh-Morgan
Goodnight Moon by Margaret Wise Brown
Happy Birthday, Moon by Fred Asch
The Mouse Party: an Open-the-Door Book,
    by Bridgette Beguino 150

Concepts Learned in

   Open and Close 158

Prop Boxes

   Going Places 158
   Going Night, Night 158
   Picnic 159

Picture File/Vocabulary . . .**159**

Rhymes/Fingerplays

   "Where Is Thumbkin?" 152

Music/Songs

   "A Tisket, a Tasket" 152
   "Good Morning to You" 151
   "If You're Happy and You Know It" 151

Toys and Materials **160**

Open and Close Baby Play
0-18 months

Materials
Small boxes, purses, bags, or pots and pans

Many opportunities exist for "open" and "close" experiences during play. Small boxes, purses, bags, pots and pans, and window curtains are just a few of the many possibilities.

Going on a Picnic
0-18 months

Materials
Picnic items
See Picnic Prop Box suggestion on page 159

Teacher Talk
Talk about opening and closing the basket. "Winston can open the basket. What do you see?"

Use items that you might bring on a picnic (blanket, plastic fruit, empty soda bottles, or colored water in bottles with tops glued). Offer very young babies objects from the basket to hold on to or to mouth. Help older babies place items in a picnic basket, close and open the top, and dump the items onto the floor.

Going Places
6-18 months

Materials
Coats, purses, toy keys, or shoes
See Going Places Prop Box suggestions on page 158

Teacher Talk
Narrate children's actions. "You put the keys in your purse. Are you ready to go?"

Use realistic items that infants associate with going places, such as coats, purses, toy keys, and shoes.

Baby's First Book

0-18 months

Materials

Paper

Paint

Tape

Contact paper

Teacher Talk

Watch the child's face and comment on his reactions. "The paint is cold! You made marks with your fingers."

Fold a piece of paper in half. Tape the edges to a table or tray on all four sides. Put a dab of washable, non-toxic paint on the paper and allow the child to explore it. When the child loses interest in the experience, remove the tape, and let the paint air dry. Position the paper vertically with the fold on the left side. Title the book with the child's name and put the date on the inside cover. Cover the book with contact paper to increase its durability. Offer the child his book to open and close. Share the book with parents to take home and read to their child. Over a period of time, each child will have an opportunity to create a book.

Infant teachers often wonder how to do art and sensory experiences with children. The idea of three or four children covered with paint can terrify the bravest teacher. Instead, view art activities as emerging projects that take place over time. Take the time to complete an art activity with one or two children at a time. Pick times that are calm and free of routines. Enjoy the experience as the children explore and discover together. Baby's First Book is an example of this kind of art experience. Gelatin Gigglers is an example of a sensory experience.

Gelatin Gigglers

6-18 months

Materials
Gelatin and materials to make it
Round dry cereal

Teacher Talk
Describe how the food feels as the child wiggles and jiggles the gelatin. "The gelatin feels soft under your fingers, Juan. What did you find?"

Gigglers are a good way for children to experience a different texture. Put a piece of round cereal in each giggler before it gels. See what the infant does when he discovers the cereal.

CURIOSITY POSSIBILITIES

Hand Hiding

0-12 months

Materials
Objects that will pass the choke tube test

Teacher Talk
"Where's the block, Angelica? There it is! Do you want to play again?"

Place an object in your hand. Let baby see what you are doing. Open your hand to reveal what is hidden. Watch the child's cues to determine how many times you repeat the interaction.

Jack-in-the-Box

6-18 months

Materials
Jack-in-the-Box

Teacher Talk
Call children's names as you interact with them. "Let's put the doll back in the box, Micheala. Ready for the surprise? Here it comes!" Use this toy to talk about "open" and "close" with infants.

Notice each child's cues to determine whether or not to continue playing. Some children may find the surprise frightening. Other infants will anticipate the surprise with glee.

?——— Pop-up Pals

6-18 months

Materials
Pop-up toy

Teacher Talk
Narrate children's actions. "Nellie, you made the dog pop up. Again? You can do it again."

Provide a pop-up toy for baby. The cause-and-effect relationship between moving something and having the figure pop up will intrigue infants.

?——— Mirror with Curtain

6-18 months

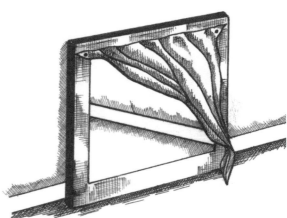

Materials
Unbreakable mirror attached to the wall
Curtain over it

Hang a curtain over the mirror that is in your classroom, so babies can discover their own image as the curtain is opened and closed. Leave the curtain opened sometimes and closed sometimes. Play peek-a-boo with the babies who discover the mirror.

?——— Boo! Boxes

6-18 months

Materials
Photographs or small acrylic mirror
Shoeboxes
Glue or tape

Teacher Talk
"Boo! Ida, I see you!"

Attach photographs to the inside lids of shoeboxes. When babies open the boxes, note the surprise on their faces when they see a face looking back, or tape a small acrylic mirror inside the lid of the shoebox. (Locker mirrors work well.)

❓ ——— Socks and Cans

12-18 months

Materials
Clean, dry, empty orange juice can
Clean white sock
Toy

Put an orange juice can (with no sharp edges) inside of a clean white athletic sock. Put a toy inside the can inside the sock and offer it to the child to explore.

LITERACY POSSIBILITIES

Happy Birthday, Moon

0-18 months

Materials
Happy Birthday, Moon by Fred Asch

Read this book to children. Observe their reaction to the story (eye contact, bouncing, cooing) and note reactions on the communication sheet. Add the book to your Books Read list (see page 431).

Goodnight Moon

0-18 months

Materials
Goodnight Moon by Margaret Wise Brown

Use this classic book to talk with children about "open" and "close." Add the book to your Books Read list.

Open and Close Books

0-18 months

Materials
Open and Close books, such as
    Arthur's Eyes by Marc T. Brown
    Arthur's Nose by Marc T. Brown
    Bright Eyes, Brown Skin by Cheryl Willis Hudson
    Close Your Eyes by Jean Marzollo
    Eyes, Nose, Ears and Toes by Jane Conteh-Morgan
    The Mouse Party: An Open-the-Door Book by Bridgette Beguino

Read any of the above books to one baby or two or three babies at appropriate times. Add to the Books Read list (see Appendix page 431).

MUSIC POSSIBILITIES

Good Morning to You
0-18 months

Materials
None needed

Sing this good morning song as babies arrive with their parents. Music can be soothing, and the ritual of separating from Mom or Dad with a song now will pay off as the child gets older and is comforted by the same separation routine used over and over again.

Good Morning to You
    Good morning to you.
    Good morning to you,
    We're all in our places
    With bright, shining faces.
    Good morning to you.

If You're Happy and You Know It
6-18 months

Materials
None needed

Sing this song with children. Add variations like open or close your eyes, hands, mouth. As infants get familiar with the song, they will respond differently. Videotape the child responding to the directions in the song. Send the videotape home for the parents to watch or put it on to play during reunions.

If You're Happy and You Know It
    If you're happy and you know it,
    Clap your hands. (clap, clap)
    If you're happy and you know it,
    Clap your hands. (clap, clap)
    If you're happy and you know it,
    Then your face will surely show it.
    If you're happy and you know it,
    Clap your hands. (clap, clap)

A Tisket, a Tasket

6-18 months

Materials
None needed

Sing this song as children play with the picnic basket.

> *A Tisket, a Tasket*
>   A tisket, a tasket,
>   A green and yellow basket.
>   I wrote a letter to my love,
>   And on the way I lost it.
>   I lost it; I lost it.
>   And on the way I lost it.
>   A little boy picked it up,
>   And put it in his pocket.

Where Is Thumbkin?

6-18 months

Materials

Use this song as the children play. Children enjoy the rhyme and repetition. Notice their reactions to fly away. Share the tune and the movements with parents.

> *Where Is Thumbkin?*
>   Where is thumbkin?
>   Where is thumbkin?
>   Here I am; here I am.
>   How are you today, sir?
>   Very well, I thank you.
>   Fly away; fly away.
>
>   Where is pointer?
>   Where is pointer?
>   Here I am; here I am.
>   How are you today, sir?
>   Very well, I thank you.
>   Fly away; fly away.
>
>   Where is tall one?
>   Where is ring finger?
>   Where is pinky?

Reaching and Grasping Rattles

0-6 months

Materials
Quilt or blanket
Rattles

Position young babies on a quilt or blanket on the floor. Shake different rattles and then place them near the babies. Observe what babies do. Record your observations on the Communication Sheet (pages 429-430).

Open and Close Box

6-18 months

Materials
Medium-size boxes
Objects to put into the boxes

Teacher Talk
Talk about what each child is doing. "Jackie can open and close the box. Open. Close. Open. Close."

Give each child an opportunity to play and strengthen arm muscles as he opens and closes medium-size boxes. Provide items to put in and take out of the box.

Shoeboxes

6-18 months

Materials
Shoeboxes with lids
Tape
Items to put into the shoeboxes

Provide shoeboxes with lids. Loosely tape one side of the lid to the box. This will make it easier for babies to open and close the shoeboxes. Provide items to put in and take out. Provide rattles that make noise to add interest.

Open/Close Eyes, Hands, Mouth
0-6 months

Materials
None needed

Teacher Talk
Talk about facial features. "Eyes. Shawn closed his eyes. Now they are open again."

Outside is a fun place to play games with infants. Open and close your mouth. Show your tongue and teeth. Talk about them. See if the baby joins you in the action. Take cues from the baby to determine if you go on to eyes and hands.

Open/Close Door
6-18 months

Materials
None needed

Teacher Talk
Describe what you are doing. "I am turning the knob, so the door will open. See how wide the door opens. Now, I am closing the door."

Before children go outside, open and close the door several times.

Open/Close Picture Book
6-18 months

Materials
Paper
Glue or tape
Photographs or magazine pictures
Scissors

Make a concept book for open and close. Use photographs of children involved in "open" and "close" activities, both inside and outside. Or, cut pictures of similar activities from appropriate magazines. Add to the book as the plan progresses. Share the book often with the children.

Open/Close Flap

6-18 months

Materials
Box, low table, or bottom shelf
Cloth

Hang a piece of cloth over the opening of a box, a low table, or the bottom shelf of a storage unit. Throughout the Possibilities Plan, change the items inside. Babies will enjoy looking many times each day to determine the surprise.

PARENT PARTICIPATION POSSIBILITIES

Supporting Possibilities

A number of different household items are needed for use in this Possibilities Plan. Ask parents to collect empty food containers, plastic soda and water bottles, boxes, curtains, cloth, and picnic items. Let parents know how the items will be used. Check all items for safety.

Baby Picnic

Ask parents to provide items for a baby picnic (banana, dry cereal, crackers, teething biscuits, meat sticks, etc.). Invite parents to join you for the picnic. Provide a shady spot, plenty of water, and a quilt or blanket. Take pictures to post in the classroom and share with parents who could not attend. Add the baby picnic to your log of parent visits or to the baby's portfolio.

Parent Postcards

Parent Postcards in this section are designed to share with parents during the Possibilities Plan. The topics are natural extensions of the activities and experiences that you are planning and implementing for the infants in the classroom. Use the postcards to connect parents to their children's learning.

Process Is the Goal

Because young children are living in the moment, the process—the experience of an activity, whether it is art, sensory, or music—is the goal. Sometimes adults have a hard time with this concept because we tend to look at the product or the accomplishment to determine whether we are pleased or displeased with our work. Young children have no interest in the final product, especially an art product. Art activities for babies are sensory in nature. They allow infants to explore the world around them.

Your child's teacher will be very careful to observe and record her or his observations of children as they interact during the day. Teachers may even take photographs to share with you to show what the process was like, even if the product isn't available.

Play is the work of children. As children play and interact with their environment and with significant adults in their lives, they are learning. As adults, we are challenged to stay in the moment just as a baby does, and enjoy the process.

TO

TO

Object Permanence

As babies develop, they learn that items hidden from their view are still there. This is called object permanence. Experiences with concepts such as open and close give babies opportunities to realize that their view of something does not determine its existence. The emergence of object permanence is an indicator of both emotional and cognitive developmental growth.

To illustrate the concept of object permanence, try using activities such as peek-a-boo with your baby. "Where's Mommy? Here she is!" If your baby is really surprised that you are still there when your hands are removed, then object permanence has not yet been acquired.

You can explore object permanence using a blanket and different rattles or cuddle toys. Show your child the toy and then place it under the blanket. Ask, "Where's the rattle?" Then pull the toy from under the blanket. "I see the rattle!" Observe your child's response.

By 12 to 14 months of age, most children begin to understand that objects don't disappear just because you can't see them. You will know when your child is developing object permanence because he or she will cry when you leave the room! The infant's crying signals that he or she is beginning to suspect that you still exist when you leave. This means the significant cognitive skill of object permanence is emerging.

Encouraging object permanence by playing these games is one more way to celebrate the many changes that are occurring with your baby.

Concepts Learned

Concepts Learned in Open and Close

I can open and close things.

Things are there when I can't see them.

I have a tongue and teeth in my mouth.

I can open and close my mouth, hands, and eyes.

Picnic baskets are full of stuff!

Outside is different from inside.

I can find things that are hidden.

Purses open and close.

Boxes open and close.

Pots and pans have lids.

I can picnic.

I can dump things out.

I can make things happen.

I can play peek-a-boo.

I have a thumb.

Doors open and close.

Resources

Prop Boxes

Going Places
  Bags   Scarves
  Billfolds   Shoes
  Hats   Toy keys
  Jackets   Wallets
  Purses

Going Night, Night
  Blankets
  Books   Cuddle toys
  Blankets   Pillows
                        Sleepy music

Picnic

Empty food containers	Picnic basket
Empty soda bottles	Paper sandwiches (sealed in bag)
Empty water bottles	Sheet/blanket/quilt
Plastic fruit	Toy binoculars

Picture File/Vocabulary

Cabinet (open and closed)

Eyes (open and closed)

Curtain (open and closed)

Hands (open and closed)

Door (open and closed)

Mouth (open and closed)

Books

Arthur's Eyes by Marc T. Brown

Arthur's Nose by Marc T. Brown

Bright Eyes, Brown Skin by Cheryl Willis Hudson

Close Your Eyes by Jean Marzollo

Eyes, Nose, Ears and Toes by Jane Conteh-Morgan

Goodnight Moon by Margaret Wise Brown

Happy Birthday, Moon by Fred Asch

The Mouse Party: an Open-the-Door Book, by Bridgette Beguino

Rhymes/Fingerplays

"Where Is Thumbkin?" (page 152)

Music/Songs

"A Tisket, a Tasket" (page 152)

"Good Morning to You" (page 151)

"If You're Happy and You Know It" (page 151)

Toys and Materials

The following purchased items are important for this Possibilities Plan:

Books about open and close
Cuddle toys
Jack-in-the-box
Pop-up pals
Prop box items
Rattles
Toy key rattles

The following gathered items will help support this Possibilities Plan:

Cloth
   Curtains
     Finger paint and paper
      Food containers
    Medium cardboard boxes
  Picnic basket and items
 Picture book
Shoeboxes
Soda bottles (filled with colored water
  and glued shut)
Water bottles (filled with water and
  glued shut)
Prop box items

CHAPTER 4

Relating to Self and Others

INTRODUCTION

During infancy, babies go from seeming to be virtually uninterested in the world that surrounds them to being intensely interested in the human world and their place in it. Relationships begin to develop seconds after birth as babies experience relating to their mothers from outside the comfort and security of the womb.

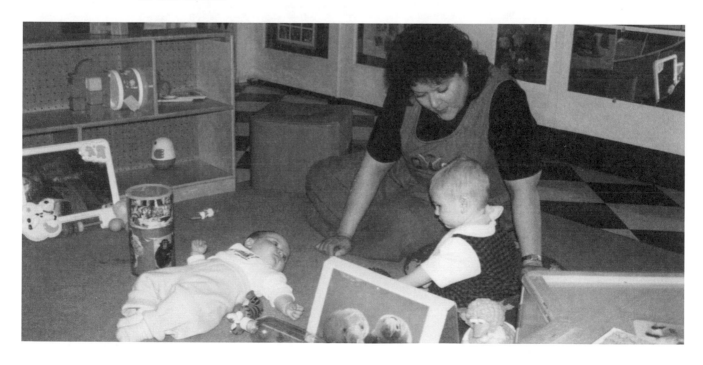

From the small circle of family, relationships widen to include extended family, neighbors, and friends, and then school and peers. As babies become mobile, their view of the world broadens rapidly.

Throughout infancy, almost everything in the baby's environment is stimulating and interesting. After babies discover other people, it is the interaction with people they seek most often and enjoy with immense pleasure.

INNOVATIONS IN OBSERVATION/ASSESSMENT

Observation/Assessment Instrument

This assessment instrument on the next page is not just a skills checklist. Instead it is designed to guide the teacher's observation of children's development through major interactional tasks of infancy. The assessment's focus is on what IS happening, not just what should happen or what will happen. Use this assessment to lead to developmentally appropriate practice.

Infant (0-18 months) Assessment

Task: Relating to Self and Others

	0-6 months	6-12 months		12-18 months
R1	a. Calms self with adult support	b. Calms self with support from adults and/or transitional objects.		c. Calms self with transitional objects.
R2	a. Unaware of own image in mirror.	b. Curious about own image in mirrors and photographs.	c. Discovers self in mirror and photographs.	d. Differentiates own image from images of others.
R3	a. Begins to demonstrate preferences for different types of sensory stimuli.	b. Prefers some types of stimuli to others.		c. Is interested in pursuing favorite stimulation activities again and again.
R4	a. Develops a multi-sensory interest in the world—wants to see, touch, mouth, hear, and hold objects.	b. Uses senses to explore and discover the near environment.		c. Uses motor movements to enhance sensory exploration of the environment.
R5	a. Play is predominantly unoccupied in nature.	b. Play is predominantly onlooker in nature.	c. Play is predominantly solitary in nature.	
R6	a. Exhibits practice play.			b. Exhibits symbolic play.
R7	a. Develops an interest in the human world.	b. Seeks interactions with responsive adults; interested also in what other children are doing.	c. Seeks most interactions with familiar adults; fascinated by what other children are doing.	d. Prefers interactions with familiar adults; resists interaction with unfamiliar adults; may be cautious with unfamiliar friends.
R8	a. Does not distinguish between needs (food, diaper changes, sleep) and wants (social interaction, a new position, holding instead of lying in the bed).	b. Begins to distinguish between needs and wants; can communicate differently about different needs and wants.	c. Uses objects, gestures, and behaviors to indicate needs and wants.	d. Uses single words to indicate needs and wants like "muk" for "I want milk", or bye-bye for "Let's go bye-bye."
R9	a. Creates mental images of emotions and emotional responses to situations.			b. Begins to understand how feelings relate to others
R10	a. Unable to negotiate interactions with peers without direct adult support and facilitation.	b. Calls for help loudly by crying or screaming when problems occur during exploration of the environment or with peers.	c. Exchanges or trades with peers to get a desired toy or material with direct adult support and facilitation.	d. Asks other children to walk away when conflict arises between children; expects the other child to do so.
R11	a. Explores environment and the things in it orally. May bite, poke, scratch, or pinch others during exploration.			b. Experiments with behavior that gets a reaction; may bite, pinch, poke, scratch during interactions with others to see what happens.

INNOVATIONS IN CHILD DEVELOPMENT

Social Development

During the first three years, the social and the emotional domains of development weave together—it is hard to know where emotional development begins or ends and social development takes over. For infants, it is the connected nature of these two domains that makes focusing on both important.

The reflexes with which a baby is born influence early social development. Crying, sucking, and other motor reflexes create connections with caregivers who are responsive to these early social attempts. Soon, though, interaction between babies and their caregivers and interaction with the environment take over as the motivation for social and emotional development.

Attachment, as discussed on pages 98-100 of Chapter 3, plays a huge role in emerging social development. So does the environment. But more than any other developmental activity or behavior, play facilitates children's social development.

Play

The development of play overlaps all areas of development—physical, social, emotional, and intellectual, which includes cognitive and language development. In fact, we often determine where a child is on one or more developmental continua by watching her play. The developmental process guides play behavior from the simple to the complex, from concentrating on the self to interacting with others, and from the concrete to the abstract (Rogers and Sawyer, 1988).

The benefits of play for children are well documented. Because play is so integrated into the developmental context, it is helpful to look at the types of play behavior and to use this knowledge to understand the social development of very young children in school.

Piaget and Play

Piaget gave us a cognitive conceptualization of play divided into three types of play behavior—practice play, symbolic play, and play-with-rules (Piaget,

1962). Practice play is composed of repetitions of the same movements and actions both with and without objects. Infants spend many hours repeating actions that interest them. Symbolic play involves the beginning of the traditional "dramatic play" where children recreate in play what they see happening in the real world. Play-with-rules is the last type of play behavior that emerges during the late preschool years. During this type of play, children began to impose rules on play to govern play or to manipulate interactions.

Parten and Play

As children develop socially, they experience six increasingly complex types of peer play (Parten, 1932). The first type is unoccupied play in which children watch others at play. Then, onlooker play emerges in which children watch others play, but seek to be near, perhaps even responding to the play of others. Solitary independent play comes next. Children play alone with objects without interacting with others, regardless of how near. Parallel activity emerges next with children playing alongside each other with similar toys—beside each other rather than with each other. In associative play, activities occur between children although no specific roles are assigned or play goal identified. Cooperative play is the sixth form of play that finds children cooperating with others to create play situations. Group membership is defined and roles are played by group members. During infancy, play is predominately unoccupied, onlooker, and solitary.

Understanding play behavior gives teachers cues as to what stage their children are socially and emotionally. Information about such behaviors facilitates fine-tuning the interactive relationship.

Six Types of Peer Play
1. Unoccupied Play
2. Onlooker Play
3. Solitary Independent Play
4. Parallel Activity
5. Associative Play
6. Cooperative Play

Vygotsky and Play

While all of these theorists support play as the link between children and the larger society, Vygotsky's sociocultural theory is based on the premise that children socially construct what they know in the context of their family and cultural experiences. In Vygotsky's theory, language is the primary strategy for communication and contact with others (Berk, 1994; Berk & Winsler,1995). In other words, Piaget said children construct knowledge by interacting with objects and perfecting errors. Vygotsky said children construct knowledge through instructions of others, and by socially interacting.

Vygotsky is best known for the idea of the zone of proximal development (ZPD), which is "the range of tasks a child cannot yet handle alone but can accomplish with the help of adults and more skilled peers" (Berk, 1994, p.30). According to Vygotsky, play creates a ZPD in the child, preparing through make-believe play for the future development of abstract thought. Supportive caregivers and more competent peers can raise the level of play children use. Called scaffolding, this support is essential to cognitive development in the early years.

Engaging in joint play with infants helps them develop skills that can later be used in social play with peers. Teachers can take turns with infants, suggesting imaginative play and selecting a level of support for play that matches the infant's abilities. All of these supportive behaviors move infants toward social play with their peers.

INNOVATIONS IN INTERACTIVE EXPERIENCES

Infants' everyday experiences stimulate all developmental domains. This overlap is precisely why teaching to stimulate emotional and social learning is so difficult to explain. Long before children begin to show others their new skills, these experiences lay the foundation for future relationship success. Infant teachers need to be attuned to the importance of everyday, yet important, experiences. They are truly the foundation upon which crucial skills and abilities grow.

Think about the following list of experiences and activities, and make sure that the classroom reflects many of them.

- ☐ Hold babies facing out to see and be seen from the safe harbor of your arms.
- ☐ Provide physical comfort to babies, both when it is needed or demanded and when it is not.
- ☐ Talk to babies during routines.
- ☐ Stimulate the senses through interaction with people, toys, and materials.
- ☐ Rotate toys and materials often enough to support new play.
- ☐ Create quiet places to play together every day with every baby.
- ☐ Establish a few consistent limits.
- ☐ Comment on what children are doing as they play.
- ☐ Imitate children's actions.
- ☐ Model play behaviors.
- ☐ Engage in joint pretend play with babies.

List of experiences and activities (continued)

☐ Serve as a secure base for exploration of the physical and social worlds.

☐ Point out interesting things in the inside and outside worlds.

☐ Support emerging symbolic play with props.

☐ Update children's preferences as they change.

☐ Provide cause-and-effect activities and experiences and toys.

☐ Put babies side-to-side and face-to-face.

☐ Respond quickly to distress.

☐ Take walks and stroller rides outdoors.

INNOVATIONS IN TEACHING

Stage 2—Discriminate Attachment: What Teachers Can Do

During this stage of attachment, babies smile, babble, coo, and respond more quickly to familiar adults. Babies show a definite preference for familiar people. Teachers can support progress during this stage by continuing to respond promptly to crying and calls for help from babies to reinforce that the world is a responsive place.

Teachers can also create a unique style of interacting with each of their babies that takes individual schedule and temperament into consideration. In other words, teachers individualize their approach to each baby in response to the baby's unique characteristics. Post pictures of the family in the child's crib, in the room, and in the family photo album (see page 65) so that parents and other familiar people in the child's world can still be close in times of need.

Play lots of action/reaction games and recite rhymes and fingerplays with surprises so children can have repeated experiences with what might happen. This kind of proactive approach prepares babies for the next stage of attachment and supports emerging emotional and social growth.

Encouraging Prosocial Behavior

Prosocial behaviors are those that precede and lead to successful social interactions. When teachers are supporting infants' social skill development, they are often validating prosocial behaviors that will predict success in future social situations. The teacher serves as an important role model for infants. The teacher's actions must coincide with the expectations she or he has for children. For example, if teachers expect children to touch each other softly or to respect each other's personal space, then they must model these social behaviors for children. Teachers have the opportunity to be an important role model for a whole range of social expectations in the classroom.

Infant teachers actively create the social climate of the classroom. They start by anticipating needs, so infants don't have to cry too long to get their needs met. They continue by getting to know individual cues and validating that communication sent via cries or nonverbal cues was received by responding promptly. Additionally, the teacher helps children solve social problems by learning new skills, including waiting a moment, trading, taking turns, and making plans.

The teacher's most important role in prosocial behavior is supporting interactions among children—enabling them to interact successfully. By being nearby to encourage early social interactions and provide protection to babies who are not able to protect themselves, the teacher helps babies see that it is worth it to try again.

Just being close to where babies are in the classroom helps facilitate early social interaction. With the teacher nearby, babies are able to try new experiences, such as looking at one another or exploring toys together on a blanket.

As babies get older, words need the support of modeling and patterning. Teachers provide support as they pattern appropriate behaviors and model appropriate responses. When teachers support early attempts at social interaction, young children develop social skills that will stay with them throughout their lives.

Making Toys and Finding Materials

Making toys and finding interesting materials for infants to manipulate and play with does not need to be an expensive or difficult task. Teachers often find that everyday discarded household materials and teacher-made toys are by far the most interesting to children. And, this approach accommodates a most important consideration for infants—the novelty of new things.

Using teacher-made toys allows teachers to use the same idea in a different way in order to interest children in activities and materials. For example, empty plastic soft drink containers can be used in many ways. Filled with water and interesting small objects that glitter and swirl when shaken, they make a good toy for a nonmobile infant to look at while on a quilt on the floor. With a short piece of twine attached to the neck, the bottle can be pulled along as a crawler moves around the room. Lined up like bowling pins, the soft drink containers make perfect targets for new walkers to push over with their hands and feet as they walk forward.

Be sure to consider the following guidelines for homemade toys:

- Make sure the toys encourage action rather than passive watching.
- If possible, make the toys responsive. If it is not possible for the toy to be responsive, plan to use it with a responsive adult close by.
- Make multiple toys while you're at it. Infants cannot wait for a turn, so don't ask them to do so.
- Work on making your toys multisensory, challenging infants with toys that have a variety of uses. That way you'll get more out of the ones you do make.
- Check each homemade toy for safety. Check it again, and have another teacher check it. Sometimes safety issues in teacher-made toys are overlooked. Get some help in insuring that the toys are safe.

Common household objects that are safe for children (even if the child decides to see how it tastes) are sometimes great toys. Some ideas for toys that can be made from common objects follow:

- **Shaker bottles**—Put small, colored pieces of dry cereal or other objects inside any clear plastic bottle. Empty, clean plastic shampoo or dishwashing detergent bottles make great toys for younger and older babies. Glue and tape the lids on tight.
- **Simple hand puppets**—Made from socks, for example, puppets are a good way for an adult to talk with a baby and are a good way for a teacher to capture baby's attention.
- **Boxes**—All shapes and sizes of boxes are appropriate for walking around or crawling into, sitting in, stacking, nesting, putting things in, and dumping them out. A shoebox with a short length of twine attached makes a good pull toy for a crawler.
- **Sorting toys**—A cardboard egg carton or a cupcake tin works well as a place to put objects (large spools, blocks, cereal). It is important that they are large enough not to be swallowed. Be sure to test each object with a choke tube.
- **Dress ups**—Babies enjoy putting on hats and carrying purses, especially if there is a mirror, so that they can see themselves.

Blocks—Use milk cartons of different sizes (half-pint, quart, half-gallon) to create blocks. Each block takes two cartons. Cut the tops off and put one bottom inside the other, so the bottoms of the cartons make the ends of the block. Put an object such as a bell inside some blocks, so that they will make a noise when shaken. Tape securely, and cover with self-adhesive paper.

Texture blocks and scraps—Cover blocks of wood (approximately 5"x 3"x ¾" and sanded to prevent splinters) with brightly colored fabric of different textures (burlap, corduroy, velvet, quilted material, voile, net).

A cup of dry cereal—How many things can a baby do with a cup of dry cereal? (Yes, one of the first things most babies would do is dump the cereal on the floor!)

Books—Use books even with very young babies. They like to look at the shapes and colors, and enjoy having teachers point out objects in the books and turn the pages to see what's next. A relatively "baby-proof" book can be made by cutting large, bright, interesting pictures from a magazine, pasting them on construction paper, covering both sides with clear self-adhesive paper, and putting the pages in a loose-leaf notebook. Old wallpaper sample books are great for infants to use by themselves to practice page-turning skills.

Hanging toys—Many common household items (paper cups, large spools, and aluminum foil pie plates) can be attached to a piece of string or yarn and hung for a very young baby to look at. When babies begin reaching (around 4 to 5 months), suspend objects, so the baby can try to reach them while lying on the floor or sitting in an infant seat. Clips to attach things from the ceiling are available at hardware stores. Bars to suspend objects can be made easily from plastic pipe.

Containers—Plastic or metal (be sure edges are smooth) containers of all sizes and shapes can be used for stacking, nesting, putting objects in, and dumping things out.

Sorting can—Cut shapes in the plastic lid of a coffee can, so only certain shapes and sizes (blocks, for example) will fit through.

Hidden objects—With the child watching, put something in a paper bag or box or under a diaper. See if she will try to find it.

The beauty of teacher-made toys is they are novel and interesting without costing much and can be discarded as they get used and worn out. New toys can be made to replace used ones, keeping the environment interesting and fun. Create lots of teacher-made toys for infants in each developmental area. Teacher-made toys keep the job of planning fresh and give both the teacher and children ways to create play together.

Guidance and Discipline

Teaching Social Problem-solving

Patterning and Modeling with Infants

During the early years, infants take much of their social learning directly from experiences. However, we often expect infants to have more sophisticated skills than they are able to acquire. What can teachers do to help children learn important social skills during this stage?

Patterning and modeling are two examples of excellent teaching strategies that are very appropriate for infant teachers to master. Patterning involves a hand-over-hand repeating of appropriate behaviors. Modeling involves showing a child what you want her to do by doing it.

Patterning is appropriate to use in showing children how to touch each other softly, how to pick up toys and materials after dumping them on the floor, or how to stand back when someone wants to come in or go out the door.

Modeling is appropriate for demonstrating the appropriate use of toys and materials, demonstrating techniques such as finger painting, brush painting, stacking blocks, pushing a ball back and forth, and so forth.

Use both often—they are powerful, particularly if you use language stimulation techniques (see page 237) such as self-talk or description along with the patterning and modeling.

Calling for Help

The tendency to call for help emerges as infants develop—we usually *hear* about problems as soon as they begin to arise. Quick response to cries when one infant gets too close, crawls or walks on another child, or gets in the way tells infants that their communication is received. When teachers validate such cries for help, children learn that the world is responsive to their needs.

Infants need to be reminded to call for help if the strategies they are using do not seem to be working. For example, when two infants want the same toy, both will grab it and begin to scream for help. Teachers must be very responsive to such situations and validate the call for help. Then, they can help children begin to understand that while grabbing didn't work, some other ideas might work.

Trading

By the time an infant approaches the end of the first year, guidance may need to be supported with appropriate discipline strategies. For infants whose expressive language skills are not yet sophisticated enough to deal verbally with their peers, trading, taking turns, and walking away are good social problem-solving strategies to teach children (Albrecht & Ward, 1989). Then, older infants need support in making plans with others to get what they want.

The concept of sharing is too advanced for infants to understand. However, trading something you have for something you want can be explained by sensitive adults who guide infants to learn this new skill. In situations where children begin shrieking as another child grabs a favored toy, the adult hands the child who is grabbing the toy another one of equal interest to trade saying, "Ask him to trade with you." Or, "Give her the doll in exchange for the book." Regular assistance with the concept of trading (which exchanges something for something rather than something for nothing) facilitates socialization skills in infants.

Taking Turns

After trading is learned, the concept of turn-taking can be introduced. Turn-taking requires children to delay gratification for a little while and participate as an onlooker until a child is ready to take a turn. Again, sensitive adults need to help children learn this skill by explaining what is happening and providing the physical support and supervision to encourage children to take turns.

Walking Away

Walking away is a technique that is used to help children begin to use words rather than actions (which are usually aggressive) to solve problems. Walking away can take two forms: I can tell you to walk away from me, or I can walk away from you if you are bothering me. Both techniques empower children to solve their own problems and to use words as problem-solving tools.

However, walking away is an adult-supported activity during infancy. Just telling an infant to walk away doesn't work. She needs the teacher's gentle support to help her do so. Also, telling your friend to walk away is a supported activity. A sensitive teacher needs to be close and remind the infant to talk to her friend who is too close and to provide the words and support the actions.

Plan-making

Finally, facilitated plan-making helps both children to get a turn. Plan-making requires adult support. Tell the children that you have an idea of how to solve the problem. Tell them that both children will get a turn. One child will get the toy for three minutes and then the teacher will help the infant give the toy to the other child for three minutes. While the second child is waiting, the teacher helps her chose another activity—even if that activity is sitting and waiting for three minutes! Plan-making keeps teachers from feeling like referees. No one loses. One child has to delay gratification but gets the teacher's help to do so. Plan-making has another important benefit. It keeps teachers from saying "NO." Having a plan is very different from not being able to do something.

Social Problem-Solving Skill Development—A Process Over Time

Step One: Calling for Help

Step Two: Trading

Step Three: Taking Turns

Step Four: Using Words

Step Five: Walking Away

Step Six: Plan-making

Handling Biting in the Classroom

Without a doubt, biting is perceived as the most common behavior problem among children under the age of three. Dealing with biting behavior is not so difficult if the developmental reasons for biting are understood and dealt with appropriately.

Although biting may not pose a problem for teachers when babies are young, biting will come to your classroom. A general discussion of handling biting throughout infancy follows. Return to this section as you need to, or as children's biting behavior moves through the stages of biting.

Understanding why children bite is the first step in preventing biting. Noted psychologists Ilg and Ames point out that biting does not mean the child is "bad" or "cruel" (1976). Instead, it is a sign of the developmental age of the child. Children bite to explore, to get reactions, and because they lack language and social skills. They are not yet able to say, "Leave me alone," or "That's my toy." As soon as they learn to tell their peers to leave them alone, to move away from children who get too close, and to negotiate turns, the frequency of biting behavior diminishes.

Three Types of Biting

Investigative/Exploratory Biting: For children between early infancy and about 14 or 15 months, biting is often a part of the investigation and exploration that defines babies' play. They are curious about things that get put into their mouths. They want to see what things taste and feel like. They are interested in exploring everything with their mouths.

Action/Reaction Biting: Children between the ages of 9 and 20 months are beginning to connect actions with reactions. They are exploring interesting combinations of actions to see what reactions they might discover. Other children provide a wide array of reactions to being bitten. When you bite down on the finger that is gingerly exploring your face, it gets a big, loud reaction from the other child and from the adults in the room.

Purposeful Biting: This kind of biting is an attempt to get what you want or to change the outcome of a situation. Purposeful biting emerges about 18 months and usually disappears as children learn language and social problem-solving skills. To adults, this stage of biting is often the most difficult to handle.

Prevention

Prevention and anticipation of biting behavior are the best ways to deal with biting. The best prevention strategy is to create an environment that spreads children throughout the available space. Because infants tend to be "groupie" in nature, (they are wherever the teacher is), it is important to arrange the classroom to limit children's ability to see everyone and everything. If children are unable to see the toys other children are playing with, they will be less likely to want to play with those specific toys and, therefore, less likely to bite to get those toys.

The best environments for infants are rooms full of "nooks and crannies" where children can play alone or with one or two playmates. Classrooms arranged in such a manner experience fewer biting episodes. Open, unbroken space only increases the tendency of infants to group together and the chances that a child will use biting behavior to meet her needs.

Anticipation

Anticipation of biting is also an important part of coping with biting behavior. Careful observation of when, where, and with whom biting occurs provides the basis for anticipating biting episodes. Once the teacher has this information, she or he will be able to limit the development of situations in which biting occurs. Separating a regular biter from her most frequent target, anticipating tired or fussy times that will likely result in conflict, and rearranging play pairs are examples of anticipation strategies for preventing biting.

Substitution

Substitution is also a strategy for helping children learn to control biting. During some ages, sore gums that need rubbing can be the cause of biting behavior. The nearest available object to soothe sore gums just might be the arms or fingers of another child. When this is the case, keep cooled teething rings or soft rubber manipulative toys available to offer to teething children.

Supervising and Shadowing Biters

The next step is a preventive one designed to bring home the fact that biting doesn't get what you think it does. Children who are biting frequently (three or more times a day for three or more consecutive days), may need increased supervision throughout the day. Shadowing the child or limiting his freedom within the classroom by having the child hold your hand as you move around the room will reinforce the idea that biting will be controlled in your classroom.

Responding to Biting

When children bite for a reaction, teachers need to go beyond just responding to the child who was bitten. Carefully plan a place to isolate the biter that removes her from the play setting and restricts her ability to play. A crib is usually effective. When a child bites, firmly say to her, "It hurts when you bite." Pick up the child and put her in the isolation place. The message you want to leave with the child is that you don't get to play freely in the classroom for a few minutes when you bite.

Because playing is much more fun than watching others play, the child ultimately gets the message that she is in control of whether or not she can continue to play. After a minute or two, remove the child from the crib or play pen and help her return successfully to her play. If the child cries or is upset by the removal, wait a minute or two for her to get under control. However, the maximum length of time in isolation should not exceed 3-4 minutes. Infants have little perspective on time and will get the point after even a brief separation.

Consistency is a critical feature in stopping biting. If more than one teacher is in a classroom, careful briefing of each staff member is critical. All staff who are in the classroom with a biting child need to respond the same way. When all staff are consistent, children will gain control over their behavior more quickly.

Finally, if biting persists, the last step is to get help. Often teachers are too close to the situation to be objective. Try having another teacher observe.

Sometimes an objective eye will pinpoint something you overlooked. If all efforts fail, call for additional assistance. Psychologists or early childhood specialists can offer insight into chronic biters and help remedy the situation.

Teacher Competencies to Support Babies
Relating to School and Teacher

Sometimes	Usually	Always	
☐	☐	☐	Spends as much or more time listening to parents as providing guidance.
☐	☐	☐	Asks questions to clarify parents' points of view or issues of concern before responding with program policies or procedures.
☐	☐	☐	Comments to parents about strengths, accomplishments, and positive attributes of the child through conversation, notes, phone calls, and so on.
☐	☐	☐	Acknowledges and compliments parents on the unique contributions they make to their child's developmental progress.
☐	☐	☐	Welcomes parents in the classroom at any time during the school day.
☐	☐	☐	Shows she or he likes children and teaches with nonverbal and verbal cues.
☐	☐	☐	Bends over, stoops down, sits, maintains eye contact while interacting with infants.
☐	☐	☐	Uses a low, calm, soothing voice.
☐	☐	☐	Avoids interruption of infants' activities; times requests wisely.
☐	☐	☐	Allows infants to follow their own routines; does not insist on scheduling compliance that conflicts with individual schedules.
☐	☐	☐	Makes mealtime and other routine interactions a time for sensory stimulation, self-help skill practice, and social interaction.
☐	☐	☐	Actively seeks meaningful exchanges with children.
☐	☐	☐	Uses floor time to build relationships with children.
☐	☐	☐	Responds to social gestures and noises of infants and elaborates on the interactions.
☐	☐	☐	Plays responsive social games.
☐	☐	☐	Takes advantage of opportunities for social play during routines.
☐	☐	☐	Structures periods of social time with other infants; remains available to support, facilitate, or interact while infants direct the activity.

Resources for Teachers

Katz, L. & P. McClellan. (1997). *Fostering social competence: The teacher's role.* Washington, DC: National Association for the Education of Young Children (NAEYC).

INNOVATIONS IN PARENT PARTNERSHIPS

School- or Teacher-initiated Possibilities

Toy Swap

Plan a toy swap for parents and children. Announce the swap day and invite all parents to participate. Check toys to be certain they are clean, safe, and appropriate for infants. If parents react favorably, plan additional toy swaps every three months or so. Another strategy for a toy swap is to place a box on a high shelf in the classroom and label it "toy swap." Suggest that parents check the box. If anything interests them, they can swap it with a toy from home. This becomes an ongoing activity, instead of a special event. As an extension of the toy swap activity, ask that parents provide discarded toys for the classroom.

Anecdotal Note Calendar

Parents love to hear news about what their child experiences and accomplishes. For this activity, use calendars with plenty of space for writing. A separate calendar is needed for each child. Calendars may be bought or created with computer programs. You may even wish to draw your own and make copies. The anecdotal comments on the calendar will make a wonderful gift for parents. Some teachers like to give the special calendars to families when it is time for birthdays or when children move away. Decorate calendars using photographs you have taken of children involved in activities in the classroom and outdoors.

What Are Anecdotal Notes?

Anecdotal notes are a special way of recording observations of children using only factual and informational data. Anecdotal notes contain observable things like what a child is doing, the expressions on her face, and the context or setting of the experience being observed. Anecdotal notes exclude judgments, value statements, and predictions. Such notes form the foundation of good information-gathering, which gives parents and teachers a clear view of what is happening to the child.

February ♥ ♥ ♥

SUN.	MON.	TUES.	WED.	THURS.	FRI.	SAT.
		1	2	3	4 went on walk to the store	5
6	7 pulled on toy bar with right hand	8	9	10	11	12
13	14 Jill likes to ride in the stroller	15	16	17 cut first tooth	18	19
20	21	22	23	24	25	26
27	28	29 rolled from front to back				

Video Diary of the Day

Ask parents to provide videotapes so you can create a video diary showing the events in each child's day. Tape activities, nap time, meals, and outdoor play. If the video camera you use does not have a date stamp, be certain to have the date included as part of the recording. Parents may be especially interested in shots that include them during arrival and departure time.

Texture Box

Create a texture box out of a shoebox and pieces of cloth. Ask parents to provide the box, as well as discarded adult clothing that their child will associate with them. Let parents know how the box and clothing will be used. Cut clothing into approximately three-inch squares. Glue the squares into and onto the shoebox using nontoxic glue. Allow the glue to dry thoroughly. Observe as the child explores the texture box. Talk about how each piece of cloth feels. Talk about the child's parents as the child touches the pieces of cloth. Use the texture box as a way for children to connect with their parents during the day.

Parent Postcards

Share Parent Postcards as parents indicate an interest, at appropriate times during the enrollment cycle, or as developmental issues arise. (See page 441-444 in the Appendix for a sample dissemination schedule.) Copy postcards. Cut if necessary. Address to parent(s) and place on the Communication Sheet or hand out personally.

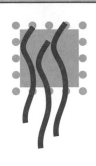

TO _____

_____

Attachment Stage 2—Discriminate Attachment: What Can Parents Do?

During stage 2 of attachment, called discriminate attachment, babies spend a lot of their time beginning to differentiate between familiar and unfamiliar caregivers. This stage lasts from 5 or 6 months until about 11 or 12 months.

This stage of attachment finds babies smiling, babbling, cooing, and responding more quickly to familiar adults. Babies show a definite preference for familiar faces and brighten considerably when a familiar face comes into view. Unlike the first stage, where almost any sensitive caregiver would do, stage 2 babies are quick to indicate with whom they would like to interact.

The following strategies will support your baby in this stage of attachment:

- Continue to respond promptly to crying and calls for help or interaction to help your baby learn that he or she can really depend on you.

- Describe what you are doing to your baby as you do it. When you can, wait for a signal from your baby that indicates that he or she is ready to be picked up or to open his or her mouth. Look for an indication that the baby is aware of what is about to happen.

- Establish an arrival and departure routine now, so it can comfort your child when he or she reaches the next attachment stage.

- Encourage the use of a security item or a favorite toy as a support for transitions.

- Play peek-a-boo games to help your baby learn that you do re-appear. These games help your baby learn that you always come back.

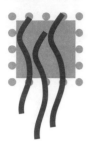

What to Expect Socially from Your Baby

For infants, learning social expectations is a slow and gradual process tied very closely to emotional development. Every parent has been puzzled when his or her delightful 9- or 12-month-old, who smiled at every responsive face for months, becomes unfriendly and downright terrified by unfamiliar people. This change in behavior represents progress in the attachment process—indicating a very positive step in emotional development. But, it isn't a good time to make new friends, change schools, move to a new room, or move to a new teacher. Social expectations for infants should be grounded in their developmental age and stage.

The following are some appropriate expectations for infants:

- Don't count on being able to make it through dinner when you go out to eat with children under two. You've seen it before—Dad eats while Mom holds or walks the baby, then they switch!

- Don't expect your infant to adjust quickly when you leave him or her in a new situation unless there are familiar adults around. For example, if your baby hasn't seen Grandma recently, he or she will probably resist going with her until they get reacquainted.

- Children are unable to share until well into the third year. Parents may help them take turns, share resources, or wait for a turn, but spontaneous sharing behavior doesn't happen consistently until after the third birthday. Stay close when your baby is near other babies to keep him or her safe.

- Manners are difficult for younger children. Eating with a utensil instead of your hands, staying at the table until you are finished, waiting for everyone to finish before getting up, and not dawdling are difficult expectations until children are older. That doesn't mean you don't have rules about these issues. It just means you will have to be the one who helps your child comply with the rules.

- Expectations such as touching softly, playing nicely, and keeping your hands to yourself are also difficult for infants. At this age most children don't really mean to pull a friend's hair. It just looks so interesting that it has to be touched. Stay close and help your child learn these skills by modeling them and facilitating their play with others.

TO

Appropriate Expectations for Infants with Friends

Infants have a very endearing quality that can cause problems for them when they are in groups. They are very egocentric—focused on themselves. They are not able, for example, to understand that the finger in their mouths might belong to another feeling person or that the baby they crawl over might not like it. Babies can't take the point of view of another child—so they need adult support to understand if they get too close or need help to be with friends.

When you get together with friends or family, remember to look at all of the babies as a group of individual, disconnected children. Stay close and help them learn the process of interacting with others as social skills emerge and grow.

Parent facilitation helps children develop a sense of "I can do it" in relation to friends. Point out when they get too close and move them further away. Help them avoid investigative biting by keeping fingers away from mouths. Put several toys out so that there is always another choice. This type of facilitation will protect infants from feeling that early social interactions are too difficult, and will support emerging social skills.

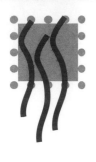

TO

Action/Reaction Biting:
Help! My Child Got Bitten, Again!

Again? You thought it was over when your child's friends finished teething and started playing with objects instead of putting them in their mouths? Well, not so. Biting to get a reaction follows investigative/exploratory biting, which usually occurs from infancy to around 14 or 15 months.

Why does biting seem to occur among children in groups at school? The simple answer to this question, according to many psychologists, is that children bite because they lack language and social skills. They view biting as a developmental phenomenon—it happens at predictable times for predictable reasons tied to children's ages and stages.

This predictable age and stage is called action/reaction biting. The most frequent reaction children create is a big response. When you bite down on the finger that is gingerly exploring your face, it gets a big, loud reaction from the other baby and from the adults in your classroom. The ruckus that is created is interesting, different, and, yes, even fun.

Children between 9 and 20 months are beginning to connect actions with reactions. They are exploring interesting combinations of actions to see what reactions they might discover. Other children provide a wide array of interesting reactions to being bitten, whether purposefully bitten or accidentally bitten. As a result, biting may be quite an interesting activity!

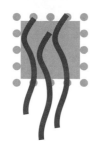

TO

What Can Teachers Do to Prevent Action/Reaction Biting?

Teachers have a variety of strategies to prevent biting. Most of their efforts will go into close supervision, careful room arrangements that spread children out in the classroom, and, most important, getting to know your baby's needs and temperament. Your child's teacher also will make sure popular toys are duplicated so that biting isn't necessary to get a toy. She or he will continue to teach your child to touch friends gently. But, even with all of these efforts, biting may still occur.

How will your teacher handle this stage of biting? The first reaction will be to comfort your child by holding and cuddling him or her. The teacher will briefly isolate the biter, so the biter gets the message that biting is not acceptable. At this stage, children also need to know that as interesting as the reaction to the bite was, the teacher does not approve of hurting others. The teacher will tell the biter that she or he doesn't like biting. We want children to get attention from positive social behaviors, not from negative ones. The message we want to send is that the teacher will spend more time with children who have positive social behaviors than those who don't.

Your child's teacher has already started to teach your child early social problem-solving skills. She or he started by responding quickly to calls for help from your child, validating that the teacher would be there when your child needed her or him. The teacher uses narration—a kind of ongoing monologue of what is going on in the child's world—to help your child learn to pick up cues about other children's feelings and reactions. Narration helps children get information to use in their interactions with their friends.

Your child's teacher will show your child how she or he wants your child to act (called modeling). The teacher will help your child repeat appropriate behaviors (called patterning) such as touching softly. Most important, the teacher will support interactions between friends by being close to them as they play and by participating in their play.

When your child is bitten, your child's teacher will always share information with you about what happened, how it was handled it, and what she or he will do to prevent it. The teacher won't be sharing with you who did the biting. Expect to receive a written report about what happened to your child. Ask your child's teacher to tell you how she or he handles biting and what the teacher will do specifically to prevent it in your child's classroom.

Connect with parents of older children who have passed through the action/reaction biting stage and lived to tell about it! They will help you put the experience in perspective.

What Can Parents Do to Prevent Action/Reaction Biting?

The first thing you can do is respond quickly when another child or a sibling hurts your child. Quick responses help children build a sense of trust that their world is a safe place to be. Then, never let your child bite you without getting a negative reaction. Tell your child that you don't like it when he or she hurts you. Remind your child that you always touch him or her softly. Then put your child down and walk away for a minute or two to communicate that biting won't get your attention.

You should also plan to work closely with your child's teacher if biting is occurring at home or in the classroom. Teachers are open to working with you to make sure biting does not become a problem. But, expect biting to come and go. It is a developmental phenomenon that will be replaced by more mature skills as your child grows and learns. Remember these important points:

- Respond quickly when another child or sibling hurts your child.

- Biting is a developmental phenomenon that comes and goes.

- Most children bite occasionally at various ages and stages.

- Your child's teacher will comfort hurt children quickly, hugging and cuddling them until they are calm.

- Expect your teacher to talk to you about any biting incident.

- Expect to see a written report.

- Biting disappears and is replaced by more mature skills as your child's skills grow.

- Be your child's first teacher about biting—don't let him or her bite you without getting a negative reaction from you.

- Give your child lots of attention and hugs for positive social behaviors, such as touching softly or taking turns with friends and siblings.

- Talk about what your child is doing and describe his or her actions and reactions, and the actions and reactions of others, as they happen.

- Model behaviors you want your child to use such as talking softly, saying please and thank you, and taking turns.

- Parents of older children can be a resource to help in understanding biting.

- Who did the biting is not as important as the teacher's plan for handling it.

- Talk to your child's teacher if you have any concerns about any of your child's behaviors.

TO

Learning Social Problem-Solving, Step One: Calling for Help

In infancy, children need constant adult supervision and support to interact successfully with other children. As they grow, they begin to learn to participate in groups with others. Participating in groups requires children to learn social problem-solving skills. Infants need adult guidance and support to be able to participate successfully in groups. But they can begin to learn discrete skills to help make life in groups less problematic.

The first step of social problem-solving is calling for help. Children, particularly those in school, need to be reminded to call for help when things get difficult. For infants, calls for help usually take the form of crying or screaming.

The tendency to call for help emerges as infants develop—we usually *hear* about problems as soon as they occur. Quick response to cries when one infant gets too close, crawls or walks on another child, or gets in the way, tells infants that their communication was received. When parents and teachers of infants validate such cries for help, children learn that the world is responsive to their needs.

Older infants need to be reminded to call for help if the things they are trying aren't working. For example, when two children want the same toy, both will grab it and begin to scream for help. Parents and teachers must be very responsive and validate the call for help. Then, you can help your child begin to understand that while grabbing didn't work, some other strategies, like taking turns, might work and that you will help him or her be successful after calling you for help.

Resources for Parents

Add these helpful books to your parent library or post this list on your parent bulletin board.

Glenn, H. and J. Nelsen. (1998). *Raising self-reliant children in a self-indulgent world.* Rocklin, CA: Prima Publishing.

Kohl, M. (1999). *Making make-believe.* Beltsville, MD: Gryphon House.

Lickona, T. (1994). *Raising good children.* New York: Bantam Doubleday Dell.

INNOVATIONS IN ENVIRONMENTS

The Role of Play Props and Play Cues in Stimulating Play

Carefully plan the classroom to take maximum advantage of children's natural desire to explore and learn. Choose simple, safe toys and ordinary objects for babies to explore and manipulate. Provide uninterrupted time, so infants can begin, explore, and elaborate without being distracted by the teacher.

Creating an environment that stimulates play is one of the important roles for teachers. Children must first feel secure in their environment. Both over-stimulation and under-stimulation are issues in school settings. Over-stimulation can occur from too much noise, light, color, and activity. Under-stimulation can occur from too little interactive experiences, physical isolation of babies in bouncers or Exer-saucers, or too few toys and materials in the environment.

Play cues or invitations can come from many sources. The first and best source of play cues is you. When the teacher picks up a toy and plays with it, it becomes very interesting to babies. Called triangulation, this

strategy for inviting play and interactions is a great way to initiate interactions with babies.

The second source of play cues or stimulation is color. Babies are drawn to high contrast images from birth. Graphics, photographs, pictures from the picture file/vocabulary (see the lists for each Possibilities Plan), and colorful toys all interest babies. Mobile babies will often scoot or crawl all the way across a room to discover something shiny or colorful.

But, color also can be overwhelming. Children benefit from color in the toys they play with and colors worn by the children and adults in the environment. They need soothing neutral colors to serve as the backdrop. Avoid adding color in bold swatches to the walls and floors of the infant classroom. This will help insure that the stimulation comes from child-directed and -initiated activity and not from the background (Cherry, 1976).

The third source of play cues is the way toys are displayed. Make toys available where children are in the classroom—on a mat or quilt on the floor, hanging from a toy bar, suspended from the ceiling, arranged on low shelves. Provide duplicate and similar toys, so they can be removed for disinfecting after they are mouthed. Separate toys on shelves, so children can consider each specific toy. Never pile toys together or place them in a toy box. How toys are displayed can invite children to move, stretch, and reach to play.

Guidance and Discipline

Room Arrangement as a Guidance Strategy

With infants, no guidance strategy is as powerful as room arrangement. The classroom environment gives children numerous clues about what to do and how to behave. Well-arranged classrooms foster self-control and adaptive behavior.

Arrangements for infants need to allow for room to play alone and alongside other children, leaving little open, nonfunctional space. The arrangement should clearly communicate the physical limits of play spaces, regulate children's behavior in each space, and control the use of materials within the space—all without direct intervention from an adult.

To evaluate whether your classroom arrangement facilitates guidance of children toward self-control, note the location of behavior problems in your classroom. If problems occur in certain areas of the room, reassess the arrangement of the physical space in the classroom. (Refer to pages 55-56 for more information on setting up environments.)

Activities and Experiences vs. Centers

Most early childhood educators think of interest or learning centers as an essential part of any classroom setting. Yet, environments for infants are different because they cannot choose to go to different areas until they are mobile. For this reason, teachers must bring the activities and experiences to the child, or they must assist the child in going to where the activities are. A wide range of activities and experiences must be available to infants. In each of the following two Possibilities Plans, *Big and Little* and *Cars, Trucks, and Trains*, activities and experiences are presented in the following areas:

- Dramatic Possibilities
- Sensory/Art Possibilities
- Curiosity Possibilities
- Literacy Possibilities
- Music Possibilities
- Movement Possibilities
- Outdoor Possibilities
- Project Possibilities
- Parent Participation Possibilities

WEB

Big and Little

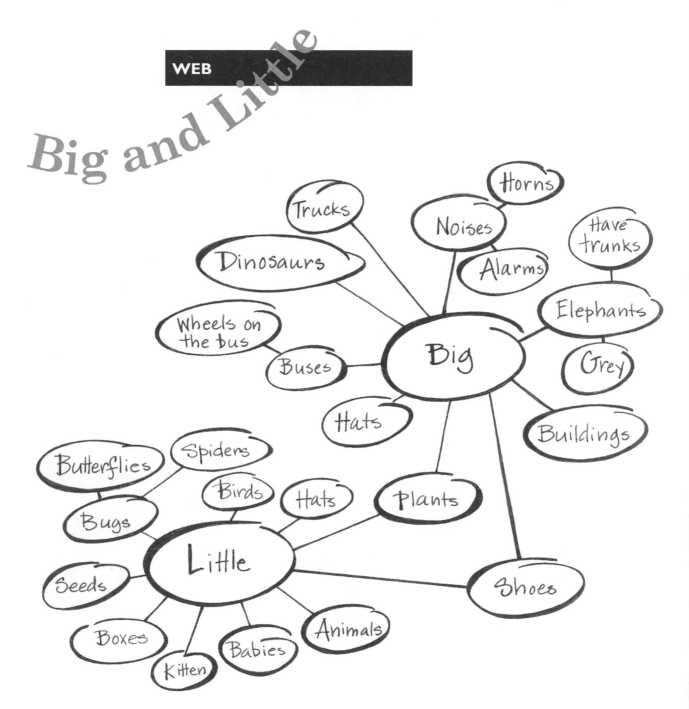

Note: Using the technique of webbing, teachers can follow the leads that children give them, as well as have an unlimited source of options. Always use the webs as a jumping-off point. The possibilities are endless!

PLANNING PAGES

Plan Possibilities

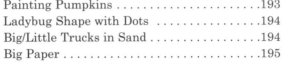

Dramatic

Little Shoes 192
Big Hats 192
Little Hats 192
Big/Little Stuffed Animals 193
Big Shoes 193

Sensory/Art

Painting Pumpkins 193
Ladybug Shape with Dots 194
Big/Little Trucks in Sand 194
Big Paper 195

Curiosity

Glitter Bottles 195
One-piece Butterfly and Truck Puzzles 195
Big/Little Boxes 196

Literacy

Big and Little 197
Teacher-made Plant and Seed Books 197
Big and Little Books 198
The Tiny Seed 198
Little Miss Muffett 198
Eensy, Weensy Spider 199

Music

Twinkle, Twinkle, Little Star 199

Movement

Sock Balls 200
Big Ride-on Trucks 200
Big and Little Boxes Inside and Outside 200

Outdoor

Washing Big/Little Trucks 201
Car Bath 201
Bird/Butterfly Wings 201

Project

Growing Plants 202
Big and Little Shoe Prints 202

Parent Participation

Shoes for Prints Project 203
Supporting Possibilities 203
Parent Postcards
Do Children Learn While They Play? 203
Transmitting Values to Children 204

Big and Little

Concepts Learned in

    Big and Little 204

Prop Boxes

    Hats 205
    Shoes 205
    Boxes 205

Picture File/Vocabulary . .205

Books

All My Little Ducklings by Monica Wellington
Big and Little by Margaret Miller 197
Big Dog, Little Dog by P.D. Eastman
Big Sister and Little Sister by Charlotte Zolotow
Enormous Turnip, The by Kathy Parkenson
Little Red Hen, The by Byron Burton
Perro Grande, Perro Pequeno by P.D. Eastman
Tiny Seed, The by Eric Carle 198

Rhymes/Fingerplays

    "Eensy, Weensy Spider" 199
    "Little Miss Muffett" 198

Music/Songs

    "Twinkle, Twinkle, Little Star" 199

Toys and Materials 206

Little Shoes
0-18 months

Materials
Small shoes such as baby booties, first shoes, and doll shoes

Teacher Talk
Talk with children as they play with the shoes. "You have the little shoes."

Add small shoes to the classroom. Baby booties, first shoes, and large doll shoes are all interesting to babies.

Big Hats
0-18 months

Materials
Adult hats
Rattles and small toys

Teacher Talk
"The rattle is in the big hat. Now it's out!"

Include adult hats for children to wear and play with in the classroom. Put rattles and small toys into the hats for children to dump or take out of the hats.

Little Hats
0-18 months

Materials
Child-size hats

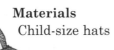

Teacher Talk
Watch for a reaction and respond by copying the child's action. "Off comes your little hat. Off comes my little hat."

Add child-size hats to the classroom. Show baby how to put the hat on your head. Then place the little hats on the baby's head.

Big/Little Stuffed Animals
0-18 months

Materials
Big and little stuffed animals

Teacher Talk
Narrate children's actions as they play with the animals. "You are carrying three little dogs, Morris." "There are the big bears, Li Ling."

Include big and little stuffed animals for dramatic play, so children can explore the concepts of big and little.

Big Shoes
12-18 months

Materials
Adult-size shoes

Teacher Talk
Describe what infants are doing. "Joanie, those are big shoes. They are like your daddy's shoes."

Add shoes that are adult size to the classroom. Children will associate these items with being "big" like their parents.
Safety alert: Remove shoestrings. Clean shoes well, spray with bleach water, and let them air dry before babies play with them.

SENSORY/ART POSSIBILITIES

Painting Pumpkins
12-18 months

Materials
Big and little pumpkins
Paintbrushes
Water
Paint

Add a big and a little pumpkin to the classroom. Offer babies the opportunity to paint them, first with dry brushes, then with water, then with paint.

Ladybug Shape with Dots

12-18 months

Materials
Red butcher paper
Scissors
Tape
Sticky dots

Cut a large ladybug shape from red butcher paper. Tape the shape to the floor in the classroom or to a hard surface outside. Help children as they stick dots on the shape. Offer dots to the babies to stick on the paper. Use different colors of dots for different children, or you may wish to label areas where children place their dots.

Photographs or narratives of how individual children reacted to the activity will be interesting for parents. Hang the ladybug on the wall or create a wall or ceiling hanging by cutting an additional ladybug shape. Glue or staple the two shapes together leaving a space of about 12" open. Stuff the shapes with crumpled newspapers and close the opening. Add legs and hang from the ceiling using heavy-duty mono-filament fishing line.

Safety alert: If children put the dots in their mouths, distract them by offering one dot to place on the paper (distraction—see page 44), or remind them to put the dots on the ladybug (redirection—see page 45). Use a hand-over-hand technique to help the baby put the dots on the paper (patterning—see page 171). If the child continues to put the dots in her mouth, put the dots away, and redirect the child to another activity.

Big/Little Trucks in Sand

12-18 months

Materials
Big and little trucks
Sand table or sandbox outside

Teacher Talk
Talk about big and little as the children play. "You have the big fire truck!" "You have the little dump truck!"

Provide big and little trucks in the sand table for sand play inside or in the sandbox outside.

 ## Big Paper

12-18 months

Materials
Paper
Tape
Large crayons or washable markers

Completely cover a table with art paper. Secure with tape. Provide large crayons or large washable markers for children to create a big picture. (Remove and put away all the caps from the markers. They are a choking hazard.) Label the different areas of the paper where children color. Hang the butcher paper up on the wall where parents can see it. Repeat the activity for several days or over several weeks until the paper is covered with special, pre-writing scribbles. Date each day additional scribbles are added.

CURIOSITY POSSIBILITIES

Glitter Bottles

0-18 months

Materials
Clean plastic soda bottles, with tops, in various sizes
Miniature objects
Glitter
Water
Glue and tape

Teacher Talk
"You are shaking the bottle. I see the little animals inside."

Make glitter bottles. Use plastic soda bottles of various sizes. Place miniature objects inside with different colors of glitter. Add water to the bottles. Glue and tape tops to the bottles securely.

One-piece Butterfly and Truck Puzzles

6-18 months

Materials
Solid color paper
Cardboard
Scissors and/or art knife
Coarse sandpaper, if needed

Teacher Talk

Talk with infants about what they are doing and about big things, like trucks, and little things, such as butterflies. "The butterflies are little, Joshua."

Create one-piece puzzles for infants. Glue a solid color paper onto a piece of cardboard. Cut a simple shape, such as a butterfly or a truck, from the center of the cardboard. (This is very easy to do using an art knife. Not in the classroom, of course!) Be certain that the inside piece fits easily into the outside piece. Sand edges with coarse sandpaper, if they don't fit easily. Or, purchase one-piece puzzles with knobs from a school supply store or catalog. Observe the way each child moves the puzzle pieces and record your observations. Children will take the puzzle pieces out first. Then, they will practice putting them back.

Big/Little Boxes

6-18 months

Materials
Big and little boxes
Sandpaper, optional
Tape, optional

Young children love to explore boxes because of the surprise of what may be inside. Use boxes that will nest inside each other. Remove staples and make boxes safe to use as toys by sanding the edges smooth with sandpaper. Reinforce with tape, if needed.

Big and Little

0-18 months

Materials
Big and Little by Margaret Miller
Paper and pen

Read this book with one child or with a few infants who show interest. Record your observations of how different children respond to books (moving to the rhythm of the language, turning pages, pointing to pictures, making sounds and words, and indicating to the teacher to read the book again). Communicate your observations to parents with the Communication Sheet (pages 429-430). Add this book to your Books Read list (page 431).

Teacher-made Plant and Seed Books

0-18 months

Materials
Poster board, cardboard, or card stock
Glue
Plants and/or seeds
Clear contact paper
Hole punch
Metal rings, or short lengths of ribbon or
      yarn

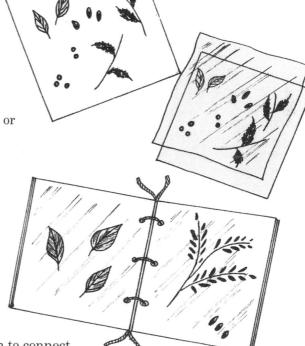

Teacher Talk
Point to objects in the book and name them. "See the leaves." "Those are seeds."

Create books using poster board, cardboard, or card stock. Glue small pieces of plants and seeds onto the pages. Cover with clear contact paper. Punch holes and use metal rings or short lengths of ribbon or yarn to connect the pages together.

Big and Little Books

0-18 months

Materials
Books about big and little, such as
> *All My Little Ducklings* by Monica Wellington
> *Big Dog, Little Dog* by P.D. Eastman
> *Big Sister and Little Sister* by Charlotte Zolotow
> *Enormous Turnip, The* by Kathy Parkenson
> *Little Red Hen, The* by Byron Burotn
> *Perro Grande, Perro Pequeno* by P.D. Eastman

Use these books to talk with children about big and little. You may also make these books using magazine pictures or pictures from the picture file.

The Tiny Seed

0-18 months

Materials
The Tiny Seed by Eric Carle
Seeds
Resealable plastic bags
Tape

Read this delightful book by Eric Carle as you talk about little seeds that grow into big plants. Seal some seeds in thick, resealable plastic bags. Then tape the edges. Let the children see the seeds before you begin the book and hold them while you read.
Safety alert: Monitor the children closely when you use props like these. If infants mouth them or begin to chew on the bags, throw them out or replace them.

Little Miss Muffett

0-18 months

Materials
None needed

Repeat this old classic as you enjoy one-on-one time with baby. The rhythm and repetition will stimulate language development and interest the baby.

> *Little Miss Muffett*
> Little Miss Muffett
> Sat on a tuffet,
> Eating her curds and whey;
> Along came a spider,
> And sat down beside her,
> And frightened Miss Muffett away.

Eensy, Weensy Spider

0-18 months

Materials
Spider shape
Tape
Copies of the rhyme

Say this rhyme with infants. Tape a spider to the window and point to it as you say the rhyme. Post the words to rhymes on the parent communication board or give individual copies to parents, so they can use the same rhyme at home. Consider adding a musical version of this classic to your music library. Then you can sing or say the rhyme.

The Eensy, Weensy Spider
   The eensy weensy spider
   Climbed up the water spout.
   Down came the rain
   And washed the spider out.

   Out came the sun
   And dried up all the rain,
   And the eensy weensy spider
   Climbed up the spout again.

MUSIC POSSIBILITIES

Twinkle, Twinkle, Little Star

0-18 months

Materials
None needed

Teacher Talk
"Abdul, I see your fingers twinkling."

Sing this song to children. Demonstrate how to "twinkle" your fingers as you sing.

Twinkle, Twinkle, Little Star
Twinkle, twinkle, little star,
How I wonder what you are!
Up above the world so high

Like a diamond in the sky.
Twinkle, twinkle, little star,
How I wonder what you are!

Sock Balls

6-12 months

Materials
Clean, old socks
Basket

Collect old socks from parents or friends.
Wash them and make them into big and little
sock balls. Put a basket of the sock balls out and give
children the opportunity to throw them. These soft sock balls
offer a good first try for tosses that go astray
more than they hit their target!

Big Ride-on Trucks

12-18 months

Materials
Big truck(s)

Teacher Talk
"You are pushing the truck. There you go, Martin. I'll wait for you over here."

Give each child an opportunity to sit on, scoot, or push a big truck. Talk about what
each child is doing.

Big and Little Boxes Inside and Outside

12-18 months

Materials
Different sizes of boxes

Teacher Talk
Talk about big and little as children play. "We are playing with big boxes. One, two,
three. Push the boxes over here."

Collect different sizes of boxes. Bring them outside for the children to move and
explore.

Washing Big/Little Trucks

12-18 months

Materials
Plastic trucks
Shallow plastic tub
Water

Teacher Talk
Talk about what you are seeing. "The trucks are in the water. You are washing the truck. Where is another truck?"

Place big and little trucks in a shallow plastic tub with a very small amount of water. Observe how children move the trucks in the water and their reactions to the experience.

Car Bath

12-18 months

Materials
Spray bottles filled with water   Scrub brushes
Washcloths   Outdoor riding toys

Teacher Talk
"Wash the cars. They need a bath!"

Provide spray bottles filled with water, washcloths, and scrub brushes, so children can clean outdoor riding toys.

Bird/Butterfly Wings

12-18 months

Materials
Paper, scissors, and tape; or scarves

Create wings to attach to children's backs and arms using paper or scarves. Encourage children to fly with their wings.
Safety alert: Always tie strings around children's bodies, never around or across the neck.

Growing Plants

6-18 months

Materials

Plant seeds

Dirt or potting soil

Unbreakable pots

Chart paper and camera

Teacher Talk

"You are looking at the plants, Le. The plants are growing tall. You see leaves."

Choose contrasting sizes of seeds (like sunflowers and zinnias) to start this project. Use the seed planting as a fun sensory experience for infants. Let them mix the seeds with the dirt in a sensory tray and then put the dirt, complete with seeds, into pots. Put in a sunny location and water as needed. Talk about the seeds/plants each day. Take babies over to look at the pot daily. Document the growth using a chart and photographs. Infants will enjoy this type of project for a long time. Save the pictures of the children looking at the growing plants to revisit the concept of growing things as the children grow. This type of resource can follow children all the way through the preschool years. Revisiting previous work is a concept made famous by the educators in the Reggio Emilia programs in Italy. It involves reconsidering children's observations over time to see how their perceptions and understanding change. Keep these photographs and this documentation to do that. **Safety alert:** Keep the pots out of reach of babies, but visible for them to see.

Big and Little Shoe Prints

12-18 months

Materials

Shoes

Washable paint

Butcher paper

Tape

Markers

Use adult and children's shoes to create a shoe print project. Allow a few children at a time to step in washable paint and walk across a large piece of butcher paper taped to the floor. Label the tracks with each child's name. After all children have had an opportunity to make little shoe prints, use adult shoes to make big shoe prints. Leave children's shoes on and stuff paper in the large shoes until they fit. Repeat the process allowing one or two children at a time to step in washable paint and then to walk across the paper. Hang the paper, so parents and children can enjoy the big and little shoe prints. **Safety hint:** This is a slippery activity. Be sure to support and guide children.

Shoes for Prints Project

Ask parents for an old pair of their shoes to use in the shoe prints project (see page 202). Plan which children will do prints on which days, so parents will only need to leave their shoes for one day. Shoes that parents are ready to discard can be used for Dramatic Play Possibilities.

Supporting Possibilities

Provide copies of the songs, rhymes, and fingerplays that children will be hearing during this plan. Also, communicate with parents the concepts being explored at school. Encourage parents to support the activities you are doing at school with similar activities at home.

Parent Postcards

Parent Postcards in this section are designed to share with parents during the Possibilities Plan. The topics are natural extensions of the activities and experiences that you are planning and implementing for the infants in the classroom. Use the Postcards to connect parents to their children's learning.

Do Children Learn While They Play?

Play is children's work. Whether it is called symbolic play, make-believe play, fantasy play, dramatic play, or imaginative play, play is central to children's development in the first three years. Play offers children a way to explore their understanding of the world in which they live.

Will your child really learn anything from playing alone, with friends, or with you? The answer is yes! Research has documented the connection between children's play behavior during the preschool years and a wide range of emerging abilities, including creativity, memory, vocabulary, reasoning, and impulse control. Research has also documented that you serve as a guide to play, increasing your child's sophistication in play as you join in.

So, make sure you play with your baby. Your playful interactions stimulate your baby's brain and form the foundation of future life skills, including academic ones.

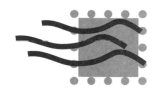

TO _____

_____

_____

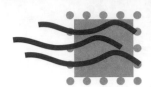

Transmitting Values to Children

Parents often ask how they can be sure that they are teaching their values to children who spend a lot of time in school. Parents have the most profound influence in their children's lives, so chances are that children will be strongly influenced by their parents' values.

Children are much more influenced by actions than by words. Telling a child to share or to be polite is far less effective than modeling those same behaviors and clearly identifying and supporting appropriate expectations. Parents of young children can relax and enjoy their time with their children. The beginning years are not a time for lectures. They are a time for closeness, hugs and kisses, and sharing your values with your child by doing what you want them to do.

TO _____
_____
_____

Concepts Learned in Big and Little

Concepts Learned

Some things are little.

Some things are big.

I have little feet.

Mommy and Daddy have big feet.

Some things grow from little to big.

Seeds are little compared to their plants.

Bugs, seeds, butterflies, and birds are little.

Trucks, elephants, and buildings are big.

Shoes can be little and big.

Seeds are planted in soil.

Seeds grow into plants.

Hats go on my head.

Shoes go on my feet.

I can paint.

I can do a puzzle.

I can take puzzle pieces out.

I can put them back.

Resources

Prop Boxes

Hats
    Hats of various sizes
Shoes
    Adult shoes
    Children's shoes
    Socks
Boxes
    Square boxes of different sizes
    Oatmeal boxes

Picture File/Vocabulary

Birds
Garden
Bugs   Hat
Buildings   Plants
Buses   Seeds
Butterflies   Shoes
Dinosaurs   Socks
Elephants   Trucks
Flowers

Books

All My Little Ducklings by Monica Wellington
Big and Little by Margaret Miller (page 197)
Big Dog, Little Dog by P.D. Eastman
Big Sister and Little Sister by Charlotte Zolotow
Enormous Turnip, The by Kathy Parkenson
Little Red Hen, The by Byron Burton
Perro Grande, Perro Pequeno by P.D. Eastman
Tiny Seed, The by Eric Carle (page 197)

Rhymes/Fingerplays

"Eensy, Weensy Spider" (page 199)
"Little Miss Muffett" (page 198)

Music/Songs

"Twinkle, Twinkle, Little Star" (page 199)

Toys and Materials

The following purchased items are important for this Possibilities Plan:

Books about big and little
Clear contact paper
Dolls
Poster board
Rattles
Resealable plastic bags
Ride-on trucks
Shallow tubs
Smaller toy trucks
Stuffed animals
Toy turtles
Yarn, ribbon, or book rings

The following gathered items will help support this Possibilities Plan:

Boxes
Plants
Plastic soda bottles of various sizes
   Prop box items
      Seeds
      Shoes

WEB

Cars, Trucks, and Trains

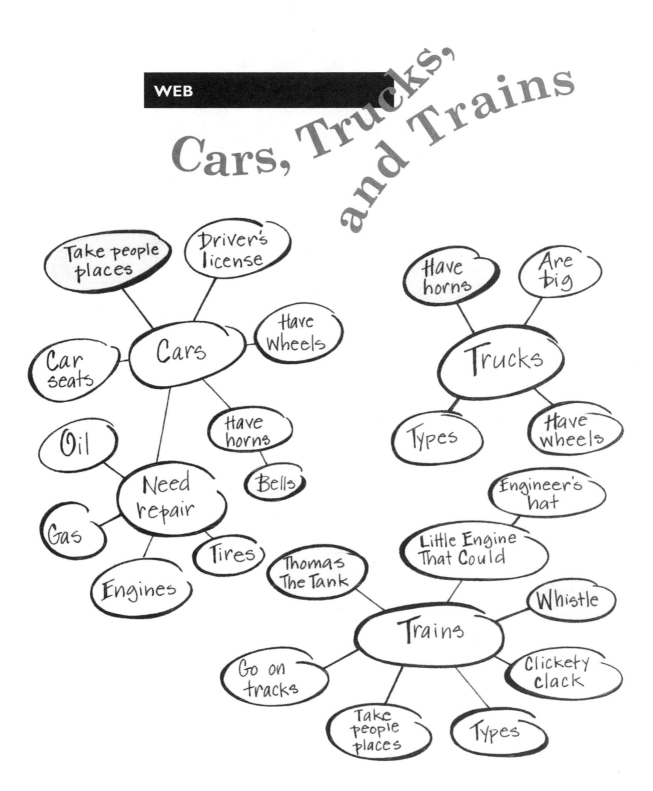

- Cars
  - Take people places
  - Driver's license
  - Have Wheels
  - Car seats
  - Have horns
    - Bells
- Need repair
  - Oil
  - Gas
  - Tires
  - Engines
- Trucks
  - Have horns
  - Are big
  - Types
  - Have wheels
- Trains
  - Thomas The Tank
  - Little Engine That Could
    - Engineer's hat
  - Whistle
  - Clickety clack
  - Types
  - Take people places
  - Go on tracks

Note: Using the technique of webbing, teachers can follow the leads that children give them, as well as have an unlimited source of options. Always use the webs as a jumping-off point. The possibilities are endless!

Plan Possibilities

Dramatic

Going on Vacation 210
Train of Car Seats 210
Construction 210

Sensory/Art

Wheel Art 211
Trucks in the Sensory Table 211
Reverse Collage 211

Curiosity

Sound Toys 212
Pop-up Pals 212
Bell on the Door 212
Busy Box 213

Literacy

Thomas the Tank 213
Cars, Trucks, and Trains Books 213
How Many Cars Do You See? 214
Drive, Drive, Drive Your Car 214
Teacher-made Vehicle Books 214

Music

Vehicle Music 215
Go In and Out the Car 215
Wheels on the Bus 215

Movement Possibilities

Scoot Toys 216

Outdoor

Bags Outside 216
Wagons 216
Watering Can for Gas 217
Honk, Honk 217

Project

Traffic Jam Book 217
Poems Learned List 218

Parent Participation

Car Seats for Train 218
Supporting Possibilities 218
Parent Postcards
    Drive-time Activities 219
    Gender Role Stereotyping 220
    Preparing for Time Away
        from Your Child 221

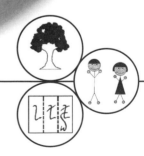

Cars, Trucks, and Trains

Concepts Learned in Cars, Trucks, and Trains 222

Prop Boxes

Going on Vacation 222
Construction 222

Picture File/Vocabulary 222

Books

All Aboard Trucks by Lynn Conrad
Big Book of Things That Go by Caroline Bingham
Big Truck, Big Wheels by Bobbie Kalman and Petrina Gentile
Chugga Chugga Choo Choo by Kevin Lewis
Construction Zone by Tana Hoban
Freight Train by Donald Crews
Peter's Trucks by Sallie Wolf
Sheep in a Jeep by Nancy Shaw
Thomas the Tank Engine by Wilbur and Vera Awdry 213
*Thomas the Tank Engine Coming and Going:
A Book of Opposites* by Wilbur and Vera Awdry
Trains by Byron Barton
Trucks by Byron Barton
Trucks by Mallory Loehr

Rhymes/Fingerplays

"How Many Cars Do You See?" 214

Music/Songs

"Drive, Drive, Drive Your Car" 214
"Go In and Out the Car" 215
"Wheels on the Bus" 215

Toys and Materials .224

Going on Vacation
6-18 months

Materials
Travel props, such as coats, purses, toy keys, bathing suits, etc.

Teacher Talk
Describe children's actions. "I saw you put the keys in your purse. Are you ready to go?"

Add realistic items that infants associate with going on vacation, such as coats, purses, toy keys, bathing suits, luggag

Train of Car Se
6-18 months

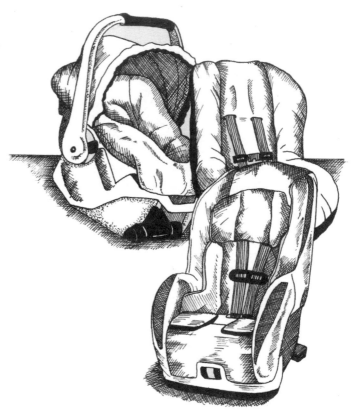

Materials
Car seats
Train whistle, optional

Use children's car seats to create a two- or three-car seat train. Talk about going on vaca Make train noises. "Chug, chu choo!" Add a train whistle to m train more realistic.

Construction
12-18 months

Materials
Toy construction props such as tool belt, etc.

Provide props appropriate for construction: hard hat, toy hammer, tape measure, clip board, tool belt, and safety glasses.

Wheel Art

6-18 months

Materials
Toy cars and trucks
Paint in a shallow container
Paper

Teacher Talk
"The truck is making lines on the paper."

Help children wheel cars and trucks through paint. Then help them roll the vehicles on paper.

Trucks in the Sensory Table

6-18 months

Materials
Cars, trucks, or trains   Sand or cornmeal

Teacher Talk
Talk with children about making tracks in the sensory tubs. "The truck is riding in the sand. You made roads with your fingers."

Add cars, trucks, or trains to the sensory table along with sand or cornmeal.

Reverse Collage

6-18 months

Materials
Clear contact paper
Pictures from magazines

Place a sheet of clear contact paper (sticky side up) on a table. Give children pictures cut from magazines to stick on the contact paper. When they have finished sticking the pictures, cover with another piece of contact paper. Attach the collage to the floor where babies can crawl over and look at the pictures. Or, display the collage where parents and children can enjoy it. Or, attach the contact paper to a window to be viewed from both sides.

Sound Toys

0-18 months

Materials
Sound toys such as rattles, bells, and music toys

Teacher Talk
"Let's wind up the toy, Alicia. Here comes the music."

Use sound toys in the classroom. Provide a wide variety, including rattles, bells, and music toys. Prepare infants for what will happen next.

Pop-up Pals

0-18 months

Materials
Pop-up toy(s)

Teacher Talk
Describe children's actions. "Nellie, you made the dog pop up. Again? You can do it again."

Provide a pop-up toy for baby. The cause-and-effect relationship between moving something and having the figure pop up will fascinate and intrigue infants.

Bell on the Door

6-18 months

Materials
Bell
String and/or strong tape

Hang a bell on the door, so children will know when someone is entering the classroom.

? _____ **Busy Box**

0-18 months

Materials
Busy box(es)

Teacher Talk
Talk about the sounds that the different activities make.

Many busy boxes have interesting sounds for infants. Place the busy box on the floor for infants who are crawling.

LITERACY POSSIBILITIES

 _____ **Thomas the Tank**

0-18 months

Materials
Thomas the Tank Engine by Wilbur and Vera Awdry

Read this book to children. Observe their reactions to the story (eye contact, bouncing, scooting, cooing) and note reactions on the Communication Sheet (pages 429-430). Add the book to your Books Read list (see page 431).

 _____ **Cars, Trucks, and Train Books**

0-18 months

Materials
Books about vehicles, such as
  All Aboard Trucks by Lynn Conrad
  Big Truck, Big Wheels by Bobbie Kalman and Petrina Gentile
  Chugga Chugga Choo Choo by Kevin Lewis
  Construction Zone by Tana Hoban
  Freight Train by Donald Crews
  Peter's Trucks by Sallie Wolf
  Sheep in a Jeep by Nancy Shaw
  Thomas the Tank Engine Coming and Going: A Book of Opposites
      by Wilbur and Vera Awdry
  Trains by Byron Barton
  Trucks by Byron Barton
  Trucks by Mallory Loehr

There are a number of quality vehicle (cars, trucks, and trains) books available. Young children often enjoy ones by Richard Scarry. Add the books to your Books Read list (see page 431).

How Many Cars Do You See?

0-18 months

Materials
None needed

Show children how you can show fingers as you say, "one, two, three."

How Many Cars Do You See?
  How many cars do you see?
  Vroom, vroom, vroom,
  One, two, three!

Drive, Drive, Drive Your Car

0-18 months

Materials
None needed

Use this variation of "Row, Row, Row Your Boat" as children play inside and outside. Share the child's response to the tune and the movements as with parents on the Communication Sheet (pages 429-430).

Drive, Drive, Drive Your Car
  Drive, drive, drive your car
  Gently down the street.
  Merrily, merrily, merrily
  Beep, beep, beep, beep, beep!

Teacher-made Vehicle Books

0-18 months

Materials
Magazines, sales flyers, newspapers
Scissors
Poster board, cardboard, card stock
Marker
Clear contact paper or resealable plastic bags
  Duct tape

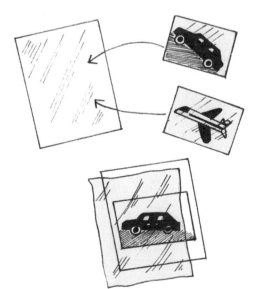

Make vehicle books by cutting out photographs from magazines, sales flyers, and newspapers and gluing them on poster board, cardboard, or card stock. Label the pictures using lowercase print. Cover the pages with clear contact paper or place in resealable plastic bags for protection. Use duct tape to attach the pages.

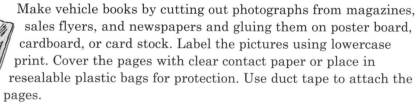

Vehicle Music

0-18 months

Materials
Music with sounds of vehicles

Provide music that has the sounds of vehicles. When the sounds (honk, honk) occur, repeat for baby and observe reactions.

Go In and Out the Car

0-18 months

Materials
None needed

Sing this variation of "Go In and Out the Window." Additional variations would be "Go In and Out the Bus" and "Go In and Out the Train."

> *Go In and Out the Car*
> Go in and out the car.
> Go in and out the car.
> Go in and out the car,
> As we have done before.

Wheels on the Bus

0-18 months

Materials
Copies of the words to the song

Sing "Wheels on the Bus." Watch for children responding to the sounds of the song. Repeat it often during this plan. Share the words with parents. They will want to use it at home or during drive time. Collect various recordings of this classic song and play different versions. The children's board book of the song also can be used.

> *The Wheels on the Bus*
> The wheels on the bus go 'round and 'round
> 'Round and 'round, 'round and 'round.
> The wheels on the bus go 'round and 'round
> All through the town.

The babies on the bus go, "waa, waa, waa,"
"Waa, waa, waa," "waa, waa, waa."
The babies on the bus go, "waa, waa, waa,"
All through the town.

The horn on the bus goes "honk, honk, honk...
The people on the bus go up and down...
The driver on the bus says, "Move on back...

MOVEMENT POSSIBILITIES

Scoot Toys
12-18 months

Materials
Scoot toys or riding toys
Bags or baskets
Items to put in bags

Teacher Talk
Talk about what each child is doing. "Scoot, scoot, Le."

Give each child an opportunity to play on scoot toys or ride-on toys. Provide items to put in and take out of bags or baskets as children play.

OUTDOOR POSSIBILITIES

Bags Outside
6-18 months

Materials
Paper bags   Toys to put in bags

Provide bags, filled with toys and rattles, so children can play fill and dump.

Wagons
12-18 months

Materials
Wagons   Blocks

Teacher Talk
"I am packing up the car, so we can go on a trip. See how much we can fit. We will unpack later."

Provide blocks, so children can fill wagons on the playground. Before children go outside, talk about filling and emptying the wagons.

 # Watering Can for Gas

12-18 months

Materials
Watering can

Use a watering can (with or without water) to put "gas" in the riding toys.

 # Honk, Honk

12-18 months

Materials
Horns

Attach horns to riding toys outside, so children can honk as they play.

PROJECT POSSIBILITIES

 # Traffic Jam Book

6-18 months

Materials
Pictures of cars, trucks, and
    trains
Glue or tape
Poster board, cardboard, or card
    stock
Hole punch
Yarn

Use pictures of cars, trucks, and trains to make a picture book.
Attach pictures to pages of poster board, cardboard, or card stock.
Use short lengths of yarn to join the pages together end to end to form a traffic jam book. Add to the book as the plan progresses.

Poems Learned List

6-18 months

Materials
Copies of poems, rhymes, and fingerplays

Create a list of poems, rhymes, and fingerplays you are using in the classroom (See Appendix pages 464-468). When you introduce a new poem, rhyme, or fingerplay, add it to the list. Post the list, so parents can see it growing. Add a copy of the poem to the child's growing portfolio.

PARENT PARTICIPATION POSSIBILITIES

Car Seats for Train

Ask parents to leave their car seats (clearly labeled with a non-toxic permanent marker) at school one day, so you can make a train. Infants will enjoy climbing into and out of the seats. This activity also works well outside. Provide a shady spot and a quilt or blanket. Take pictures of the train in use.

Supporting Possibilties

A number of different items are needed for use in this plan. Ask parents to collect magazine pictures of cars, trucks, and trains. Let parents know how the items will be used.

Parent Postcards

Parent Postcards in this section are designed to share with parents during the Possibilities Plan. The topics are natural extensions of the activities and experiences that you are planning and implementing for the infants in the classroom. Use the Postcards to connect parents to their children's learning.

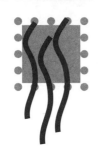

TO

Drive-time Activities

Often during the course of a Possibilities Plan, we will share with you a particular story, rhyme, song, or book that is being used in the classroom. This is so you will have an opportunity to support what the teacher is doing in the classroom. In addition, your child will feel comfortable with familiar elements like "Twinkle, Twinkle, Little Star" or "The Wheels on the Bus." A good time to use these familiar songs, rhymes, and fingerplays is during "drive time."

For parents of very young children, the time spent going to and from work can be a frustrating time of day. Your baby wants to see more of you than the back of your head, and traffic can make the quick drive home an arduous journey.

While you are on the road, talk with your baby about your day, your baby's day, what you are seeing out the window, and what you will both do when you get home. Often just the sound of your voice will be enough to calm baby and make the time go faster. Also, try some classic songs and rhymes, and see what reaction you get. Using the same rhymes and fingerplays we use at school will be fun because your baby has already been introduced to them. Don't let drive time be boring! Sing, talk, and rhyme away the time! Here's a rhyme your child will love.

There Was a Little Turtle Who Lived in a Box

There was a little turtle who lived in a box,
He swam in the water and climbed on the rocks.
He snapped at a mosquito; he snapped at a flea;
He snapped at a minnow; and he snapped at me.
He caught the mosquito; he caught the flea;
He caught the minnow, but he didn't catch me!

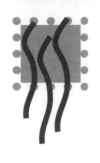

TO

Gender Role Stereotyping

From a very early age, many parents seem to be concerned about blue and pink. Whole nurseries and wardrobes are planned around the boy or girl issue. The concern doesn't stop there. Often parents are concerned about their young children's sexual orientation. When they see boys playing with purses and girls playing with trucks, they worry about the future.

Adults observe particular characteristics in young children and attribute them to the fact that a child is male or female. But, gender identification is not firmly established until children are older. In the early years they will take on the many roles they see adults around them using without awareness of the typical or stereotypical gender of those roles. Before age 5, this is normal. Later, children will begin to decide on activities and experiences based on the gender of who plays the role. For now, encourage your child to play however he or she wants to play.

Both girl and boy infants need a wide range of physical, intellectual, emotional, and social experiences. Of course we want girls to grow up to be competent physically, and we certainly want boys to grow up to be loving and affectionate. Thus, we must give both boys and girls chances to become the best individuals they can be. This will be accomplished through allowing many varied experiences, instead of limiting girls to playing house and boys to building with blocks.

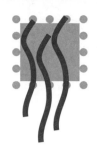

TO
_____
_____

Preparing for Time Away from Your Child

As more and more parents are required to travel with their jobs, the issue of leaving a child for extended periods of time becomes an important one. What can parents do to make the absence more bearable? The simple answer: plan ahead.

Very young children have difficulty with time concepts. This is one reason why arrival and departure times at school are so important. Infants need to know that schedules are predictable and that parents will return. The trick with trips is being honest, but not telling young children too far in advance. Make arrangements for your child to be with someone familiar, in familiar surroundings, and on a familiar schedule.

The day before the trip, talk with your child. Say when the trip will be and where you will be going. Be reassuring as to who will care for your child and where your child will be. Tell why you must go (for example, for your job) and that you will telephone (as often as you can). Don't promise what you cannot deliver. Let your child know that you love him or her even when you are apart.

Details are important. Little things, such as having the usual clothes and shoes become more essential when a parent is away. Give your child a security item that will be comforting and will remind your child of you (a pillowcase, a photograph, or a T-shirt, for example). Be certain that your child has his or her usual security items, also.

Far in advance, write down information such as emergency phone numbers, medical conditions, and where special items are located. Then have a good trip, knowing that you have done your best to prepare.

Concepts Learned in Cars, Trucks, and Trains

Cars and trucks have wheels.

Wheels go 'round and 'round.

Cars and trucks have horns.

Horns go beep, beep.

Vehicles break and need repair.

Trains have whistles.

I can pretend.

People take vacations.

I can get in my car seat.

I can get out of my car seat.

I can make tracks with car and truck wheels.

I can gas up my car.

Things stick to sticky paper.

Bells ring.

Resources

Prop Boxes

Going on Vacation

Bags   Scarves

Empty sunscreen bottles   Shoes

Hats   Sunglasses

Jackets   Toy keys

Maps   Travel brochures

Purses

Construction

Clip board   Safety glasses

Gloves   Tape measure

Hard hat   Toy hammer

Lunch box

Picture File/Vocabulary

Cars   Map

Construction site   Trains

Gas station   Travel brochures
Highway   Trucks
Horns   Whistle
Luggage

Books

All Aboard Trucks by Lynn Conrad
Big Book of Things That Go by Caroline Bingham
Big Truck, Big Wheels by Bobbie Kalman and Petrina Gentile
Chugga Chugga Choo Choo by Kevin Lewis
Construction Zone by Tana Hoban
Freight Train by Donald Crews
Peter's Trucks by Sallie Wolf
Sheep in a Jeep by Nancy Shaw
Thomas the Tank Engine by Wilbur and Vera Awdry (page 213)
Thomas the Tank Engine Coming and Going: A Book of Opposites by Wilbur
     and Vera Awdry
Trains by Byron Barton
Trucks by Byron Barton
Trucks by Mallory Loehr

Rhymes/Fingerplays

"How Many Cars Do You See?" (page 214)

Music/Songs

"Drive, Drive, Drive Your Car" (page 214)
"Go In and Out the Car" (page 215)
"Wheels on the Bus" (page 215)

Toys and Materials

The following purchased items are important for this Possibilities Plan:

Books about vehicles
Busy box
Pop-up pals
Prop box items
Rattles
Sound toys
Toy key rattles

The following gathered items will help support this Possibilities Plan:

Bells
Car seats
Contact paper
Prop box items
Resealable plastic bags
Small trucks and cars
Vehicle pictures
Watering can
Whistles
Yarn, ribbon, or book rings

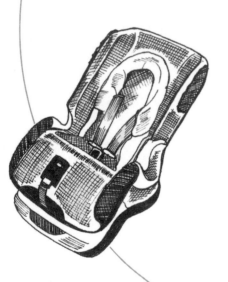

CHAPTER 5

Communicating with Parents, Teachers, and Friends

INTRODUCTION

Newborns arrive in this world able to communicate with others primarily through language such as crying. During infancy, though, this changes. A major transition from having almost no understanding of spoken language, to understanding spoken

words, and then to expressing their knowledge of language with their own words is completed.

Infancy is a critical period for the acquisition of language. The window for learning language opens at birth and closes around 18 to 24 months. After this period, language still can be acquired, but it is a much more difficult process.

Stimulating language is a crucial task for infant teachers. Unless babies understand how language functions in their world and how important language is, they will not learn to use it. But communicating is not an isolated skill. It is a reciprocal task— communicating with someone who responds in kind. Creating this interactive dialogue is the first step down the road of learning to communicate.

Intellectual development is also critical during infancy. Emerging understanding of brain development in the early years confirms that these years are learning years. Although not as visible to parents and teachers as skill acquisition in the emotional, physical, and language domains, the future of cognitive skills is being developed during infancy.

Brain connections called synapses are developing from all of things babies see, touch, taste, hear, feel, and experience. These connections must be used again and again to remain useful and viable. Teachers and parents provide the stimulation process that reinforces these new connections. Enabling babies to experience and repeat sensory stimuli forms the foundation of future cognitive development.

INNOVATIONS IN OBSERVATION/ASSESSMENT

Observation/Assessment Instrument

The assessment instrument on the next page is not just a skills checklist. Instead it is designed to guide the teacher's observation of children's development through major interactional tasks of infancy. The assessment's focus is on what IS happening, not just what should happen or what will happen. Use this assessment to lead to developmentally appropriate practice.

Infant (0-18 months) Assessment

Task: Communicating with Parents, Teachers, and Friends

	0-6 months			6-12 months		12-18 months
CM1	a. Gazes at familiar faces.	b. Responds to facial expressions of familiar faces.	c. Occasionally engages in reciprocal communication with facial expressions, vowel sounds, and voice inflection.	d. Frequently engages in reciprocal communication using facial expressions, inflection, and vowel and consonant sounds.		e. Imitates and jabbers in response to familiar voices.
CM2	a. Makes sounds		b. Imitiates intonational and inflectional vocal patterns.	c. Develops holophrasic speech—words that convey complete sentences or thoughts.	d. Uses the same word to convey different meaning.	e. Develops telegraphic speech where 2 or 3 words are used as a sentence.
CM3	a. Listens to familiar people's voices when they talk.		b. Shows understanding of simple phrases by responding or reacting.	c. Points or looks at familiar objects when asked to do so.		d. Follows commands with visual cues or context cues.
CM4	a. Babbles motorically, acoustically, and visually simple sounds like (m), (p), (b), (n) at the beginning of words and vowel sounds like (ah), (oh), (uh).			b. Babbles sounds like (w), (k), (f), (t), (d) at the beginning of words and vowels sounds like (eh), (ee); strings sounds together (ba-ba-ba-ba-ba) and practices sounds in a wide variety of ways.		
CM5	a. Responds discriminantly to voices of mother and father.		b. Turns toward and responds to familiar voices and sounds.	c. Prefers familiar sounds and voices.		d. Directs vocalizations toward familiar people and objects in the environment.
CM6	a. Experiments with babbling and cooing.		b. Inflection is added to babbling and cooing.			c. Single words or phrases are understandable to familiar adults; strangers may not understand these words.
CM7	a. Looks at picture books.		b. Listens to books when read by a familiar adult.		c. Points to pictures.	d. Turns pages.

INNOVATIONS IN CHILD DEVELOPMENT

Brain Growth and Development

With the advent of new imaging technologies, neurobiologists have discovered exciting information about how the brain develops. Many of these discoveries have validated premises long held as important by early childhood teachers. New knowledge indicates that brain development is the result of a complex dance between the genetic makeup of a child, which is fixed at conception, and the child's experience, which is open to many possibilities. Scientists have always thought that this dance was a lifelong one. Brain research has now confirmed that what happens to children in the first ten years of life has a profound impact on the way the lifelong dance proceeds.

Before a child is born, neurons or brain cells are developed. After birth, synapses develop between the neurons. As stimulation occurs, millions of connections are developed creating networks for coordination and communication. This is a "use it or lose it" time. Neurons that aren't stimulated simply don't get connected and never have another chance to do so. So the early experiences that babies have directly effect the way their brains develop and how many networks are created. Early stimulation, therefore, has lifelong impact on babies—impacting the abilities the child will have as an adult.

After the initial connections are forms, the brain begins a lifelong process of improving the connections or highways between neurons and connecting smaller roads to larger one. For the next 10 years are so, well-stimulated neural pathways become larger, stronger, and more coordinated while un- or under-stimulated ones are abandoned.

Another important finding of brain research is that there are prime times for acquiring different kinds of knowledge and skills—an optimum time for stimulating and enriching children's learning (Shore, 1997). Because this is the case, negative experiences or the lack of stimulation during these prime times increases the risk of lifelong consequences for children. For very young children, two important optimum times take place before age three. The first is the foundation of emotional development that begins at birth and begins to diminish at age 2. The second is the foundation of language development that opens at birth and begins to diminish at about age 6. As a result, supporting the development of attachment between infants and their primary caregivers and stimulating language development are critical curricula for infants.

Language Development

From birth to 18 months, children go from being nonverbal to communicating effectively with words—often speaking in 2- to 3-word sentences. To the casual observer, this rapid growth may seem like magic. But, like all areas of development, language follows predictable growth patterns that we can identify and follow. Children learn to use language by having adults use language with them. In other words, communicating with children teaches them to communicate with us and with others.

Good teachers talk spontaneously to infants. They narrate what is going on in the classroom, talk about what children are doing, and respond to vocalizations from the child regardless of how understandable these early utterances are. Infant teachers quickly learn not to feel self-conscious about talking to children who do not talk back. They know that the baby perceives the tone and timbre of their voice, their facial expressions, and their body language. The words teachers use mean a lot to children. Good teachers also understand that talking to infants is the best way to help them learn language.

Reciprocity—the back-and-forth of interactions between infants and their teachers—is most important in encouraging language development. No child will learn to use language in an environment that does not have a responsive adult to stimulate and respond to early attempts to communicate.

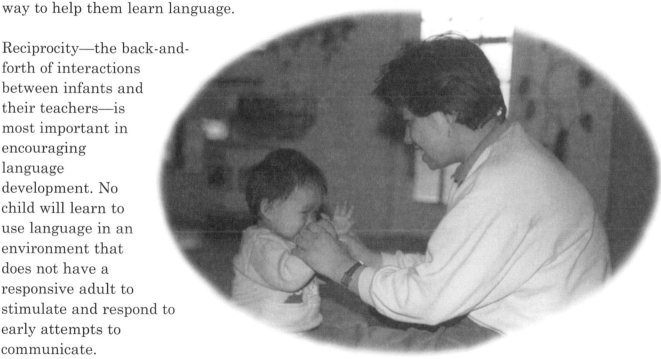

During the first three years of life, children typically go from babbling to using grammatically correct sentences. As magical as this rapid growth seems, it follows the same developmental guidelines of all growth.

In general, the sequence of acquisition of speech sounds follows these developmental principles:

1. motorically simple to motorically complex; for example, (m) as in mama to (kw) as in queen

2. acoustically simple to acoustically complex; for example, (p) as in pie to (thr) as in throw
3. visible to less visible; for example, (b) as in boy to (r) as in red

The sequence of sound articulation is also predictable. During the first four years, a child will master the following groups of sounds:

(b), (p), (d), (t), (g), (k), (f), (m), (n), (ng), (w), (h), (y)

Other sounds are mastered after the fourth year.

Children's language behaviors also follow a predictable developmental pattern. The following language behaviors can be expected to emerge within one to three months following chronological ages:

AGE	LANGUAGE BEHAVIORS
BIRTH-6 MONTHS	• Responds to familiar voices. • Changes cry with emotional state. • Turns eyes and head toward the source of sound. • Is aware of the sounds he makes. • Makes soft vowel sounds: uh, ah.
7-10 MONTHS	• Turns head and shoulders toward soft, familiar sounds. • Imitates intonational patterns of familiar phrases using some vowel and consonant patterns. • Practices a variety of intonational and inflectional patterns. • Understands simple phrases such as bye-bye, no-no, and his own name. • Directs vocalizations toward people and familiar objects in the environment.
11-16 MONTHS	• Says first words, da-da, ma-ma, muk (milk), etc. • Uses several words correctly and consistently. • Points or looks to familiar objects when asked to do so. • Imitates and jabbers in response to human voice. • Frowns when scolded. • Imitates sounds he hears: moo, baa baa, etc. • Expresses bodily needs with nonverbal and verbal responses.
16-18 MONTHS	• Begins to identify body parts; is able to point to eyes and nose. • Uses several meaningful words that may not be articulated correctly such as ba-ba for bottle, muk for milk, etc. • May use one word to represent several things, including wa-wa for I want water, look at the water, and I spilled the water.

As these skills emerge, children's language becomes more intelligible. Expect about 20-25% of an 18-24-month-old's language to be understandable to strangers. This percentage goes up to 60-65% of a 2 ½-year-old's language that is understandable to strangers, and 75-90% of 3-4-year-old's language.

Expressive and Receptive Language

Children have two different types of language skills. One type is children's expressive language skills, meaning those things the child can say, the size of the spoken vocabulary, and the grammar and syntax of language. Receptive language skills refer to language that is understood by children, regardless of their expressive ability. Very young children learn the meaning of language, like "no" or "go bye-bye," before they are able to say those words themselves. So, stimulation of both expressive and receptive language is of critical importance. Most of an infant teacher's efforts go into creating receptive language skills. Teachers need to be skilled in using a wide variety of language stimulation techniques (see pages 237-238) that support emerging receptive and expressive language.

Intellectual Development

The intellectual development of infants is stimulated by virtually everything a teacher does with children in the classroom. In fact, during the first two years of life, intellectual and language development is stimulated naturally as children explore and interact with the environment, exploring their place in it.

According to Jean Piaget, the most noted scholar of cognitive development in very young children, children learn cognitive skills by making mistakes, by actively experimenting with the real world, and by trying to understand how things work (Piaget, 1977). Active experimentation is the best form of intellectual stimulation. There is no need for infant teachers to worry about teaching children numbers, colors, or any academic skills. These concepts will emerge when children are older. Experiences with real things, with concrete objects, and with the environment in which infants live are the best ways to stimulate intellectual development.

The chart on the next page summarizes Piaget's sensori-motor stage of cognitive development;

Piaget's Sensori-motor Stages of Cognitive Development

Overview	Birth-2 years	• Adaptation (through assimilation and accommodation) to environment does not include the use of symbols or oral language. • Child develops schema (cognitive pictures).
Simple Reflex Stage	Birth -1 month	• Reflex actions are practiced to become more efficient; child begins to exercise reflexes. • Lacks object permanence; if object can be seen, it exists. If not seen, it does not exist.
Primary Circular Stage	1-4 months	• Child repeats reflexive behavior as well as other pleasant behavior (for example, sucking). • Object permanence advances—perceives object as having its own separate existence. • Continues to gaze at spot where object was, as if expecting it to return.
Secondary Circular Stage	4-10 months	• Behaviors discovered by chance are repeated to produce interesting results. Child is beginning to understand that something happens as a result of his actions. • Object permanence advances—looks for removed object where it was last seen.
Coordinate Secondary Stage	10–12 months	• Beginning to see what Piaget calls "intelligent behavior." Behavior is intentional—it has a goal. • Object permanence advances—object has own existence. Child searches for object in the last place seen. • Imitation of models increases.
Tertiary Circular Stage	12-18 months	• Actively experiments with environment; varies responses to obtain interesting results. • Uses trial-and-error techniques. • Object permanence advances—follows visual sequential displacement of objects.
Imagery Stage	18 months - 2½ years	• Begins transition to symbolic thought. Vocabulary grows rapidly. Uses formed mental images to solve problems. • Thought processes relate to concrete experiences and objects. • Object permanence advances—searches for objects when displacement is visible.

INNOVATIONS IN INTERACTIVE EXPERIENCES

Brain research and theories of language acquisition and intellectual development suggest that early stimulation of language and cognition results in many advantages for babies later in life. For language, this means giving the baby many repeated experiences with language—hearing it used, being included in communication, having nonverbal cues interpreted correctly, and receiving encouragement for communication attempts whether verbal or nonverbal. Infant teachers must view their communication—all of it—as including the baby.

Stimulating cognitive development almost comes naturally as children begin the exploration of the world around them. The role of the infant teacher is to support and extend these explorations as curriculum—helping infants accomplish early exploration successfully. Later, the teacher will actually structure and support exploration as it becomes physical. As always, the integrated nature of development is seen in the intersection of physical development—as babies begin to move around, cognitive skills—as their interest in finding and exploring the world grows, and language skills—as the labels and names of things become interesting and as babies learn that what they say has broader meaning in the adult world.

Because infant teachers begin communicating with babies before they develop expressive language skills, it is important to plan experiences that support reciprocal communication and receptive and expressive language acquisition. Make these experiences a part of every infant's daily curriculum. It is also important to plan for and support exploration—the foundation of expanding and coordinating networks in babies' brains.

The following are all important interactive experiences for babies.

- ☐ Make eye contact with babies.
- ☐ Narrate routines as you implement them.
- ☐ Coo and converse with babies.
- ☐ Look at objects and label them.
- ☐ Repeat word attempts made by babies.
- ☐ Stress single words (holophrases) in your speech.
- ☐ Sing to babies, move with babies, and use fingerplays as stimulation activities.
- ☐ Expand telegraphic speech by adding words and repeating baby's utterances.
- ☐ Interpret nonverbal cues and give them word descriptions.

The following are all important interactive experiences for babies. (Continued)

☐ Respond to babies' actions.

☐ Ask the child to show you, take you to, or to point to objects of interest.

☐ Play "what if" games.

☐ Support emerging concentration skills by not interrupting babies when they are playing (working).

☐ Time interruptions to avoid distracting babies from interesting tasks.

INNOVATIONS IN TEACHING

What Does Brain-based Care and Early Education Look Like?

Brain-based curricula looks like developmentally appropriate curricula. It supports teachers in spending time with children to develop close connections. Children's brains work best in the context of healthy relationships. Warm, consistent, responsive care makes brain growth and development emerge as nature planned. So the time teachers spend connecting, really connecting to babies, learning to read cues, observing babies play, and cuddling them is curricula for babies' brains.

Using warm, responsive touch to stimulate neural connections is an important teaching skill. Rough, insensitive touch, however infrequent, puts children at risk for shutting down the emotional connections that are forming between adults and children. Gentle, responsive touch stimulates and strengthens the emerging connections between neurons.

Talking to and with children is crucial to the future development of language—both the primary language of the family and secondary language of the community or society. Starting with gazing at each other, adults and children begin the communication process and tell each other that messages are being sent and received. Then, using language with children—functionally—to get needs met and understand the world around them is important. Language stimulation techniques such as description, self-talk, and expansion (see pages 235-238) strengthen neural connections and capitalize on this prime time.

Stimulation that matches the child's interest and ability without overwhelming or overstimulating is another part of brain-based curricula. This goodness of fit refers to the match between the child's individuality and the actions and interactions of the teachers. Individualizing these interactions is crucial to brain development because of the risk of interrupting or negating the neural development under way.

Stimulating Developmental Growth

To stimulate development, teachers balance two key roles—interacting and observing. The teacher also must be sensitive to the timing of interactions and be aware of the whole group while interacting with one or two children. The following are guidelines for stimulating developmental growth:

- Make friendly overtures to children, such as eye contact, smiling, and attention to clothes or belongings. These overtures show children that you are friendly and interested in their activities.

- Sit on the floor near infants who are playing. Get down on their level.
- Offer or display materials that are appropriate to the child's age. Children view this as an invitation to play.
- Demonstrate the uses of playthings (especially if they are ignored). Show how to use a rattle, drive a car, or pull a string on a pull toy. This gives children an idea about where to begin.
- Prevent interruptions by adults or children when a child is attempting to use a toy. Let

children create their own learning experiences.

- Encourage reluctant or distracted children to try or to complete a task. This helps them focus on the experience at hand and may build confidence in using materials.

- Be available to consult on a problem or share a discovery with children. If the teacher is nearby and watching, children come to feel that the teacher is personally interested and able to help when needed.

- Use language whenever it can be a simple and comfortable part of the experience. This stimulates understanding and adds information and vocabulary to the child's thinking and doing activities.

- Introduce related materials, activities, or ideas when children are temporarily uninvolved or indicate that they are tired of the materials available for play. A different sounding rattle or a new block shape adds interest to the child's play and extends the experience.

- When children are unable to do what they started, guide them to a similar but easier task. This prevents the kind of frustration that can reduce motivation for a second attempt.

- Plan new activities and materials. Variety is as important to infants as familiarity in maintaining their learning momentum.

- Attend to every child every day. Be certain the interaction reaches and stimulates every infant, not just those who demand it.

- Be conscious of the next steps in the child's developmental sequence. The teacher's readiness to move on when the child is willing and able can ensure continued developmental progress.

Early Identification of Developmental Challenges

Teachers have many opportunities to observe children as they grow and learn. Occasionally, these observations cause teachers to have questions concerning how babies are developing. When you notice that a baby is outside of the age range for accomplishing a task or skill on the observation/ assessment instrument, remember that differences in development are normal. For example, if a baby is 7 months old and does not display the tasks or skills on the 6-12-month section, continue careful observations and data collection. You are probably observing the differences in the individual pace of development. If this trend continues and the baby is still not demonstrating tasks and skills within his chronological age range, talk to the child's parents about your observations. You might want to suggest that the parents discuss what you have observed with their pediatrician.

Children who are six months or more behind their chronological age need to be evaluated further to determine if the delay you are observing is related to maturational factors or a developmental delay. Early identification of developmental delays is an important role for teachers. They are not diagnosticians, but they are excellent observers. Often intervention can completely remediate problems that are discovered early. Your careful observations can support parents in making sure that their child's needs are met.

Techniques for Stimulating Language Development

The field of speech and language development offers several indirect language stimulation techniques that infant teachers will find extremely useful. These techniques, called description, parallel talk, self-talk, expansion, and expansion plus, direct the teacher's language behaviors and encourage the emergence of language.

- *Description*—Description is a technique in which the teacher narrates or describes what is going on in the child's world by putting word labels on things. For example, if a child looks toward the door as a parent enters the room, the adult might say, "That's Jenny's mother. She must be here to pick up Jenny." Description is also helpful in communicating what Gerber (1979) termed mutual respect. Mutual respect advocates telling children what will happen to them before it happens and waiting for the child to indicate that he is ready. A teacher might say, "It's time for a diaper change," as a description of what will happen to the child. Then, a respectful teacher waits before continuing, so the child can stop his activity and indicate he is ready. The teacher then describes each step of the diaper change as it occurs, "Off come your pants. Here's the clean diaper. All done!"

- *Parallel Talk*—Parallel talk is a short phrase that focuses on the child's action. Parallel talk usually begins with "you." For example, "You're turning over from your back to your front," is parallel talk. Others might be, "You're putting the Duplos in the bucket," "You've got the baby doll," or "You pulled off your shoe." Focusing on the action helps the child put word labels on behavior.

- *Self-Talk*—Self-talk focuses on adult behavior, labeling and describing what the adult is doing. Teachers who use self-talk usually start their utterances with "I." For example, a teacher might say to a child who is getting fussy, "I'll be over to pick you up as soon as I put these toys back on the shelf," or "I'm picking up the toys and then I'll pick you up!"

- *Expansion and Expansion Plus*—Expansion and expansion plus are extremely useful techniques to use with children when their vocabularies begin to grow. These techniques take what the child says and expand on it (expansion) or add to what the child says (expansion plus). For example, when a child says, "muk," the teacher might say, "You want more milk," or "Jason needs milk, please," to expand what the child says. If the child says, "Outside," the teacher might say, "You'd like to go outside." For expansion plus, the teacher adds a little more to the sentence a child uses. An example might expand, "Go bye-bye," uttered by the child, to "It's time to get your things and go bye-bye." Expansion and expansion plus restate what the child says in complete and sometimes expanded sentence form.

Notice that these techniques require nothing of the child. The child is not asked to repeat the larger sentence, to repeat the label of an object identified by description, or to respond further to the teacher. These techniques are stimulation approaches that add information to the child's language skills and foster future language development. The techniques are not designed to be used as drills or exercises for very young children.

What Does Attachment Have to Do with Intellectual and Language Development?

The previous section focused on the acquisition of language and emergence of cognitive skills. Why, then, are we now talking about attachment, a part of social emotional development? The reason is simple. Because development is so integrated, it is very difficult to consider one area without considering another. This integration is clear in the connections between emotional growth, cognitive growth, language growth, and physical growth.

During the third stage of attachment, called separation anxiety, a key intellectual skill enables babies to understand that their parents have not just disappeared—they have gone away. This cognitive skill is called object permanence. It connects with emerging emotional skills and all of a sudden, babies are crying when they realize that their parents or most familiar caregiver is no longer visible. Throw in emerging motor skills that allow the child to crawl after a departing parent or teacher and you can clearly see that development across areas is connected.

Separation Anxiety: What Can Teachers Do?

Separation anxiety is a difficult time for both teachers and parents because children cry during transitions to and from school. Both adults would really like the child to separate easily and without tears. It is the teacher's job to help parents understand the normalcy of these new behaviors and how they herald the emergence of new skill development in emotional, cognitive, and language domains. Try some of the following strategies to address separation anxiety.

- Limit the number of unfamiliar people who are in the child's space at one time. Let visitors say hello from the door instead of entering the classroom.

- Always tell your babies when you are leaving the classroom—even if it makes them cry. This develops a sense of trust that you will do what you say you will and, in the long run, shortens the crying time.

- Don't sneak out of the classroom for breaks when babies aren't looking. Tell them you are leaving and when you will return.

- Help babies say goodbye to their parents and to you when you leave with lots of hugs and kisses.

- Spend lots of floor time with babies as they explore and discover the environment and the world. Exploration is a marvelous distraction and can re-orient the child from being upset to being interested in an activity after you leave.

- Give babies lots of experience with action/reaction toys and games such as peek-a-boo and find-the-doll-under-the-blanket. These experiences give children opportunities to practice the emerging skill of understanding that objects have permanence and do not disappear simply because they are not visible.

- Celebrate reunions! Make a big point of reuniting, so babies clearly know you are glad to see them and that you came back, just like you said you would.

Simplifying Piaget

Alice Honig, a noted early childhood specialist, simplifies Piaget's theories by synthesizing the learning tasks of childhood into 12 categories (Honig, 1982). Some infant teachers will find that they already spend an enormous amount of time exposing infants to these learning tasks. Each should be incorporated in planned interactions with children throughout the day.

1. Learning to make groups
2. Learning to separate parts from the big group
3. Learning to line up objects in a logical order
4. Learning time relationships
5. Learning about places and how space is organized
6. Learning what numbers mean
7. Learning to recognize change
8. Learning to use body parts together
9. Learning to reason

10. Learning to use imagination
11. Learning language and using books
12. Learning social skills

Understanding these learning tasks of the first three years allows teachers to capitalize on emerging skills by developing appropriate curriculum plans. Each of these tasks offers numerous opportunities to enhance the intellectual development of very young children.

Multiple Intelligences

Gardner's theory of multiple intelligences proposes that children have several kinds of intelligence that operate at the same time in complementary ways (Gardner, 1983). But many of the intelligences, such as logical-mathematical and spatial intelligence, seem to apply to older children, not to infants. Can we apply these ideas to younger children?

Gardner's Multiple Intelligence

Intelligence	Description
Linguistic	Sensitivity to the meaning and order of words
Logico-mathematical	Ability to handle chains of reasoning and recognize patterns and order
Musical	Sensitivity to pitch, melody, rhythm, and tone
Bodily-kinesthetic	Ability to use the body skillfully and handle objects adroitly
Spatial	Ability to perceive the world accurately and to recreate or transform aspects of that world
Naturalist	Ability to recognize and classify the numerous species of an environment
Interpersonal	Ability to understand people and relationships
Intrapersonal (also called emotional intelligence by Goleman)	Access to one's emotional life as a means to understand oneself and others.

According to Gardner, children have lots of different types of intelligence, not just one or two types. Some children have lots of musical intelligence while others have lots of logical or mathematical intelligence. Theorists and researchers who think children have multiple intelligences believe that there are many ways for children to learn and for teachers to teach.

All of the multiple intelligences begin at birth. Early indicators of different intelligences can be seen in infants in many ways. Some infants are watchers—they like to watch other infants try new things. Others are doers—they have to be in the middle of any experience, embracing it all. Still others listen carefully to what goes on around them before they begin to interact. These differences emerge from the individual's unique collection of intelligences and are part of what makes each of us different from one another.

One type of intelligence—intrapersonal intelligence—is a crucial type of intelligence to support during the early years. Also called emotional intelligence, this intelligence includes self-awareness, managing emotions, emotional self-control, recognizing emotions in others, and handling relationships (Goleman, 1998). Goleman believes that every interaction between infants and their parents and teachers carries emotional messages that can influence emotional intelligence. If messages are positive and responsive, infants learn that the world is a supportive and caring place. If children receive curt, insensitive responses, or worse, abusive or cruel responses, these emotional encounters will negatively mold children's views of relationships. Both of these experiences affect functioning in all realms of life, for better or worse.

The theory of multiple intelligences offers teachers of infants a wonderful framework for interacting with and teaching them. It is very freeing for teachers to know that it is acceptable to treat children differently—when the treatment matches the child's learning style.

Gardner's theory also proposes that interaction is cumulative—every one matters. Our actions, reactions, plans, and schedules tell children if and how much we care for them.

This theory validates what every infant teacher knows—every baby is unique. Such ideas help us to understand individual children better and modify our programs to fit each child rather than requiring children to fit into our programs. Further, the theory of multiple intelligences helps us support parents in viewing their child's unique skills rather than comparing their child to other children—a wonderful way to guarantee that cumulative interactions of important caregivers positively affect children's potential.

Books for Babies

Children, even babies, need to have stories read to them every day. Experiences with books help young children develop important pre-reading skills, so make books a part of the classroom every day.

Realize, though, that infants view books as consumable. Paper books won't last long because they will be mouthed and pages will be torn. Nevertheless, infants are learning that print goes from left to right and from top to bottom, and that books are read right side up. They are learning how to turn pages and that the book goes from the front to back. Later, children will learn the meaning of the story is in the print—not in the illustrations. Then, they will learn that letters make words and that words make sentences.

Try some of the following ideas for reading to babies:

- In the beginning, don't read. Point! Name objects while you point to pictures on the page. Reading pictures is an important pre-reading skill that infants will perfect first.

- Put life into your reading. Vary your voice tone. Give voices to different pictures and characters. Have fun!

- Start with easy-to-read, bright, and simple picture books. In most cases, you needn't bother with the text until babies can sit through looking at the pictures of the whole book. Then, abbreviate the text, keep it simple, and move quickly to keep children's interest.

- Move your finger across the page to show that reading is taking place. This helps your child learn left-to-right progression—a key pre-reading skill.

- Point out familiar things first. Eyes, animals, mother, daddy, baby, car, and so on that are familiar to children's experience will keep their attention. Then, gradually add unfamiliar pictures and words as you re-read the book.

- Don't stay on one page too long. Four seconds is about long enough for very young children. For now, limit your reading to one page at a time. But over time, start to connect one page with the next, so children will see the relationship between characters or objects on subsequent pages.

Start with books that can be used for different purposes. For example, if an alphabet book has animals (like bears or tigers) that are associated with letters, use the book to explore the different sounds animals make as well as reading the book to associate the letter with the animal.

Teacher Competencies to Support Communicating with Parents, Teachers, and Friends

Sometimes	Usually	Always	
☐	☐	☐	States directions in positive terms.
☐	☐	☐	Communicates effectively with children and adults.
☐	☐	☐	Speaks in simple, understandable terms.
☐	☐	☐	Understands how to use voice as a teaching tool.
☐	☐	☐	Mediates communication between children to foster social communication and interaction.
☐	☐	☐	Uses nonverbal techniques to communicate desired behavior.
☐	☐	☐	Uses existing materials and equipment effectively.
☐	☐	☐	Devises new materials to stimulate and challenge children.
☐	☐	☐	Rotates and adapts materials to insure children's interest.
☐	☐	☐	Encourages language by repeating infant vocalizations, adding new sounds, naming objects, expanding the child's language, and narrating events relevant to the child.
☐	☐	☐	Avoids baby talk. Uses "parentese," the high-pitched, slow-paced, exaggerated enunciations that make speech easier for babies to understand.
☐	☐	☐	Uses language in context without unnecessary repetitions.
☐	☐	☐	Responds to infant communications in a variety of ways such as vocalizations, facial expressions, and body language.

Resources for Teachers

Bodrova, E., & D. J. Leong. (1996). *Tools of the mind: The Vygotskyian approach to early childhood education.* Englewood Cliffs, NJ: Prentice Hall.

Goleman, D. (1998). *Emotional intelligence.* New York: Bantam Books.

Honig, A., & H.E. Brody. (1996). *Talking with your baby: Family as the first school.* Syracuse, NY: Syracuse University Press.

Mitchell, G. (1998). *A very practical guide to discipline with young children.* Glen Burnie, MD: Telshare.

National Association for the Education of Young Children. (1996). *Responding to linguistic and cultural diversity.* Washington, DC: National Association for the Education of Young Children (NAEYC).

Rockwell, R., D. Hoge, & B. Searcy. (1999). *Linking language and literacy: Simple language and literacy activities throughout the curriculum.* Beltsville, MD: Gryphon House.

Shore, R. (1997). *Rethinking the brain: New insights into early development.* New York: Families and Work Institute.

INNOVATIONS IN PARENT PARTNERSHIPS

School- or Teacher-initiated Possibilities

Picture Book Exchange

Plan a book exchange where parents bring in books and exchange them for others. This can be accomplished by inviting parents to bring in their books all at the same time, or by providing a decorated box and having the activity be ongoing.

Trash as Treasure

Decorate a paper trash bag to send home for storing discarded items that you can use for the children at school. You may want to attach or include a list of everyday items that you can use, such as cardboard tubes, clean plastic bottles, magazines, boxes, and so on.

Coupon Exchange

Provide a diaper coupon exchange by providing a place on a bulletin board or a basket where parents can leave coupons they don't need and pick up coupons they do need.

Visiting Reader

Invite parents to sign up to read in the classroom. They may bring a favorite book or choose one from the school library when they arrive. Or, ask parents to bring one of their child's favorite books to school, so you can read it to the baby during the day. This will make a connection between home and school for the baby.

Parent Postcards

Share Parent Postcards as parents indicate an interest, at appropriate times during the enrollment cycle, or as developmental issues arise. (See pages 441-444 in the Appendix for a sample dissemination schedule.) Copy postcards. Cut if necessary. Address to parent(s) and place on communication sheet or hand out personally.

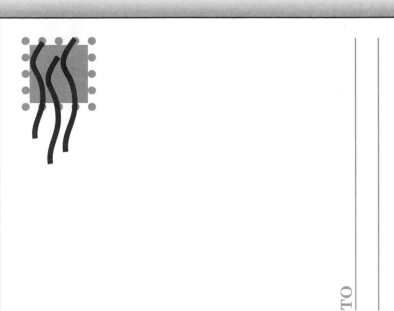

TO

What Is Developmentally Appropriate Care and Early Education for Infants?—The Role of the Teacher

Developmentally appropriate practice (DAP) is educational jargon referring to a particular approach to care and early education that has found wide acceptance in the United States. Noted early childhood specialists say DAP is the way to go. But, what is DAP for infants and how does it apply to your child? To answer this question, let's take a look at what developmentally appropriate care and early education for infants looks like and how it might be different from teaching practice in programs for older children.

The role of the teacher is viewed in a special way in developmentally appropriate infant programs. The teacher's job is to support the development of relationships between parents and their child, between the school and home, and between the teacher and the child. These mutually beneficial relationships begin with the teacher's intimate knowledge about the child, his or her family, and the child's experience at school. When teachers have these important relationships with families, they are able to modify the child's daily experience to match the child's individual developmental needs. This congruence between what a child needs and what the program provides is the foundation of developmentally appropriate practice.

Another important role of the teacher is that of a decision-maker. Teachers make decisions constantly as they care for infants. Is that cry a fussy cry? A hungry cry? A physical discomfort cry? An "I'm sleepy" cry? Each of these situations requires a different response and leads the teacher to act differently. If the baby is hungry, a bottle may be warmed. If the child is sleepy, the teacher may get the baby's blanket and pacifier and began to rock the child to sleep. This dynamic decision-making process requires that teachers draw upon their knowledge of your child, of child development,

What Is Developmentally Appropriate Care and Early Education for Infants?—The Role of the Teacher (continued)

of best care and education practices, and of the family's cultural and social expectations for the child.

The teacher's role often looks different from the role of teachers of older children. For example, direct instruction—the teacher telling the child information that is important—is less prevalent. When observed over time, the role of the teacher looks much more like a dance—approaching the child who needs attention, observing children who are busy and involved with objects or activities to see how the children respond, helping children be close together in groups, intervening when children get too close, helping a child learn a discreet task (like putting a round block in the round hole), and so on. The dance is sometimes fast and hectic, sometimes slow and soothing.

Teachers have another important role in infant programs. That role is assessment of learning and development. In order to know which role to play, which activity to do, which toy to offer, which child to approach, which child to leave alone with a discovery, teachers are constantly assessing children's learning and using that information in their teaching.

TO

TO
_____
_____

What Is Developmentally Appropriate Care and Early Education for Infants?—The Role of Curriculum (Activities and Experiences)

The content of curriculum for infants is not the same as for older children. During the first three years of life, children learn in a variety of ways. They learn by interacting with and acting on their environment—touching, tasting, smelling, feeling, manipulating, and seeing the world around them. This interaction with people and things forms the core of curriculum for very young children.

While good early childhood settings may look similar to one another, part of curriculum is preparing the environment to have pleasing, stimulating, and interesting objects in it. What is available, what gets added or taken away, what is new, and what is familiar are all important parts of curriculum for infants. Adults plan experiences that will be fun to do alone, with a caring adult, or with a friend.

Curriculum for infants is less didactic—or teacher-directed—than it is in the preschool classroom. Teachers of infants do direct instruction with children all the time, but not with a group. Direct instruction is usually at the child's initiation or request and usually with only a few other interested children. Infant teachers read books, play with children, help children play with each other and with interesting toys, count, sing, repeat fingerplays and rhymes, try new motor skills or perfect emerging ones, go outside, drink bottles, eat lunch, and build with and manipulate objects. This is the curriculum for infants.

School for infants looks very different from school for preschoolers or school-agers. This difference is not an accident—it is desirable. It reflects what we know to be the best way to approach the care and early education of children under three years of age.

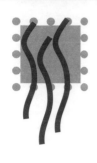

TO _____

Using Found and Discarded Items for Toys

Parents want to give their children what is best for them. Sometimes when we try to give a special gift, our child doesn't seem to cooperate. Instead of finding the new toy interesting, the child may find the box interesting, disappointing parents in the process!

Many items commonly found around the home are very interesting to infants. Pots and pans are a favorite and offer a wonderful diversion during meal preparation. Smaller ones are easier to handle and create less of a danger of pinched fingers. The shiny surfaces allow children to see their own reflections, and the noise is an added bonus.

Boxes are wonderful toys that can be used in a wide variety of ways. They can be used for stacking, carrying, nesting, filling, dumping, and matching. Large boxes make wonderful toys to climb into and out of. Very large boxes make great playhouses. Remove all staples, reinforce with tape, and eliminate all rough edges. Don't forget to add doors and windows.

Plastic bottles are another favorite of young children. Smaller ones can be filled with glitter and water to make interesting toys. Larger bottles are great for carrying around, rolling, hitting, and knocking over. Securely glue caps onto the bottles because their small size makes them a choking hazard.

The key to using found and discarded items as toys is being open to the limitless opportunities and the imagination of a child! Think of the difference between a child having a toy phone that is always a phone and a box that can be a house, a car, a truck, a train, a trunk, a step, and so on. It is the open-ended nature of these items that makes them better than many bought toys, and a great way for your child to learn.

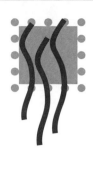

TO

Good Books for Babies

Reading to young children is a great way to get them interested in books. In fact, early experiences with books help ensure that children will have successful literacy experiences later. Books are essential for the development of young children's language and literacy skills.

What kinds of books do young children need? Children explore everything with their mouths. Books will be explored in this same way as well. For this reason, books such as cloth books, vinyl books, and chubby board books are all appropriate for young infants.

Simple books are best. Books with realistic (not cartoon) illustrations are recommended. Expect children to want to read the same books over and over again. This is not a problem. Children learn from repetition (and adults get to practice patience with the repetition)!

Realize that books really are consumable. They won't last long because babies are just beginning to develop emergent reading skills. Books will be mouthed, and pages will be torn. As they develop page-turning skills, books will be ruined. Still, infants are learning that print goes from left to right and from top to bottom, and that books are read right side up. They are learning how to turn pages and that the book goes from the front to back. Then, children will learn the meaning of the story is in the print–not in the illustrations. Finally, they will learn that letters make words and that words make sentences.

When reading to your child, first read the title and the author. Then talk about what the book may be about. Read page by page, pointing out things of interest in the story, as well as the illustrations. Young children have a much bigger receptive vocabulary than expressive vocabulary. They will understand far more words than they can speak. Read the book with expression. And enjoy this wonderful, close time with your child.

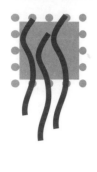

TO
_____
_____

Attachment Stage 3—Separation Anxiety: What Can Parents Do?

An amazing change begins to occur to infants as they approach the end of the first year. Smiling, cooing, responsive babies, who were friendly to almost every smiling face, begin to be wary of strangers and new situations. And they begin to prefer one parent's support. Further, they begin to prefer that one person to others for comforting or particular routines.

Characteristics such as these indicate that your baby is in the third stage of attachment. During this stage, babies show a clearly defined preference for parents and familiar adults. Friendliness toward strangers declines. Babies use parents as a secure base and hide their heads, hold on tight, and turn away from strangers.

This behavior is good news! It means your baby's emotional development is proceeding normally. Take these changes in your baby's behavior into consideration as you take him or her out into the broader social world. Parents can try some of the following strategies to help baby handle this stage of attachment.

- Accept your baby's cool response to unfamiliar adults. Don't push or encourage interaction until the baby seems ready to initiate it.

- Give your baby time to adjust to new people before they try to hold or interact with him or her. Let your baby stay close when a new person is around; use supportive, encouraging, nonverbal cues like eye contact or smiling and nodding your head if your baby decides to let the stranger approach and interact. Allow your baby to set the pace—if he or she doesn't want to go to a new person, respect your child's decision and try again later.

- Explain what is going on to grandparents, friends, or relatives who do not see the baby often enough to be familiar to him or her. It is a developmental stage—not a rejection of their interest.

- Always alert your child to your departure. He or she may object, but your baby will also learn that you can be trusted to do what you say you will do.

TO

How Babies Learn

Opportunities to touch should include a variety of textures such as smooth floors, textured upholstery, squishy things like cereal, warm bath water, cold metal or door frames and furniture, and soft blankets and cuddle toys. Remember that all of the baby's body is sensitive to touch—not just the hands. Feet, tummies, and cheeks respond to the powerful stimulation of touch.

Opportunities to taste and explore with the mouth are innate in babies. From the first reflexive rooting response to nursing or drinking a bottle, oral stimulation provides a primary means of exploration and sensory input. Everything in the environment is a source of oral stimulation. The parents' challenge is to make sure mouthed objects are safe and sanitary.

Opportunities to scan the environment interest babies from the moment of birth. Very young babies calm themselves by visually seeking interesting and engaging things. An early favorite is the face—particularly mom's or dad's face. Provide lots of gazing into each other's eyes. Patterns and high contrast like black on white with red highlights provide early practice with visual acuity. Babies are also good spectators. They like to be where the action is and love to watch what is going on around them, even without direct interaction with others.

Young children's hearing is sensitive to the sounds and noises around them—and can easily be overwhelmed. Limit background noises from radio and television while providing a wide variety of auditory input from human voices—particularly using the native language of the family. Natural sounds like rain on a windowpane or wind rustling a tree branch also will interest infants.

Opportunities to explore the environment are crucial to babies' early learning. Offer plenty of action-reaction toys, rattles, and musical toys. As infants become mobile, a major challenge for parents is how to balance safety issues with exploration needs. Experience and practice are primary learning strategies. Children who have too little opportunity for exploration may experience delays in learning new skills.

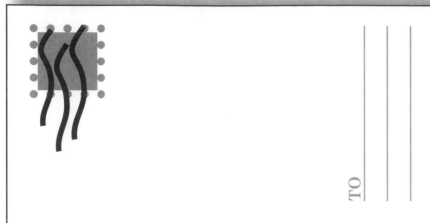

The Amazing Infant Brain

Everyone is talking about the brain! New imaging techniques such as PET scans are providing neurobiologists with fascinating new information about how the brain develops. This research confirms that the early years are learning years and that parents and teachers need to make them count.

Brain development is the result of a complex dance between the genetic makeup of a child, which is predetermined, and the child's experience, which is open to many possibilities. Scientists have always thought of this dance as a lifelong one. They now know that what happens to a child in the first 10 years of life has profound impact on the way the lifelong dance proceeds.

Before a child is born, neurons or brain cells are developed. It is after birth that connections (called synapses) are developed between the neurons. From birth to about a year, millions of connections between neurons are developed—almost like making roads between towns and communities. During this stage of brain development, it is a "use it or lose it" time. Neurons that aren't stimulated simply don't get connected to other neurons.

After these initial connections are formed, the brain begins the process of improving the connections or highways between neurons and connecting smaller roads to larger ones. As this process progresses, communication and coordination among areas of the brain begin. For the next 10 or so years, well-stimulated neural pathways get bigger, stronger, and more coordinated, while under-stimulated ones are abandoned.

What makes brains strong and capable? Experience is the chief architect of the brain. Stimuli from people, places, and things provide the nutrients for healthy brain development. Parents have the unique responsibility of providing infants with some of their early experiences. What a wonderful thing for parents to know—the way parents provide early experiences to children develops their brains!

Brain research indicates that there are critical periods or learning windows for certain areas of the brain. For children under three, two major critical periods occur. The first is the foundation of emotional development, which opens at birth and closes around 18 months. The second critical period is the foundation of language development, which opens at birth and begins to close around age 6. During these critical periods, parents need to be particularly attuned to how children's experiences are stimulating the brain.

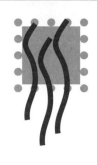

TO

Supporting Brain Development at Home

What kinds of experiences do the best job of supporting brain development? Time, touch, talk, and training are the important sources of brain growth and development.

Time—Consistent, warm, responsive caregiving is so important to children's brains during the first three years. As every infant parent knows, responsive caregiving takes time and can't be rushed. Investing in the time it takes to make nursing or drinking a bottle an interactive, warm experience is not a waste of time. It is a wonderful way to develop young children's brains.

Touch—The very young child takes in experience through all of the senses—touch, taste, smell, sight, and sound. The brain picks up critical messages from touch. Taking the time to hold infants, spending time being gently physical with toes, fingers, arms and legs, touching the body to send positive messages to the developing pathways of the brain are all teaching at its best. Remember that touch is an important communication. Warm and soft touches send very different messages from rough, insensitive touches. Spend time with your baby stretching, wiggling, rolling from side to side, batting at objects, and reaching to improve the communication between areas of the brain, which coordinate these skills. Holding hands is a crucial touching experience as baby pulls to a stand and begins to walk.

Talk—Pay attention to communication. Repetition forms connections in the brain as babies are communicating all the time. The challenge is to read the verbal and nonverbal cues and interpret them accurately. Talk to your baby. Describe what you are doing as you do it. "I'm going to pick you up now to change your diaper." Narrate what you see your child doing as he or she does it. "You are looking at the light—isn't it bright!" Respond to sounds and noises as if they were words, sentences, and thoughts—because they are!

Training—The brain's connections are easily disconnected or abandoned if they are not stimulated. So very young children need lots of practice. Your baby will like doing things again and again. In fact, this repetition is sometimes a frustrating part of parenting because children like to do both fun and interesting things again and again and irritating and inappropriate things again and again! Viewing this repetition as brain training helps parents embrace and tolerate it. Experiences that happen many times make connections, communication, and coordination among the areas of the brain stronger and more capable—actually enhancing children's potential in the process.

Appropriate Expectations for Learning Academic Skills

Many child development specialists believe that the foundation for learning is built during the first three years of life. This may be a scary thought because the academic experiences we remember started at age 5 or 6. We think we have no idea how to teach our babies.

Everything parents do with their children is teaching. Start by teaching your baby that you love him or her. Then teach your baby to depend on you. Then teach him or her how to play with objects. Then teach your baby how to scoot to get something, and so forth. What you may not realize is how important these early skills are for later learning.

Each time you interact with your baby, you are teaching. And each positive, playful experience a child has builds potential for academic readiness and success. Here's a list of activities that is guaranteed to lay the foundation for success in academic skills after age six. Do these now and wait until your child is ready for direct instruction in academic preparation—in about six years!

- Read to your child every day.

- Share your work with your baby. When you sort laundry, give your baby a pile of socks to play with and manipulate. When your baby is older, ask him or her to put the socks in a different pile than the towels, or count out forks for the table, plates as you take them out of the dishwasher, and stop signs as you drive along to school.

- Comment on what you are doing and why. It offers children ideas about connections that will have more meaning later.

- Use discarded cereal boxes, cartons, and cans to create fun playthings.

- Hold your child every day. Take the time to reconnect emotionally. Eye contact is very important. Supporting emotional development is one of the most important things parents can do to prepare their children for academic success. Emotionally stable children make good students.

- Avoid teaching by telling too much at this stage. The early years are years of doing and experimenting—not being taught by telling.

TO _____

Teaching Your Child to Read

It starts early. You want the very best for your child—the best start, the best support, the best education, and the best experiences. Sometimes it seems like parenting is a quest to figure out what to do and when to do the things that will insure that your child gets the best that you can offer.

Well, here's the good news. Teaching your child to read is a very simple process. Surprised? Puzzled? Most parents are. Reading seems like such a complex set of skills. How can we be a part of making it happen without expert assistance from educators? Only one activity predicts success in reading; being read to by parents. Research into early literacy and reading has repeatedly found that children whose parents read to them every day are the best readers during the elementary years.

The reason for this is simple. When you read to your children, you are introducing them to the function of the written word. They are learning that letters have meaning and make words. This lesson is the first lesson in reading and writing. So get out a book and read!

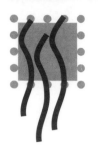

TO

Teaching Your Child to Write

Writing is the other half of reading. Once children learn that symbols (letters and numbers) have meaning, they become interested in representing those symbols in writing. Like reading, learning to write is a process that begins by understanding the function of writing—why adults do it.

During infancy, your child's writing skills will be limited to scribbling and making marks on paper with a variety of writing implements—crayons, markers, pencils, chalk, and so forth. To encourage writing skills, let your child write when you write. For example, when you make a grocery list, give your child a piece of scrap paper and a non-toxic marker and have him or her make a list. Or, when you sit down to pay the bills, give your child some pretend checks to write or pretend bills to pay right along with you. (Junk mail works well for this!) Whenever you use your writing skills, set your child up to use his or hers with you.

Expect your child's writing to be illegible well into the fourth year. Then, you may begin to see the letters of their names and drawings that you can recognize. Rather than focusing on whether you can read your child's writing, ask your child to tell you what it says. Remember, functional writing—applying meaning to symbols—is what is important in early writing. As long as your child thinks his or her marks have meaning, the process of learning to write is right on track!

Resources for Parents

Add these helpful books to your parent library or post this list on your parent bulletin board.

Schiller, P. (1999). ***Start smart: Building brain power in the early years.*** Beltsville, MD: Gryphon House.

Silsberg, J. (1999). ***125 brain games for babies.*** Beltsville, MD: Gryphon House.

INNOVATIONS IN ENVIRONMENTS

Creating a Classroom that Values Multiple Intelligence

What does a classroom that understands multiple intelligences look like? Infant classrooms are characterized by individual, intimate interactions between teachers and children. Children are allowed to follow their own schedules for eating, sleeping, and playing, rather than following a superimposed schedule that is required by the adults. These routines are conducted intimately, one or two infants are eating while another one or two are playing on the floor, and another baby is taking a nap. Rarely, if ever, are children under the age of 2 required to do the same thing at the same time in the same way as all of the other children in the group.

Teachers who understand multiple intelligences recognize that different babies like different types of stimulation. For example, a baby with highly complementary spatial and body kinesthetic intelligence might love exploring tight spaces like the inside of boxes, underneath a table, and behind furniture. Another baby, who has complementary spatial and logico-mathematical intelligence might prefer to mouth and manipulate items in an open space. These examples illustrate the individual nature and variety of multiple intelligences.

Activities and Experiences vs. Centers

Most early childhood educators think of interest or learning centers as an essential part of any classroom setting. Yet, environments for infants are different because they cannot choose to go to different areas until they are mobile. For this reason, teachers must bring the activities and experiences to the child, or they must assist the child in going to where the activities are. A wide range of activities must be available to infants, but the environments are different. In each of the following two Possibilities Plans, *Storybook Classics* and *Sounds*, activities and experiences are presented in the following areas:

- Dramatic Possibilities
- Sensory/Art Possibilities
- Curiosity Possibilities
- Literacy Possibilities
- Music Possibilities
- Movement Possibilities
- Outdoor Possibilities
- Project Possibilities
- Parent Participation Possibilities

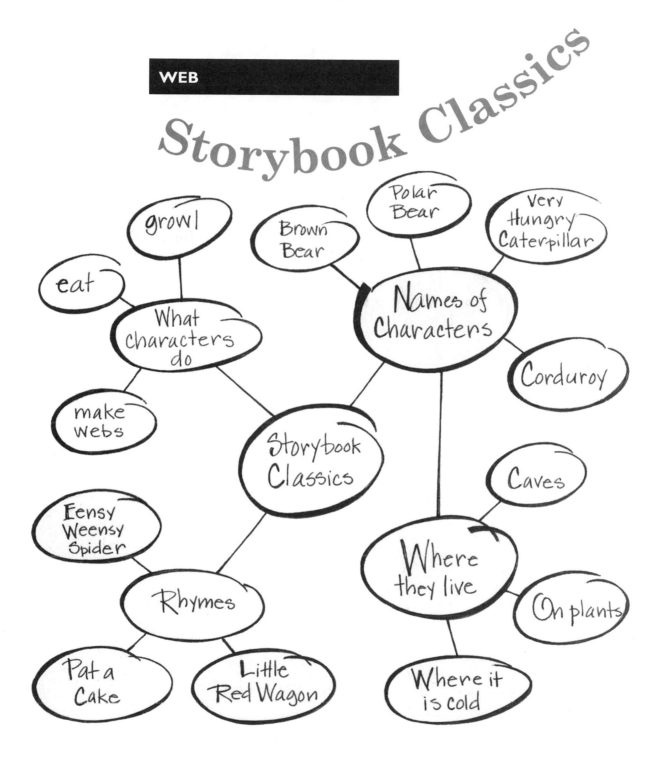

Storybook Classics

growl

eat

What characters do

make webs

Brown Bear

Polar Bear

Very Hungry Caterpillar

Names of Characters

Corduroy

Storybook Classics

Eensy Weensy Spider

Rhymes

Pat a Cake

Little Red Wagon

Caves

Where they live

On plants

Where it is cold

Note: Using the technique of webbing, teachers can follow the leads that children give them, as well as have an unlimited source of options. Always use the webs as a jumping-off point. The possibilities are endless!

PLANNING PAGES

Plan Possibilities

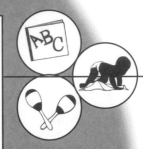

Literacy

Accordion Books 267
Junk Mail Page Turning 267
Cereal Box Books 267
Logo Books 268
Book Buddies 268
My Very First Mother Goose Book 268
Growl Like a Bear .268
Storybook Classics Books 269

Music

Greg and Steve Record 269
Favorite Songs 269

Movement

"Pat-a-Cake" Clapping 270
Follow the Bear Tracks 271
Red Wagon Rides 271
Bears and Boxes 271

Dramatic

Bear Play 262
Bear Cave 262
Props from Stories 262
Teddy Bear Picnic Inside .263

Sensory/Art

Rain Water 263
Corduroy Texture Board .263
Painting/Coloring the
    Bear Cave 264
Foot Painting 264
Porridge Play 265

Curiosity

Bear Puppets 265
Very Hungry
    Caterpillar Puppet 266
One-piece Puzzles 266

Outdoor

Play Gym 272
Storybooks Outside 272
Teddy Bear Stroller Ride 272

Project

Sound Acquisition Chart 273
Brown Bear Painting Book 273

Parent Participation

Supporting Possibilities 273
Guest Readers 274
Parent Book Recordings 274
Teddy Bear Picnic with Parents 274
Parent Postcards
    Tips for Reading to Your Infant 275

Storybook Classics

Books

Brown Bear, Brown Bear by Bill Martin, Jr. 262
Clifford the Big Red Dog by Norman Bridwell
Corduroy by Don Freeman 262
If You Give a Mouse a Cookie by Laura J. Numeroff
Little Engine That Could, The by Watty Piper
My Very First Mother Goose Book
    by Iona Archibald Opie 268
On the Day You Were Born by Debra Fraser
Pat the Bunny by Dorothy Kunhardt
Runaway Bunny by Margaret Wise Brown
Very Busy Spider, The by Eric Carle
Very Hungry Caterpillar, The by Eric Carle 266

Concepts Learned in
Storybook Classics . .276

Prop Boxes

Picnic 276
Storybooks 277

Picture File/Vocabulary . .277

Rhymes/Fingerplays

"Little Miss Muffett" 265
"Pat-a-Cake" 270

Music/Songs

"Brown Bear" song by Steve and Greg 269
"Bumping Up and Down in
   My Little Red Wagon" 270
"Eensy Weensy Spider" . . . . .263 and 270
"Ring Around the Rosie" 270

Toys and Materials 278

Bear Play

0-18 months

Materials
Stuffed bears
Books about bears, such as
   Brown Bear, Brown Bear by Bill Martin, Jr.
   Corduroy by Don Freeman

Teacher Talk
"Allison, you have three stuffed bears to play with. What a big hug!"

Many of the books and stories from this Possibilities Plan have bears as a part of the fun. Examples include *Brown Bear, Brown Bear,* "Teddy Bear, Teddy Bear," and *Corduroy.* Add stuffed bears to the classroom for infants to touch, hold, look at, and carry around. Safety alert: Be sure all stuffed animals have no small parts that might present a choking hazard if they fall off the stuffed animals.

Bear Cave

6-18 months

Materials
Cardboard box
Scissors or sharp knife (for teacher use on

Provide a cardboard box with an archway out to represent a cave. Remove staples, reinforce with tape, and cover or smooth rough edges.

Props from Stories

6-18 months

Materials
Stuffed bears, caterpillars, and other items related to books

Provide items associated with the stories read during this Possibilities Plan. In addition to the stuffed bears, add other characters and items found in the stories such as caterpillars, a red wagon, pretend or real arrowroot cookies, large toy spiders, and even picnic supplies.

Teddy Bear Picnic Inside

12-18 months

Materials
Play picnic materials (see pge 276)
Stuffed bears

Provide picnic materials for children. A blanket spread on the floor and a basket with plates and pretend food will provide play cues to infants.

SENSORY/ART POSSIBILITIES

Rain Water

6-18 months

Materials
Watering can
Water

Use a watering can and tepid water to provide a sensory experience for young children. Observe the reaction as you sprinkle water onto baby's legs and arms. Cleanup will be easier if the activity is done outside. Infants can pat and explore the very interesting feel of water. Talk about rain as babies play. Recite "Eensy, Weensy Spider" during the activity. Begin this activity as an individual one and gradually add children as infants' experience with water play increases.

> *The Eensy, Weensy Spider*
> The eensy weensy spider
> Climbed up the water spout.
> Down came the rain
> And washed the spider out.
>
> Out came the sun
> And dried up all the rain,
> Then the eensy weensy spider
> Climbed up the spout again.

Corduroy Texture Board

0-18 months

Materials
Pieces of corduroy cloth
Poster board
Non-toxic glue

Teacher Talk

Talk with infants about the feel of the cloth. "The corduroy is soft. You are touching the yellow corduroy."

Thoroughly glue squares of corduroy cloth onto poster board. Encourage infants to feel the texture of the cloth.

Painting/Coloring the Bear Cave

12-18 months

Materials
Cardboard box (see Bear Cave, page 262)
Brown paint and brushes, or brown crayons or markers
Camera and film

Let one or two children at a time paint or color the box that will be used as a bear cave. Use washable, nontoxic brown paint or crayons that can be cleaned up easily, or plan the whole activity for outside time. Follow the children's lead. They will let you know when they are ready to end the activity and move on. Take photographs and write comments on the Communication Sheet (pages 429-430) about how children react to the activity. Post photographs where parents can see what children are doing during the day.

Foot Painting

6-18 months

Materials
Paper
Tape
Paint
Marker

Teacher Talk

Narrate children's actions. "You painted with your feet on the wall. I see your toes wiggle."

Tape paper to the wall, so children can paint with their feet. Very young children may be in a bouncy chair. Older children can lie on their backs. Label the section of the paper where each child paints. Repeat this activity with different babies, different paint colors, and additional opportunities to practice painting with feet.

Porridge Play

6-18 months

Materials
Porridge

On one of the days that you read "Little Miss Muffett," plan time for children to experience the feel of porridge. Place a small amount in one hand. Observe the child's reaction. If the child is interested, add porridge to the other hand or put some on the chair tray or tabletop.

Little Miss Muffett
Little Miss Muffett
Sat on a tuffet,
Eating her curds and whey;
Along came a spider,
And sat down beside her,
And frightened Miss Muffett away.

CURIOSITY POSSIBILITIES

Bear Puppets

0-18 months

Materials
Bear puppets or stuffed bear
Glove or mitten
Scissors
Needle and thread

Use purchased bear puppets as you ⌐
classic stories, or create bear puppet⌐
stuffed bears by ripping the seam al⌐
bottom of the toy. Insert a glove or m⌐
the ripped seam in the toy and sew i⌐
securely to the opening of the glove. ⌐
may be necessary to remove some of ⌐
stuffing. **Safety note:** On a regular ⌐
basis, inspect both bought and create⌐
toys for safety.

? _____ # Very Hungry Caterpillar Puppet
6-12 months

Materials
Caterpillar puppet
The Very Hungry Caterpillar by Eric Carle

Teacher Talk
"You are petting the puppet, Lakeshia. Look at the pretty colors."

Use a caterpillar puppet as you read the book. Put the puppet out in the classroom. When babies pick it up to play with, go over to them with the book, and read it. Or, point to the caterpillar puppet and then to the one in the book. Watch whether the baby looks in the book for more caterpillars. Some commercial puppets can change from a caterpillar to a butterfly.

? _____ # One-piece Puzzles
12-18 months

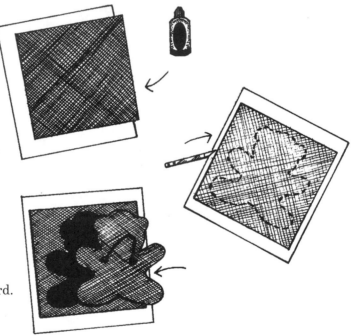

Materials
Solid-color paper
Cardboard
Glue
Scissors

Teacher Talk
Talk with infants about what they are doing. "The smaller piece fits into the bigger one. That's the way to move it around until it fits."

Create one-piece puzzles for infants. Glue a solid color paper onto a piece of cardboard. Cut a simple shape of a bear from the center of the cardboard. (This is very easy to do using an art knife, but not in the classroom, of course.) Be certain that the inside piece fits easily into the outside piece. Observe the play with the puzzle. The simple puzzle may be a new skill for some children, so observe for what Gonzalez-Mena & Eyer (1989) call "optimal stress." Optimal stress is very much like Vygotsky's "zone of proximal development (ZPD)" (Berk, 1994)—that point at which a given activity is neither too hard nor too easy. Observe children with puzzles to prevent frustration or add more complex puzzles if the babies figure out the very simple ones.

Accordion Books

0-18 months

Materials
Cardboard
Catalog or magazine pictures
Glue
Markers
Clear contact paper

These books are great for babies who are lifting their heads, turning heads from side to side, or pushing up on their hands and forearms. They are also good for children who are beginning to perfect their page-turning skills. Use cardboard in a long strip. Fold the paper back and forth like an accordion. Add simple catalog or magazine pictures to each section of the book. Label each picture. Cover with clear contact paper to make the book last longer. Talk about the pictures in the book as the infant looks at it. Place the book to the baby's right, left, or straight ahead to encourage gazing. Note which picture or photo keeps the baby's attention. Communicate your observations to parents on the Communication Sheet (pages 429-430).

Junk Mail Page Turning

6-18 months

Materials
Junk mail

Use appropriate junk mail, so children can practice turning pages (without tearing classroom books).

Cereal Box Books

0-18 months

Materials
Infant cereal boxes   Scissors
Hole punch   Yarn or metal rings

Teacher Talk
"Rice cereal is good."

Cut out the front panels of infant cereal boxes to make books for infants. Punch holes in the sides of the panels and use short lengths of yarn or metal rings to join them together. Stand books in front of infants where they eat cereal each day. With older infants, use popular children's cereal boxes.

Logo Books
12-18 months

Materials
Toy-store and fast-food logos
Cardboard
Glue
Hole punch
Yarn or metal rings

Create books from familiar toy-store and fast-food logos. Glue the logos onto the fronts and backs of heavy pieces of cardboard. Talk about the familiar stores and restaurants as the book is opened and closed.

Book Buddies
12-18 months

Materials
Books
Older children

Children will enjoy having older children pretend to read to them. Create a system of book buddies, allowing only one older buddy at a time in the classroom.

My Very First Mother Goose Book
0-18 months

Materials
My Very First Mother Goose Book by Iona Archibald Opie

Use this book to talk about different classic rhymes. Pick one rhyme to read regularly. Repetition increases interest and infants will begin to anticipate the rhymes.

Growl Like a Bear
0-18 months

Materials
Bear Cave (see page 262)
Stuffed bears

During one-on-one time, take the baby over to the cave with the stuffed bears. Growl like a bear. Observe the baby's reaction. If baby responds, continue the game. Use the stuffed bears to make different kinds of growls.

Storybook Classics Books
0-18 months

Materials
Books such as
> *Clifford the Big Red Dog* by Norman Bridwell
> *Little Engine That Could, The* by Watty Piper
> *On the Day You Were Born* by Debra Fraser
> *Pat the Bunny* by Dorothy Kunhardt
> *Runaway Bunny* by Margaret Wise Brown

Read these books to one infant or a group of two or three infants at appropriate times. Add to Books Read list (see Appendix page 431).

MUSIC POSSIBILITIES

Greg and Steve Record
0-18 months

Materials
"Brown Bear" song from *Playing Favorite* (Youngheart Records) by Greg and Steve

Play the "Brown Bear" song in conjunction with the corresponding *Brown Bear* activities. Watch for children responding to the sounds of the music. Repeat it often and share the words with parents. They will want to use it at home or during drive time.

Favorite Songs
0-18 months

Materials
Words to songs (see next page)

Use the following classics during this Possibilities Plan. Share them with parents. Children will enjoy the rhythm and action of the songs: "Eensy Weensy Spider," "Bumping Up and Down in My Little Red Wagon," and "Ring Around the Rosie." The children will be entertained as the teacher actually does the actions.

The Eensy Weensy Spider
The eensy weensy spider
Climbed up the water spout.
Down came the rain
And washed the spider out.

Out came the sun
And dried up all the rain,
And the eensy weensy spider
Climbed up the spout again.

Bumping Up and Down in My Little Red Wagon
Bumping up and down in my little red wagon,
Bumping up and down in my little red wagon,
Bumping up and down in my little red wagon,
Won't you be my darlin'?

Ring Around the Rosie
Ring around the rosie,
A pocket full of posies.
Ashes, ashes,
We all fall down!

MOVEMENT POSSIBILITIES

"Pat-a-Cake" Clapping

0-18 months

Materials
None needed

Practice pat-a-cake with infants. Observe the baby's response as the actions become familiar. Share the baby's reaction with parents using the Communication Sheet (pages 429-430).

Pat-a-Cake
Pat-a-cake, pat-a-cake, baker's man,
Bake me cake as fast as you can.
Pat and roll and mark it with "B."
Put it in the oven for baby and me.

 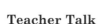

Follow the Bear Tracks
12-18 months

Materials
Paper
Scissors
Tape or clear contact paper

Teacher Talk
"You are following the bear tracks. Out the door you go, Kimbo. We'll play in the grass."

Attach bear prints to the floor in the classroom leading outside. Also, attach bear prints outside leading to the door. Point to the bear tracks and encourage babies to follow them.

Red Wagon Rides
12-18 months

Materials
Wagon

Give children who are able to sit unattended rides in the wagon. Sing, "Bumping Up and Down in My Little Red Wagon." Give the bears and children rides inside and outside, too.

> *Bumping Up and Down in My Little Red Wagon*
> Bumping up and down in my little red wagon,
> Bumping up and down in my little red wagon,
> Bumping up and down in my little red wagon,
> Won't you be my darlin'?

Bears and Boxes
12-18 months

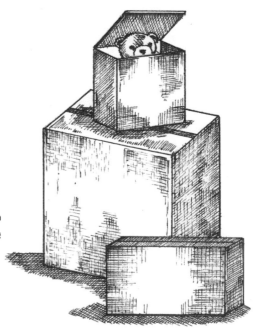

Materials
Large boxes
Stuffed bears

Teacher Talk
"Where are the bears? You found them."

Hide bears in large boxes. Encourage children to find the bears. You may need to show the infants where the bears are and then put them back in the boxes.

Play Gym

0-6 months

Materials
Play gym
Mat or quilt

Bring a play gym outside. Moving activities to the outside adds novelty. Put the play gym on a mat or quilt in the shade. Encourage the baby to reach for items on the play gym.

Storybooks Outside

0-18 months

Materials
Books
Blanket

Spread a blanket on the grass. Bring storybooks outside and enjoy them with the children. Follow the interests of the babies.

Teddy Bear Stroller Ride

0-18 months

Materials
Stroller
Stuffed bears

Teacher Talk
Talk about the things you see. "The birds are in the branches. See them fly away."

Take babies and bears outside for rides in the strollers.

PROJECT POSSIBILITIES

Sound Acquisition Chart

0-18 months

Materials
Paper
Marker

Create a sound acquisition chart for each infant in the classroom.
(Use the chart on page 230 of this chapter or make up your own
chart.) As each child masters a new sound, circle the sound, and date
it. Parents will delight in the progress their child makes. For older
infants, write their new words on a vocabulary list and date them.
Add the lists or charts to the children's portfolios.

Brown Bear Painting Book

6-18 months

Materials
Paints in the colors used in *Brown Bear, Brown Bear* by Bill Martin, Jr.
Brushes
Paper
Hole punch
Yarn or metal rings

Use the sequence of colors used in the book *Brown Bear, Brown Bear*
for art activities. Write the color words on the bottom of each page
after children paint with each particular color. Create a title page
and join the book together using short lengths of yarn or metal rings.
Read the book with children. Also, read the book when parents join
babies for a teddy bear picnic.

PARENT PARTICIPATION POSIBILITIES

Supporting Possibilities

Ask parents to loan teddy bears and to collect large and medium
boxes, picnic items, a blanket or checkered tablecloth, and corduroy
cloth scraps. Let parents know how the items will be used.

Guest Readers

Invite parents to come into the classroom and read to children. They may bring a favorite book or use one of the favorites in the classroom.

Parent Book Recordings

When parents come into the classroom to read, make a recording. If parents are unable to read in the classroom, provide a portable tape recorder, so they can audiotape reading a book at home for you to use in the classroom.

Teddy Bear Picnic with Parents

Invite parents to a picnic with their children. Serve very simple sandwiches for parents and include all the bears collected for this Possibilities Plan.

Parent Postcard

The Parent Postcard in this section is designed to share with parents during the Possibilities Plan. The topic is a natural extension of the activities and experiences that you are planning and implementing for the infants in the classroom. Use the Postcard to connect parents to their children's learning.

TO

Tips for Reading to Your Infant

- In the beginning, don't read. Point! Name objects while you point to pictures on the page. Reading pictures is an important pre-reading skill that your child will perfect first. Later, your child will realize that the meaning is in the words and the pictures illustrate the meaning.

- Put life into your reading. Vary your voice tone. Give voices to different pictures and characters. Have fun!

- Start with easy-to-read, bright, and simple picture books. In most cases, you needn't bother with the text until your child can sit through looking at the pictures of the whole book. Then, abbreviate the text, keep it simple, and move quickly to keep your child's interest.

- Move your finger across the page to show that reading is taking place. This helps your child learn left-to-right progression—a key pre-reading skill.

- Point out familiar things first. Eyes, animals, mother, daddy, baby, car, and other things that are familiar will keep your child's attention. Then, gradually add unfamiliar pictures and words as you read the book again.

- Don't stay on one page too long. Four seconds is about long enough for very young children. Initially, limit your reading to one page at a time. But over time, start to connect one page with the next so your child will see the relationship between characters or objects on subsequent pages.

- Start with books that can be used for different purposes. For example, if a book tells a story about animals, use the book to explore the different sounds animals make as well as to tell the story.

When you don't feel like reading to your child, remember that many requests for story time are really requests for holding, cuddling, and getting reconnected emotionally. In this situation, pick a very familiar book and let your child read to you. Your child will get the holding he or she needs, and you will marvel at how rapidly your child's emergent reading skills are growing.

How much time is enough? This question plagues many working parents who wonder if the time they spend with their child is enough. Start by spending 10 or 15 minutes a day reading and looking at books with your baby. Then, as he or she grows, add 5 minutes every 6 months until you are reading to your child at least 30 minutes a day. But don't worry about the time. If you can't find 30 minutes, grab 5 minutes here and 10 minutes there to add up to a half-hour a day.

Don't forget nursery rhymes and fingerplays as reading activities. Use these childhood traditions as springboards to create your own rhyme memories with your child.

Concepts Learned

Concepts Learned in Storybook Classics

I can listen to my teacher read stories.

I can listen to Mom/Dad read stories.

Stories can be about different things.

I can bounce to the words in songs and rhymes.

Teddy bears are good to hug.

I can ride in a wagon.

I can hold a book.

I can look at words and pictures in a book.

Things change when I go outside.

My body fits inside things.

I can paint.

I can ride in a wagon.

I can sing.

I can do fingerplays.

I can climb in a bear cave.

I can make puzzles.

I can make sounds.

I can turn pages.

I can "read" pages.

I can turn pages in a book.

I can paint with my feet.

I can identify my cereal box.

I can hide.

I can follow bear tracks.

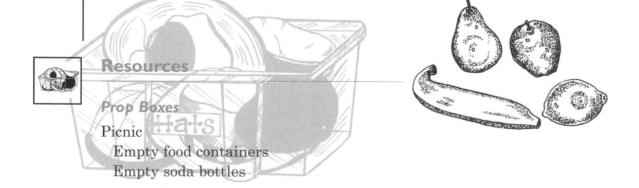

Resources

Prop Boxes

Picnic
　　Empty food containers
　　Empty soda bottles

Empty water bottles
Paper sandwiches (sealed in bag)
Picnic basket   Stuffed bears
Plastic fruit   Toy binoculars

Storybooks
Puppets relating to stories   Toys relating to stories (caterpillar
  (caterpillar, spider, turtles,   spider, turtles, bears)
  bears)   Variety of bought storybooks
Sheet/blanket/quilt   Variety of teacher-made storybooks
Storybooks

Picture File/Vocabulary

Bear   Flowers
Butterfly   Picnic
Caterpillar   Spider
Cave   Turtle

Books

Brown Bear, Brown Bear by Bill Martin, Jr.
Clifford the Big Red Dog by Norman Bridwell
Corduroy by Don Freeman
If You Give a Mouse a Cookie by Laura J. Numeroff
Little Engine That Could, The by Watty Piper
My Very First Mother Goose Book by Iona Archibald Opie
On the Day You Were Born by Debra Fraser
Pat the Bunny by Dorothy Kunhardt
Runaway Bunny by Margaret Wise Brown
Very Busy Spider, The by Eric Carle
Very Hungry Caterpillar, The by Eric Carle

Rhymes/Fingerplays

"Little Miss Muffett" (page 265)
"Pat-a-Cake" (page 270)

Music/Songs

"Brown Bear" song by Steve and Greg (page 269)
"Bumping Up and Down in My Little Red Wagon" (page 271)
"Eensy Weensy Spider" (pages 263 and 270)
"Ring Around the Rosie" (page 270)

Toys and Materials

The following purchased items are important for this Possibilities Plan:

Activity gym
> Blank tapes
> > Caterpillar/butterfly puppet
> > Large butcher paper
> > Poster board
> > Storybooks
> > Stuffed bears
> Tape recorder
> Toy turtles

Yarn or metal rings

The following gathered items will help support this Possibilities Plan:

Blanket or tablecloth

Cereal boxes

Fast food and toy store logos

Junk mail booklets

Large box for cave
> Medium boxes for hiding bears
> > Prop box items

Sounds

WEB

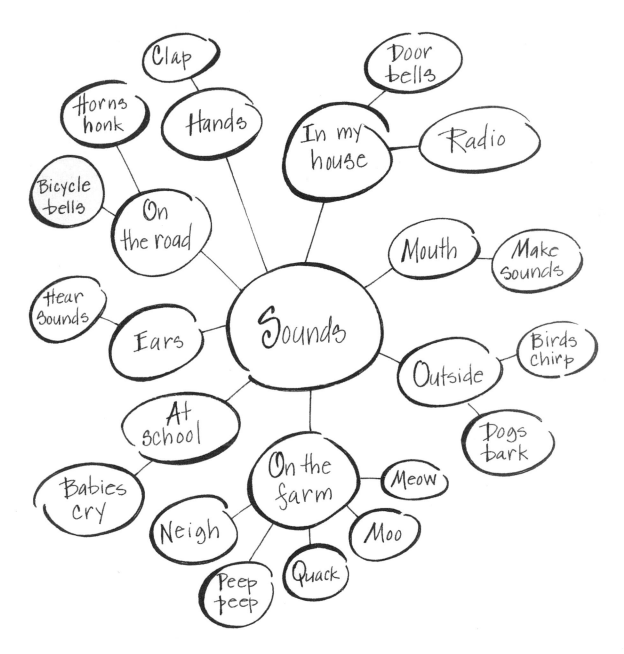

Note: Using the technique of webbing, teachers can follow the leads that children give them, as well as have an unlimited source of options. Always use the webs as a jumping-off point. The possibilities are endless!

Plan Possibilities

Dramatic

Toy Phone 282
Animals 282
Sounds Tape 282
Sounds All
   Around 282
Teacher-Made
   Sound Objects . .283

Sensory/Art

Ringing Bouncy
   Chair 283
Bell Necklace 284
Bubble Wrap 284

Curiosity

Bell from Ceiling . .284
Jack-in-the-Box . . .285
Pop-up Pals 285
Hidden Alarm
   Clock 285

Literacy

Sound Books 286
Thundercake Book 286
Clap Your Hands Book 286
I Hear 286
Moo, Baa, La la la 287
Sounds Books 287

Music

Wrist Rattles 287
Instrument Music 288
Contrast Music 288
Old MacDonald
   Had a Farm 288
Open, Shut Them 289
Thomas Moore Music 289
Where Is Thumbkin? 289

Movement

Musical Pat Mats 290
Chime Ball 290
If You're Happy and
   You Know It 291
Popcorn Poppers 291
Rhythm Instruments
   for Infants 291

Outdoor

Wind Chimes 292
Water Play with Sounds 292
Row, Row, Row Your Boat 292
Outside Sounds 292

Project

Music Art 293

Parent Participation

Parent Tape 293
Supporting Possibilities 293
Movie Day 294
Parent Postcards
   Watch Those Ears! 294
   Sound Opportunities 295

Sounds

Concepts Learned in Sounds 296

Prop Boxes

    Sounds 296

Picture File/Vocabulary 296

Books

Animal Sounds by Aurelina Battaglia
Clap Your Hands by Lorinda B. Cauley 286
Cow That Went Oink, The by Bernard Most
Polar Bear, Polar Bear, What Do You Hear? by Bill Martin, Jr.
Doorbell Book, The by Jan Pienkowski 286
I Hear by Helen Oxenbury 286
Moo, Baa, La la la by Sandra Boynton 287
Peek a Moo by Bernard Most 287
Thundercake by Patricia Polacco 286
Who Says "Quack"? by Jerry Smith

Rhymes/Fingerplays

    "Open, Shut Them" 289

Music/Songs

    "If You're Happy and You Know It" 291
    "Old MacDonald Had a Farm" 288
    "Row, Row, Row Your Boat" 292
    "Where Is Thumbkin?" 289

Toys and Materials 298

Note

Videotape record, photo record, or make an anecdotal record of the Sounds Possibilities Plan. Parents will enjoy seeing children involved in all the various activities and experiences. Either make duplicates or plan an event when parents can view the videotape, photographs, or anecdotal records at the same time.

Toy Phone
0-18 months

Materials
Toy phone(s), without cords

Teacher Talk
"Ring, ring! I hear the telephone. Now where is that phone?"

Pick up the phone and talk. Then give the phone to a child.

Animals
0-18 months

Materials
Toy farm animals

Teacher Talk
"Bark, bark. The dog is barking."

Include toy animals that could be on Old MacDonald's Farm. Make the animal sounds as you introduce the toys.

Sounds Tape
0-18 months

Materials
Tapes
Tape player

Create different atmospheres for dramatic play by playing environmental sounds on the tape player. Make the props in the area match the sounds you are playing. Add stuffed animals when you play nature sounds and add vehicles when you play traffic sounds.

Sounds All Around
6-18 months

Materials
Bells, rattles, squeak toys
Purses, bags, pockets

Teacher Talk

"You put the key rattles in your purse. Are you ready to go?"

Add sound items (such as bells, rattles, and squeak toys) that infants can hide, find, and/or explore in purses, bags, and pockets.

Teacher-made Sound Objects
6-18 months

Materials
Boxes, plastic bottles
Items that rattle, ring, or squeak
Glue and tape

Teacher Talk
Talk about the sounds that children are making. "Hear the rattle of the bottle? You are making the sound when you move the bottle."

Many opportunities exist for sound exploration during play. Collect boxes from food items and plastic bottles. Place items inside the boxes and bottles that will rattle, ring, or squeak. Glue and tape the tops securely.

SENSORY/ART POSSIBILITIES

Ringing Bouncy Chair
0-6 months

Materials
Bouncy chairs
Bells
Tape or string

Attach large bells to the bouncy chairs in the classroom. Observe the baby's reactions to the sounds the bells make as the baby bounces. Record your observations on a Communication Sheet (pages 429-430).

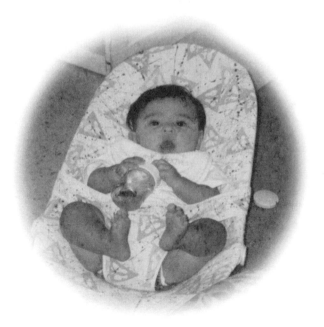

Bell Necklace

0-18 months

Materials
Bell necklace

Teacher Talk
"Winston is looking at me. He hears the sound of the bell."

Wear a bell necklace. Observe how babies will orient themselves toward the sound of the bell. Check to see that all babies respond to the sound after being introduced to the bell. If not, share your observations with parents, and encourage them to have the baby's hearing checked.

Bubble Wrap

6-18 months

Materials
Bubble wrap
Tape

Teacher Talk
Talk about the feel and the sound of the bubbles as the baby kicks. "Listen, Ashley. Did you hear the sound of the bubbles popping?"

Tape bubble wrap to a low area on the wall. Position a baby in a bouncy seat such that the child's feet can kick the bubble wrap. For mobile infants, tape the bubble wrap to the floor or table. Encourage children to pop the bubbles. See what happens as the babies step on the bubble wrap. **Safety alert:** Check regularly to make certain the bubble wrap is not loose or slippery.

CURIOSITY POSSIBILITIES

Bell from Ceiling

0-12 months

Materials
Bell
Bungee cord

Attach a bell from the ceiling using a bungee cord. During regular classroom routines ring the bell. Let children ring the bell as you hold them.

Jack-in-the-Box

6-18 months

Materials
Jack-in-the-box

Teacher Talk
Use children's names as you interact with them. "Let's put the doll back in the box, Suzette. OK, let's get ready for the pop!"

Use a jack-in-the-box to talk about sounds with infants. Notice each child's cues to determine whether or not to continue play. Some children may find the surprise frightening. Other infants will anticipate the surprise with glee.

Pop-up Pals

6-18 months

Materials
Pop-up toy

Teacher Talk
Narrate children's actions. "Billie Jo, you made the ball click. Again? You can do it again."

Provide a pop-up toy for baby. The cause-and-effect relationship between moving something and having the figure pop up will fascinate and intrigue infants. Let babies know what is about to happen before it does.

Hidden Alarm Clock

6-18 months

Materials
Alarm clock
Videotape, optional

Teacher Talk
"I hear an alarm clock. Let's find it. Bo, will you help me find the sound?"

Hide an alarm clock that is set to ring in about 10 minutes. When the alarm rings, observe the reactions of the children to the sound. Invite children to find the clock. Videotape children as you repeat the activity again.

Sound Books

0-18 months

Materials
Sounds books, such as
The Doorbell Book by Jan Pienkowski

Teacher Talk
"Ding dong. Hear the doorbell, Amy? You are touching the doorbell."

Use sound books (where the child touches something on a page and the book makes a sound). A good example is *The Doorbell Book*. Add all the books you read to your Books Read list (see page 431).

Thundercake Book

0-18 months

Materials
Thundercake by Patricia Polacco

Read this book to children. Add it to the Books Read list (see page 431) posted in the classroom. Point out the Books Read list to parents when they come into your classroom.

Clap Your Hands Book

0-18 months

Materials
Clap Your Hands by Lorinda Bryan Cawley

Teacher Talk
"You can clap you hands, Keesha. Let's clap hands together."

Read this book to children. Encourage them to clap their hands as you are reading.

I Hear

0-18 months

Materials
I Hear by Helen Oxenbury

Read this book to children. Talk about the different sounds and make sounds. Add the book to the Books Read list (see page 431) in the classroom.

Moo, Baa, La la la

0-18 months

Materials
Moo, Baa, La la la by
Sandra Boynton or *Peek a
Moo* by Bernard Most

Teacher Talk
"Moo, moo. The cow goes moo."

Read either of these delightful books.
Encourage children to make the animal
sounds.

Sounds Books

0-18 months

Materials
Books such as
   Animal Sounds by Aurelina Battaglia
   Cow That Went Oink, The by Bernard Most
   Polar Bear, Polar Bear, What Do You Hear? by Bill Martin, Jr.
   Who Says "Quack"? by Jerry Smith

Read any of the above books to one baby or two or three babies at
appropriate times. Add to the Books Read list (see Appendix page
431).

MUSIC POSSIBILITIES

Wrist Rattles

0-6 months

Materials
Wrist rattles

Use wrist rattles to provide sound
experiences for young babies. Show baby
that her wrist rattle will sound when she
moves. Observe to see if baby moves on
her own to make the noise.

 ___ # Instrument Music

6-18 months

Materials
Recorded music
Tape or CD player

Teacher Talk
Talk about the different instrument sounds. "Boom! Boom! Boom! I hear the sound of the drum."

Play music that has different instruments playing at different times. Label the instruments as they play.

 ___ # Contrast Music

0-18 months

Materials
Recorded music
Tape or CD player

As you play a wide variety of music, talk about contrasting characteristics: loud and soft, high and low, fast and slow.

 ___ # Old MacDonald Had a Farm

6-18 months

Materials
Farm animals

Sing this song as you introduce different animal toys in the classroom: puppets, stuffed animals, and plastic animals.

> *Old MacDonald Had a Farm*
> Old MacDonald had a farm,
> E-I-E-I-O.
> And on his farm he had some cows,
> E-I-E-I-O.
> With a moo-moo here and a moo-moo there,
> Here a moo, there a moo, everywhere a moo-moo.
> Old MacDonald had a farm,
> E-I-E-I-O.

Continue with other animals:
> Sheep...baa-baa....
> Pigs...oink-oink....
> Ducks...quack-quack....
> Chickens...chick-chick....

Open, Shut Them

0-18 months

Materials
None needed

Sing this song often during the day. Emphasize the claps. Show children how you can show your thumb and hide your thumb as you open and close your hands.

> *Open, Shut Them*
> Open, shut them, open, shut them,
> Give a little clap.
> Open, shut them, open, shut them,
> Put them in your lap.
>
> Creep them, creep them, creep them, creep them,
> Right up to your chin.
> Open wide your smiling mouth,
> But do not let them in.
>
> Creep them, creep them, creep them, creep them,
> Past your cheeks and chin.
> Open wide your smiling eyes,
> Peeking in-BOO.

Thomas Moore Music

0-18 months

Materials
Thomas Moore tapes or CDs

Use selections of music from Thomas Moore. Talk about how he sings in a low voice.

Where Is Thumbkin?

0-18 months

Materials
None needed

Use this rhyme as children play inside and outside. Children will enjoy the rhythm and repetition. Notice their reactions to "fly away." Share the tune and the movements with parents.

> *Where Is Thumbkin?*
> Where is thumbkin?
> Where is thumbkin?

Here I am; here I am.
How are you today, sir?
Very well, I thank you.
Fly away; fly away.

Where is pointer?
Where is pointer?
Here I am; here I am.
How are you today, sir?
Very well, I thank you.
Fly away; fly away.

Continue with other fingers:
Where is tall one?
Where is ring finger?
Where is pinky?

MOVEMENT POSSIBILITIES

Musical Pat Mats
0-12 months

Materials
Pat mats

Provide musical pat mats for infants. Musical pat mats are available commercially from school supply companies and some toy stores. When different areas are touched on a pat mat, different sounds are produced. Place babies near the mat on their tummies, or close to the musical pat mat, so they may roll over and make the mat play. Observe reactions to making the music start over and over again.

Chime Ball
0-12 months

Materials
Chime ball

Teacher Talk
Talk about the sounds the ball makes. "Lee is rolling the ball. Listen to the sound the ball makes."

Roll the ball on the floor near an infant. Watch how the infant notices the ball and the sound it makes.

 # If You're Happy and You Know It
0-18 months

Materials
None needed

Sing this song and do the actions with children. Clap your hands; stomp your feet; wiggle your fingers.

> *If You're Happy and You Know It*
> If you're happy and you know it,
> Clap your hands. (clap, clap)
> If you're happy and you know it,
> Clap your hands. (clap, clap)
> If you're happy and you know it,
> Then your face will surely show it.
> If you're happy and you know it,
> Clap your hands. (clap, clap)

Continue with other movements:
> Stomp feet
> Wiggle your fingers

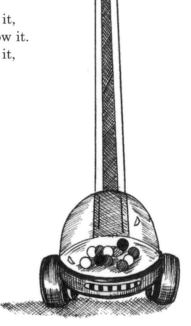

 # Popcorn Poppers
12-18 months

Materials
Popcorn poppers

Provide popcorn poppers (push toys with balls that pop up) for older children to push while sitting and standing.

 # Rhythm Instruments for Infants
12-18 months

Materials
Rhythm instruments

Teacher Talk
"Sally, you are shaking the bells. Ring, ring."

Encourage children to move by using appropriate instruments for infants. Hands, feet, bells, shakers, hand drums, and rattles will make a nice rhythm band.

Wind Chimes

0-18 months

Materials
Wind chimes

Teacher Talk
"You are pointing at the wind chimes, Eric. The wind is making them move and make a beautiful sound."

Hang wind chimes outside, so children can hear the sounds of the chimes as they play.

Water Play with Sounds

6-18 months

Materials
Small plastic tubs
Water toys
Tape player
Tape of water or ocean sounds

Provide a water play experience by using small plastic tubs. Take the tape player outside and play rain or ocean sounds as children play.

Row, Row, Row Your Boat

6-18 months

Materials
Boxes

Sing this song as children play. Provide boxes for children sit in.

> *Row, Row, Row Your Boat*
> Row, row, row your boat
> Gently down the stream.
> Merrily, merrily, merrily, merrily,
> Life is but a dream.

Outside Sounds

0-18 months

Materials
Quilt or blanket

Teacher Talk

"The bird is singing in the tree. Sally, you are looking at the bird."

Lie on a quilt or blanket with the children. Encourage everyone to listen for the outside sounds.

PROJECT POSSIBILITIES

Music Art

6-18 months

Materials
White butcher paper
Crayons or markers
Recorded music
Tape or CD player

Completely cover a table with white butcher paper or tape a very large piece of paper on the floor. Play different types of music on different days (jazz, blues, opera, and ballads). Use a different color for each different type of music. Label the paper with children's names, dates, and type of music played. Play similar music as parents arrive or depart and direct parents' attention to the emerging project. Hang the art, so parents can enjoy it.

PARENT PARTICIPATION POSSIBILITIES

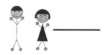

Parent Tape

Record parents' voices on a tape to play during the day.

Supporting Possibilities

Ask parents to collect empty food containers, plastic soda and water bottles, and boxes. Let parents know how the items will be used.

Movie Day

Invite parents to come and see the videotape, photos, documentation, or notes you have made of children during the Sound Possibilities Plan. Serve refreshments.

Parent Postcards

Parent Postcards in this section are designed to share with parents during the Possibilities Plan. The topics are natural extensions of the activities and experiences that you are planning and implementing for the infants in the classroom. Use the Postcards to connect parents to their children's learning.

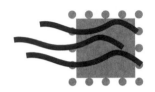

Watch Those Ears!

Parents of very young children have so many concerns: school, emotional development, health, time, work. Then baby starts having ear problems, and the concerns double.

The following signs may indicate that a child has an ear infection.

 Baby may get fussy and pull on ears.

 Baby may cry, especially at mealtime (sore throat) or at bedtime (drainage).

 Hearing may be lessened (baby doesn't turn head when you speak).

Fevers over 100 degrees Fahrenheit may occur (particularly in the afternoon).

What can be done? Often, your pediatrician will prescribe an antibiotic to combat the infection. Your child's medical history and the severity of the infection will determine the medicine prescribed. Follow directions precisely because dosage and duration will vary. Complete the full dosage. Failure to do this is the major cause of recurrence—the infection never really leaves. Many doctors are slower to prescribe antibiotics than they once were, citing the case of antibiotic-resistant infections. In any case, some untreated ear infections can be dangerous, so parents need to take them seriously.

Many children have chronic problems with ear infections. These can be caused by allergies, the formation of the inner ear, or a particular susceptibility to infections. The final result may be ear tubes, but this is a decision you will need to make with your child's doctor.

Because ear infections can affect a child's hearing in both the short and long term, they may result in a delay in language development or even some speech difficulties. So watch those ears!

TO _____

_____

_____

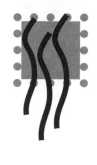

TO

Sound Opportunities

Before birth, babies are able to hear and make sounds. After birth, sound-making abilities continue to expand. Create an environment for your baby that encourages sound explorations. Try some of the following sound opportunities with your child.

Parent-made Rattles—Create rattles by placing objects that will ring or rattle in boxes or plastic bottles. Secure the top with glue and tape.

Sound Invitations—Invite baby to make sounds with his or her body. Depending on age, your baby may be able to clap hands, click tongue, or stomp feet. Demonstrate the activity first and then watch your baby to see if he or she is interested. Often this will turn into an exchange. You clap–baby claps. You stomp–baby stomps.

Sing and Dance—Sing to your child (talent isn't required) and dance with him or her. He or she will enjoy the sounds as well as the movement.

Musical House—Play appropriate music periodically for baby. Classical music is wonderful. The majority of children's music is great for older infants.

Paper Crumples—Sound activities are often action-reaction in nature. Give your baby a piece of paper to crumple and observe the reaction. Supervise closely, so baby won't eat the paper.

Sounds invite young children to explore their world. Enjoy being a part of that exploration.

Concepts Learned in Sounds

Concepts Learned

Many things make sounds.

Some sounds are loud.

Some sounds are soft.

Some sounds are high.

Some sounds are low.

Some sounds are fast.

Some sounds are slow.

I can make sounds with my body.

I can clap my hands.

I can listen to music.

I can find things that are hidden.

Animals make sounds.

I can move to music.

Toys can make sounds.

Resources

Prop Boxes

Sounds
 Bells
  Bicycle bell
  Doorbell
  Rain stick
  School bell
  Sound books
  Sound toys (squeak toy, rattle)

Picture File/Vocabulary

Bells

Cars

Cats

Chickens

Cows

Dogs

Ducks
Goats
Horses
Musical instruments
Ocean
People clapping
People dancing
Rain
Rattles
River
Sheep
Trucks

Books

Animal Sounds by Aurelina Battaglia
Clap Your Hands by Lorinda B. Cauley
Cow That Went Oink, The by Bernard Most
Doorbell Book, The by Jan Pienkowski
I Hear by Helen Oxenbury
Moo, Baa, La la la by Sandra Boynton
Peek a Moo by Bernard Most
Polar Bear, Polar Bear, What Do You Hear? by Bill Martin, Jr.
Thundercake by Patricia Polacco
Who Says "Quack"? by Jerry Smith

Rhymes/Fingerplays

"Open, Shut Them" (page 289)

Music/Songs

"If You're Happy and You Know It" (page 291)
"Old MacDonald Had a Farm" (page 288)
"Row, Row, Row Your Boat" (page 292)
"Where Is Thumbkin?" (page 289)

Toys and Materials

The following purchased items are important for this Possibilities Plan:

Animal puppets
Animal toys
Bell necklace
Chime ball
Jack-in-the-box
Music tapes (classical, jazz)
Popcorn poppers
Pop-up pals
Prop box items
Rattles of various types
Sound books
Sound toys (rattle, squeak, crunch)
Stuffed animals
Tapes of nature/weather sounds
Wind chimes
Wrist rattles

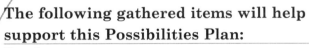

The following gathered items will help support this Possibilities Plan:

Butcher paper
Drums made from oatmeal boxes
Food containers (filled with rattle materials
   and glued shut)
Medium cardboard boxes
Prop box items
Soda bottles (filled with rattle
   materials and glued shut)
Water bottles (filled with rattle
   materials and glued shut)

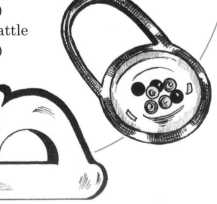

CHAPTER 6

Moving Around

INTRODUCTION

As babies grow, they are able to exert more and more control over their environments. Initially, they have very little influence and spend energy learning to control and experience moving with their bodies. Discovering toes and fingers, making sounds, wiggling, tracking an object visually are all wonderful experiences of discovery.

As babies master fine motor skills, they are able to pick up objects and even turn the pages of a book. As babies master gross motor skills, they are able to roll, crawl, and then finally walk.

Alternately, motor skills development causes frustration and excitement, challenges and successes, tears and joy. These exciting physical changes lead babies to explore the physical world and begin to understand, appreciate, and explore its many wonders.

INNOVATIONS IN OBSERVATION/ASSESSMENT

Observation/Assessment Instrument

This assessment instrument is not just a skills checklist. Instead it is designed to guide the teacher's observation of children's development through major interactional tasks of infancy. The assessment's focus is on what IS happening, not just what should happen or what will happen. Use this assessment to lead to developmentally appropriate practice.

Moving Around Home and School

	M1	M2
0-6 months	a. Holds head away from shoulder. b. Holds head steady side to side. c. Holds head up when lying on stomach. d. Rolls from back to front. e. Rolls from front to back.	a. Eyes and head follow motion. b. Holds rattle. c. Exchanges objects between hands. d. Uses pincer grasp to pick up small items.
6-12 months	f. Scoots on stomach. g. Sits with support. h. Sits without support. i. Crawls after ball or toy. j. Pulls to a stand.	e. Picks up toys and objects. f. Dumps objects out of containers. g. Puts objects back into containers. h. Scribbles.
12-18 months	k. Lowers back down to squatting position. l. Walks with support. m. Walks without support. n. Squats down and stands back up. o. Climbs into a chair. p. Kicks ball.	j. Turns pages in cardboard book. k. Unbuttons large buttons. l. Completes puzzles with 2-3 pieces.

INNOVATIONS IN CHILD DEVELOPMENT

Physical Development

During the first year and a half of life, the child's body changes dramatically. Seemingly helpless newborns grow into physically competent 18-month-olds. As with all development, physical development follows predictable developmental patterns even though individual progress may be highly variable.

For physical development in general, and motor development specifically, the sequence of development is from the head to the foot and from the center to the periphery of the body (this is called the cephalocaudal/proximodistal trend). During infancy, children develop their bodies from the top down and from the center out. For example, most children can swipe at objects by the age of 5-6 months, pick up objects between the thumb and forefinger by about 11-12 months, and hold a spoon by about 16 months, illustrating the proximodistal trend. Similarly, children roll over by about 5-6 months, sit without support by about 7-8 months, pull to a stand by about 10-12 months, and walk by 12-16 months, illustrating the cephalocaudal trend.

Both of these trends are affected by each child's unique pace through the developmental sequence, the unevenness of development in general, and the opportunities available for experience, and practice of emerging skills. In other words, children continue to have an individual pace in acquiring skills, and experience and practice can support or hinder motor development. For example, children who do not have opportunities to be on the floor to develop their motor skills may seem to lag behind those who do.

The milestones of physical development are usually broken down into two major components—gross motor and fine motor. Gross motor development refers to the large muscles of the legs, arms, and torso, whereas fine motor refers to the smaller muscles of the body including the muscles in the hands, feet, and eyes. Physical development milestones for both gross and fine motor development from birth to age 18 months are listed below.

Physical Development Milestones

AGE	FINE MOTOR SKILLS	GROSS MOTOR SKILLS
BIRTH-6 MONTHS	• Holds rattle. • Eyes and head follow. • Grasp objects.	• Turns head from side to side. • Holds head and chest up when lying on stomach. • Swipes at objects. • Rolls from back to side.
6-12 MONTHS	• Feeds self dry cereal or crackters • Exchanges objects between hands. • Picks up toys and objects. • Points. • Puts objects in containers. • Drinks from a cup.	• Scoots on stomach. • Holds bottle. • Sits without support. • Crawls after ball or toy. • Pulls self to standing position. • Walks with support.
12-18 MONTHS	• Uses spoon. • Turns pages of cardboard books. • Stacks blocks. • Scribbles with crayon.	• Walks without support. • Squats down and stands back up. • Carries large objects around. • Kicks a ball.

Infant Nutrition

What Do Infants Really Need to Eat?

Pediatric advice about what infants should eat varies widely. The American Academy of Pediatrics recommends that babies be fed breast milk if at all possible. Breast milk is easier on the child's stomach and digestive system, provides optimal nutrition for growth and development, and provides some protections for young babies from illness.

Some mothers are unable to nurse. Others are uncomfortable with nursing and expressing milk. When this is the case, formula is substituted for breast milk.

The following is a recommended 24-hour food guide for infants. Use it along with the information gathered from parents as a resource to help determine the nutritional needs of the infants in your classroom.

	0-6 months	6-12 months	12-18 months
Breast Milk or Formula	16-32 oz. in 5-10 feedings from breast or bottle.	24-40 oz. in 3-5 feedings from breast, bottle or cup.	20-24 oz. from cup. May add whole milk.
Water	2-4 oz. in hot weather.	Offer between feedings.	Offer between feedings.
Cereals and Breads	1-3 tablespoons with breast milk or formula once a day.	1-4 tablespoons twice a day.	4 servings in three feedings.
Fruits and Vegetables	None.	½-1 cup of strained, pureed, or mashed vegetables (dark yellow, orange, or green), or fresh or cooked fruits in two to three feedings.	4 servings in three feedings.
Meats and Protein	None.	½ cup of yogurt.	2 servings in two or three feedings.

Adapted from Kendrick, Kaufman, and Messinger, 1988 and Wong, Hockenberry-Easton, Winkelstein, Wilson, & Ahmann, 1999

Breastfeeding Issues

When mothers choose breastfeeding for their infants, teachers need to understand basic health and safety precautions for breast milk. Mothers who are nursing can bring freshly expressed milk to school in labeled, dated storage containers. Freshly expressed milk may be stored up to 72 hours at 39 degrees Fahrenheit. Once it is warmed for the baby to drink, it can be stored at room temperature for six hours. Do not return warmed milk to the refrigerator or reuse it after it has been at room temperature over six hours (La Leche League International, 1990; Morris, 1995; Wong, et al, 1999).

If mothers choose to bring in frozen breast milk, it can be stored at –20 degrees Fahrenheit until it is ready to be used to feed the baby. Encourage mothers to freeze milk in small containers of 2-4 ounces and to date the storage containers. Smaller amounts defrost more quickly and result in less waste.

To defrost frozen milk, place it in the refrigerator until it is defrosted (this may take up to 12 hours) or place the milk in a container of warm water. Do not use hot water to defrost milk because the milk may lose some of its immunological components.

Never microwave breast milk or any other kind of formula! Changes in the composition occur in the microwaving process. Further, the milk may have hot spots that can cause serious burns.

Defrosted breast milk can be stored for 24 hours in the refrigerator. Once it is warmed, it must be served to the baby or discarded. It cannot be stored at room temperature or returned to the refrigerator for later use.

Formula-feeding Issues

Formula is an alternative to breast milk. Consider the following safety precautions to keep formula-fed babies healthy. Formula that is warmed for an infant cannot be saved. Discard any leftovers in the bottle if the formula is not consumed in one feeding.

Safe Breast Milk and Formula Use

Type of Milk	Storage	Shelf Life After Warming
Freshly expressed breast milk	Keeps 72 hours in refrigerator.	Store at room temperature for up to 6 hours, then discard.
Frozen breast milk	Up to 1 month. Defrost in refrigerator or in warm water.	None. Discard after warming if not consumed. Do not return to refrigerator.
Formula	Check labels.	None. Discard after warming if not consumed. Do not return to refrigerator.

Formula should be warmed in a hot water bath. Microwaves are unsafe for warming milk. Most pediatricians recommend that children learn to drink their bottles at refrigerator temperature to avoid problems with the shelf life of formula.

Ready-to-feed formula typically can be kept refrigerated for 24 hours once opened. Discard formula that is not consumed within the suggested time period. Check expiration dates on powdered or concentrated formula to insure that the formula is fresh.

Mix formula according to the manufacturer's instructions. Concerns about underfeeding or overfeeding children typically relate to mixing errors. Use the measuring spoons provided by the manufacturer to measure formula.

Infant Health

Health Policies

When to send children home and when to let them stay at school is one of the most important decisions an infant teacher must make. And, the decision is complicated by a host of additional factors, including the family's lifestyle, the location of the parents' work, and the ability of the family to make contingency plans for sick children.

Every school needs a carefully crafted set of health policies. Clear policies are used as the foundation for determining whether or not a child can stay in school when she becomes ill or exhibits symptoms indicating the onset of illness. Policies should be developed in conjunction with consulting physicians and reviewed regularly to make sure that the latest information is used. Policies should be shared with parents in written form during the enrollment and discussed with parents in detail by the child's teacher during gradual enrollment.

The Pennsylvania chapter of the American Academy of Pediatrics has published excellent guidelines for parents and caregivers to follow to protect both well and ill children (APHA/AAP, 1992). Though not a substitute for advice from a physician, it is an excellent starting place for writing policies that are sound and supportable. But, like so many things in infant education, health policies are only guidelines to use to make good decisions about whether a child's needs can be met at school. Children's individuality and the teacher's attitude toward demanding children are variables that cannot be reduced to rules and regulations.

Helping teachers understand how to make decisions about sending children home works better than trying to make health policies cover each and every potential situation.

Illness and the Very Young Child

Every teacher has heard the accusation. "She got sick at school." The comment is usually followed by, "My doctor says she shouldn't be in a school setting." Teachers are often in the position of helping parents understand the infectious disease process and what steps are taken to prevent the spread of contagious diseases at school. Teachers also find that they are often the ones identifying the onset of illness.

Babies spit up all of the time. Spitting up is normal if it is intermittent and occurs after feeding times. Vomiting is different. Vomiting involves repeated, forceful emptying of the stomach caused by spasms in the digestive tract.

Loose stools are also a normal part of babies' experience. Breast-fed babies have very little form to their stool, and most babies have watery bowel movements. Diarrhea, though, is emptying of the bowel caused by spasms in the intestinal tract that are more frequent than normal for the child.

The hardest part of understanding the spread of contagious disease is that children who do not look sick can be spreading infection by leaving their secretions around the environment. Typically, children are contagious before they show signs of illness. This makes careful observation and effective sanitation procedures in the infant classroom even more important.

Illnesses in the first six months of a child's life are treated differently by the medical community because very young children have immature immune systems. As a result, they can get sicker more quickly than they would after the immune system begins to mature.

The Disposable Glove Debate

Some health professionals recommend that teachers always wear disposable gloves while diapering to protect them from contamination. Because of the frequency of diapering, the intimate nature of the diapering procedure and the possibility for one-to-one interaction to occur, gloves for routine diapering are not recommended. Careful handwashing (including the use of nailbrush) after diapering is encouraged, monitored, and expected. As long as the teacher's hands are free of cuts or sores and the child who is being diapered is healthy, gloves are not needed for routine diapering (APHA/AAP, 1992).

There are exceptions to this rule. When blood or blood containing body fluids are present, teachers should wear gloves or create barriers between themselves and blood. When gloves are used, they must be discarded after a single use and careful handwashing should still occur (Ratler, 1994).

Infant teachers need to be excellent observers of children's behavior to support parents in early intervention if an illness is suspected. In general, infants under six months should see a physician if they have a temperature over 101 degrees under the arm (axillary) or have other symptoms of illness like irritability, crying that cannot be soothed, frequent loose stools, coughing, wheezing, repeated vomiting, and so on.

As children get older, parents and teachers become better able to differentiate behaviors and symptoms that indicate the onset of illness in children. In fact, teachers and parents often report that they are able to anticipate when a child is getting ill by observing changes in behavior, schedule, or temperament.

Infectious diseases are diseases caused by infection with specific microorganisms like viruses, bacteria, fungi, or parasites. Contagious diseases are infectious diseases that are spread from one person to another (Kendrick, Kaufman, and Messinger, 1988). The challenge for infant teachers is to prevent the spread of contagious diseases by careful sanitation procedures and appropriate health practices.

Preventing the onset and spread of infectious and contagious disease is partially under the control of the teacher. Careful handwashing procedures and good environmental sanitation form the first line of defense.

Get a Choke Tube and Use It!

One of the greatest risks to very young children is choking. Infant environments are often part of schools that serve older children. Many of the toys and materials that are appropriate for preschool children pose choke threats to infants.

Every infant classroom needs to have a choke tube out and available at all times. Anytime a teacher sees small items in the room, she or he should use the tube to check the item for safety. If the item fits inside of the tube, it fails the choke test and poses a choke hazard to infants. Remove it immediately from the room. If no choke tube is available, a toilet paper tube is a conservative approximation of a choke tube and can be used until a choke tube is purchased.

INNOVATIONS IN INTERACTIVE EXPERIENCES

Physical development is one of the domains of development that responds so well to experience and practice. Babies who are always in baby bouncers, car seats, swings, and Exer-saucers have little opportunity for motor practice.

Practice is what wires the connections in the brain to bring muscles under voluntary control. In other words, babies need to repeat motor movements again and again. Movement sends messages to the developing brain to strengthen the connections between neurons. These connections are the roadways that send instruction to the muscles about what to do. Muscles come under voluntary control as these pathways become stronger.

Teachers must provide numerous opportunities for infants to practice motor skills every day. They are the foundation upon which crucial skills and abilities grow. Teachers might also want to use this list to make notes on the Communication Sheet (see pages 429-430 in the Appendix) to document the types of experiences children had during the day.

Be sure to plan experiences such as these for babies every day. In addition, don't hesitate to do them over and over again.

- ☐ Strengthen back and stomach muscles.
- ☐ Encourage arm and foot motions.
- ☐ Encourage flexibility.
- ☐ Provide exercise for arms and legs.
- ☐ Offer practice reaching.
- ☐ Provide toys to pull and push.
- ☐ Help babies practice squatting then standing then squatting.
- ☐ Add surprises to favorite experiences.
- ☐ Place babies on the floor regularly.
- ☐ Support babies check-in behavior.
- ☐ Provide challenges for small muscles in the hands.
- ☐ Limit time in restrained equipment such as bouncers, Exer-saucers, and swings.

INNOVATIONS IN TEACHING

Encouraging Independence and Autonomy

From birth, children have feelings about themselves. If they feel they can make things happen, succeed in trying new things, surmount obstacles, and solve problems, they will likely develop positive feelings about themselves. Finding a thumb or finger to suck allows a baby to soothe herself, rather than just waiting for someone to do the soothing. Crying when you are hungry will alert teachers to give you a bottle, rather than just waiting until someone feeds you. Smiling and cooing at someone's face gets them to smile and coo back at you. From these early attempts at independence comes a view of self that says, "I can!"

Success in achieving age- and stage-appropriate autonomy and independence throughout childhood has a profound impact on the way children mature. They are naturally motivated to make things happen. If their early attempts are successful and fulfilling, children will continue to grow and develop competence. If their early efforts are unsuccessful and frustrating, children will carry this failure and the negative views of self with them into adulthood.

Children get feedback about attempts at independence from parents and other important caregivers. When teachers support emerging independence, they are expressing their confidence in the child's ability. Such expression creates the desire to increase independent behaviors and helps children feel successful, further enhancing self-esteem and self-confidence.

Teach discrete skills in small increments. If the child wants to hold her own bottle, help her get her hands in the right position and support the first attempts. If a child wants to feed herself, offer food that is just the size for fingers and put a spoon on the plate, too. After perfecting finger feeding, offer the spoon as the next step.

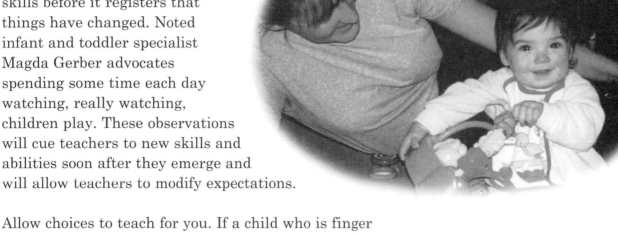

Frequently reassess where children are. Growth and development is a dynamic process. Children often develop new skills before it registers that things have changed. Noted infant and toddler specialist Magda Gerber advocates spending some time each day watching, really watching, children play. These observations will cue teachers to new skills and abilities soon after they emerge and will allow teachers to modify expectations.

Allow choices to teach for you. If a child who is finger feeding wants to try a spoon, let the child get the food all over the high chair as she learns to hold the spoon level all the way to the mouth. This kind of experiential learning takes place all the time and is very empowering for children. It teaches children to persist until they accomplish a new skill and that practice is worthwhile and fun.

Nutrition

Introducing Solid Foods

The following suggestions for feeding infants should be taken into consideration.

- Allow the child to decide when she has had enough. Do not continue to feed children who indicate they have had enough. Signs of fullness include turning away, arching the back, spitting out food, irritability, fidgeting, and so on.
- Pour baby food into a bowl to feed babies. The saliva left on the spoon contaminates the food left in the jar. If served from the jar, discard food

that is not finished in one serving. Feed solids from a spoon. Have two available—one for you and one for the baby to hold during mealtime.

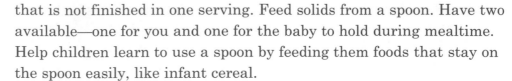 Help children learn to use a spoon by feeding them foods that stay on the spoon easily, like infant cereal.

Offer finger foods as a part of the meal as soon as the child is ready for them.

Offer a cup of fluids to children over 9 months. Baby food is thick and sometimes needs to be washed down. In addition, the child gets experience drinking from a sippy cup.

Take your time feeding children. Talk to them, ask them questions, and point out things in the environment. In short, make mealtime pleasant and unhurried.

Give children who are not being fed a role in other children's mealtime. (Remember, children do not all eat at once. They eat on their own individualized schedules.) They can hold an extra spoon, hold the lid to the baby food jar, hand a baby a washcloth to clean up after eating, or sit nearby playing with a manipulative toy or rattle.

Hold babies to feed them their bottles. Never prop them. Try to keep children from drinking lying down to prevent middle ear contamination from the milk that can lead to middle ear infections. Offer children who hold their own bottles a place to lie down that elevates the head.

Consider bottle feedings with younger children just as important as mealtimes with older children. These are opportunities to maximize the child's experience with her teacher and to give each child a special time alone with the teacher. Use this time to gaze into the baby's eyes and make a real connection through eye contact.

Health

Handwashing and Diapering Procedure

1. Gather all of the supplies needed.
2. Wash your hands with soap, rinsing well with running water. Dry hands well with disposable toweling, then, turn off the running water with the towel covering the handle. Discard the paper towel. Remember, handwashing throughout the day is the most important method for controlling illness.
3. Cover the changing area with disposable paper. Computer paper, newspaper, or commercially prepared changing papers are all acceptable covers.
4. Pick the child up and put her on the changing table. Hold the child by the abdomen with one hand.
5. Remove the soiled diaper and place on the paper covering the diaper-changing table away from the infant's hands and face.

6. Wash the child's bottom and genitals with warm water, using soap and paper towels, washcloths, or wipes.

7. Pat the bottom dry with paper towels or a clean washcloth.

8. Now, dispose of the soiled diaper in a plastic bag and then in a closed container located within easy reach of the table.

9. Put on a clean diaper.

10. Examine clothes. Change any soiled or wet clothes.

11. Wash the child's hands with soap and water. Make this easy by taking time to set this up so that the child can reach the sink, soap, and toweling. By getting children into the habit of washing after diapering now, they will remember it after toileting later. If the child is too young to stand, wash hands with a wet paper towel.

12. Return the child to a comfortable play area or assist with the transition back to the group.

13. Remove the changing table paper. Wipe the table top and any other surfaces that came in contact with the diaper (like the lid of the trash can), with a weak bleach solution (¼ cup to 1 gallon of water). Also wipe the exteriors of the entire changing station.

14. Wash your hands with soap under running water, drying thoroughly and shutting off the water with the paper towel.

15. Mark the child's Communication Sheet (see pages 429-430 in the Appendix). Record the type of diaper change (urine or bowel movement) and the time.

Daily Health Conversations

An important part of every separation from parents and reunion with school should be a discussion about health. This conversation has two goals. The first is to make sure the parent who is dropping off the child at school shares information about the time spent at home. The second is to make sure the baby is healthy enough to stay at school.

When the school day starts, teachers need the following information about time spent at home:

- What time the baby went to sleep and how long she slept,
- What time the diaper was last changed,
- What time the child was last fed and how much was eaten,
- Changes in the child's behavior and disposition, and
- Any special instructions for the child's day.

Collecting this information is important because children's health and behavior at home are often indicators of their health and behavior at school.

Use a quick health check that can be completed before parents leave for the day as an integral part of parent's drop-off procedure. The check includes a quick look at the child's general physical condition for indicators of health problems. Place a hand on the child's abdomen to determine if she is running a temperature, and look at the face, eyes, the skin on the abdomen, and the inside of the arms to screen for signs of infectious or contagious disease like rashes, bumps, or blisters.

Talk with the parent in detail about the child's behavior and disposition. Irritability, sleep interruptions, and changes in general demeanor and mood can be cues to the baby's general health. Ask the parent if the child is on any medication.

Health checks won't prevent children from getting sick during the school day, but they will help spot ill children who are exhibiting symptoms. Health checks further assure parents that you are diligent about preventing the spread of disease.

Making Determinations about Sending Children Home

When teachers consider sending children home, a number of criteria need to be taken into consideration. Some of those are:

- **Symptom severity.** Severity of symptoms refers to the number and type of symptoms as well as the intensity of the symptoms. In general, the more symptoms a child has or the more intense the symptoms, the more comfortable the teacher can be with a "go home" decision.
- **Time of the day.** Symptoms that begin at the end of the school day pose a different picture than symptoms that begin early in the school day. Some symptoms unrelated to disease onset can be cyclical, like having a fever after a temper tantrum or waking from a nap with a elevated temperature. Children who began to get sick late in the day can probably stay at school until their parents pick them up. When this occurs, teachers need to make sure to tell the parents whether or not the child can return to school the next day if symptoms subside.
- **Speed of onset of symptoms.** Symptoms that emerge rapidly need to be recorded on the child's chart and watched for 15 to 30 minutes to determine if they go away or get worse. Don't forget to record what happens after the time lapse as well, particularly if you decide not to send the child home.
- **Daily pattern of behavior.** All symptoms need to be compared with the child's pattern of behavior. Two weeks of communication sheets should be kept handy. Then, teachers can look back to bring behavior changes or symptoms into focus in the broader perspective. If symptoms have a pattern (like loose stools every afternoon after eating spinach at lunch),

you can be fairly sure they are not the result of onset of illness.

- **Consistency with health and sick child policy.** Schools have health and sick child policies for a reason. It is to protect teachers and other children from the spread of contagious disease WHEN SOMETHING CAN BE DONE TO IMPACT THAT SPREAD.

- **Sanitation procedures.** Because many of the types of diseases that are contagious are contact borne, carefully follow sanitation procedures such as handwashing, toy washing, and disinfecting the diaper changing area.

- **Review health policies.** The first thing a teacher should do if a child exhibits symptoms is READ the school's health policies to determine if it provides any guidance for the situation the teacher is considering. If the policy is clear-cut and the child is exhibiting the symptoms listed, the child should be sent home. If the policy is not clear-cut, teachers may want to check out their preliminary decision with others before acting. Getting a second opinion helps teachers gain confidence in their ability to make good decisions about whether a child should be sent home or not.

- **The family's unique situation.** Some families have several options for the care of sick children; others do not. Think in terms of helping the family when at all possible. Sending children home must be viewed in light of what the parents are likely to be able to handle, particularly if the child's needs can be met in the center. Children who are too ill to be cared for at school need to be at home. But those decisions are usually easy to make. It is more difficult to determine whether mildly ill children or those who are only exhibiting one or two symptoms should stay at school. Letting the child's teacher and the parents make that decision in conjunction with the school's health policy seems appropriate.

- **Communicate with parents.** Parents should be informed about changes in children's health status as changes occurs, even if a change does not require the child to go home. Notification of parents enables them to begin to plan ahead should they decide the child should be at home. It allows the parents time to call their physician for advice or an appointment, and it makes the stay-at-school/send-home decision a shared one—made by the people who know the child best and who can determine if the child needs special care at home. It allows the child's teacher to consider the needs of the whole group of children. If the teacher feels she or he cannot meet the child's needs, the teacher is free to say so to the parents and get their assistance in developing other strategies for getting the child's needs met.

- **Notify other parents of illness incidents.** When a child is sent home for a specific illness or when a contagious disease is documented, parents of other children should be notified. Notification serves two purposes. One is to give parents advance warning of possible contagious diseases that their children have come in contact with as soon as they are exposed.

Letting parents know in advance what to look for can limit the number of children who come to school when they are contagious because parents notice symptoms more readily when they are alerted to them. Second, parents who work often need advance warning of impending absence from their jobs. Notification allows them to make some contingency plans if their child gets ill. Use the Communication Sheet (see page 430 in the Appendix) to make a note for parents to read upon reuniting with their baby.

Safety

Bottle Safety at School

There is no place for glass bottles in the school setting. Plastic ones are widely available and should always be used in school. All personal items from home need careful labeling with permanent markers to prevent mistakes in feeding children.

Warming bottles. The American Academy of Pediatrics does not recommend using a microwave to warm bottles. Microwaves cause hot spots and may result in burning the infant's mouth. Use a warm water bath (around 105 degrees Fahrenheit) to warm the bottles or serve at refrigerator temperature.

Feeding infants. Hold infants while feeding with a bottle. Although children can hold their bottles easily around 6 months or so, infant teachers should be in no hurry to allow them to do so. Drinking from the bottle is one of the times teachers can spend intimately interacting with babies by gazing, smiling, singing, or just being "with" the baby while they eat.

As infants grow, they will enjoy drinking from a bottle while they relax and gaze around the room. To prevent contamination of the middle ear, prop babies' heads up a little with a small pillow. This will prevent milk from tracking up the Eustachian tube into the middle ear and growing bacteria. Stay close as babies eat and maintain eye contact to reinforce cuddling while eating.

Make eating time relaxed and individualized. Create a place for eating in your classroom that is out of the traffic pattern. Resist the urge to restrict babies in bouncer seats when they are eating. Restrictions like these discourage infants from beginning and ending their feedings as they are ready and places the responsibility for determining when the baby is through on the teacher.

Bottles for children under 12 months of age should only contain breast milk or formula. The American Academy of Pediatrics suggests offering juice to babies in a cup after six months of age. Juice fed to infants from bottles is associated with dental caries, and excess juice ingestion is associated with abdominal pain, diarrhea, bloating, and increased likelihood of childhood obesity.

When babies become mobile enough to crawl around the room, they will often want to take their bottles along with them. In the school setting, crawling or walking around with the bottle in the mouth poses the risk of falling and injuring the soft tissues around the mouth. Require children to lie down or sit comfortably with a slightly elevated head during the entire process. If the child doesn't want to comply, she is probably not quite ready to eat. Take the bottle away and give the infant some additional time before you try again.

Guidance and Discipline

Natural and Logical Consequences

Applying natural and logical consequences is a great tool for teachers to use to help children gain self-control. A natural or logical consequence is a consequence that emerges from the situation. This important teaching skill is not one of the easiest ones to learn. And it takes time, practice, and careful response. The example to the right illustrates the concept of logical consequences.

An infant pulls on your earring as soon as she gets picked up. After you take her hand and remind her to leave the earring alone, the baby pulls again on the earring. You put the baby down, saying, "I can't hold you if you pull on my earring. It hurts!" The logical consequence of not listening to your request is to be put down where she cannot reach your earring.

Notice that there is no power struggle or disapproval in this situation. The consequences emerge from the situation and are responded to firmly but calmly. As a result, children learn to control their own behavior slowly over time as they are reminded of the consequences, both by your words and your actions.

Setting Appropriate Limits

Teachers have two reasons to set rules and limits. The first reason is to protect children and keep them safe—reason enough for a good set of limits. The second reason teachers set limits is to help children grow toward self-control. Where do you start to establish reasonable limits and rules for your classroom? Rules should have the following elements (Marion, 1998):

- **First, rules and limits must be humane.** There is no place for rules that are punitive in nature and/or make children feel bad about themselves. Humane rules do not humiliate, embarrass, belittle, or degrade the child. An example of an inhumane rule: "Babies who cry don't get to play." This kind of rule has no place in school.

- **Second, limits should not be arbitrary.** Each rule should have several good reasons for existing. An example of an arbitrary rule: "I won't pick you up unless you stop crying."

- **Third, rules should be overt, out in the open, not hidden.** Children, particularly very young children, cannot guess what the rules are. They need to be told, reminded, and reminded again. (Yes, even if it takes thousands of reminders!) For example, if crawling around with your bottle dangling from your mouth isn't allowed because you might fall on your mouth and injure your gums or teeth, then babies need to be reminded about the rule when you hand them their bottles. Then help them settle into a place to drink them. To determine if your rules are overt, simply watch children's behavior. If your rules are clear, most children will be learning to follow them when given supportive reminders by adults.

- **Fourth, limits should be clearly stated and enforceable.** Rules should refer to the expected behavior and be clear enough for children to know immediately when they have broken the rule. An example of a clearly stated rule with a reference to behavior: "Leave the sand in the sandbox or I will have to ask you to play somewhere else." Rules that end in threats like, "I'll never let you play in the sand again," are ineffective because they are unenforceable, and very young children don't have the self-control to resist putting the sand in their mouths.

- **Fifth, rules should be accompanied by reasons.** Research has shown that children who are given the reasons behind the rules are more likely to listen and follow the rules later without adult reminders. It is important to be brief and to the point. Children need one good reason for each rule, not three or four. Using the previously stated sand rule, an example might be: "Leave the sand in the sandbox. When you throw it, someone's eyes could be badly hurt."

- **Sixth, remember to update your rules.** This is particularly important during the first three years when children are maturing and developing so quickly. As children mature, the limits imposed on them should be updated. As new skills emerge, limits should reflect those new skills. For example, infant skills change quickly during the first 18 months. As children perfect new skills, like crawling or taking first steps, update your rules. You might say, "Hold my hand while we walk outside" to a new walker, then drop the rule when she becomes steadier on her feet.

- **Finally, rules and limits should be firmly enforced.** As children grow, they will test limits that adults set for them. If teachers use repressive controls like coercion, testing will continue. If teachers do not set limits and do not enforce rules, children will heed no adult guidance. Firm, consistent responses to broken rules will result in children who learn to follow the rules set for them by their teachers.

The easiest way to enforce the limits you've set is to move the child to another setting when out of bounds behavior occurs. This technique uses logical consequences to help children remember the rules. If the child is throwing sand, take her by the hand and ask her to find another place to play until she can remember the sandbox rules. If the child is climbing without holding on, take the child off of the climbing structure and ask her to find another place to play until she can remember the rule about holding on tightly.

Infants will need frequent reminders of your rules and support in complying with them. They are unable to do so just because you say so. Combine your rules with physical action (holding a child by the hand, moving a child to another place), and, later on, infants will remember and comply.

Teacher Competencies to Support Babies Learning to Move

Sometimes	Usually	Always	
☐	☐	☐	Is aware of the activities of the entire group even when dealing with a part of it; positions self strategically, looks up often from involvement.
☐	☐	☐	Establishes and carries out reasonable limits for children and activities.
☐	☐	☐	Uses nonpunitive ways of dealing with behavior; can exert authority without requiring submission or undermining the child's sense of self.
☐	☐	☐	Redirects, distracts, or channels inappropriate behavior into acceptable outlets. Anticipates confrontations between children and intervenes before aggressive behavior arises.
☐	☐	☐	Anticipates problems and plans to prevent their re-occurence.
☐	☐	☐	Does not avoid problem situations, can generate alternative ideas, and implement and evaluate solutions selected.
☐	☐	☐	Reinforces appropriate behavior by encouraging children's appropriate behavior.
☐	☐	☐	Uses praise and encouragement effectively; differentiates between the behavior and the child when using praise.
☐	☐	☐	Guides children to work out increasingly effective ways of making social contacts and solving social problems.
☐	☐	☐	Sees that children are dressed appropriately for existing temperatures throughout the day.
☐	☐	☐	Models the behavior being encouraged and taught to children.
☐	☐	☐	Assures that all children have frequent opportunities for success.
☐	☐	☐	Provides regular and varied outdoor experience.
☐	☐	☐	Provides ample opportunity for and encouragement of large muscle activity.
☐	☐	☐	Knows a variety of guidance techniques such as redirection, distraction, ignoring, using room arrangements and schedules to support appropriate behavior, and uses each appropriately.
☐	☐	☐	Helps parents develop realistic expectations for children's behavior in ways that help avoid disciplinary problems.

Resources for Teachers

Adams, C. & E. Fruge. (1996). *Why children misbehave.* Oakland, CA: New Harbinger.

Dreikurs, R. (1964). *Children: The challenge.* New York: Hawthorne/Dutton.

Kendrick, A.S., R. Kaufman, & K.P. Messinger. (1988). *Healthy young children: A manual for programs.* Washington, DC: National Association for the Education of Young Children (NAEYC).

Marion, M. (1998). *Guidance of young children.* St. Louis, MO: Mosby.

Mitchell, G. (1998). *A very practical guide to discipline with young children.* Glen Burnie, MD: Telshare.

INNOVATIONS IN PARENT PARTNERSHIPS

School- or Teacher-initiated Possibilities

Tie Snakes

Ask parents to provide one of Dad's (or another special family member's) discarded ties to make a stuffed toy snake. (This can also work with Mom's scarf.) The tie needs to be washable and have no loose parts. First, wash each tie by hand. Then stuff the ties with fiber fill. Fold each end of the tie back toward the center and sew or glue securely to the body of the tie. Examine all seams to be certain they are secure. Avoid sewing buttons as features on the snake as they pose a choke hazard. If you wish to add features, embroider them on the larger end, or add them with non-toxic permanent markers.

Parent Participation Possibilities

Happy Hour

Invite parents to visit the classroom one afternoon during departure time for Happy Hour. Serve refreshments. Play the song "Shake It All About" (on many records, tapes and CDs, including *Greg and Steve's Body Rock Dance*). Ask parents to dance with their babies. They also may enjoy "Do the Opposite" from the same album. Take photographs and display them in the classroom. Point to them and talk with children about the Happy Hour Dance.

Parent Postcards

Parent Postcards can be shared with parents as they indicate an interest, at appropriate times during the enrollment cycle, or as developmental issues arise. (See pages 441-444 in the Appendix for a sample dissemination schedule.) Copy postcards. Cut if necessary. Address to parent(s) and place on Communication Sheet or hand out personally.

Appropriate Expectations for Self-Control

An important developmental task is learning the expectations of the family and society and matching behavior to the rules. Knowledge about these important expectations comes from exposure to expectations and support with compliance from supportive adults. Children are not born able to comply with the rules of the world; they construct this knowledge through interactions and experiences that expose them to the rules and behavioral expectations that accompany rules (for example, be quiet in church; sit down to eat, and so on). This process is called the internalization of control—becoming able to comply with expectations without reminders or support.

Infants are almost totally controlled externally—that is, they depend on others to keep them safe, support them in following established rules, and succeed in interactions with others. How, then, do they learn to internalize rules?

The answer is simple. They learn to internalize the rules by having the rules consistently and constantly applied and followed. For example, when an older infant picks up the television remote control, most parents take it away and tell the child that the control is for adults and not babies and then put it out of reach. This rule will be pointed out a thousand times over the next few months.

As the baby gets older, he or she will pick up the remote, turn to Mom and Dad to see if they will follow the rule, and then play with it even though he or she knows the remote is off limits. This illustrates the external nature of self-control. The infant has learned that there is a rule pertaining to the remote control but has not internalized the rule. Internalization means that the child can control his or her actions without adult support.

Infants still need external support to comply with rules, even when they have figured out what the rules are! In addition, they need many, many reminders to confirm that the rule really does apply every time.

TO

Natural and Logical Consequences

Natural and logical consequences are the best tools for parents to help their child gain self-control. A natural or logical consequence is a consequence that emerges from the situation. This important parenting skill is not one of the easiest ones to learn. It takes time, practice, and careful response. The following examples illustrate the concept of logical consequences:

An infant pulls on Mommy's earring as soon as he or she gets picked up. After Mommy takes her hand and reminds her to leave the earring alone, the baby pulls again on the earring. Mom puts the baby down, saying, "I can't hold you if you pull on my earring. It hurts!" The logical consequence of not listening to Mommy's request is to be put down where you cannot reach her earring.

Notice that that there is no struggle for power in this situation. The consequences emerge from the situation and are responded to firmly but calmly. As a result, children learn to control their own behavior slowly over time as they come to understand the reasons they should do so and understand the consequences of not doing so.

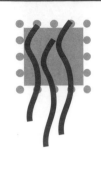

TO

Setting Appropriate Limits

Parents have two reasons to set rules and limits. The first reason is to protect children and keep them safe—reason enough for a good set of limits. The second reason is to help children grow toward self-control. Where do you start to establish reasonable limits and rules for your home? Start by following these rules about rules.

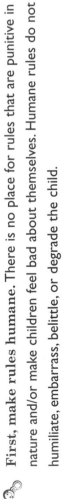

First, make rules humane. There is no place for rules that are punitive in nature and/or make children feel bad about themselves. Humane rules do not humiliate, embarrass, belittle, or degrade the child.

Secondly, limits should not be arbitrary. Rules should convey to children that you make rules thoughtfully, not just because you can.

Third, rules should be out in the open, not secret. Children, particularly very young children, cannot guess what the rules are. They need to be told, reminded, and reminded again. (Yes, even if it takes thousands of reminders!)

Fourth, limits should be clearly stated and enforceable. Rules should refer to the expected behavior and be clear enough for children to know immediately when they have broken the rule. Avoid don't rules, such as: don't run, or don't stand on the couch. Try to state your rules from a positive perspective (walk in the house, sit on the couch).

Fifth, rules should be accompanied by reasons. Research has shown that children who are given the reasons behind the rules are more likely to listen and to follow the rules without parental reminders. But, be brief and to the point. Children need one good reason for each rule, not three or four.

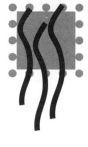

TO

Setting Appropriate Limits (continued)

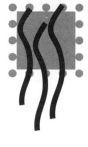 **Sixth, remember to update your rules.** This is particularly important during the first three years when children are maturing and developing so quickly. Limits should reflect new skills. For example, very young children need strict climbing rules like, "Hold on tightly with both hands when you climb." As children become proficient in climbing, the rule can simply be, "Climb safely."

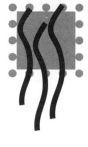 **Most important, rules and limits should be firmly enforced.** As children grow, they will test limits that parents set for them. If parents do not set limits and do not enforce rules, children will heed no adult guidance. Firm, consistent responses to broken rules help children learn to follow the rules set for them by their parents.

Very young children get a sense of security and support from parental rules. Part of your child's rule testing is an attempt to confirm that you will set limits and keep him or her safe. Children who don't have an ordered, disciplined life struggle to find out where the limits are by testing harder and longer. Setting limits along with enforcing them is a very loving and responsive thing to do.

TO

Coping with Ear Infections

Parents of very young children have so many concerns: school, emotional development, health, time, work. When a baby starts having ear problems, the concerns increase.

How can you discern if your child has an ear infection? Look for these symptoms:

- Baby may get fussy and pull on ears.
- Baby may cry, especially at mealtime (sore throat) or at bedtime (drainage).
- Hearing may be lessened (baby doesn't turn head when you speak).
- Fevers over 100 degrees Fahrenheit may occur (particularly in the afternoon).
- Baby may experience uncontrolled crying.
- Baby may become lethargic.

What do you do? First, the pediatrician will examine each ear and eardrum to see if there is evidence of an infection. The doctor will probably prescribe an antibiotic to combat the infection. Your child's medical history and the severity of the infection will determine the medicine prescribed.

If an antibiotic is prescribed, follow directions precisely because dosage and duration vary. Complete the full dosage. Failure to do this is the major cause of recurrence—the infection doesn't get resolved. Many doctors are slower to prescribe antibiotics than they once were. They are concerned about antibiotic-resistant infections.

Some children have chronic problems with ear infections. These can be caused by allergies, the formation of the inner ear, or a particular genetic susceptibility to infections. If infections reduce exploratory behavior because balance is affected, or if language does not emerge, the final result may be ear tubes. This is a difficult decision you will need to make in consultation with your child's doctor.

Ear infections can affect a child's hearing, both short and long term. Chronic infections may result in delayed language development or speech difficulties. So watch those ears!

Resources for Parents

Add these helpful books to your parent library or post this list on your parent bulletin board.

Adams, C. & E. Fruge. (1996). **Why children misbehave: and what to do about it.** Oakland, CA: New Harbinger.

Honig, A. (1989). **Love and learn: Discipline for young children.** Washington, DC: National Association for the Education of Young Children (NAEYC).

National Association for the Education of Young Children. (1998). **Helping children gain self-control.** Washington, DC: National Association for the Education of Young Children (NAEYC).

Shelov, S. (1998). **Caring for your baby and child.** New York: Bantam, Doubleday, Dell.

INNOVATIONS IN ENVIRONMENTS

Environmental Sanitation

Environmental sanitation involves two steps. The first is removing the warm, moist conditions under which microorganisms thrive and grow. The second is destroying or removing microorganisms that arrive at school through the respiratory tract (via secretions from the mouth, nose, lungs, or eyes), through the intestinal tract (via stool), through direct contact or touching, and through contact with blood.

Classrooms need to be well ventilated with fresh air, and children need opportunities to go outside often. As doors are opened for children to move inside and outside, fresh air is introduced into closed, centrally air-conditioned classrooms, airing out the collected airborne contaminants.

Sanitation procedures should require sanitation of surfaces that children touch, including the floors, walls, and furniture as well as the toys and materials that children put in their mouths or touch with their hands. Further, diapering and eating areas should be as far away from each other as possible and need thorough sanitizing after each use. Bleach solution is usually the sanitizing agent of choice because it is inexpensive and easy to mix. Use ¼ cup of bleach to 1 gallon of water mixed fresh daily as a sanitizing solution.

Bringing Indoor Materials Outside

Outdoor time is very important for young children; babies need to go outside each day (preferably in both the morning and afternoon). However, avoid the middle of the day, and always protect baby's skin with sunscreen or a hat.

When thinking of outdoor play, many teachers think of traditional physical education activities. These, of course, are not appropriate for babies. They, instead, need opportunities for sensory and physical stimulation. The very same activities that babies need and enjoy inside are appropriate when they go outside. Try some of these activities:

- Books outside provide a special time for reading on a blanket.
- Play gyms provide opportunities to stretch and move outside in the fresh air.
- Dramatic play takes on a new dimension when activities take place under a shade structure or tree.
- Messy art projects that may be difficult to do in the classroom are often easier to clean up outside.

Bringing indoor materials outside helps to provide rich learning experiences for babies outdoors. Teachers, through their careful planning and thoughtful interactions, support children as they develop socially, emotionally, physically, and intellectually when they are both in the indoor and outdoor learning environment.

Activities and Experiences vs. Centers

Most early childhood educators think of interest or learning centers as an essential part of any classroom setting. Yet, environments for infants are different because they cannot choose to go to different areas until they are mobile. For this reason, teachers must bring the activities and experiences to the child, or they must help the child go to where the activities are. A wide range of activities and experiences must be available to infants, but the environments are different. In each of the following two Possibilities Plans, *Competent Me* and *Windows, Walls, Doors, and Hallways*, activities and experiences are presented in the following areas:

- Dramatic Possibilities
- Sensory/Art Possibilities
- Curiosity Possibilities
- Literacy Possibilities
- Music Possibilities
- Movement Possibilities
- Outdoor Possibilities
- Project Possibilities
- Parent Participation Possibilities

Competent Me

WEB

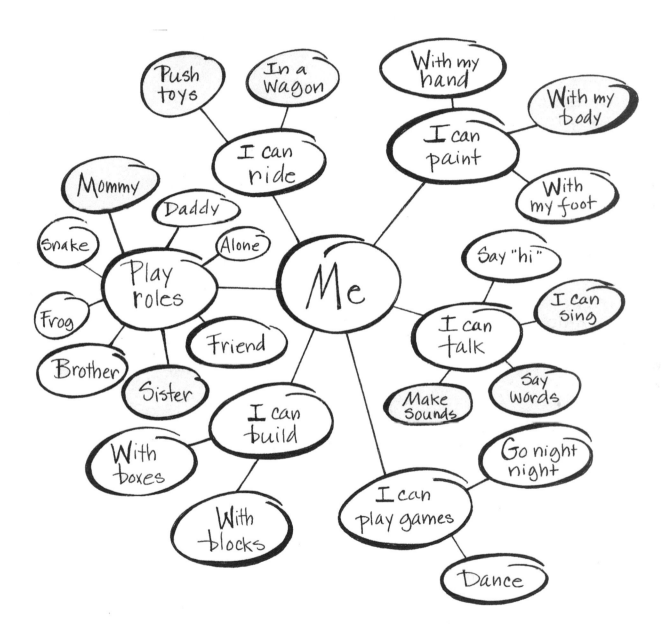

Note: Using the technique of webbing, teachers can follow the leads that children give them, as well as have an unlimited source of options. Always use the webs as a jumping-off point. The possibilities are endless!

Plan Possibilities

Dramatic

Shopping Bag Fill
    and Dump 330
Cooking 330
Cleaning 330
Building 330

Sensory/Art

Toes in Flour/Powder 331
Fingers in Flour 331
Circle Picture 332
Scrap Collage 332
Self-portrait 332

Curiosity

Foot Rattles 332
Telephone Play 333
Food Containers 333
Nesting Cans and Boxes 333

Literacy

No! No! No! 334
You Can't Catch Me 334
Picture Blocks 334
Competent Me Books 334

Music

Shaking Rattles 335
Food Container Rattles 335
If You're Happy 335
Head, Shoulders, Knees,
    and Toes 336

Movement

Pat-a-Cake 336
Stuffed Sacks to Carry 337
Box and Lid Match 337
Phone Book Tearing 337
Paper Ball Toss 337
Dump and Load
    Laundry Hamper 338

Outdoor

Bouncy Seat Barefoot 338
Texture Walk 338
Pumpkin Carry 338
Outside Play Gyms 339

Project

Developmental Banners 339
"I Can" Cans 339

Parent Participation

Pockets for Wall Hanging 340
Walking Chart 340
Supporting Possibilities 340
Shadow Child 340
Picture Necklace 340
Parent Postcards
    Encouraging Independence
        and Autonomy 341
    Continuing to Support
        Independence and
        Autonomy 342

Competent Me

Concepts Learned in

Competent Me 343

Prop Boxes

Cooking 343
Cleaning 344
Construction 344

Picture File/Vocabulary 344

Books

Can You Hop? by Lisa Lawston
Catch Me If You Can by Bernard Most
Dressing by Helen Oxenbury
No! No! Jo! by Kate McMullen
No! No! No! by Anne Rockwell. 334
You Can't Catch Me by Rosanne Litzinger 334

Rhymes/Fingerplays

"Pat-a-Cake" 336

Music/Songs

"If You're Happy and You Know It" 336
"Head, Shoulders, Knees, and Toes" 336

Toys and Materials 345-6

Shopping Bag Fill and Dump
6-18 months

Materials
Shopping bags with handles
Small boxes or manipulatives to put into the bags

Provide shopping bags with handles and small boxes or manipulatives. Show children how to pick up items and fill the bags after they have been dumped out.

Cooking
6-18 months

Materials
Realistic kitchen items, such as pots, pans, cardboard food boxes, etc.

Teacher Talk
Narrate children's actions. "Pots have lids. Yes Jojo, you can make noise with the pot and lid."

Add realistic kitchen items, such as pots, pans, plastic bowls, cans, cardboard food boxes, and cookbooks to the classroom. Observe for skills such as taking off lids, putting lids on pots, and matching the right lid to the right pot.

Cleaning
6-18 months

Materials
Spray bottles with water, cloths, brooms, hand towels, etc.

When providing materials for cleaning, be certain that all chemicals have been completely cleaned from the containers. Spray bottles with water, cloths, hand brooms, hand mops, hand towels, and soap containers will all add to the fun. Describe children's actions as you play with them and the props.

Building
6-18 months

Materials
Toy construction items such as plastic hammers, pliers, measuring tape, etc.

Toy construction items such as plastic hammers, pliers, and measuring tapes make building fun. Also add construction hats, blocks, and trucks that can be pushed or pulled.

Toes in Flour/Powder

0-6 months

Materials
Flour or powder
Shallow plastic tub
Bouncy seat or
    jumper

Teacher Talk
"The flour (or
powder) feels
soft under your
feet, Jacque.
You wiggled
your toes!"

Put flour or
powder in a
shallow plastic
tub. Place under a
child in a bouncy
seat or jumper.
Describe how the flour
(or powder) feels as the
child wiggles his toes. Be
certain the powder is non-toxic.

The Use of Food in Classroom Activities

Some early childhood educators object to the use of real food materials in activities for children either because of their sensitivity to the issue of hunger in the world or because they are concerned that children will be confused by food that is not meant to be eaten. Food included in this curriculum is used because it works beautifully as a manipulative activity and it is an extremely inexpensive source of sensory stimulation. Educators with objections can find substitutes for the materials listed. Alternatives are sometimes included in the activities.

Fingers in Flour

6-18 months

Materials
Flour or powder
Wading pool
Paper and pen

Allow children to explore a
small amount of flour (or
powder) in a wading pool with
you very close by watching,
commenting, and supervising for
safety. Be certain the powder is
non-toxic. Describe children's actions as you observe
curiosity, smiles, wiggles, and bounces. Record your
observations on the Communication Sheet (pages 429-430).

Circle Picture

6-18 months

cut hole in center of paper.

Materials
Large sheet of paper
Art materials such as crayons,
     markers, etc.

Cut a hole in the middle of a very
large sheet of paper. Place a child in
the hole with art materials such as
tempera paint in paint cups and a paintbrush, or
chalk or crayons, depending on the child's age and abilities.
Label the section each child paints, colors, or marks.

Scrap Collage

6-18 months

Materials
Scraps of paper and fabric
Clear contact paper

Help children place items from the scrap box on the sticky side of a sheet of clear
contact paper. Talk about the colors and shapes of the scraps. This activity will help
children develop pincer grasp.

Self-portrait

12-18 months

Materials
Paper or a mat
Full-length unbreakable mirror
Paint and brushes

Cover the area of the floor in front of a full-length unbreakable mirror with paper or a
mat. Provide paint and brushes, so children can create a self-portrait on the surface of
the mirror.

CURIOSITY POSSIBILITIES

Foot Rattles

0-6 months

Materials
Wrist rattles

Place wrist rattles on young babies' ankles. Gently shake feet to show how the sound is made. Watch how baby responds. Record response on Communication Sheet (pages 429-430).

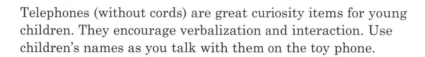

Telephone Play
6-18 months

Materials
Toy telephones without cords

Teacher Talk
"Hello. Hello, John. You are talking on the phone."

Telephones (without cords) are great curiosity items for young children. They encourage verbalization and interaction. Use children's names as you talk with them on the toy phone.

Food Containers
6-18 months

Materials
Boxes
Items to put into the boxes
Paper and pen

Provide boxes for children to explore. Add surprise items to the food boxes, such as unbreakable hand mirrors, small animals, and small vehicles. Be certain that all items are safe and do not present choke hazards. Replace surprises often for children to rediscover. Record search-and-find skills such as looking where toys were the last time or searching for hidden objects.

Nesting Cans and Boxes
12-18 months

Materials
Cans and boxes

Teacher Talk
Talk about what children are doing. "Yes, Amy. You placed the little box inside the big box."

Provide numerous cans and boxes, so children can nest them. Support babies as they practice this skill.

No! No! No!
0-18 months

Materials
No! No! No! by Anne F. Rockwell

Read this delightful book that explores the words young children hear so often. Younger infants will like being read to, and older infants will relate to the experiences described in the book.

You Can't Catch Me
0-18 months

Materials
You Can't Catch Me by Rosanne Litzinger

Read this book with individual children or with two or three children at a time. Put feeling and expression into the words.

Picture Blocks
0-18 months

Materials
Small boxes
Newspaper
Tape
Photographs
Clear contact paper

Collect a small box for each b and stuff each with newspape Tape the boxes shut. Attach b sides of the box and cover wit pictures and talk with babies photos.

Competent Me Books
0-18 months

Materials
Books such as
Can You Hop? by Lisa Lawston   *No! No! Jo!* by Kate McMullen
Catch Me If You Can by Bernard Most   *You Can't Catch Me* by Rosanne Litzinger
Dressing by Helen Oxenbury

Read one of these books at appropriate times. Add to Books Read list
(see Appendix page 431).

MUSIC POSSIBILITIES

 ## Shaking Rattles
0-6 months

Materials
Rattles

When older babies are making noise with noisemakers, give younger
babies rattles to shake.

 ## Food Container Rattles
6-18 months

Materials
Empty cardboard food containers
Items to put inside, such as plastic blocks,
    large buttons, etc.
Tape

Teacher Talk
"That box makes a soft sound. That one makes
a loud sound!"

Use empty cardboard food containers to make
rattles. Place items (too large to pass through a choke
tube) inside the boxes. Tape them securely.

 ## If You're Happy
6-18 months

Materials
None needed

Teacher Talk
"I see you clapping your hands. Can you stomp your feet?"

Sing this happy song to children and encourage them to make the
movements as you move.

If You're Happy and You Know It
    If you're happy and you know it,
    Clap your hands. (clap, clap)
    If you're happy and you know it,
    Clap your hands. (clap, clap)
    If you're happy and you know it,
    Then your face will surely show it.
    If you're happy and you know it,
    Clap your hands. (clap, clap)

Head, Shoulders, Knees, and Toes

12-18 months

Materials
None needed

Teacher Talk
"Where's your head, Michael? That's right. You touched your head."

Sing this rhyme and show babies the movements.

Head, Shoulders, Knees, and Toes
    Head, shoulders, knees, and toes,
    Head, shoulders, knees, and toes,
    And eyes and ears and mouth and nose.
    Head, shoulders, knees and toes, knees and toes.

MOVEMENT POSSIBILITIES

Pat-a-Cake

0-6 months

Materials
None needed

Teacher Talk
"You're playing pat-a-cake, Chelsea. This is fun."

Play pat-a-cake with young babies.

Pat-a-Cake
    Pat-a-cake, pat-a-cake, baker's man,
    Bake me cake as fast as you can.
    Pat and roll and mark it with "B."
    Put it in the oven for baby and me.

Stuffed Sacks to Carry

6-18 months

Materials
Paper sacks
Newspaper
Packing tape

Stuff paper sacks of all sizes with crumpled newspaper and tape with wide packing tape. Children will enjoy moving and carrying the paper blocks.

Box and Lid Match

6-18 months

Materials
Small and medium boxes with lids

Provide small and medium boxes for children to hold or to use to practice taking lids off and putting them on.

Phone Book Tearing

6-18 months

Materials
Used phone book

Show children how to tear pages from a phone book and crumple the pages into balls.

Paper Ball Toss

6-18 months

Materials
Used copy paper crumpled into balls
Basket

Teacher Talk
Talk with children about what they are accomplishing. "You can drop the paper ball in the basket. You did it!"

Show children how to drop the paper balls into a basket.

Dump and Load Laundry Hamper
6-18 months

Materials
2 safe, lightweight, large laundry baskets
Dress-up clothes

Provide two safe, lightweight laundry baskets, so children can take dress-up clothes from one hamper and place them in the other. They also will enjoy dumping out and loading up baskets. Model the process and describe your actions.

OUTDOOR POSSIBILITIES

Bouncy Seat Barefoot
0-6 months

Materials
Bouncy seat

Position young babies in bouncy seats. Take off their shoes and socks, so they can feel the grass as they bounce.

Texture Walk
6-18 months

Materials
None needed

Take infants on a texture walk outside (dirt, grass, sand, bark, mulch). Talk about the different textures the children see or gently help the baby touch the textures with her hand.

Pumpkin Carry
6-18 months

Materials
Pumpkins, coconuts, squash, corn, etc.
Wagon
Non-toxic markers, optional

Teacher Talk
Talk with children about what they are doing. "That is a big pumpkin. You are sitting on it."

Provide real pumpkins, coconuts, squash, and corn for children to carry and place in the wagon. Drawing with markers (remove caps as they present a choking hazard) on a pumpkin or squash will also be fun for children.

Outside Play Gyms
6-18 months

Materials
Play gyms
Blankets or quilts

Take play gyms from the classrooms outside and place them on blankets or quilts in the shade. Children will enjoy the change to the outdoors.

PROJECT POSSIBILITIES

Developmental Banners
6-18 months

Materials
Large piece of paper
Art materials, such as crayons, markers, etc.

Create banners to celebrate accomplishments in the classroom. "Brandon is walking!" "Leesha is sitting alone!" "Kendra has her first tooth!" Parents will enjoy learning about the accomplishments of their children and others in the classroom.

"I Can" Cans
6-18 months

Materials
Index cards
Pen or pencil
Coffee cans
Patterned contact paper or wallpaper scraps

Another way to document and celebrate children's accomplishments is by writing on an index card when the event occurs. For example, you may write something such as, "July 6th, John rolled over from back to front."

Make the "I Can" cans by covering coffee cans with patterned contact paper or wallpaper. Use the "I Can" cans as part of your parent-teacher conferences.

Pockets for Wall Hanging

Ask parents to provide discarded clothing with pockets. Make a wall hanging using a piece of heavy cloth. Attach the pockets to the cloth and hang in the classroom or secure to the floor. Provide items for children to place in pockets and take out of pockets. Or put pictures of Mom and Dad covered in clear contact paper inside pockets for children to discover. Talk with children about their parents as they play. Tell parents how the pockets will be used during the day to make the connection between the child's parents and school.

Walking Chart

Make an age chart of the children in your classroom. Mark the onset of walking for each child. This will highlight the range involved in normal development.

Supporting Possibilities

A number of different items are needed for use in this Possibilities Plan. Ask parents to collect empty food containers, empty cleaning containers, newspapers, phone books, boxes with lids, cleaning containers, coffee cans, and pockets from discarded clothing. Let parents know how the items will be used. Thoroughly inspect all items for safety before using them in the classroom.

Shadow Child

Invite parents to come into the classroom and shadow their child. This will give them a real appreciation of the many activities involved in the day at school. Ask parents to sign up, so there won't be too many people in the room at one time.

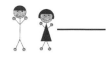

Picture Necklace

Make necklaces for parents by using lengths of yarn, children's photographs, poster board, a permanent marker, and clear contact paper. Glue each child's photograph to poster board and print the child's name underneath it. Print parent names above the picture. Have necklaces available for Parent Meetings and other school events.

Parent Postcards

Parent Postcards in this section are designed to share with parents during the Possibilities Plan. The topics are natural extensions of the activities and experiences that you are planning and implementing for the infants in the classroom. Use the Postcards to connect parents to their children's learning.

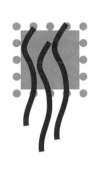

TO

Encouraging Independence and Autonomy

What are some of the ways parents can support emerging independence and autonomy? During the first year of life, infants are learning that they can trust the world in which they live to be a safe and responsive place. Quick responses to crying, sensitive matching of what you do to what the baby needs, and warm, caring, soothing, holding, and cuddling help children feel that they can trust the world to be a safe place. Support, love, attention, and affection in the early months are the cornerstones for future independence and autonomy.

Near the end of the first year, children begin to resist being helped by their parents. This behavior signals the beginning of a significant stretch for autonomy and independence and huge growth in several domains of development. Parents know when this happens. They pick their baby up, and he or she immediately wants to get down. They try to put on their child's shoes, and he or she grabs the shoes and attempts to put them on.

Encourage these early tries. Tell your child "nice try," even if the child doesn't succeed at first. Follow his or her lead on tasks where there is interest. Monitor your child's frustration, though, allowing just enough to keep interest but not so much that your child gets discouraged. Expect failure and mistakes, particularly in early attempts at a new skill. Noted psychologist Jean Piaget believed that children learn primarily by making mistakes and coming up with their own corrections. Making your own mistakes and figuring out solutions can be fun!

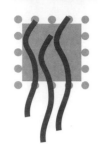

Continuing to Support Independence and Autonomy

Avoid taking over when your child makes a mistake. Let your child know you have confidence in his or her ability. Encourage your child to keep trying or to try again. Verbal support provides important feedback that you really feel your child can succeed. Talk children through what they are doing by describing their actions. "You've almost got your foot in the shoe," or "You finished all of your bottle!" These verbal cues help children see the impact of their actions as they occur and encourage a better understanding of how things work.

Expect regression as children learn and lose skills. Most emerging skills need repeated practice to be added to a child's developmental skill repertoire. Your child may accomplish a task once (like being able to sleep through the night or hold his or her own bottle) and then be unable to repeat that success in many subsequent tries. Your child may also lose interest in tasks for quite some time. This is a part of the natural process of learning and developing. Don't be alarmed when regression or loss of interest occurs.

Support and encourage early attempts at independence and autonomy, even though you may ultimately have to help complete the task. Early independence needs support even if the results are not quite what you expected. Success in putting on Daddy's shoes or finding one's own pacifier indicates progress toward independence. Validate these important steps as they occur with hugs, smiles, and encouragement.

TO

Concepts Learned in Competent Me

Concepts Learned

Clothes have pockets.

I can put things in pockets.

I can take things out of pockets.

I can put things in a bag.

I can put clothes in a hamper.

I can paint.

I can play outside.

I can listen to stories.

I can move to music.

I can put a box in a box.

I can put a can in a can.

I can pretend to garden, build, cook, and clean.

I can make noise with noisemakers and rattles.

Pots and pans have lids.

I can put a lid on a box.

I can feel flour/powder.

I can tear paper.

I can crumble paper into a ball.

I can carry things.

Resources

Prop Boxes

Cooking

Dishcloths

Dish towels

Empty food containers

Pans

Pots

Real and toy vegetables

Recipe cards

Utensils

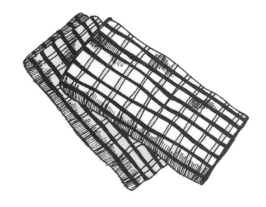

Cleaning
  Empty cleaning containers
  Hand broom
  Rags

  Small mop
  Squirt bottles
  Towels

Construction
  Blocks
  Construction hat
  Construction magazines/catalogs
  Paper plans or maps

  Small tape measure
  Toy tools
  Toy trucks

Picture File/Vocabulary

Babies involved in activities
Clothes with pockets
Construction site
Fruits
Kitchen
Laundry day
People on the telephone
Person building with tools

Person cleaning
Person cooking
Person gardening
Plants
Pots and pans
Tools
Trucks
Vegetables

Books

Can You Hop? by Lisa Lawston
Catch Me If You Can by Bernard Most
Dressing by Helen Oxenbury
No! No! Jo! by Kate McMullen
No! No! No! by Anne Rockwell (page 334)
You Can't Catch Me by Rosanne Litzinger (page 334)

Rhymes/Fingerplays

"Pat-a-Cake" (page 336)

Music/Songs

"If You're Happy and You Know It" (page 336)
"Head, Shoulders, Knees, and Toes" (page 336)

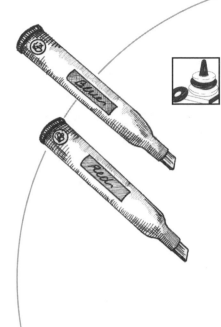

Toys and Materials

The following purchased items are important for this Possibilities Plan:

Art paper

Blocks

Books about babies

Books about mommies and daddies

Bouncer seats

Construction hats

Noisemakers

Play gyms

Toy telephone

Rattles

Ring-o-Links or other
   manipulatives

Telephone rattle

Toy Construction items

Toy tools

Trucks

Washable finger and tempera paint

Washable markers

The following gathered items will help support this Possibilities Plan:

Basket
Cleaning containers
Coffee cans
Contact paper or
 wallpaper scraps
Discarded clothes with pockets
 Dramatic play clothes
 Flour or powder
 Food containers for rattles
Gardening catalogs and magazines
Index cards
Newspapers
Paper scraps
Photographs of children in classroom
Pots and pans with lids
Prop box items
Shopping bags with handles

Windows, Walls, Doors, and Hallways

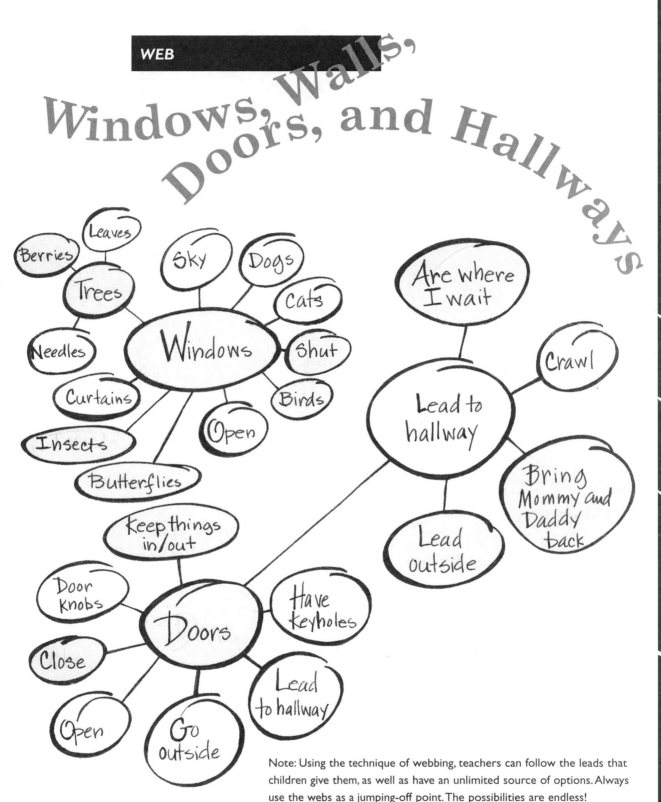

Windows
- Leaves
- Berries
- Trees
- Sky
- Dogs
- Cats
- Shut
- Needles
- Curtains
- Birds
- Open
- Insects
- Butterflies

Lead to hallway
- Are where I wait
- Crawl
- Bring Mommy and Daddy back
- Lead outside

Doors
- Keep things in/out
- Door knobs
- Have keyholes
- Close
- Open
- Go outside
- Lead to hallway

Note: Using the technique of webbing, teachers can follow the leads that children give them, as well as have an unlimited source of options. Always use the webs as a jumping-off point. The possibilities are endless!

Plan Possibilities

Dramatic

Sock Puppets 350
Box House 350
Window View 350
Where's Baby? 351
Cleaning Up 351
Swinging Door 351

Sensory/Art

Corn Pat 352
Cornhusk Painting 352
Plunger Art 352

Curiosity

Peek-a-Boo 353
Moving in the Mirror . . .353
Tape Grasp 353

Literacy

I See the Moon 354
Jack and Jill 354
Building a House 354
Doorbell Book 355
Books About Windows,
   Walls, Doors, and
   Hallways 355

Music

Go In and Out the
   Window 355
Are You Sleeping? 356

Movement

Pat-a-Cake 356
Johnny Jumper 356
Turntable Merry
   Go Round 357
Suspended Beach Ball 357

Outdoor

Blanket Talk 358
Stroll with Baby Dolls 358
Carrot Top Painting 358
Outside Squirt Bottles 359
Window Cleaning 359

Project

Memory Collage 359
How Tall? 360

Parent Participation

Front or Back Door Book . .360
Supporting Possibilities . . .360
Workday at School 360
Parent Postcard
   Childproofing Your Home 361

Windows, Walls, Doors, and Hallways

Concepts Learned in

Doors, Walls, Windows,

and Hallways. 362

Prop Boxes

Cleaning Up 362

Picture File/Vocabulary . . 363

Books

Bridges Are to Cross by Philemon Sturges 355
Building a House by Byron Barton 354
Door Bell, The by Jan Pienkowski 355
Harold and the Purple Crayon
    by Crockett Johnson
Houses by Claude Delafosse
Humpty Dumpty and Other Rhymes
    edited by Iona Opic

Rhymes/Fingerplays

"I See the Moon" 354
"Jack and Jill" 354
"Pat-a-Cake" 356

Music/Songs

"Are You Sleeping?" 356
"Go In and Out the Window" 355

Toys and Materials 364

Sock Puppets

0-6 months

Materials
Baby socks
Non-toxic permanent markers
Paper and pen

Teacher Talk
"See the face on the puppet, Wilson. It moves when you move your hand."

Draw faces on baby socks with permanent marker. Place them on baby's hands. Notice if the baby notices or focuses on either of the puppets. Record your observation.

Box House

6-18 months

Materials
Large cardboard box
Sharp knife or scissors (teacher only)
Pillow, dolls, blanket, etc.

Teacher Talk
"You're looking out the window, Shelton." "Dirk, you're sitting by the wall."

Make a house out of a cardboard box. Include a door and windows. Provide a pillow, cradle, dolls, and a blanket. Label the parts of the box house as children play. Supervise closely. Remove the roof if necessary.

Window View

6-18 months

Materials
Window or paper and markers

Teacher Talk
"The red wing blackbirds are at the bird feeder. When you clap your hands, they fly away."

If there is a window in the classroom, point to things outside and talk about them. If there is no window, take a walk outdoors with babies.

Where's Baby?
6-18 months

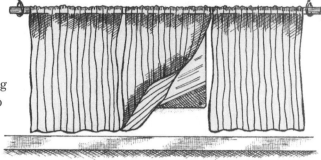

Materials
Curtains
Unbreakable mirror or pictures of babies

Teacher Talk
"Would you like to look for the baby? The picture of the baby is under the curtain. You found the baby!"

Create places of interest by hanging small sets of curtains convenient to babies as they sit or walk. Place a mirror or a picture of a baby under each curtain. Make a game by saying, "Where's baby?" and open the curtain. Continue to play if baby shows interest.

Cleaning Up
6-18 months

Materials
Box or basket
Empty, washed, cleaning containers

Use the cleaning-up prop box, so children can have housekeeping experiences. Check to be certain all items pass the choke test.

Swinging Door
12-18 months

Materials
Sturdy furniture
Large pieces of cardboard or side of a box
Tape

Using classroom furniture, tape, and the side of a box create a swinging door that opens into the space for dramatic play.

Corn Pat

0-6 months

Materials
Ear of corn

Teacher Talk
"The kernels of corn are yellow and smooth, Dawn."

Place baby's hand on an ear of corn. Talk about the feel of the silk, husk, and kernels. **Safety alert:** If individual kernels of corn fall off, be careful babies do not put the kernels into their mouths.

Cornhusk Painting

12-18 months

Materials
Cornhusks
Paper
Paint
Paper plates

Provide very large pieces of paper that completely cover a low table or a section of the floor. Place a blob of paint on a paper plate and help each child dip the end of the cornhusks into the paint. Then children can paint with the corn. **Note:** Early art experiences for infants are actually sensory in nature. Use washable, safe materials for all activities.

Plunger Art

12-18 months

Materials
Large piece of paper
Tape
Small, clean plungers
Paint
Paper plates

Teacher Talk
Talk about the process as you help the children. "The plunger made a circle on the paper, Keisha. Do you want to do another one?"

Secure a large piece of paper to a table or floor. Use small clean plungers to dip into paint and then stamp on the paper. This is a great activity for outside.

Peek-a-Boo

0-6 months

Materials
None needed

Play a game of peek-a-boo! Observe baby's reaction to determine if you should continue.

Moving in the Mirror

6-18 months

Materials
Unbreakable mirrors in different sizes and shapes

Provide many types of mirrors for children to explore. Very large mirrors mounted on the wall will give children opportunities visually to orient themselves to adults from different areas in the room. They also will be able to see themselves as they practice their moving skills. Talk with children about what they are seeing. Make a note when the child first discovers her own image in the mirror.

Tape Grasp

6-18 months

Materials
Wide masking tape

Teacher Talk
"Good job. You took the tape off the door."

Place short pieces (about 2" long) of wide masking tape on the door of the classroom. Only stick about half the length of the tape down. Show children how to use a pincer grasp (thumb and forefinger) to take the tape off the door. Supervise closely, so tape doesn't go in children's mouths.

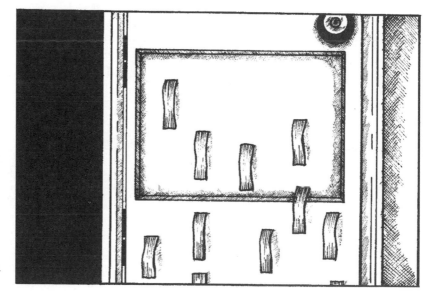

___ ## I See the Moon

0-18 months

Materials
None needed

Repeat this rhyme with babies. Point to the window and to yourself at appropriate times in the rhyme. Hug baby when
you finish the rhyme.

> *I See the Moon*
> I see the moon.
> The moon sees me.
> God bless the moon,
> And God bless me.

 ___ ## Jack and Jill

0-18 months

Materials
None needed

Recite this poem for children at
different times during the day. Observe
children's reactions as you say the
words.

> *Jack and Jill*
> Jack and Jill went up the hill,
> To fetch a pail of water;
> Jack fell down and broke his crown,
> And Jill came tumbling after.

 ___ ## Building a House

0-18 months

Materials
Building a House by Byron Barton

Share the book with each baby or with two or three babies at a time. Observe for skills such as pointing to pictures, saying sounds or words, and turning pages. Communicate your observations to parents on the Communication Sheet (pages 429-430).

Doorbell Book

12-18 months

Materials
The Door Bell by Jan Pienkowski

Young children love to explore sound books. Observe children's reactions to the sound of the doorbell in the book.

Books About Windows, Walls, Doors, and Hallways

0-18 months

Materials
Books about windows, walls, doors, and hallways, such as
>*Bridges Are to Cross* by Philemon Sturges
>*Building a House* by Byron Barton
>*Door Bell, The* by Jan Pienkowski
>*Harold and the Purple Crayon* by Crockett Johnson
>*Houses* by Claude Delafosse
>*Humpty Dumpty and Other Rhymes* by Iona Opie

Teacher Talk
"This book has lots of doors in it. We go out the door when we go outside." Talk about concepts whenever appropriate.

Use books that explore a variety of architectural forms or specific forms including windows, walls, doors, or hallways.

MUSIC POSSIBILITIES

Go In and Out the Window

0-18 months

Materials
None needed

Sing this song at appropriate times during the day. Point to the window as you sing.

>*Go In and Out the Window*
>>Go in and out the window.
>>Go in and out the window.
>>Go in and out the window,
>>As we have gone before.

 ## Are You Sleeping?

0-18 months

Materials
None needed

Sing this song when children are playing Night! Night! (page 63). Talk with parents about the songs and rhymes you use with children during the day. Make a copy of the words to send home to parents.

> *Are You Sleeping?*
> Are you sleeping,
> Are you sleeping,
> Brother John, Brother John?
> Morning bells are ringing,
> Morning bells are ringing.
> Ding, ding, dong!
> Ding, ding, dong!

MOVEMENT POSSIBILITIES

 ## Pat-a-Cake

0-6 months

Materials
None needed

Play pat-a-cake with infants and use a hand-over-hand approach to move their hands to the words. Observe baby's reactions to determine whether to continue.

> *Pat-a-Cake*
> Pat-a-cake, pat-a-cake, baker's man,
> Bake me cake as fast as you can.
> Pat and roll and mark it with "B."
> Put it in the oven for baby and me.

 ## Johnny Jumper

6-12 months

Materials
Johnny Jumper
Mirror, optional

Teacher Talk

Talk about what the infant is doing. "You are bouncing in the Johnny Jumper. Up and down, Marissa." "Look at Harris in the mirror on the wall."

Give each child an opportunity to bounce in the Johnny Jumper to strengthen leg muscles. Position a mirror nearby on the wall, so the child can watch herself jump. **Note:** Children should be in the Johnny Jumper no longer than 10 to 15 minutes.

Turntable Merry Go Round

6-18 months

Materials
Stuffed animal
Turntable or lazy Susan

Position a stuffed animal on a turntable or lazy Susan. Turn so the stuffed animal is in front of the baby. Turn again, so the stuffed animal is in front of you. Watch the baby's reaction to determine if you should continue the activity.

Suspended Beach Ball

12-18 months

Materials

Beach ball
String
Tape

Teacher Talk

Talk with babies about what they are doing as they hit the ball. "You hit the ball, Thomas. Can you hit it again?"

Suspend a beach ball from the ceiling in the classroom so that walking infants can hit it.

Blanket Talk

0-6 months

Materials
Blanket

Teacher Talk
Follow the baby's line of sight and talk about all the many things you can see outside. "You are looking at the tree, Thomas. The bird is on the branch."

Spread a blanket on the grass and place babies on it.

Stroll with Baby Dolls

6-18 months

Materials
Dolls
Stroller

Teacher Talk
Talk about what you are seeing outdoors. "I see a big truck!" "Look, a squirrel!"

Take infants and baby dolls outside for a stroll in the stroller.

Carrot Top Painting

6-18 months

Materials
Carrots with tops
Sharp knife (teacher only)
Paint
Paper plates
Paper
Tape

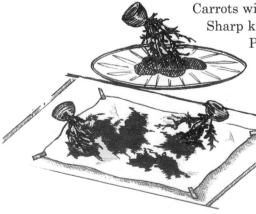

Cut the tops, with greens still attached, off carrots. Squirt some washable paint on a paper plate. Show babies how to dip the carrot tops in the paint and then rub them on large pieces of paper taped to the sidewalk.

Outside Squirt Bottles

12-18 months

Materials
Squirt bottles
Cool water

Provide squirt bottles with cool water in them. Show babies how to squeeze the bottles to make water come out. Examine all tops to be certain that they pass the choke test.

Window Cleaning

12-18 months

Materials
Sponges
Plastic bucket
Water (just a little)
Small plastic squeegee

Provide sponges, water, and a small plastic squeegee, so children can wash windows.

PROJECT POSSIBILITIES

Memory Collage

0-18 months

Materials
Large piece of paper
Pictures, photographs, and other creations from throughout the year
Poster tape

Create a collage by using a large piece of paper. Gather materials from the last year in your classroom. If you are borrowing materials from children's portfolios, be certain that materials have names, labels, and dates. Arrange the materials on the paper. Use a material, such as poster tape, that will attach papers to the large piece of paper and then let you remove materials, so you can place materials back in portfolios. Also, include any photographs that show activities in the classroom. Point to pictures and materials during the day and talk about them with children.

How Tall?

0-18 months

Materials
Strips of paper
Tape
Markers

Create individual growth charts for babies using strips of paper. Quarterly, measure and mark the charts. Lay babies on charts until they can stand safely. Include the date and anything memorable about the baby's reaction. Use the same procedure each time, so children will develop a familiarity with the process. Share the growth charts with parents during conferences.

PARENT PARTICIPATION ACTIVITIES

Front or Back Door Book

Provide a Polaroid camera and film. Send home with parents and ask them to take a picture of their front or back door. When all the photographs have been taken and returned to the classroom, place them in heavy-duty resealable plastic bags. Make a book by joining pages together with metal rings, short lengths of yarn, or duct tape. Talk to parents about how the pictures are used during the day to keep the connection between the child's family and the school.

Supporting Possibilities

A number of different items are needed for this Possibilities Plan. Ask parents to collect magazine pictures of doors, walls, windows, and hallways that can be mounted or covered with clear contact paper and displayed in the classroom. Also, ask parents to collect discarded baby socks, a large cardboard box, a medium cardboard box, discarded curtains, carrots with tops, corn in husks, squirt bottles, sponges, and plastic squeegees. Let parents know how the items will be used in *Windows, Walls, Doors, and Hallways*.

Workday at School

Invite parents to participate in a workday at the school. Ask parents to sign up for one hour. If parents are unable to help, ask if they can provide snacks or cleaning materials.

Parent Postcard

The Parent Postcard in this section is designed to share with parents during the Possibilities Plan. The topic is a natural extension of the activities and experiences that you are planning and implementing for the infants in the classroom. Use the Postcard to connect parents to their children's learning.

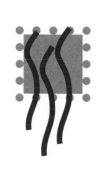

TO _____

Childproofing Your Home

As young children become more mobile, parents must childproof their homes. While babies are young, childproofing generally means being certain that dangerous materials are not allowed near babies. However, mobile children can find many dangers for themselves. For this reason, the entire house must be considered.

Many childproofing items are available from toy stores. Items include electric plug covers, cabinet locks, doorknob covers (to prevent a child from being able to twist the knob and enter or exit a room), and drawer locks. Materials high on a shelf are not necessarily out of reach. Be especially careful about cleaning materials.

Water is a great danger—even the water in the toilet. Because older babies are so top-heavy, they are in danger of leaning into a toilet or bucket and not being able to get out. Keep bathrooms off limits, and keep buckets empty and stored where babies cannot reach them. Young children need constant supervision. Never leave a child alone near water even for a minute. Not only large pools, but also wading pools and tubs are dangerous.

Choking hazards are a major source of danger for young children. Mouthing objects is one way your child learns about the world around him. Practically everything that goes in a baby's hand also goes in his or her mouth. To test for whether an item is a choke hazard, buy a commercial choke tester. If the item being tested fits entirely into the tube, it is a danger to your child. If a choke tester is not available, use an empty toilet paper tube. This tester is not exactly the same as a choke tube, but it is a good estimate.

Finally, walkers are a major concern. Despite the name, walkers do not actually help children learn to walk. Instead, they often make walking more difficult because of the positioning of the child. Walkers *are not recommended.* They are especially dangerous if floors are at different levels or if stairs are present.

It is an exciting time when your child starts to crawl and walk. Take the time to prepare your home for the adventure!

Concepts Learned

Concepts Learned in Doors, Walls, Windows, and Hallways

I can look out windows.

I can go in and out of doors.

I can paint with a plunger.

I can paint with a carrot top and with cornhusks.

I can play pat-a-cake.

I can play with puppets.

I can look at books.

I can squirt water.

School has doors.

School has walls.

School has windows.

School has hallways.

I can ride in a stroller.

I can climb in a box.

I can see myself in the mirror.

I can jump in the Johnny Jumper.

I can sit and play in the Exer-saucer.

I can play peek-a-boo.

I can see down hallways.

I can crawl down hallways.

I can read books.

I can hit a beach ball.

I can squirt water bottles.

Resources

Prop Boxes

Cleaning Up

Cloths	Empty, washed, cleaning containers
Dustbuster toy	Scrubber
Duster	Vacuum toy

Picture File/Vocabulary

Babies inside
Cleaning materials
Dolls
Doors
Hallways
Outdoor scenes
Puppets
Walls
Windows

Books

Bridges Are to Cross by Philemon Sturges
Building a House by Byron Barton (page 354)
Door Bell, The by Jan Pienkowski (page 355)
Harold and the Purple Crayon by Crockett Johnson
Houses by Claude Delafosse
Humpty Dumpty and Other Rhymes edited by Iona Opie

Rhymes/Fingerplays

"I See the Moon" (page 354)
"Jack and Jill" (page 354)
"Pat-a-Cake" (page 356)

Music/Songs

"Are You Sleeping?" (page 356)
"Go In and Out the Window" (page 355)

Toys and Materials

The following purchased items are important for this Possibilities Plan:

Beach ball
Blanket
Books about windows, walls, doors, and
    hallways
Exer-saucer
Finger paint and tempera paint
Johnny Jumper
Large drawing paper
Large wall mirrors
Polaroid camera and film
Small mirrors
Stroller

The following gathered items will help support this Possibilities Plan:

Baby pictures
Baby socks
Carrots with tops
Corn in husks
Curtains
Empty cleaning items (soap, dishwashing
    detergent, etc.)
Magazine pictures of windows, walls, doors,
    and hallways
Masking tape
Prop box items
Sponges and squeegees
Squirt bottles
Turntable

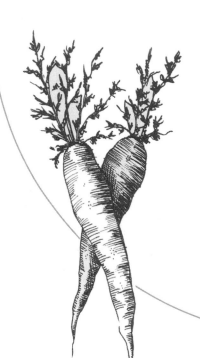

CHAPTER 7

Expressing Feelings with Parents, Teachers, and Friends

INTRODUCTION

Babies begin expressing their feelings and emotions right after birth. They communicate clearly whether an experience is a pleasant one or not! Infants often look like pure emotions when they screw up their faces and begin to cry. As they grow and mature, infants begin to differentiate feelings and pair those feelings with physical expressions that convey the differences between one emotion and another.

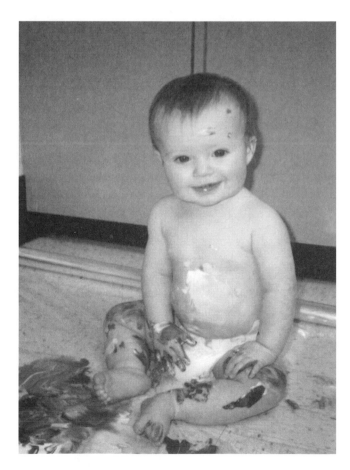

Learning to express oneself and to identify and understand emotions is a crucial part of growing up. For infants, this process is an emerging one—one that changes over time in the context of other developmental changes taking place.

New interest in the effects of emotions on the developing brain has put the emotional development of infants in the spotlight. During the first three years, the brain grows to about two-thirds of its full size and evolves in complexity at a greater rate than it ever will again. Key learning takes place in several important developmental domains during the period of infancy, including emotional learning. Pediatricians, educators, and other specialists emphasize the importance of supporting emotional learning in infants right from the start. In addition, these experts view emotional intelligence as important as physical, cognitive, and language ability.

INNOVATIONS IN OBSERVATION/ASSESSMENT

Observation/Assessment Instrument

The assessment instrument on the next page is not just a skills checklist. Instead it is designed to guide the teacher's observation of children's development through major interactional tasks of infancy. The assessment's focus is on what IS happening, not just what should happen or what will happen. Use this assessment to lead to developmentally appropriate practice.

Infant (0-18 months) Assessment

Task: Expressing Feelings with Parents, Teachers, and Friends

	0-6 months	**6-12 months**	**12-18 months**
E1	a. Begins to self-regulate; calms self after sensitive response from a caring adult.	b. Expects adults to respond to social cues such as vocalization, gestures, or cries	c. Knows which behaviors will make caregivers react in certain ways (for example, which actions will make you laugh and which ones will make you say "stop").
E2	a. Develops an interest in the world; is alert to sounds, touch, and faces.	b. Explores the environment; picks up objects of interest, then moves on to other objects.	c. Plays in a focused, organized manner.
E3	a. Gazes at faces with interest; smiles responsively.	b. Reaches up to indicate an interest in being held; is interested in social interaction with familiar adults.	c. Uses physical behavior (such as crawling over and pulling up) to establish closeness to caregivers.
E4	a. Seeks interactions with familiar people; vocalizes in response to vocalization.	b. Seeks to explore interesting toys, objects, and people.	c. Responds to limits that are set verbally; complies only with support from adults.
E5	a. Emotional reactions continue for a minute or two after an adult responds; does not recognize the change in state immediately.	b. Begins to coordinate behavior and emotions by acting on feelings; connects physical actions with needs (for example, goes over to the refrigerator to indicate interest in food or drink).	c. Recovers from emotional outbursts in a few minutes most of the time.

INNOVATIONS IN CHILD DEVELOPMENT

Emotional Development

Developmental theory tells us that children move through a predictable sequence of steps as they mature. These steps are observable and can be charted. Likewise, developmental theory tells us that each and every individual has his own pace of development. This holds true for the emotional area of development also.

Because infants are so dependent on adults to meet their immediate needs, their teachers need to be aware of this sequence of development, sensitive to the child's individual pace of development, and adept at determining ways to stimulate and challenge the emergence of skills.

Stanley Greenspan, noted developmental psychologist, describes the stages in the following way (Greenspan, 1994). In the first three months of life, infants learn to calm themselves and develop a multisensory interest in the world (touching, hearing, tasting, smelling, seeing, feeling). They are already able to express their personality by demonstrating individual preferences for certain kinds of sensory experiences.

The second stage of emotional development is what Greenspan calls "a time of falling in love." This stage lasts from months two through seven. At this time, infants develop a joyful interest in the human world. They use each of the senses to engage the adults in their world in interaction. Although objects in the world are interesting also, infants would much rather respond to an adult, particularly a familiar one. This striking preference for interactions with familiar adults is an important and crucial step in emotional development.

In the third stage, babies develop intentional communication. They begin to seek a cause-and-effect relationship with the most familiar adults in their lives. In seeking a dialogue with the human world, infants want their caregivers to know, for example, when they are hungry as opposed to when they want to be held. If parents and teachers are proficient at interpreting children's communication cues and responding appropriately to them, children learn that there are social laws for successful

interaction and they begin to follow these laws to get their needs met. As adults respond differently to infant communication cues (feed them when they are hungry and hold them when they need comforting), children learn to distinguish between their own needs and feelings. This stage lasts from months 3 to 10 and overlaps stage two.

In the fourth stage, which emerges from 9 to 18 months, infants learn how to coordinate their behavior with their emotions. And, because they are becoming more organized, they are able to use objects and take the initiative. An organized sense of self begins to emerge. The infant begins to link together units of cause-and-effect into chains. He will grab the teacher's hand and take the teacher over to his cubbie, point to the bottle, and say "muk" instead of merely crying for something to drink.

INNOVATIONS IN INTERACTIVE EXPERIENCES

Children's experiences at school have so much to do with the way they will grow and develop. If they experience school as negative, frustrating, or insensitive, they will view the learning process as overwhelming and insurmountable. If, on the other hand, their experiences are supportive, nurturing, and positive, human development has an almost perfect plan for growing and learning. In fact, during the first three years, development unfolds naturally for most children.

Many teachers view the activities they plan as the most important part of their job. Although this task is important, remember that infants are experiencing all the time—not just when teachers are providing direct stimulation. This curriculum advocates thinking about and planning for everything that can, by the nature of the setting (school vs. home), contribute to children's development and the teacher's relationship with the child and the family. What is outside the realm of activities in the classroom (for example, a child who takes longer to prepare to transition to another place, a child who naps much longer or shorter than expected, a child who is suddenly fascinated with an earthworm) is all curriculum. Children are always learning, and it is the teacher's job to support that learning in whatever forms it may take.

Life's minutiae build to create experiences. Infant teachers must be attuned to these everyday, yet important, experiences. They are truly the foundation upon which crucial skills and abilities grow. Think about the following list of experiences and make sure that the classroom reflects many of them.

- ☐ Label expressions of emotions, for example, "What a happy smile," or "That face is angry."
- ☐ Act authentically.
- ☐ Support practice play that deals with emotional issues.
- ☐ Prepare infants before strangers enter the classroom. Stay close to them, support their interests, and protect them from getting overwhelmed.
- ☐ Keep a predictable schedule during the school day. Times may vary, but the sequence stays the same.
- ☐ Prepare children when the teacher moves around the room. Take them with you when you can and prepare them in advance when you can't.
- ☐ Embrace separation anxiety as a normal part of emotional development.
- ☐ Stay nearby when babies are playing on the floor together. Facilitate appropriate behavior.
- ☐ Support appropriate interactions through patterning and modeling.
- ☐ Provide multisensory experiences for babies.
- ☐ Spend floor time with infants.
- ☐ Support emerging creativity by letting children choose their activities among a selected range of appropriate ones.
- ☐ Validate novel ways of doing things. When babies make things happen in a new or different way, recognize and celebrate their excitement.

INNOVATIONS IN TEACHING

Stimulating Emotional Development

Babies from birth through 3 months need to have opportunities to learn to calm themselves and to receive and respond to stimulation from the world. Learning to calm oneself does NOT mean that babies need to cry for a while before their teachers respond to them. On the contrary, they need prompt, quick attention to distress, so they can begin to feel the difference between comfort and discomfort. At this stage, a crying baby will continue to cry for a minute after being picked up because he does not recognize the change right away. Babies need practice determining when something has changed their situation and will learn to respond more quickly to the change.

Babies need plenty of sensory stimulation—seeing, hearing, touching and being touched, and smelling. Create and produce these experiences for infants. For example, hang an unbreakable mirror in the crib to catch indirect light and reflect the baby's face or a mobile overhead to attract visual attention. Give infants things that make noise when they are touched such as certain rattles, soft grab toys, and crib gyms. Music is important during this period; however, it must be more than just background noise (babies can't tune it out as well as adults can).

Babies need teachers who talk to them, touch them, snuggle them close, and challenge each of their senses to respond. In preparation for the next stage, very young infants need many real interactions with teachers, particularly the teachers with whom they will spend a major part of the day. Because emotional stages tend to overlap, infants begin to develop an intense interest in the human world while interacting with adults during this first stage. If children don't demand the adult's attention, it needs to be available anyway to stimulate social-emotional development.

From 2 to 7 months, babies need someone to fall in love with at the school—a special, caring, interesting, consistent person who woos the child's love and interest. Assigning a primary teacher is the first step in making sure the child at this stage has his needs met and his social-emotional growth facilitated. The rest comes naturally for most children. Ira Gordon (1970) calls the interaction during this stage "ping-ponging." The teacher smiles at the baby—the baby smiles back—the baby coos—the teacher talks back to him. This type of interaction forms the best environment possible to help infants continue to develop.

Senses need to be involved in stimulation, too. Touching, tasting, smelling, hearing, and seeing the world about them are a very important part of this stage. Opportunities to do so should be numerous and repetitive so that infants have many sensory experiences. By this stage, children should spend very little time in their cribs except when they are sleeping. Awake time should be spent near adults, watching, hearing, touching, smelling, tasting, and experiencing their environment and the things adults offer children.

From 3 to 10 months, babies need plenty of opportunities to see what happens if.... They are beginning to seek out cause-and-effect relationships, and the classroom should be full of them. Push-pull toys, squeak toys, adults who play hide-and-seek, water to pour, blankets to pull, and so forth. Babies also need alert, attentive teachers who don't wait until the infants are too tired to go to sleep or too hungry to eat. They need adults who can read their nonverbal cues and anticipate their needs. If adults can learn to do this, children will learn it also as they mature.

Getting a copy of the baby's regular schedule from his parents will help the teacher develop this sensitivity to cues. If you know a baby is likely to be hungry about 11:00 a.m., you can make sure the bottle is warmed and ready about 10:50 a.m. so that there is no waiting when the hunger bells go off. The same is true of elimination, sleeping, irritability, and so on. This is why primary teachers want to know everything about a baby that his parents can share. It makes the job of reading cues so much easier.

From 9 to 14 months, the organized sense of self begins to show itself in assertive exploration of everything. The infant begins to test limits and attempts to control and manipulate the world around him—including the adults in it. Firm, consistent limits are important even in situations when children are practicing being the boss or testing their independence. Notice once again the overlapping of stages. This stage is emerging between 9 and 14 months.

Make it a teaching practice to do floor time with the babies in your group. Fifteen to 20 minutes a day should be standard curriculum in your classroom!

Floor Time as a Practice

This curriculum proposes that floor time be used as a practice that supports children's emotional development. Floor time looks something like this. One or two children who are fed, rested, and ready to play join the teacher in an area of the classroom that is conducive to positive interaction. The teacher starts the practice of floor time by watching, listening, and being with the baby or babies. The teacher lets the child or children direct the time together. If a baby smiles at the teacher, the teacher smiles back. If a baby reaches out to be picked up, the teacher picks him up. Following the child's lead is the important part of floor time.

When babies pick up objects or toys, the teacher expands and extends the play to enhance the child's experience. For example, if the baby is kicking toys that jingle with his feet, the teacher might watch, smile when the toy jingles, and clap his hands indicating that the success of the kick was right on target.

Interactions such as these support infants' interest in the social world and validate that the teacher is going to support being a part of the social world. These interactions also fill children with feelings of competence. Once initiated through a supportive adult, the child will be able to reconnect with the feeling without the adult's support at a later time.

Beyond Products: Supporting Emerging Creativity in Young Children

When does creativity begin? Is it always present, or do teachers help it develop? The educators at Reggio Emilia believe that creativity is not an exceptional occurrence but a characteristic way of thinking, knowing, and making choices that is innate in all children (Edwards, Gandini & Forman, 1994). Viewed this way, creativity is part of the childhood experience—not something that teachers need to teach children during the early childhood years.

Creativity is the production of novel thoughts, solutions, and products based on previous experience and knowledge. Creativity is the integration of learning and creative thoughts, solutions, and products—not artistic creativity, or musical creativity, or movement creativity, and so on. Viewed this way, creativity *is* an early childhood experience and can be part of every teacher's classroom.

What can teachers do to foster integration of creativity and learning? Start with choice. Creativity blossoms when children are free to choose what to do, when to do it, how to do it, whom to do it with, and where to do it! Think about the infant classroom and the activities and experiences you plan for children. How often do you allow children to choose not only what, but also where, when, how, and with whom to do it?

Create an environment that fosters stability and novelty? Is that possible?! Aren't stability and novelty opposite ends of the same continuum? Children benefit from the stability of knowing where things are, where they will sleep, and the novelty of new, interesting, and unusual toys and experiences they encounter. Consider the following diagrams.

STABILITY———————→ NOVELTY

Teaching strategies that support emerging creativity in infants include listening and observing. Teachers who talk too much can't foster creativity. Listening, really listening, and observing children as they become fascinated by their own ideas and skills, encourages creativity. From this fascination comes wonderful observations by the child, clear insight from the teacher about what the child was trying to do, and wonderful questions to pose as children play.

Look for ideas, not answers. It is the process—the exploration—that leads to learning, not isolated facts presented to children during teacher-directed times. Instead of telling children how things work, let them find out. Instead of showing children where things are, let them search for them. Instead of anticipating the infant's next move, wait to see if it unfolds the way that you thought it might.

Repeat experiences often. Project Possibilities in each chapter are examples of ways to stimulate creativity with repeated experiences. Repetition develops a crucial creative skill—persistence to task. Task persistence leads children to explore, fostering creativity.

Validate children's novel ideas and ways of doing things. Children who scoot on their bottoms instead of crawling on hands and knees are still getting from place to place. Infants who repeat favorite activities again and again are still practicing important tasks. Don't be in a hurry to narrow children's activities into what you or parents expect. Instead, wait with patience as creativity takes its course.

Guidance and Discipline

Managing Normal Aggression in Very Young Children

Aggression is a normal part of young children's experiences. Aggression results from powerful emotions that are not yet under the child's direct control. Children hit, pinch, bite, slap, and grab when their emotions cause them to act before they can think about doing something different.

Children learn to manage aggression when supportive adults help them learn other skills and connect consequences with aggression. Using aggression to stop aggression only teaches children that they must submit to adults who are bigger and more powerful. It does not help children gain control over aggressive behavior or replace it with more appropriate skills. Replacing aggressive behavior with more sophisticated skills is a process. Learning to express feelings appropriately is a lifelong task. The first steps are taken in the first three years.

The following are some examples of ways supportive teachers can meet aggression with consequences from the earliest stage.

🌐 When a baby bites your finger, exploring the feel of pressure on his gums, say that biting hurts and put the baby down. Tell the baby that your finger is not for biting, and don't let the baby put your finger in his mouth again. What babies learn is the consequence of biting—close contact between teacher and baby goes away for a minute.

🌐 When an older infant pokes a finger in your nose, ears, eyes, or mouth, take his hand firmly in yours and say that you will hold hands until he can keep his fingers out of your face. Every time you get poked, hold the baby's hands away from your face saying, "I'll hold your hands if you can't keep them out of my eyes." After trying this for a while, tell the older infant that you must hold hands when you pick him up because you don't want fingers in your nose, and so on. After doing this a few times, give the older infant a chance to keep his hands to himself. If he doesn't, repeat the process.

🌐 When an older infant grabs a toy away from a friend, explain that the friend had the toy first and return the toy to the friend. Offer another idea about how to get the toy back. Tell the infant to put out his hand, asking the friend with a gesture to put the toy in his hand. If the older infant falls apart when you do this, remove him from the situation until he is calm enough to return to play.

Early experiences with the consequences of aggression help children learn over time that aggressive behavior doesn't accomplish much. After this lesson is learned, children can begin the process of becoming assertive enough to prevent being victimized and authoritative enough to be seen as a leader. Both of these important lessons will never be learned unless both teachers and parents help children learn to manage normal aggression and convert it into constructive assertion and leadership.

Conferencing with Parents of Infants

Parent conferences are an accepted part of school. Conferences form the foundation of the communication system between parents of infants and the programs in which children spend their day. But, the length of the care and early education day and the busy schedules of working parents often leaves teachers wondering how to make this crucial part of the program a viable one.

Communicating with Parents of Infants Is Different

For parents of infants, parent conferences are actually part of a broader communication and conferencing system. The system is based on five underlying assumptions. The first assumption is that communication, and therefore, conferencing, needs to take place more often. The twice-a-year format of preschool conferences is simply inadequate for both infants and their parents.

The second assumption is that family systems have many adjustments to make as they transition to parenthood. Parenting in the United States is a lonely endeavor. Close relatives, neighborhoods as community, and same-age and stage friends have gone the way of the dinosaurs for most families. Further, the workplace is only just beginning to understand the challenges working parents are facing, and many families are separated from the support systems that once made parenting a shared experience. As a result, schools are the places new families connect with resources to help them become good parents. This new reality puts even more pressure on schools as they attempt to meet these new demands.

The third assumption is that parents of infants are different than parents of older children. There is little argument that this is true, particularly for first-time parents. The question is what to do about it without wearing out teachers.

The fourth assumption is that a wider variety of formats is required for communicating and conferencing with parents of infants. One type of communication and conferencing is not enough.

A fifth assumption is that a communication and conferencing system has to provide a wider range of resources in a wider variety of formats. Parents of infants want and need more. They need more information from a wider variety of sources. They want more time to discuss their ideas and concerns with caring teachers. They need more support in understanding development and much more opportunity to understand the difference between their "ideal" view of what parents can or should do and what is realistic or practical to do.

Conferences Are Parent Education

Conferences are a component of parent education. There are five goals of parent education:

1. To help parents develop self-confidence in their own parenting style;
2. To increase their understanding of child development;
3. To enhance parenting skills so that parents are able to support their child's increasing developmental competence;
4. To empower parents to make good parenting decisions and choices; and
5. To connect parents to resources.

To address each of these goals, it is necessary to re-conceptualize conferencing into a broader system.

Re-conceptualizing Conferencing

Re-conceptualizing conferencing into a more multidimensional approach lessens the feeling of being overwhelmed by infant parents. Parent communication and conferencing is an ongoing, two-way communication system between parents, the school, and the teacher. The communication system should include four types of communication and conferencing:

1. Formal face-to-face conferences with written documentation;
2. Informal conferences in a written format;
3. Formal oral conferences that occur at checkpoints in the school schedule; and
4. Informal oral conferences that occur as a part of the regular interface between the parent and the teacher.

Let's look at each of these types of communicating and conferencing.

Formal Conferences with Written Documentation

This is the traditional conference. Parents and the teacher sit together to review some sort of written evaluation of the child's developmental repertoire. Anecdotal notes by the teacher, normative developmental assessment with checklists, and summaries of the child's developmental stage are common components of this type of conference. Formal conferences with written documentation are an important part of the parent education process because it validates the importance of parental understanding of the child's age and stage.

What is often missing from the formal conference is an opportunity for the parents of the infant to let teachers know about their feelings, issues, or concerns. Formal conferences are often directed by the teacher, who shares information she or he has collected with the parents. To help make

---

Open-ended Conference Questions

- What are your observations about your child's experience at school?
- What are his or her most interesting characteristics?
- What concerns do you have about your child?
- What questions do you have about how your child spends his or her day?
- What plans should we make for your child in the next few weeks or months?
- Has anything changed in your family that we should be aware of?
- What has been your child's response to other children in the program?
- Is there anything we should change about your child's day at school?

parents a part of the formal conference process, before the conference ask them to identify things they would like to include or discuss. A series of open-ended questions to think about before the conference might be helpful to parents to stimulate their thinking about what they might want to discuss.

Informal Conferences with Written Documentation

It seemed like it started all at once for Ying Chu. One day, she began to cry loudly when her mother or father dropped her off at school or came in the door to pick her up. The teacher reported similar behavior from Ying Chu during the day. She said that every time she moved away, Ying Chu started to scream and cry, particularly when the teacher was helping another baby.

Ying Chu's mother was distressed with this change. Until that point, everything had been going fine. She wondered where this behavior was coming from and was considering looking for another school for her child.

Every perceptive infant teacher knows that Ying Chu is experiencing separation anxiety—the normal separation behavior that accompanies the attachment process. Why then, didn't Ying Chu's mother know what was going on?

Infants change so dramatically during the first three years. They go from helpless, dependent, puzzling newborns to walking, talking, and interacting toddlers. This is a dramatic and rapid process with many developmental changes and dilemmas. Parents, particularly first-time parents, need opportunities to understand and support this rapid developmental growth.

Because this development takes place so quickly, it must be shared as it happens. Parents of infants need help seeing the little changes that indicate developmental growth, not just the easily observable milestones like pulling to a stand or walking. Informal written communication can fill this role. This communication is also called anecdotal notes (see page 428 in the Appendix). Observations of what happened, when it happened, where it happened, and with whom it happened are written down to consider later for implications or conclusions.

Seizing the opportunity to share this type of developmental data on a regular basis creates a wonderful dialogue between parents and teachers. Try using an inexpensive notebook for each infant. Start by writing one anecdotal note a week on each child. Then send the notebook home and ask the parents to write one anecdotal note about what happens at home. This back and forth of observations—not opinions or judgments—hones skills for both parties. Teachers learn to observe babies' behavior as a source of notes, and parents become good observers of their child's developmental growth.

Something else also happens. Parents get a glimpse of what teachers do all day besides diaper, feed, and hold infants. Informal written communication reinforces that observing is a crucial part of the teacher's role as well as communicating that parents are important sources of information about their child's development. It also gives teachers the perfect opportunity to share other resources with parents. Written materials, videotapes, reference books, professional organizations, and support from other parents with similar experiences can all be offered to enhance the parent education process.

Ying Chu's parents needed opportunities to note her increasing discomfort with arrival and departure, to discuss separation anxiety and how normal it is, to read about separation anxiety, and to talk to other parents whose child is through this stage. Ying Chu's family would be more knowledgeable and less worried about this emerging emotional developmental milestone if these types of conferences had occurred.

Formal Oral Conferences

Madeline and Raj, parents of Amanda, have been enrolled since their baby was six weeks old. At about six months, they requested a conference with the infant coordinator to discuss concerns they were unable to work out with their teacher.

Conversation during the conference revealed that the family was satisfied with the routine care that their daughter was getting and happy with the teacher's relationship with the Amanda. It also revealed that they had no concerns about their child's safety or health, and that they felt the teacher did a good job of communicating with them about Amanda's daily patterns of eating, sleeping, and diaper changes.

What then was the problem? Madeline had seen another teacher reading a story to one of her babies and was extremely concerned that Amanda was never read to at school. Because she had never seen it, it wasn't happening. In spite of notes to the contrary on the daily communication sheet and posted curriculum plans indicating which books were being read, Madeline and Raj were concerned about their child's cognitive and language growth because they hadn't observed it happening.

As this vignette illustrates so vividly, points of view can be very different. For this family, all of the usual concerns were absent. Health and safety, attention, written information about the child's daily schedule, and so on were of no concern. One observation during arrival or departure led them to conclude that their child was in some way left out of an important developmental experience.

What we share with parents is as important as what we don't share. Every teacher of infants knows that early exposure to books is an important curriculum activity that fosters a love of reading in later life. Books are read to infants in schools every day. But how often do we share with parents that we read to their child every day?

Building in checkpoints for regular exchanges between parents and their child's teachers is an important part of the conferencing system. T. Berry Brazelton (1992) identified touchpoints that offer pediatricians an opportunity to discuss upcoming developmental changes and progress. Perhaps we need a touchpoints-like approach to formal oral conferencing!

Consider formal oral conferences at the end of the first full week of school, one month later, and at least quarterly thereafter. In addition, formal oral conferences might be helpful any time something is going to change—like a teacher's schedule or a change in staffing.

Although this seems like a lot of conferences, they can take place fairly simply by telephone. The scheduling problems of face-to-face conferences can be almost completely avoided.

Frequent connections such as these confirm that everyone is on the same page and that nothing is going on that needs attention. Structure the conferences so similar topics are covered each time. Setting up the conference this way will encourage efficient use of the time allotted and prevent overlooking emerging problems. Keep the notes from the conversation each time to analyze for trends, continued concerns, or perhaps, even compliments to share with other teachers.

Informal Oral Conferences

Informal oral conferences that occur as a part of the regular interface between parents and the child's teacher are the last type of conference. These take place daily during arrival or departure time. Don't overlook them as important, and don't overlook them as conferences. Parents get their view of their child's experiences from these verbal exchanges. The amount and accuracy of these conversations can either build confidence or concern.

Confidence builds as the infant teachers show their connection with the baby. Concern builds if opening and closing teachers aren't reliable reporters of the child's experience or can't share information with parents when asked.

Operational supports help. Written communication systems such as Communication Sheets (see pages 429-430 in the Appendix), telephone calls from the child's primary teacher who arrives after the parent drops off the child or before the child leaves, and varying schedules so parents see their child's teacher either upon arrival or departure all help. And, this is an ongoing staff development issue. Helping early and late teachers see the importance of arrival and departure interactions as crucial parent conferences is a topic worth discussing often.

Parents of infants do require teachers to invest in building a relationship. The outcome of the investment is parents whose parenting skills grow as their baby matures and develops. Taking the time to set up and implement a multidimensional conferencing system makes conferences become parent education.

Preventing Child Abuse and Neglect

Child Abuse Prevention

The safety and well-being of the children in school is a foremost concern and, therefore, child abuse reporting laws must be taken very seriously. Staff are required by federal law and often, state or local laws, to report any suspected child abuse, regardless of who is the suspect or where the abuse may have occurred. The teacher or the school does not make a judgment about actual abuse. It is the responsibility of the appropriate agency to investigate the allegation and make a judgment. The role of program staff is to report any conditions that indicate the possibility of suspected abuse or neglect.

Documentation of Suspected Abuse

The best way to assure thorough and accurate documentation of suspected child abuse is to have a system for anecdotally recording data on each child in the classroom on a regular basis. Communication sheets serve well for this purpose. Record any and all information related to the child as it comes to a teacher's attention. For example, if a child arrives in your classroom with a scratch on his cheek, a quick note of the date, the time, and a description of the scratch is recorded under the teacher comments section. Facts, not opinions, are recorded. Note the example on the right.

John arrived at the center at 7:55 a.m. When he took off his hat, a silver dollar-size bump and bruise were noticed above his right eye. His mother reported that he had walked into the corner of the dining room table over the weekend.

This account is accurate and nonthreatening. It indicates when and where the injury was noticed and establishes the explanation given for the injury. It does not indicate that John is abused or neglected. It is just a record of the incident. If John had repeated injuries, suspicious injuries, or considerably different behavior after the injury, a report to the appropriate agency may be necessary. The better the records, the more likely the child's best interest will be served.

The same is true for even minor injuries that occur at the school. Record the information for the parent to review when picking up the child. Under no circumstances should accident information be hidden. Even minor injuries deserve reporting to parents.

Teacher Competencies to Support Infants Expressing Feelings with Parents, Teachers, and Friends

Sometimes	Usually	Always	
☐	☐	☐	Checks infants periodically for wetness; asks the child first if he needs changing.
☐	☐	☐	Assures that children have frequent opportunities for success. Delights in each child's success, expresses kindness and support when children are struggling with developmental challenges, and supports children in learning from their mistakes.
☐	☐	☐	Uses vocabulary, materials, activities, and experiences that are suitable for the age, stage, temperament, and learning styles of children in her or his group.
☐	☐	☐	Exhibits flexibility in carrying out activity and experience plans.
☐	☐	☐	Shows imagination and spontaneity in building on children's interests for developing curriculum rather than depending exclusively on pre-prepared curriculum.
☐	☐	☐	Plans, implements, and evaluates parent-teacher conferences, intake interviews, and gradual enrollment.
☐	☐	☐	Plans, implements, and evaluates parent participation activities.
☐	☐	☐	Models the recognition and expression of feelings by naming her or his own feelings.
☐	☐	☐	Uses modeling and patterning as strategies for helping babies interact successfully.
☐	☐	☐	Understands that social roles and expectations for children in their family setting may be different from what is expected at school. Helps children make the transition between these two different sets of expectations and helps children behave appropriately in each.
☐	☐	☐	Serves as a social model by building a relationship with each child and family and by maintaining positive relationships with other teachers. Provides children with a break from social interaction or over-stimulation as needed.
☐	☐	☐	Watches and observes children at play and throughout the school day.

Resources for Teachers

Goleman, D. (1995). *Emotional intelligence.* New York: Bantam Doubleday Dell.

Goleman, D. (1998). *Working with emotional intelligence.* New York: Bantam Doubleday Dell.

Greenspan, S. & N.T. Greenspan. (1994). *First feelings: Milestones in the emotional development of your baby and child.* New York: Penguin.

INNOVATIONS IN PARENT PARTNERSHIPS

School- or Teacher-initiated Possibilities

Emotions Pictures

Ask parents to provide at home pictures of their child expressing different emotions. Or, they may provide photographs of family members showing intense emotions. Or, they can cut pictures from magazines of different emotions. Label the pictures with the emotion illustrated. Cover them with clear contact paper and post them around the room, so you can point to the pictures as you talk about emotions.

Muffins for Mom

Invite mothers to a "Muffins for Mom" informal breakfast. Make preparation easy and expect breakfast to be brief. Express your appreciation for what each mom does to support her child's learning throughout the year. A thank-you note to moms is always appreciated!

Doughnuts for Dad

Invite fathers to a "Doughnuts for Dad" informal breakfast. Make preparation easy and expect breakfast to be brief. Express your appreciation for what dads do to support their child's learning throughout the year. A thank-you note to dads is always appreciated! **Note:** With Muffins for Mom and Doughnuts for Dads, be sensitive to family configurations of the children in your class. An uncle or grandparent who is raising the child, or a same-gender parent all need to be included.

Parent Postcards

Parent Postcards can be shared with parents as they indicate an interest, at appropriate times during the enrollment cycle, or as developmental issues arise. (See pages 441-444 in the Appendix for a sample dissemination schedule.) Copy postcards. Cut if necessary. Address to parent(s) and place on Communication Sheet or hand out personally.

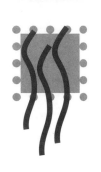

TO

Managing Normal Aggression in Very Young Children

Every parent dreads the day when the teacher reports that his or her child is responsible for hurting another child. But that day will come. Aggression is a normal part of young children's experiences. Aggression results from powerful emotions that are not yet under the child's direct control.

Children hit, pinch, bite, slap, and grab when their emotions cause them to act before they can think about doing something else.

Children learn to manage aggression when supportive adults help them learn other skills and connect consequences with aggression. Using aggression to stop aggression only teaches children that they must submit to adults who are bigger and more powerful. It does not help children gain control over aggressive behavior or replace it with more appropriate skills. Learning to express feelings appropriately is a lifelong task. Replacing aggressive behavior with more sophisticated skills is a process. The first steps are taken during the first three years.

The following are some examples of ways supportive parents can meet aggression with consequences from the earliest stage.

- When your baby bites your finger, exploring the feel of pressure on his or her gums, say that biting hurts, and put the baby down. Tell your baby that your finger is not for biting, and don't let the baby put your finger in his or her mouth again. What babies learn is the consequence of biting—close contact between parent and baby goes away for a minute.

TO

Managing Normal Aggression in Very Young Children (continued)

When your older infant pokes a finger in your nose, ears, eyes, or mouth, take his or her hand firmly in yours and say that you will hold hands until he or she can keep fingers out of your face. Every time you get poked, hold the baby's hands away from your face saying, "I'll hold your hands if you can't keep them out of my eyes." After trying this for a while, tell your older infant that you must hold hands when you pick him or her up because you don't want fingers in your nose, etc. After doing this a few times, give your older infant a chance to keep hands to him- or herself. If your child doesn't, repeat the process. The consequences of poking mom's or dad's eyes is that the baby's hands get held to prevent poking.

When your infant grabs his or her sibling by the hair and pulls, separate the two and hold the child whose hair was pulled until he or she calms down and gets under control. Help the older sibling tell the infant to stop pulling hair without being aggressive or hurting the baby—by using words. Tell both children, "Pulling hair didn't solve the problem." Then offer an alternative such as, "Call me when you need help getting a toy back."

Early experiences with the consequences of aggression help children learn over time that aggressive behavior doesn't accomplish much. After this lesson is learned, children can begin the process of becoming assertive enough to prevent being victimized and authoritative enough to be seen as a leader. Both of these important lessons will never be learned unless parents and teachers help children learn to manage normal aggression and convert it into constructive assertion and leadership.

Resources for Parents

Add these helpful books to your parent library or post this list on your parent bulletin board.

Brazelton, T. B. (1992). *Touchpoints: The essential reference.* Reading, MA: Addison-Wesley.

Goleman, D (1995). *Emotional intelligence.* New York: Bantam Doubleday Dell.

Greenspan, S. & N.T. Greenspan. (1985). *First feelings: Milestones in the emotional development of your baby and child.* New York: Viking.

INNOVATIONS IN ENVIRONMENTS

Windows and Natural Light

Our colleagues at Reggio Emilia were right! The Reggio classrooms for infants and toddlers are bright, open spaces, well lighted with natural light. These educators feel that seeing the day wax and wane is a part of very young children's discoveries about the world in which they live. Now, brain research has documented the incredible value of natural light. Children with natural light and windows in their room have been reported to do better on academic tasks and learn more readily when new information is presented to them (Houston Chronicle, 1999).

Not Too Much Stuff

The arrangement of toys and materials on storage units and shelves varies considerably for infants. Nonmobile infants need resources available near the areas they are playing, so teachers can replace toys that have lost appeal or have been discarded. Mobile infants need a more limited selection of toys arranged enticingly on low shelves. They tend to play with toys, then drop them, and move on. When they do, classrooms with too much stuff become cluttered and uninviting.

Open baskets and clear containers make it possible for mobile infants to identify what is available. They also allow teachers to change often what is presented to babies and to re-sort toys back into their storage containers after sanitizing.

Activities and Experiences vs. Centers

Most early childhood educators think of interest or learning centers as an essential part of any classroom setting. Yet, environments for infants are different because they cannot choose to go to different areas until they are mobile. For this reason, teachers bring the activities and experiences to the child, or they assist children in going to where the activities are. In each of the following two Possibilities Plans, *Senses* and *Bubbles, Mud, and Puddles*, activities and experiences are presented in the following areas:

- Dramatic Possibilities
- Sensory/Art Possibilities
- Curiosity Possibilities
- Literacy Possibilities
- Music Possibilities
- Movement Possibilities
- Outdoor Possibilities
- Project Possibilities
- Parent Participation Possibilities

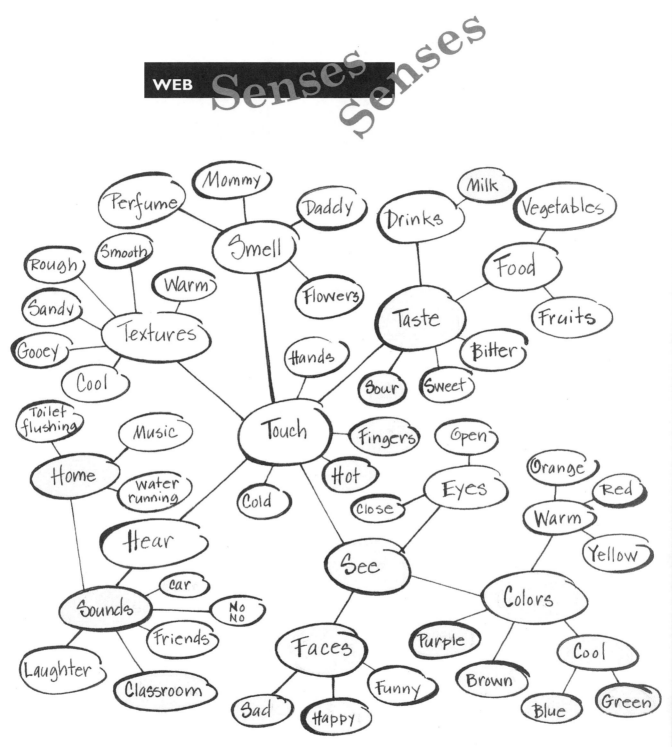

WEB

Senses Senses
Senses

Note: Using the technique of webbing, teachers can follow the leads that children give them, as well as have an unlimited source of options. Always use the webs as a jumping-off point. The possibilities are endless!

PLANNING PAGES

Plan Possibilities

Dramatic

Rattles 392
Dramatic Rattles 392
Prop Box Fun 392
Special Scents 393
Toy Binoculars 393
Teacher-made Binoculars 393

Sensory/Art

Flour/Powder Pat 394
Shredded Paper in the
   Sensory Table 394
Gelatin Blocks 394
Scented Finger Painting 395
Texture Wall 395

Curiosity

Peek-a-Boo Tube 395
Tracking Tube 396
Mirror Play 396
Wrapping Toys 397

Literacy

Chocolate-Covered Cookie Tantrum .397
Texture and Activity Books 397
No, No, No! 397
Senses Books 398
Eye Winker, Tom Tinker 398
Clap, Clap, Clap Your Hands 398

Music

Where Is Thumbkin? 399
Where Is Baby? 399
Old MacDonald Had a Farm 400
Baby Bumblebee 400

Movement

Johnny Jumper 401
Carpet Squares 401
Rattles and Drums Band 401

Outdoor

Change Perspective 402
Fence Painting 402

Project

Body Painting 402
Water Paints 403

Parent Participation

Handkerchief from Home 403
Handkerchief Return 403
Invitation to Visit 404
Parent Postcard
   Cooking with Kids 404

Senses

Concepts Learned in

Senses **405**

Prop Boxes

Things That Go on My Hands! 405
Things That Go on My Head! . .405
Things That Go on My Feet! . .405

Picture File/Vocabulary **406**

Books

Bright Eyes, Brown Skin by Cheryl Willis Hudson
Chocolate Covered Cookie Tantrum
   by Deborah Blumenthal 397
Clap Your Hands by Lorinda Bryan Cauley 398
My Five Senses by Aliki
My Five Senses by Jan Belk Monclure
No, No, No! by Anne Rockwell 397
No! No! Jo! by Kate McMullen
Pat the Bunny by Dorothy Kunhardt 397
Touch Me by Eve Witte and Pat Witte 397

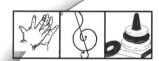

Rhymes/Fingerplays

"Clap, Clap, Clap Your Hands" 398
"Eye Winker, Tom Tinker" 398

Music/Songs

"Baby Bumblebee" 400
"Old MacDonald Had a Farm" 400
"Where Is Baby?" 399
"Where Is Thumbkin?" 399

Toys and Materials **407**

Rattles

0-6 months

Materials
Rattles

Use rattles to show action-reaction for young infants. Gently shake the baby's rattle and then pause to see if he will want to do the same. Observe baby to see if he is ready to play.

Dramatic Rattles

6-18 months

Materials
Clean, empty of baby lotion, shampoo, etc.
Items to place inside the containers
Glue and tape

Teacher Talk
Talk with children about what they are doing. "You're shaking the box, Elizabeth. Rattle! Rattle! Listen to the sound the box makes!"

Clean, empty containers of baby lotion, shampoo, baby powder, and food items will make excellent noise items. Place different items inside the containers. Then securely glue and tape the tops.

Prop Box Fun

6-18 months

Materials
See suggestions for prop boxes on page 405

Use materials from prop boxes for Things That Go on My Head, Things That Go on My Hands, and Things That Go on My Feet to help children explore their senses.

_____ **Special Scents**

6-18 months

Materials
Extracts, flower-scented water, etc.
Classroom cloths
Paper and pen

Provide special scents on the cloth items children will play with. Use scents such as lemon, vanilla, and rosemary. Observe and record children's reactions on the Communication Sheet (page 430) or on an Anecdotal Record (page 248).

 _____ **Toy Binoculars**

12-18 months

Materials
Toy binoculars

Teacher Talk
Talk about what children can see through the lenses. "Look at the pretty leaves, Carey. It's easier to see them through the binoculars."

Interact with children as they play with toy binoculars.

 _____ **Teacher-made Binoculars**

12-18 months

Materials
Cardboard tubes
Tape

Make binoculars by taping together cardboard tubes for children to play with.

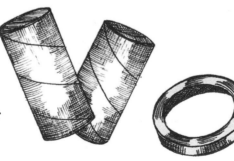

Flour/Powder Pat

0-6 months

Materials
Shallow tub
Flour or powder

Teacher Talk
Talk about how soft the flour/powder is on baby's skin.

Place baby's hand in a shallow tub of flour or powder. If you are using powder, be certain that the powder is non-toxic.

Shredded Paper in the Sensory Table

6-18 months

Materials
Shredded paper
Sensory table

Use shredded paper that is cut in long strips. Place paper in the sensory table for a very different tactile experience for infants.

Gelatin Blocks

6-18 months

Materials
Gelatin blocks

Teacher Talk
Talk about the feel of the gelatin. "Anetria, I see you touching the gelatin. Look at it wiggle!"

Provide gelatin blocks on the chair tray, table, or in the sensory table for an interesting sensory experience.

Scented Finger Painting

6-18 months

Materials
Large pieces of paper
Finger paint
Added scents, such as vanilla, cinnamon, lemon, etc.

Teacher Talk
Watch the children's reactions, and then talk with them about their reactions. "Bo, you are shaking your head. The paint smells like vanilla."

Early art experiences for infants are actually sensory in nature. Provide very large pieces of paper that completely cover a low table or a section of the floor. Use washable, safe finger paint. As a variation, add items with interesting scents to the paint (cinnamon, vanilla, lemon).

Texture Wall

6-18 months

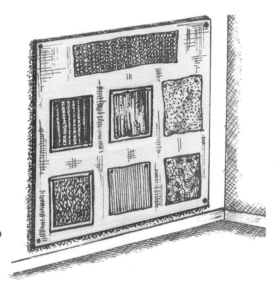

Materials
Large box
Scissors
Cloths, sandpaper, bark, etc.
Glue
Tape

Create a texture wall using a panel from a very large box. Glue a variety of cloths and other items (sandpaper, bark, fabric, paper) to the cardboard. Attach the panel to a low area of the wall, so babies can explore it.

CURIOSITY POSSIBILITIES

Peek-a-Boo Tube

0-6 months

Materials
Clear plastic cylinders   Construction paper
Tennis ball   Glue
Strong clear tape

Use a clear plastic cylinder (such as tennis balls, socks, or underwear may be packaged in). Place a piece of construction paper inside the cylinder to cover half of the inside. Place a tennis ball in the container. Glue the container shut and cover with strong, clear tape, such as book tape. When the ball rolls into the section with the paper, it will hidden. When the ball rolls into the clear section, the ball will be visible. Play a Where's the Ball? also known as Ball Peek-a-Boo! Watch to see if the baby visually tracks the ball.

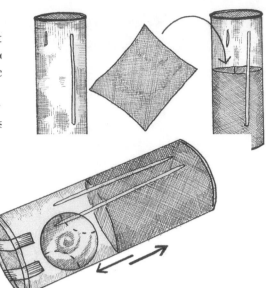

? _____ Tracking Tube
0-6 months

Materials
Tracking tube

Teacher Talk
Talk about what the baby is seeing. "The red ball is moving, Tommy. You are looking at the ball as it moves."

Provide a tracking tube so baby can practice tracking (following an object as it moves).

? _____ Mirror Play
6-18 months

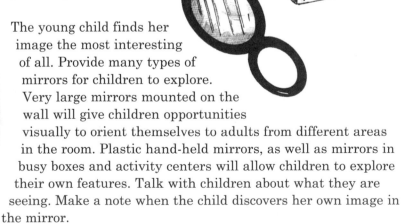

Materials
Unbreakable mirrors
Paper and pen

The young child finds her image the most interesting of all. Provide many types of mirrors for children to explore. Very large mirrors mounted on the wall will give children opportunities visually to orient themselves to adults from different areas in the room. Plastic hand-held mirrors, as well as mirrors in busy boxes and activity centers will allow children to explore their own features. Talk with children about what they are seeing. Make a note when the child discovers her own image in the mirror.

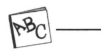 **? ____ Wrapping Toys**

12-18 months

Materials
Wrapping paper
Tape

Teacher Talk
"That is the truck, Scott. You found the truck!"

Wrap toys to add novelty. Any non-toxic paper will do. Many babies will be more interested in the paper than the item they unwrap.

LITERACY POSSIBILITIES

 ABC ____ Chocolate-Covered Cookie Tantrum

0-18 months

Materials
Chocolate-Covered Cookie Tantrum by Deborah Blumenthal

Read the book to each baby or to two or three babies at a time. Watch for skills such as pointing to pictures, saying sounds or words, and turning pages. Communicate your observations to parents on the Communication Sheet (pages 429-430).

ABC ____ Texture and Activity Books

0-18 months

Materials
Books such as *Pat the Bunny* by Dorothy Kunhardt

Young children love to touch books that have different textures and activities added to the pages. Books such as *Touch Me* and *Pat the Bunny* are two good examples that baby will enjoy. Read the book to each baby or to one or two babies at a time.

 ABC ____ No, No, No!

0-18 months

Materials
No, No, No! by Anne Rockwell

Children begin to hear NO very early. This book puts nos into perspective with the underlying reason that there have to be some rules in the world. Read the book when you hear no—either from parents, teachers, or children themselves.

Senses Books

0-18 months

Materials
Books about the senses, such as
Bright Eyes, Brown Skin by Cheryl Willis Hudson
My Five Senses by Aliki
My Five Senses by Jan Belk Monclure

Read one of these books at an appropriate time. Add to Books Read list (see Appendix page 431).

Eye Winker, Tom Tinker
0-18 months

Materials
None needed

Repeat this rhyme with infants as they explore their facial features in the mirror or as you sit with a baby in your lap, gazing at his face.

> *Eye Winker, Tom Tinker*
> Eye winker, Tom tinker,
> Nose smeller, mouth eater,
> Chin chopper, gully, gully, gully!

Clap, Clap, Clap Your Hands
6-18 months

Materials
None needed

Use this rhyme as you model clapping hands with infants.

> *Clap, Clap, Clap Your Hands*
> Clap, clap, clap your hands
> Clap your hands together.
> Clap, clap, clap your hands
> Clap your hands together.

Also, read *Clap Your Hands* by Lorinda Bryan Cauley.

Where Is Thumbkin?

0-18 months

Materials

None needed

Sing this song and do the motions for babies. It will give young babies an opportunity to practice visual tracking. Other children may bounce or move to the sounds of the music. Emphasize the motions as you sing.

Where Is Thumbkin?

Where is thumbkin?	Where is pointer?
Where is thumbkin?	Where is pointer?
Here I am; here I am.	Here I am; here I am.
How are you today, sir?	How are you today, sir?
Very well, I thank you.	Very well, I thank you.
Fly away; fly away.	Fly away; fly away.

Where is tall one?

Where is ring finger?

Where is pinky?

Where Is Baby?

0-18 months

Materials

None needed

Sing this variation of "Where Is Thumbkin?" as children are playing. Observe each child's reactions when he hears his name. Talk with parents about the songs and rhymes you use with children during the day. Make a copy of the words to send home to parents.

Where Is Baby?

Where is baby? (Insert infant's name)
Where is baby?
Here I am; here I am.
How are you today, sir?
Very well, I thank you.
Fly away; fly away.

Old MacDonald Had a Farm
0-18 months

Materials
Tape or CD with song on it, optional
Tape or CD player, optional
Toy animals from the song

Play this song on a tape or CD, or sing the song. Hold different toy animals as they come into the song.

> *Old MacDonald Had a Farm*
> Old MacDonald had a farm,
> E-I-E-I-O.
> And on his farm he had some cows,
> E-I-E-I-O.
> With a moo-moo here and a moo-moo there,
> Here a moo, there a moo, everywhere a moo-moo.
> Old MacDonald had a farm,
> E-I-E-I-O.

Continue with other animals:
> Sheep...baa-baa....
> Pigs...oink-oink....
> Ducks...quack-quack....
> Chickens...chick-chick....

Baby Bumblebee
0-18 months

Materials
None needed

Sing this song to children. Later, practice making a buzzing sound. First model for children. Then use a hand-over-hand approach to help them participate. Observe their reactions to determine if you should continue singing.

> *Baby Bumblebee*
> I'm bringing home a baby bumblebee,
> Won't my mommy be so proud of me?
> I'm bringing home a baby bumblebee,
> "Ouch! It stung me!"

Johnny Jumper
6-12 months

Materials
Johnny Jumper
Unbreakable mirror

Teacher Talk
Talk about what the infant is doing. "You are bouncing in the Johnny Jumper. Up and down, Morgan."

Give each child an opportunity to bounce in the Johnny Jumper to strengthen leg muscles. Position a mirror nearby on the wall, so the child can watch himself jump. **Note:** Children should be in the Johnny Jumper no longer than 10 to 15 minutes. Remove the child immediately if he begins to object.

Carpet Squares
6-18 months

Materials
Carpet samples
Tape
Paper and pen

Secure carpet sample squares to the floor. Include different textures (patterned, high pile, low pile). Notice if babies feel the changes in the texture. Record reactions on the Communication Sheet (pages 429-430).

Rattles and Drums Band
12-18 months

Materials
Teacher-made rattles and drums
Tapes or CDs of lively music
Tape or CD player

Use different teacher-made rattles and drums as noisemakers. Play lively music on the tape or CD player as your little band plays.

Change Perspective

0-12 months

Materials
Blanket

Teacher Talk
Talk about trees, clouds, and other items outside. "You are looking at the tree, Su Lin. The breeze is blowing the branches."

Spread a blanket on the grass and place babies on it.

Fence Painting

6-18 months

Materials
Paper
Tape
Paintbrushes
Water or paint, optional

Tape paper low on the fence. Give children paintbrushes, with or without water or paint, so they can experience painting outside.

PROJECT POSSIBILITIES

Body Painting

0-18 months

Materials
Large pieces of paper
Non-toxic, washable paint
Paintbrushes
Tape
Permanent marker

Provide times during the day where children can body paint. Use only non-toxic, washable paint. Strip one or two infants to their diapers. Introduce babies individually to experiencing paint on their skin. Very young babies may be placed on their tummies with paper and paint under their legs and arms. Older babies can scoot or crawl over the paper. Hang the body paint pictures on the wall. The next time you want to body paint, use the same paper and a different color of paint. Date the picture each time a child adds to it. **Safety Alert:** Some children will want to taste the paint. Distract them by pointing to the paint on the paper. Redirect them by saying, "Paint with your fingers," or "Paint with your toes!" Make sure to alert parents to painting activities because some paint pigment may still end up in the stool of children. Post the non-toxic label to assure parents that the paint will cause no harm.

Water Paints

12-18 months

Materials
Large piece of paper
Paintbrush
Squeeze or squirt bottles
Towels for cleanup

Washable tempera paint
Tape
Water

Paint a large piece of paper completely with washable tempera paint. Let the paint dry completely. Hang the paper low on a fence or outside wall. Give children a variety of squeeze and squirt bottles filled with water. They squirt the paint-covered paper. Some children will want to slide their hands on the paint as it gets wet. A fun variation is to put the paint on the paper in layers. Then, as children add the water, a different color paint will appear.

PARENT PARTICIPATION POSSIBILITIES

Handkerchief from Home

Ask parents to provide a cotton handkerchief that has Mom's perfume or Dad's cologne or aftershave on it. The handkerchief will be used during the day to provide a connection for the child to home. Tell parents the handkerchief will be used later in an art project. Label each handkerchief with the child's initials to avoid confusion.

Handkerchief Return

After the scent of the perfume, cologne, or aftershave has faded, use the handkerchiefs to make a surprise for Mom and Dad. Use the handkerchiefs for children to make a

Jamie 6/2/00

handprint. Label the print with the child's name and date. Surprise parents with the handkerchief as a gift on Mother's Day, Father's Day, their birthdays, or on the anniversary of the child's enrollment in school.

Invitation to Visit

Parents are usually in a hurry during arrival and departure time. Often, they think that the level of intensity and noise at these times is indicative of the entire day. Try inviting parents to come during the day to visit their child and observe the wonderful things that occur at times other than arrival and departure. Add this visit to your Parent Visit Log (see page 434 in the Appendix) in the child's portfolio.

Parent Postcard

The Parent Postcard in this section is designed to share with parents during the Possibilities Plan. The topic is a natural extension of the activities and experiences that you are planning and implementing for the infants in the classroom. Use the Postcard to connect parents to their children's learning.

Cooking with Kids

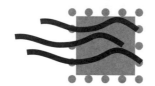

Meal preparation time can be a wonderful time to spend with your young child. Often by this time of the day, your baby will be ready to have your undivided attention, and sharing you is not an option! So what can baby do while dinner is being prepared?

Very young babies will enjoy being where the action is! Position your child so he or she can see what you are doing. Talk about what you have been doing during the day. Sing songs that your child has been hearing at school. Label the items you are using in the kitchen and connect with your baby using eye contact.

Older babies will enjoy doing what you do. Small pots and pans will make great toys to play with while you are cooking. Talk about what you are doing and what you see your child doing. Open up the pantry and allow your child to play with cans. They roll, which is fun for babies, and they stack, which is a skill that takes a great deal of practice.

The main objective is calm time together to reconnect after your busy day. Your baby will enjoy your attention and will come to look forward to this special time you have together.

TO _____

_____

_____

Concepts Learned in Senses

Concepts Learned

I can do things with my hands and my feet!

I can move to music.

I can smell with my nose.

I can see with my eyes.

I can taste with my mouth.

I can touch with my fingers.

Different things feel different.

I can look at the sky, trees, and grass.

I can make sounds with rattles.

I can paint inside.

I can paint outside.

I can see myself in the mirror.

I can bounce with my legs in the Johnny Jumper.

Resources

Prop Boxes

Things That Go on My Hands!
  Bangle bracelets
  Gloves
  Mittens
  Wrist rattles
Things That Go on My Head!
  Bows
  Hats
  Scarves
  Sunglasses
Things That Go on My Feet!
  Boots
  Heels
  Sandals
  Socks
  Tennis shoes

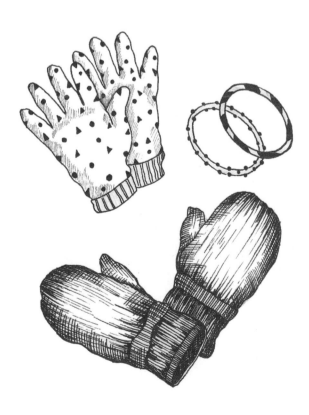

Picture File/Vocabulary

Babies inside
Babies outside
Babies with different facial expressions
Binoculars
Eyes
Faces
Feet
Handkerchief
Hands
Mouth
Nose
Truck

Books

Bright Eyes, Brown Skin by Cheryl Willis Hudson
Chocolate Covered Cookie Tantrum by Deborah Blumenthal (page 397)
Clap Your Hands by Lorinda Bryan Cauley (page 398)
My Five Senses by Aliki
My Five Senses by Jan Belk Monclure
No, No, No! by Anne Rockwell (page 397)
No! No! Jo! by Kate McMullen
Pat the Bunny by Dorothy Kunhardt (page 397)
Touch Me by Eve Witte and Pat Witte (page 397)

Rhymes/Fingerplays

"Clap, Clap, Clap Your Hands" (page 398)
"Eye Winker, Tom Tinker" (page 398)

Music/Songs

"Baby Bumblebee" (page 400)
"Old MacDonald Had a Farm" (page 400)
"Where Is Baby?" (page 399)
"Where Is Thumbkin?" (page 399)

Toys and Materials

The following purchased items are important for this Possibilities Plan:

"Old MacDonald" tape or CD

Books about emotions

Books about senses

Finger paint and tempera paint

Hand-held mirrors

Johnny Jumper

Large wall mirrors

Rattles

Shallow tubs

Wrist rattles

The following gathered items will help support this Possibilities Plan:

Blanket or quilt

Cardboard tubes

Carpet samples

Clear plastic tennis ball tube

Cuddle toys

Empty bath items (lotion, shampoo, soap, powder)

Empty food containers (oatmeal boxes, macaroni boxes, salt boxes)

Prop box items

Shredded paper

Unflavored gelatin

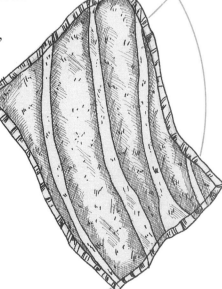

WEB

Bubbles, Mud, and Puddles

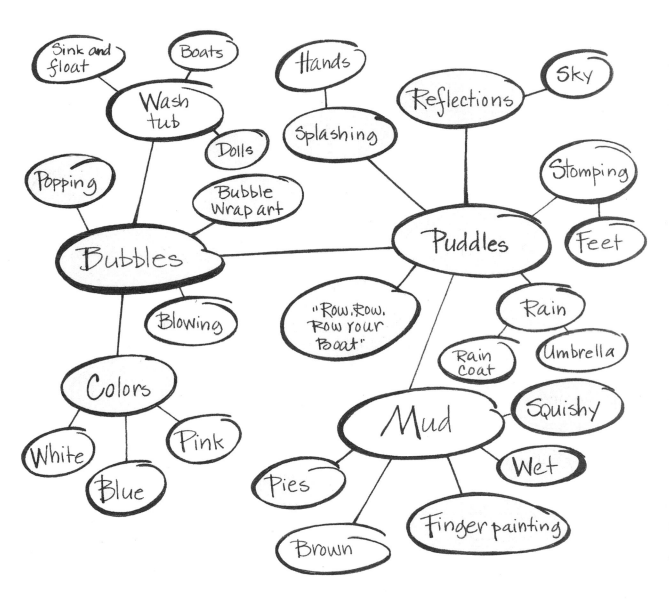

Note: Using the technique of webbing, teachers can follow the leads that children give them, as well as have an unlimited source of options. Always use the webs as a jumping-off point. The possibilities are endless!

PLANNING PAGES

Plan Possibilities

Dramatic

Umbrella 412
Cleaning Up 412
Rain Gear 412

Sensory/Art

Cool Toothpaste in Baggie 412
Warm Toothpaste in Baggie 413
Paint in Squirt Bottles 413
Clean Mud .413
Rain Play 414
Feather Duster Painting 414

Curiosity

Sock Puppet 414
Glitter Bottles 415
Slow Glitter Bottles 415

Literacy

By the Seashore 415
Tubby Tugboat 416
Baby's Bath 416
Bubbles, Puddles, and Mud Books . .416
Jack and Jill 416
Rub-a-Dub-Dub 417

Music

Chime Rattles 417
Row, Row, Row Your Boat 417
Bottle Rattles 418
Five Little Ducks 418

Movement

Clap Your Hands 419
Mud Digging 419
Colored Water Bottles 419

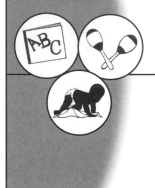

Outdoor

Floating Fish 420
Scrubbing Rocks 420
Painting with Water 420

Project Possibilities

Wrapping Paper for Parents 421
Bubble Time 421

Parent Participation Possibilities

Items for Dramatic Possibilities 421
Supporting Possibilities 422
Bubble Party 422
Parent Postcards
    When Your Child's Teacher Leaves 423
    When Your Child's Day Is Lengthened . . .424

Bubbles, Mud, and Puddles

Concepts Learned in Bubbles, Mud and Puddles **424**

Prop Boxes

Cleaning Up 425

Picture File/Vocabulary . . .**425**

Books

Baby's Bath by Judy Nayer
By the Seashore by Maurice Pledger 415
Clap Your Hands by Lorinda Bryan Cauley 419
Clifford Counts Bubbles by Norman Bridwell
Clifford's Bath by Norman Bridwell
Duck Song by Kenneth Grahame
I Don't Want to Take a Bath by Julia Sykes
Jumbo-shaped Board Books: Tugboat
    by Wilfried Wood 416
Max's Bath by Rosemary Wells
Pete's Puddles by Harriet Roche
Puddles by Jonathan London
Rain Song by Lezlie Evans

Rhymes/Fingerplays

"Jack and Jill" 416
"Rub-a-Dub-Dub" 417

Music/Songs

"Five Little Ducks" .418
"Row, Row, Row Your Boat" 417

Toys and Materials **426**

Umbrella

0-18 months

Materials
Umbrella
String and/or tape
Recording of nature music

Hang an umbrella from the ceiling and play nature music (a rainstorm would be great!). **Note:** Keep umbrella out of the reach of all children in the classroom.

Cleaning Up

12-18 months

Materials
Empty, washed, cleaning containers, etc.

Give children empty, washed cleaning containers and cloths, so they can pretend to clean up.

Rain Gear

12-18 months

Materials
Rain gear and/or boots

Include child-size rain gear and boots, so children can play.

Cool Toothpaste in Baggie

6-18 months

Materials
Toothpaste
Resealable plastic bag
Refrigerator

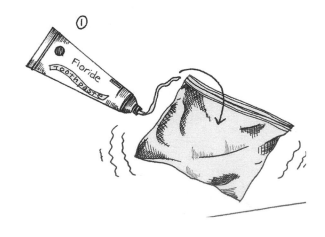

Place a small amount of toothpaste in a resealable plastic bag. After sealing the bag, also tape it shut. Place the baggie in the refrigerator until it becomes cold. Allow children to explore the baggie as you watch, comment, and supervise for safety. Describe children's actions. As you observe curiosity, smiles, and surprise, record your observations on the Communication Sheet (pages 429-430).

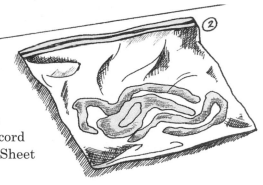

Warm Toothpaste in Baggie

6-18 months

Materials
Toothpaste	Resealable plastic bag
Sunny windowsill	Tape

Place a small amount of toothpaste in a resealable plastic bag. After sealing the bag, tape it shut. Place the baggie on a windowsill in the sun or in a hot water bath until it becomes warm. Allow children to explore the baggie as you watch, comment, and supervise for safety. Describe children's actions. As you observe curiosity, smiles, and surprise, record your observations on the Communication Sheet (page 430) or on an Anecdotal Record (page 428).

Paint in Squirt Bottles

6-18 months

Materials
Squirt bottles	Tempera paint
Paper	Tape

Fill squirt bottles about half full with tempera paint. Tape large pieces of art paper to the floor, so children can paint with the bottles or finger paint on the paper.

Clean Mud

12-18 months

Materials
Toilet paper	Water
Ivory soap	Grater

Teacher Talk
"John Wesley is squeezing the clean mud through his fingers. What fun!"

Create clean mud for the sensory table by combining small bits of toilet paper, water, and shaved Ivory soap. Supervise closely as children explore the texture of the mixture. Distract ("Stir the mud with this spoon, Allison."), redirect ("Here is your pacifier. It goes in your mouth."), or impose consequences ("The mud stays in the sensory table. If you can't keep it out of your mouth, I will move you away from playing here.") with infants who will not leave the clean mud in the sensory table.

Rain Play

12-18 months

Materials
Sensory table
Containers
Water

Put containers and water in the sensory table. Encourage children to make rain by turning the containers upside down. Include bottles with holes punched in the top, as well as things like plastic salt and pepper shakers.

Feather Duster Painting

12-18 months

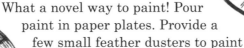

Materials
Small feather dusters   Paint
Paper plates   Paper

What a novel way to paint! Pour paint in paper plates. Provide a few small feather dusters to paint with. First demonstrate how to use the feather duster by dipping it in a blob of paint, then dabbing the paint on paper.

CURIOSITY POSSIBILITIES

? _____ Sock Puppet

0-6 months

Materials
Child's sock
Scissors
Non-toxic permanent marker

Give young babies a sock puppet made from a child's sock. Cut five holes in the end of the sock, so the baby's fingers will slip through. Then draw a face on the palm side of the sock using a nontoxic permanent marker. Observe to see how baby responds to the puppet. Record responses on Communication Sheet (page 430) or on an Anecdotal Record (page 428).

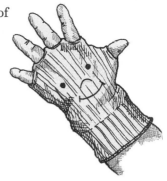

? —— Glitter Bottles
0-18 months

Materials
Water
Small, clear plastic soda bottle
Glue and tape

Cooking oil
Confetti glitter

Teacher Talk
"Kevin, you are rolling the bottle on the floor. Look at all the glitter!"

Place equal parts water and cooking oil in a small clear plastic soda bottle. Add large confetti glitter. Glue and tape the bottle top. Talk with infants about what they see.

? —— Slow Glitter Bottles
0-18 months

Materials
Small, clear, plastic soda bottle
Glitter

Corn syrup
Glue and tape

Teacher Talk
Talk about how slowly the glitter moves in the bottle. "You are watching the glitter, Boone."

Place corn syrup in a small clear soda bottle. Add glitter. Glue and tape the bottle top.

LITERACY POSSIBILITIES

By the Seashore
0-18 months

Materials
By the Seashore by Maurice Pledger

Talk about water and sand as you read this book with a few children at different times during the day.

Tubby Tugboat

0-18 months

Materials
Jumbo-shaped Board Books: Tugboat by Wilfried Wood

Read this delightful board book to babies. Talk about what the little boat does to help the big ships.

Baby's Bath

0-18 months

Materials
Books about bath time, such as
    Clifford's Bath by Norman Bridwell
    Max's Bath by Rosemary Wells
    I Don't Want to Take a Bath by Julia Sykes

Babies will enjoy these books about this familiar routine.

Bubbles, Puddles, and Mud Books

0-18 months

Materials
Books about Bubbles, Puddles, and Mud, such as
    Clifford Counts Bubbles by Norman Bridwell
    Duck Song by Kenneth Grahame
    Pete's Puddles by Harriet Roche
    Puddles by Jonathan London
    Rain Song by Leslie Evans

Read children books that include bubbles, puddles, and mud. Relate the experiences children have had as you read the books.

Jack and Jill

0-18 months

Materials
None needed

Recite this rhyme with children. Watch for indications that children would like you to repeat the rhyme.

> *Jack and Jill*
>   Jack and Jill went up the hill,
>   To fetch a pail of water;
>   Jack fell down and broke his crown,
>   And Jill came tumbling after.

Rub-a-Dub-Dub

0-18 months

Materials
None needed

Recite this rhyme with children.

> *Rub a Dub, Dub*
> Rub a dub, dub,
> Three men in a tub,
> The butcher,
> The baker,
> And the candlestick maker.

MUSIC POSSIBILITIES

Chime Rattles

0-6 months

Materials
Chime rattles

Give younger babies chime rattles to shake. First demonstrate the interesting sound by gently shaking the rattle. Then observe to see if baby responds.

Row, Row, Row Your Boat

0-18 months

Materials
None needed

Sing this song to children as you make rowing motions with your arms. Observe to see if children move to the sound of the music. Record your observations.

> *Row, Row, Row Your Boat*
> Row, row, row your boat
> Gently down the stream.
> Merrily, merrily, merrily, merrily
> Life is but a dream.

Bottle Rattles

0-18 months

Materials
Empty plastic bottles or jars
Items that fit inside the bottles
Glue and tape

Use empty plastic bottles or jars
to make rattles. Place items
inside the bottles. Glue and tape
them securely. "That bottle makes a
soft sound. That one makes a loud
sound!"

Five Little Ducks

0-18 months

Materials
Rubber ducks, optional

Sing this song with children. If desired, provide rubber ducks for children to hold as
you sing.

Five Little Ducks
Five little ducks went out to play,
Over the hill and far away.
Mama Duck called with a quack, quack, quack.
And four little ducks came swimming back.

Four little ducks went out to play,
Over the hill and far away.
Mama Duck called with a quack, quack, quack.
And three little ducks came swimming back.

Three little ducks went out to play,
Over the hill and far away.
Mama Duck called with a quack, quack, quack.
And two little ducks came swimming back.

Two little ducks went out to play,
Over the hill and far away.
Mama Duck called with a quack, quack, quack.
And one little duck came swimming back.

One little duck went out to play,
Over the hill and far away.
Mama Duck called with a quack, quack, quack.
And five little ducks came swimming back!

 ___ **Clap Your Hands**

0-6 months

Materials

Clap Your Hands by Lorinda Bryan Cauley

Teacher Talk

"You are clapping your hands, Amanda. This is fun."

Read *Clap Your Hands.* Show baby how to do the physical activities illustrated in the book.

 ___ **Mud Digging**

6-18 months

Materials

Mud
Shallow plastic tubs
Plastic shovels

Teacher Talk

Talk about what each child is doing. Remind children to keep the mud in the sand and water table or tub. "Not for your mouth, Kevin Michael. Use the shovel to dig."

Give each child an opportunity to play and strengthen arm muscles by digging in mud in shallow plastic tubs. Always be near and attentive. Provide items to bury and then discover.

 ___ **Colored Water Bottles**

0-18 months

Materials

Clear plastic bottles
Colored water
Glue and tape

Partially fill plastic bottles of various sizes with colored water. Glue and tape closed. Children will enjoy gazing at, rolling, and carrying the bottles.

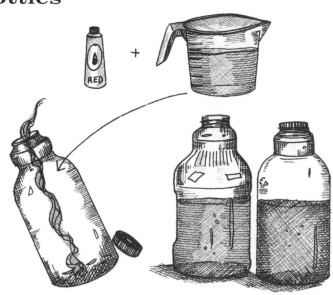

Floating Fish

6-12 months

Materials
Shallow tubs
Plastic fish that float

Teacher Talk
"You put the fish in the water, Julian. Look! It is floating."

Put about two inches of water in shallow tubs. Give children fish that will float in the water. Supervise closely.

Scrubbing Rocks

12-18 months

Materials
Small buckets
Water
Sponges and cloths
Rocks or other objects

Put a small amount of water in small buckets. Add sponges and cloths. Show children how to scrub large rocks or other objects outside. Add more water as needed.

Painting with Water

12-18 months

Materials
Shallow containers
Water
Large clean brushes

Put a small amount of water in shallow containers. Provide very large, clean brushes, so children can paint with water outside. The fence, the outside wall, riding toys, and walkways will all change color as the children water "paint" them.

Wrapping Paper for Parents

6-18 months

Materials
Large pieces of paper
Tape
Paint
Paintbrushes
Marker
Ribbon

Tape very large pieces of art paper to the floor or wall. Over a period of time, introduce babies to repeated sensory experiences using paint. Put children's names on the sheets, so they can get the same one each time. When each paper is almost completely covered with paint, roll it up and tie it with a ribbon. Send it home for parents to use as wrapping paper.

 Bubble Time

12-18 months

Materials
Bubble wands
Non-toxic bubble solution

Blowing bubbles is a fun but often difficult task for young children. Provide many opportunities for children to blow bubbles. First, hold the bubble wand and blow the bubbles yourself. Blow bubbles away from the child's face. Observe the baby's reaction to determine what you do next. Later, you may offer the wand and see if baby wants to blow. Repeat this experience with babies on a regular basis and watch their interest and skill grow.

PARENT PARTICIPATION POSSIBILITIES

 Items for Dramatic Possibilities

Ask parents to gather items related to water (raincoat, rain boots, floats, oars) and loan them to your classroom during this Possibilities Plan. Thoroughly inspect all items before using them in the classroom.

Supporting Possibilities

Ask parents to collect empty plastic bottles (of all sizes), as well as metal or plastic salt shakers, water bottles, and cardboard tubes. Let parents know how the items will be used. Thoroughly inspect all items for safety before using them in the classroom.

Bubble Party

Invite parents to come to a bubble party one afternoon. If the weather is good, put quilts or blankets on the grass and provide bubble solution and a wand for each parent. Take pictures as parents interact with their children.

Parent Postcards

Parent Postcards in this section are designed to share with parents during the Possibilities Plan. The topics are natural extensions of the activities and experiences that you are planning and implementing for the infants in the classroom. Use the postcards to connect parents to their children's learning.

TO

When Your Child's Teacher Leaves

It may be your worst fear. Your infant has really started to adjust to school while you are at work. Then, wham! Something changes. Your child's favorite teacher leaves. You have a big project at work that requires a lot of extra time (and lengthens your child's day at school). The director tells you a classroom change is coming up. Change is a challenge to everyone—children, teachers, and parents. Having a teacher leave is like riding up an escalator that jerks to a stop. Everything seems so unsure. What can parents do to help their baby cope with change?

First of all, remember that everything isn't changing. As important as the teacher-child relationship is, it is one part of the big picture. Other areas will stay constant. Your child's schedule will probably remain the same. So, too will the daily routine, the other children in the group, and the other adults in the classroom. Most important, you will stay constant. Continuity of group, schedule, activities, and friends can form a strong foundation for children to begin to adjust to a departing teacher. Work to keep as many other parts of your child's life as consistent as possible to help him or her adjust to a change in teachers.

Second, view adjusting to change as a transition. It may take as much as two to six weeks for everything to settle down again after a favorite teacher departs. Children are learning to accommodate changes. Adults may not like change, but they have many more adjustment skills than children do. In this case, time is a good friend.

Third, keep your schedule predictable. When your child loses a special teacher, he or she may wonder if you are going to leave, too. Keeping to your regular arrival and departure schedule reassures your child that you will be there for him or her. Say goodbye when you leave in the morning. Never sneak out while your child is playing. He or she may cry when you leave, but you will be able to remind your child that you will be back, reinforcing that you will always be there for him or her.

Fourth, welcome the new teacher. Your child will be cautious at first and will be looking to you for cues as to whether the new teacher is acceptable. Greet the teacher warmly, talk with her or him, and tell her or him about your child. Give your child a chance to warm up before you encourage him or her to interact with the new teacher. Don't push too hard for interaction between your child and the new teacher. Adjustment to change takes time.

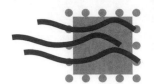

When Your Child's Day Is Lengthened

Infants get better at handling change when parents and teachers make change a positive experience. Your child will have many changes in his or her life. Early experience with smooth, facilitated transitions will prepare him or her for adjusting to the inevitable change that permeates our lives.

Very young children have little perspective on time, but they have a powerful sense of sequence. Just watch an infant room. Although the children can't tell you with words who will come in the door next, the right child will be waiting close to the door for his or her parents to arrive. Even young children know the sequence of who arrives in what order.

Try to let your child's teacher know if your routine is going to change. Sometimes teachers can offset your child's discomfort about changes by preparing him or her for the change. Your child's teacher can alert your child that you will be a little out of sequence today and keep him or her from going into the waiting mode too soon.

TO _____
_____
_____

Concepts Learned in Bubbles, Puddles, and Mud

Concepts Learned

I can squeeze mud.

Rain is water.

I can play with water.

I can paint with big brushes.

I can look at books.

I can move to music.

Some things are cool.

Some things are warm.

I can blow bubbles.

I can clean.

Different textures feel different.

I can pretend.

Resources

Prop Boxes

Cleaning Up
Cloths
Dustbuster toy
Duster

Empty, washed, cleaning containers
Scrubber
Vacuum toy

Picture File/Vocabulary

Babies
Bubbles
Clouds
Families cleaning
Lake

Mud puddles
Rain
River
Trees

Books

Baby's Bath by Judy Nayer
By the Seashore by Maurice Pledger (page 415)
Clap Your Hands by Lorinda Bryan Cauley (page 419)
Clifford Counts Bubbles by Norman Bridwell
Clifford's Bath by Norman Bridwell
Duck Song by Kenneth Grahame
I Don't Want to Take a Bath by Julia Sykes
Jumbo-shaped Board Books: Tugboat by Wilfried Wood (page 416)
Max's Bath by Rosemary Wells
Pete's Puddles by Harriet Roche
Puddles by Jonathan London
Rain Song by Lezlie Evans

Rhymes/Fingerplays

"Jack and Jill" (page 416)
"Rub-a-Dub-Dub" (page 417)

Music/Songs

"Five Little Ducks" (page 418)
"Row, Row, Row Your Boat" (page 417)

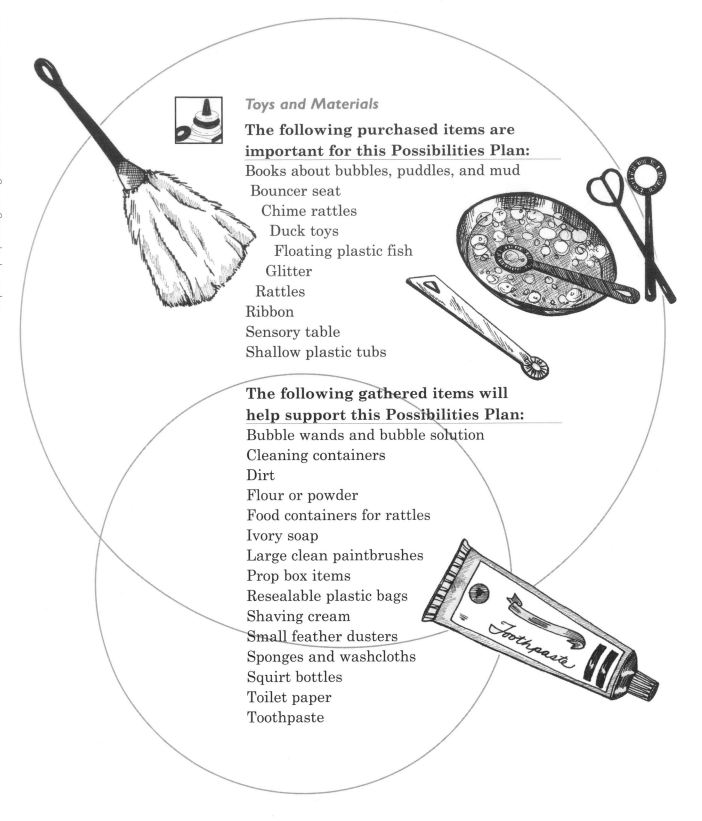

Toys and Materials

The following purchased items are important for this Possibilities Plan:

Books about bubbles, puddles, and mud
Bouncer seat
Chime rattles
Duck toys
Floating plastic fish
Glitter
Rattles
Ribbon
Sensory table
Shallow plastic tubs

The following gathered items will help support this Possibilities Plan:

Bubble wands and bubble solution
Cleaning containers
Dirt
Flour or powder
Food containers for rattles
Ivory soap
Large clean paintbrushes
Prop box items
Resealable plastic bags
Shaving cream
Small feather dusters
Sponges and washcloths
Squirt bottles
Toilet paper
Toothpaste

Appendix Contents

Sample Forms
    Anecdotal Record 428
    Communication Sheet 429
    Books Read List 431
    Parent Visit Log 434
    Accident/Incident Report 432
Observation/Assessment Instruments 435-440
Dissemination Schedule for Postcards 441
Possibilities Planning 445
    Sample Lesson Plan 448-451
Concepts Learned in Each Possibilities Plan 452-463
Songs, Poems, Rhymes, and Fingerplays 464-468
Resources and References 469-474

Anecdotal Record

INNOVATIONS

Child _____ Date _____ Time _____

What I observed

_____

_____

_____

_____

_____

_____

_____

_____

_____

_____

Teacher

Reprinted with permission from Innovations: The complete Infant Curriculum

INNOVATIONS

Anecdotal Record

Child _____ Date _____ Time _____

What I observed

_____

_____

_____

_____

_____

_____

_____

Teacher's Name _____ **Assessment References**

_____

Reprinted with permission from Innovations: The Comprehensive Infant Curriculum

Communication Sheet

INNOVATIONS

Appendix

CHILD'S NAME

FOR THE WEEK OF

DAY	BREAKFAST		TOTAL HOURS SLEPT	BEHAVIOR CHANGES NOTICED		PARENT COMMENTS/INSTRUCTIONS	FOODS EATEN		DIAPER CHANGES		NAPTIME		TEACHER COMMENTS
							SOLIDS	LIQUIDS			START	WOKE	
M	YES	NO		YES	NO				WET	BM			
T	YES	NO		YES	NO				WET	BM			
W	YES	NO		YES	NO				WET	BM			
Th	YES	NO		YES	NO				WET	BM			
F	YES	NO		YES	NO				WET	BM			

Reprinted with permission from Innovations: The Comprehensive Infant Curriculum

Communication Sheet

CHILD'S NAME _____ **FOR THE WEEK OF** _____

DAY	BREAKFAST		TOTAL HOURS SLEPT	BEHAVIOR CHANGES NOTICED		PARENT COMMENTS/INSTRUCTIONS	FOODS EATEN		DIAPER CHANGES		NAPTIME		TEACHER COMMENTS
	YES	NO		YES	NO		SOLIDS	LIQUIDS	WET	BM	START	WOKE	
M													
T													
W													
Th													
F													

Reprinted with permission from Innovations: The Comprehensive Infant Curriculum

Books Read List

Book Title	Date
1.	
2.	
3.	
4.	
5.	
6.	
7.	
8.	
9.	
10.	
11.	
12.	
13.	
14.	
15.	
16.	
17.	
18.	
19.	
20.	
21.	
22.	
23.	
24.	
25.	
26.	
27.	
28.	
29.	
30.	

Reprinted with permission from Innovations: The Comprehensive Infant Curriculum

Accident/Incident Report

(for school records)

Name of injured child
_____

Date of accident/incident
_____

Location of accident (address)
_____
_____

Site of accident (place in school)
_____
_____

What happened? Describe what took place.
_____
_____
_____
_____
_____
_____
_____
_____

Why did it happen? Give all of the facts—why? where? what? when? who? etc.
_____
_____
_____
_____
_____
_____
_____
_____
_____
_____

Reprinted with permission from Innovations: The Comprehensive Infant Curriculum

Accident/Incident Report (cont'd.)

What should be done to prevent this accident from recurring?

If the accident involved a child, how was the parent notified and by whom?

What was the parent's reaction?

What has been done so far to correct the situation?

With whom was this accident discussed, other than the child's parents?

Reported by   Date

Parent Visit Log

Teacher _____

Date	Name of Parent	Activity
1.		
2.		
3.		
4.		
5.		
6.		
7.		
8.		
9.		
10.		
11.		
12.		
13.		
14.		
15.		
16.		
17.		
18.		
19.		
20.		
21.		
22.		
23.		
24.		
25.		
26.		
27.		
28.		
29.		
30.		

Reprinted with permission from Innovations: The Comprehensive Infant Curriculum

Observation/Assessment Instruments

Task: Separating from Parents

	0-6 months	6-12 months		12-18 months
S1	a. Little or no experience with separating from Mom and Dad; accepts sensitive care from substitute.	b. Some experience with separating from Mom and Dad; prefers familiar caregiver, but accepts sensitive care from substitute.	c. More experience with separating from Mom and Dad; resists separating; shows distress upon separation, and takes time to adjust.	d. Experienced with separating from Mom and Dad; resists initial separation, but adjusts after only a few moments.
S2	a. Startled by new sounds, smells, and people.	b. Orients toward new or interesting stimuli.		c. Seeks new and interesting stimuli.
S3	a. Accepts transitions without notice.	b. Reacts with discomfort during the transition.	c. Resists transition preparation as well as the transition.	d. Anticipates transitions when preparation activities begin. If preparation is to a preferred, familiar activity, transition is accepted.
S4	a. Displays indiscriminate attachment; will accept sensitive care from most familiar adults; exhibits preference for Mom, Dad, or familiar caregiver if present.	b. Displays discriminate attachment; will still accept care from sensitive caregivers, but prefers care from Mom, Dad, or familiar caregivers.		c. Separation anxiety emerges; resists approaches by unfamiliar adults and resists separation from Mom, Dad, and familiar caregivers. Cries, clings, calls for parents when they leave the child's view.
S5	a. Unpredictable daily schedule.	b. Patterns in daily schedule emerge around eating and sleeping.		c. Daily schedule is predictable. Eating and sleeping patterns are relatively stable and predictable.
S6	a. Feeds from breast or bottle.	b. Begins to take baby food from a spoon; begins to sip from a cup.		c. Drinks from bottle and/or cup; eats finger foods.
S7	a. Plays with objects within visual field; bats at objects with hands and feet.	b. Manipulates, mouths, and plays with objects; likes action/reaction toys. Plays with objects then drops them to move on to new objects. May return to objects again and again.		c. Plays with favorite things again and again. Likes to dump out objects and play with them on the floor. Considers all objects and toys in the environment personal play choices, even when being played with by others.

	0-6 months		6-12 months	12-18 months
C1	a. Does not resist separating from parents.		b. Resists separating from parents; resists comfort from primary teacher.	c. Resists separating from parents; accepts comfort from primary teacher.
C2	a. Accepts transition from parent to teacher.		b. Maintains physical proximity to primary teacher during separation.	c. Seeks primary teacher's support in separating.
C3	a. Comforts after a period of distress.		b. Comforts quickly after being picked up.	c. Comforts when needs or wants are acknowledged by caregiver.
C4	a. Is unaware of friends in classroom.		b. Visually notices friends in classroom.	c. Gets excited about seeing friends; seeks physical proximity.
C5	a. Uses parents and teacher physically to support exploration of the environment; explores objects placed nearby parents and teachers.		b. Uses parents and teacher visually to support exploration of the environment; manipulates objects found in environment.	c. Explores the environment independently; responds to play cues presented by adults.
C6	a. Focuses on face-to-face interaction.	b. Tracks moving object up and down and right to left.	c. Watches people, objects, and activities in immediate environment.	d. Initiates interactions with people, toys, and the environment.
C7	a. Objects exist only when in view.	b. Objects perceived as having separate existence.	c. Looks where objects were last seen after they disappear.	d. Follows visual displacement of objects.
C8	a. Thinks object disappears when it moves out of view.	b. Looks where object was last seen after it disappears.	c. Follows object as it disappears.	d. Searches for hidden object if the disappearance was observed.

Infant (0-18 months) Assessment

Task: Relating to Self and Others

	0-6 months	6-12 months		12-18 months
R1	a. Calms self with adult support	b. Calms self with support from adults and/or transitional objects.		c. Calms self with transitional objects.
R2	a. Unaware of own image in mirror.	b. Curious about own image in mirrors and photographs.	c. Discovers self in mirror and photographs.	d. Differentiates own image from images of others.
R3	a. Begins to demonstrate preferences for different types of sensory stimuli.	b. Prefers some types of stimuli to others.		c. Is interested in pursuing favorite stimulation activities again and again.
R4	a. Develops a multi-sensory interest in the world—wants to see, touch, mouth, hear, and hold objects.	b. Uses senses to explore and discover the near environment.		c. Uses motor movements to enhance sensory exploration of the environment.
R5	a. Play is predominantly unoccupied in nature.	b. Play is predominantly onlooker in nature.	c. Play is predominantly solitary in nature.	
R6	a. Exhibits practice play.			b. Exhibits symbolic play.
R7	a. Develops an interest in the human world.	b. Seeks interactions with responsive adults; interested also in what other children are doing.	c. Seeks most interactions with familiar adults; fascinated by what other children are doing.	d. Prefers interactions with familiar adults; resists interaction with unfamiliar adults; may be cautious with unfamiliar friends.
R8	a. Does not distinguish between needs (food, diaper changes, sleep) and wants (social interaction, a new position, holding instead of lying in the bed).	b. Begins to distinguish between needs and wants; can communicate differently about different needs and wants.	c. Uses objects, gestures, and behaviors to indicate needs and wants.	d. Uses single words to indicate needs and wants like "muk" for "I want milk", or bye-bye for "Let's go bye-bye."
R9	a. Creates mental images of emotions and emotional responses to situations.			b. Begins to understand how feelings relate to others
R10	a. Unable to negotiate interactions with peers without direct adult support and facilitation.	b. Calls for help loudly by crying or screaming when problems occur during exploration of the environment or with peers.	c. Exchanges or trades with peers to get a desired toy or material with direct adult support and facilitation.	d. Asks other children to walk away when conflict arises between children; expects the other child to do so.
R11	a. Explores environment and the things in it orally. May bite, poke, scratch, or pinch others during exploration.			b. Experiments with behavior that gets a reaction; may bite, pinch, poke, scratch during interactions with others to see what happens.

Infant (0-18 months) Assessment

Task: Communicating with Parents, Teachers, and Friends

	0-6 months			6-12 months		12-18 months
CM1	a. Gazes at familiar faces.	b. Responds to facial expressions of familiar faces.	c. Occasionally engages in reciprocal communication with facial expressions, vowel sounds, and voice inflection.	d. Frequently engages in reciprocal communication using facial expressions, inflection, and vowel and consonant sounds.		e. Imitates and jabbers in response to familiar voices.
CM2	a. Makes sounds	b. Imitiates intonational and inflectional vocal patterns.		c. Develops holophrasic speech—words that convey complete sentences or thoughts.	d. Uses the same word to convey different meaning.	e. Develops telegraphic speech where 2 or 3 words are used as a sentence.
CM3	a. Listens to familiar people's voices when they talk.	b. Shows understanding of simple phrases by responding or reacting.		c. Points or looks at familiar objects when asked to do so.		d. Follows commands with visual cues or context cues.
CM4	a. Babbles motorically, acoustically, and visually simple sounds like (m), (p), (b), (n) at the beginning of words and vowel sounds like (ah), (oh), (uh).			b. Babbles sounds like (w), (k), (f), (t), (d) at the beginning of words and vowels sounds like (eh), (ee); strings sounds together (ba-ba-ba-ba-ba) and practices sounds in a wide variety of ways.		
CM5	a. Responds discriminantly to voices of mother and father.	b. Turns toward and responds to familiar voices and sounds.		c. Prefers familiar sounds and voices.		d. Directs vocalizations toward familiar people and objects in the environment.
CM6	a. Experiments with babbling and cooing.	b. Inflection is added to babbling and cooing.				c. Single words or phrases are understandable to familiar adults; strangers may not understand these words.
CM7	a. Looks at picture books.	b. Listens to books when read by a familiar adult.			c. Points to pictures.	d. Turns pages.

Infant (0-18 months) Assessment

Task: Moving Around Home and School

	0-6 months	6-12 months	12-18 months
M1	a. Holds head away from shoulder. b. Holds head steady side to side. c. Holds head up when lying on stomach. d. Rolls from back to front. e. Rolls from front to back.	f. Scoots on stomach. g. Sits with support. h. Sits without support. i. Crawls after ball or toy. j. Pulls to a stand.	k. Lowers back down to squatting position. l. Walks with support. m. Walks without support. n. Squats down and stands back up. o. Climbs into chair. p. Kicks ball.
M2	a. Eyes and head follow motion. b. Holds rattle. c. Exchanges objects between hands. d. Uses pincher grasp to pick up small items.	e. Picks up toys and objects. f. Dumps objects out of containers. g. Puts objects back into containers. h. Scribbles.	i. Turns pages in cardboard book. j. Unbuttons large buttons. k. Completes puzzles with 2-3 pieces.

Infant (0-18 months) Assessment

Task: Expressing Feelings with Parents, Teachers, and Friends

	0-6 months	**6-12 months**	**12-18 months**
E1	a. Begins to self-regulate; calms self after sensitive response from a caring adult.	b. Expects adults to respond to social cues such as vocalization, gestures, or cries	c. Knows which behaviors will make caregivers react in certain ways (for example, which actions will make you laugh and which ones will make you say "stop").
E2	a. Develops an interest in the world; is alert to sounds, touch, and faces.	b. Explores the environment; picks up objects of interest, then moves on to other objects.	c. Plays in a focused, organized manner.
E3	a. Gazes at faces with interest; smiles responsively.	b. Reaches up to indicate an interest in being held; is interested in social interaction with familiar adults.	c. Uses physical behavior (such as crawling over and pulling up) to establish closeness to caregivers.
E4	a. Seeks interactions with familiar people; vocalizes in response to vocalization.	b. Seeks to explore interesting toys, objects, and people.	c. Responds to limits that are set verbally; complies only with support from adults.
E5	a. Emotional reactions continue for a minute or two after an adult responds; does not recognize the change in state immediately.	b. Begins to coordinate behavior and emotions by acting on feelings; connects physical actions with needs (for example, goes over to the refrigerator to indicate interest in food or drink).	c. Recovers from emotional outbursts in a few minutes most of the time.

Dissemination Schedule for Postcards

There are two ways to disseminate Parent Postcards. The first strategy is to begin the dissemination along with the child's enrollment in school. If children enroll as infants, this strategy works well. It allows the teacher to select postcards that are appropriate to the child's situation, the family's interests and parent education needs, and the school's desire to share information. When used in this fashion, postcards can be viewed as roughly chronological in order. (The Postcard schedule on the next three pages follows this chronological order.)

A second strategy for disseminating Postcards is to do so by topic as needs or interests arise. This approach allows teachers to pick and choose topics and postcards that fit individual families' experiences and needs.

If you choose to disseminate as needs arise, notice that the Postcards are typically disseminated before the need to know and understand emerges chronologically. This makes the Postcards anticipatory preparation for the next stage and, therefore, parent education at its best. Don't hesitate to give parents a postcard more than once—repetition assures that parents will have more than one opportunity to get, understand, and use the information provided. Some issues arise repeatedly and strategies to use need to be refreshed.

Use the Postcards in the Possibilities Plan when you are doing related activities and experiences with children.

Finally, supplement the Postcards printed in this curriculum with articles, ideas, and information from other sources. There are many wonderful materials for parents available. When you discover one, add it to the curriculum to strengthen and supplement the topics that are included here.

Separating from Parents–months 1-3

Create a Separation and Reunion Ritual
Arrival and Departure Routines ARE Transitions
Call If Your Plans Change
Develop a Backup Plan
Thumb and Finger Sucking
Always Say Goodbye
Pacifiers
Security Items

Postcards in the Separating Possibilities Plans

Me! Possibilities
Helping Your Baby Develop a Positive Sense of Self
Every Child Is Unique!

Mommies and Daddies Possibilities
You Are Your Child's Best Teacher
Including Children in Routines

Connecting with School and Teacher–months 4-6

Just How Long Will Adjustment Take?
Facilitating Adjustment
Attachment Behavior, Stage 1–Indiscriminate Attachment: What Can Parents Do?

Postcards in the Connecting Possibilities Plans

Inside and Outside Possibilities
Controlling Transition Stress
Car Seat Safety

Open and Close Possibilities
Process Is the Goal
Object Permanence

Relating to Self and Others–months 7-9

Attachment Stage 2–Discriminate Attachment: What Can Parents Do?
Appropriate Expectations for Infants with Friends
Action/Reaction Biting: Help! My Child Got Bitten, Again!
What Can Teachers Do to Prevent Action/Reaction Biting?
What Can Parents Do to Prevent Action/Reaction Biting?
Learning Social Problem-Solving Step One: Calling for Help

Postcards in the Relating to Self and Others Possibilities Plans

Big and Little Possibilities
Do Children Learn while They Play?
Transmitting Values to Children

Cars, Trucks, and Trains Possibilities
Drive-time Activities

Gender Role Stereotyping

Preparing for Time Away from Your Child

Communicating with Parents, Teachers, and Friends–months 10-12

What Is Developmentally Appropriate Care and Early Education for Infants?–The Role of the Teacher

What Is Developmentally Appropriate Care and Early Education for Infants?–The Role of Curriculum (Activities and Experiences)

Using Found and Discarded Items for Toys

Good Books for Babies

Attachment Stage 3–Separation Anxiety: What Can Parents Do?

How Babies Learn

The Amazing Infant Brain

Supporting Brain Development at Home

Appropriate Expectations for Learning Academic Skills

Teaching Your Child to Read

Teaching Your Child to Write

Postcards in the Communicating Possibilities Plans

Storybook Classics Possibilities

Tips for Reading to Your Infant

Sounds Possibilities

Watch Those Ears!

Sound Opportunities

Moving Around–months 13-15

Appropriate Expectations for Self-control

Natural and Logical Consequences

Setting Appropriate Limits

Coping with Ear Infections

Postcards in the Moving Around Possibilities Plans

Competent Me Possibilities

Encouraging Independence and Autonomy

Continuing to Support Independence and Autonomy

Windows, Walls, Doors, and Hallways Possibilities

Childproofing Your Home

Expressing Feelings with Parents, Teachers, and Friends–months 16-18

Managing Normal Aggression in Very Young Children

Postcards in the Expressing Feelings Possibilities Plans

Senses Possibilities

Cooking with Kids

Bubbles, Mud, and Puddles Possibilities

When Your Child's Teacher Leaves

When Your Child's Day Is Lengthened

Possibilities Planning

Like the old saying goes, "If we fail to plan, we plan to fail." Even though *Innovations: The Comprehensive Infant Curriculum* is emergent in nature, planning is crucial. In fact, we see planning as being even more important when curriculum is emergent. To adequately prepare, teachers need to be aware of options and how, when, and where these options might present themselves. Viewed this way, curriculum is as much about what teachers do before interacting with children as it is about what teachers do during and after interactions.

The purpose of a Possibilities Plan is to focus attention on all of the dimensions of planning and to support the process of planning curriculum. In addition, the plan supports teachers' efforts to make both parents and other teachers aware of the focus, events, activities, experiences, and interactions that are being considered and provided for babies. The Possibilities Plan includes all the different aspects of curriculum presented in *Innovations: The Comprehensive Infant Curriculum.*

Unlike traditional lesson plans that provide only activities, the Possibilities Plan provides the big picture of possibilities that might emerge. It may cover a week, 2 weeks, or even a month. Possibilities Plans are designed to be living documents. Teachers may make additions, changes, or corrections to reflect children's experiences, reactions, preferences, emergent ideas, and changing development. You may find it helpful to use one color pen for your original Possibilities Plan, then other color pens to make changes in the plan that result from children's reactions or that influence what happens next, as well as to show how the children respond or react to what actually happens in the classroom.

The following list provides an overview of the different sections of the Possibilities Plan. Use the Possibilities Plan as it is (feel free to make additional copies), or modify it to reflect your individual differences or preferences in format or space.

Parent Possibilities: Because parents are children's first and most important teachers, the Possibilities Plan begins with the parent involvement section. Include suggestions for both teacher-initiated activities as well as parent participation possibilities. Be sensitive to the range of parents' abilities to participate in activities by planning many different options.

Environmental Possibilities: The Comprehensive Infant Curriculum views environmental planning, preparation, and modification as a major responsibility for all teachers. Our colleagues in Reggio Emilia view the environment as the "extra" teacher in any classroom. A well-planned environment can communicate volumes to children, even very young children. Planned and prepared thoroughly and thoughtfully, the environment can support children's play and work, teachers' activities and work, and parents' comfort. When inadequately planned and prepared, environments can interfere or even conflict with children's ideas, development, and activity as well as with teachers' goals and parents' comfort. Included in this section are equipment and materials to make, add, take away, and change. When regularly considered, changes and modifications like these will keep the environment fresh and interesting for babies, their parents, and their teachers.

Observation/Assessment Possibilities: A major focus of this curriculum is observation and assessment. Use indicators from the various developmental continua to cue teachers' observation as well as to create anecdotal documentation of children's emerging skills, abilities, reactions, responses, and emergent activities. A copy of the complete assessment form follows. Complete an assessment on each child for his or her portfolio and use it to discuss your observations and children's emerging skills with parents at formal conferences. Use the Possibilities Plan and the Communication Sheet to record brief notes concerning individual children's development and experiences or reactions to the plan.

Interactive Experiences: Each chapter in the curriculum includes a list of important interactive experiences for young children. Often, these experiences emerge from warm, caring interactions and are rarely the result of planning or formal activities. Because the quality of children's experiences are so important and cumulative, it is important to remind teachers and parents that these interactions ARE curriculum. Use the lists in each developmental task as well as ones that emerge uniquely from your interactive teaching style and list them for parents (and other teachers) to see. This validates these important experiences and reminds everyone that warm, positive interaction is the foundation of early childhood EDUCATION.

Web: A sample web is provided for each Possibilities Plan. Use it or create your own web including ideas and activities that your babies might enjoy as well as to open up emergent possibilities. Then, you might use different ink colors to show how the web grows or changes as children show preferences for activities, experiences, materials, and so on. Further, these beginning webs can be used later as a platform for future planning as children grow and learn.

Possibilities: Choose from the many different possibilities provided. Initially, use the age guides at the beginning of each activity, then modify activities based on your observations of babies' responses. Because so much of an infant's day is involved with routines (diapering, feeding, napping, and so on), you may only need only a few activities listed here. Remember the value of repetition for early brain development. Never hesitate to repeat popular activities more than once a day or for many subsequent days. At the same time, remember the value of novelty—add variety to children's day to gently excite and challenge emerging skills and prevent boredom. Finally, include plenty of time for children to explore the stimulating environment you have planned and prepared.

Books: Include children's books that are favorites and that will support the other activities that your babies will be experiencing. Read to children individually or in small groups each and every day.

Picture File/Vocabulary: Write the new vocabulary words you will be using in this section and indicate the pictures you will add to the classroom from your picture file. Including these additions to the plan will not only cue parents that you are supporting vocabulary development (and receptive language) but also that you are adding a wide variety of interest and images to the environment. It also gives parents an opportunity to support your teaching by adding photos and pictures from home and to replicate these early literacy ideas at home.

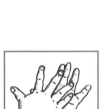

Rhymes/Fingerplays and Music/Songs: Include rhymes and music that you will be using during the course of the plan. Writing the titles of these important literacy activities down here and placing copies of the rhymes, fingerplays, and/or songs on the parent bulletin board or on the Communication Sheet support developing literacy and reinforce parents as primary educators of their children.

Prop Boxes: Items included in individual prop boxes can be listed in this section. Prop boxes are valuable resources for teachers because they help you collect, organize, and store materials and resources. Start by developing one prop box and you will be hooked! Storing items in clear plastic containers aides in quick identification of resources as curriculum emerges in your classroom. Listing prop boxes on your Possibilities Plan will also remind parents to support the collection of these valuable teaching resources.

When you are finished considering all of these possibilities, you will have a rich and interesting plan for you and your babies. Then, it will be time to relax and enjoy the educational experiences that you have prepared for children in your group—knowing that everything you do IS curriculum.

INNOVATIONS

Class _____
Teacher _____
Possibility Plan _____

Possibilities Plan

Parent Possibilities

Teacher-Initiated

Parent Participation

Innovations in Environments

Observation/Assessment Possibilities

Interactive Experiences

-1-

Reprinted with permission from Innovations: The Comprehensive Infant Curriculum

Possibilities Plan

Web

Dramatic Possibilities

Art/Sensory Possibilities

Curiosity Possibilities

Music Possibilities

Movement Possibilities

Literacy Possibilities

Outdoor Possibilities

Project Possibilities

Books	**Picture File/Vocabulary**

Rhymes & Fingerplays	**Music/Songs**	**Prop Boxes**

-2-

Class _____
Teacher _____
Possibility Plan _____

Possibilities Plan

Parent Possibilities   Me!

Teacher-Initiated   Parent Picture book

Parent Participation
Ask parents for items to add to the "Things that Go on My Head" prop box.

Innovations in Environments

Add rattles.
Add mirrors.
Collect empty bath items.
Add sleep items.

Take out exersaucer, bouncer.
Make Smelling Game, page 65.

Collect pots and pans to use with "Pots and Pans" by Patricia Hubbell

Observation/Assessment Possibilities

Tameka= S1c, S2b, S3b, S4c, S5b, S6b, S7b
Joseph= S1c, S2b, S3b, S4c, S5b, S6b, S7b
Trevarious= S1c, S2b, S3b, S4c, S5b, S6b, S7b
Sue= S1c, S2b, S3b, S4c, S5b, S6b, S7b
Observe transitions—Joseph, Sue
Observe outdoor floor time—Trevarious

Interactive Experiences

—leave a written record of Tameka's for other teachers
—use routines for interaction and learning with Joseph, Sue
—provide physical and visual support for new experiences (foot painting) for Trevarious

-1-

Reprinted with permission from Innovations: The Comprehensive Infant Curriculum

Possibilities Plan

Web	Me!

Dramatic Possibilities Bathing Baby 62, Taking Things Off 62

Art/Sensory Possibilities Drawing 63, Foot Painting 64

Curiosity Possibilities Peek-a-boo 64, Mirror Play 64

Music Possibilities Johnny Works with One Hammer 68

Movement Possibilities Johnny Junper 69

Literacy Possibilities Parent Picture Book 65, On the Day I was Born 66

Outdoor Possibilities View from a Blanket 70, Outside Doll Baths 70

Project Possibilities Repeated Foot Painting 71

Books	Picture File/Vocabulary	
On the Day I was Born 　by Debi Chocolate From Head to Toe by Eric Carle Pots and Pans by Patricia Hubbell	Babies Eyes Faces Noses	Babies Outside Hands Mouths Ears

Rhymes & Fingerplays	Music/Songs	Prop Boxes
Eye Winker, Tom Tinker	Johnny Works	Things That Go On My Head Things That Go On My Hands

-2-

Concepts Learned in Me!

I can do things with my hands and my feet!

Some babies have teeth; some don't.

I can smell with my nose.

I can see with my eyes.

I can taste with my mouth.

I can take things off (socks, shoes, hats)!

I can put things on (hats, sunglasses)!

I can go to sleep.

I can eat.

I have a bellybutton!

I can see myself in the mirror.

I can bounce with my legs in the Johnny Jumper.

I can make things rattle.

I can bathe my baby doll.

I can put my baby to sleep.

I can paint with my hands and my feet.

I can play peek-a-boo!

I can stroll in a stroller.

I can eat with a spoon!

Concepts Learned In Mommies and Daddies

Concepts Learned

Mommies and daddies come back.

A child has a mommy and a daddy.

Mommies and daddies are special

Mommies and daddies do different things.

Families love babies and help them.

Mommies and daddies garden, cook, clean, work, and camp out.

Textures feel different.

I can pretend.

Mommies and daddies have car keys.

Pots and pans have lids.

Picnic baskets are full of stuff!

Things float.

I can shake a rattle.

I can dig in the dirt.

I can turn the pages in a book.

I can clean.

I can use the telephone.

I can empty and fill the picnic basket.

Concepts Learned in Inside/Outside

Concepts Learned

I can put things inside other things.

Keys go inside a purse or pocket.

Things change when I go outside.

Things change when I go inside.

My body fits inside things and outside things.

Cars and trucks have insides and outsides.

Insides are different from outsides (boxes, food jars, and bottles).

I can go bye-bye.

I can go shopping.

Water can be warm or cool.

The sky is outside.

I can squeeze a squirt bottle.

My body makes prints,

I can climb in my car seat.

Briefcases have thins inside.

Purses have things inside.

Boxes open and close.

I can kick my feet and make noise with ankle rattles.

I can make puzzles.

I can take tops off.

Concepts Learned in Open and Close

Concepts Learned

I can open and close things.

Things are there when I can't see them.

I have a tongue and teeth in my mouth.

I can open and close my mouth, hands, and eyes.

Picnic baskets are full of stuff!

Outside is different from inside.

I can find things that are hidden.

Purses open and close.

Boxes open and close.

Pots and pans have lids.

I can picnic.

I can dump things out.

I can make things happen.

I can play peek-a-boo.

I have a thumb.

Doors open and close.

Concepts Learned in Big and Little

Some things are little.

Some things are big.

I have little feet.

Mommy and Daddy have big feet.

Some things grow from little to big.

Seeds are little compared to their plants.

Bugs, seeds, butterflies, and birds are little.

Trucks, elephants, and buildings are big.

Shoes can be little and big.

Seeds are planted in soil.

Seeds grow into plants.

Hats go on my head.

Shoes go on my feet.

I can paint.

I can make a puzzle.

I can take puzzle pieces out.

I can put puzzle pieces back in the puzzle.

Concepts Learned in Cars, Trucks, and Trains

Concepts Learned

Cars and trucks have wheels.

Wheels go 'round and 'round.

Cars and trucks have horns.

Horns go beep, beep.

Vehicles break and need repair.

Trains have whistles.

I can pretend.

People take vacations.

I can get in my car seat.

I can get out of my car seat.

I can make tracks with car and truck wheels.

I can gas up my car.

Things stick to sticky paper.

Bells ring.

I can count one, two, or three.

Concepts Learned in Competent Me

Concepts Learned

Clothes have pockets.

I can put things in pockets.

I can take things out of pockets.

I can put things in a bag.

I can put clothes in a hamper.

I can paint.

I can play outside.

I can listen to stories.

I can move to music.

I can put a box in a box.

I can put a can in a can.

I can pretend to garden, build, cook, and clean.

I can make noise with noisemakers and rattles.

Pots and pans have lids.

I can put a lid on a box.

I can feel flour/powder.

I can tear paper.

I can crumble paper into a ball.

I can carry things.

Concepts Learned in Doors, Walls, Windows, and Hallways

Concepts Learned

I can look out windows.

I can go in and out doors.

I can paint with a plunger.

I can paint with a carrot top and with
cornhusks.

I can play pat-a-cake.

I can play with puppets.

I can look at books.

I can squirt water.

I can ride in a stroller.

I can climb in a box.

I can see myself in the mirror.

I can jump in the Johnny Jumper.

I can sit and play in the Exer-saucer.

I can play peek-a-boo.

I can see down hallways.

I can crawl down hallways.

I can read books.

I can hit a beach ball.

I can squirt water bottles.

Concepts Learned in Senses

Concepts Learned

I can do things with my hands and my feet!

I can move to music.

I can smell with my nose.

I can see with my eyes.

I can taste with my mouth.

I can touch with my fingers.

Different things feel different.

I can look at the sky, trees, and grass.

I can make sounds with rattles.

I can paint inside.

I can paint outside.

I can see myself in the mirror.

I can bounce with my legs in the Johnny Jumper.

Concepts Learned in Bubbles, Puddles, and Mud

Concepts Learned

I can squeeze mud.

Rain is water.

I can play with water.

I can paint with big brushes.

I can look at books.

I can move to music.

Some things are cool.

Some things are warm.

I can blow bubbles.

I can garden.

I can camp.

I can clean.

Textures feel different.

I can pretend.

Concepts Learned in Storybook Classics

Concepts Learned

I can listen to my teacher read stories.

I can listen to Mom/Dad read stories.

Stories can be about different things.

I can bounce to the words in songs and rhymes.

Teddy bears are good to hug.

I can ride in a wagon.

I can hold a book.

I can look at words and pictures in a book.

Things change when I go outside.

My body fits inside things.

I can paint.

I can ride in a wagon.

I can sing.

I can do fingerplays.

I can climb in a bear cave.

I can make puzzles.

I can make sounds.

I can turn pages.

I can "read" pages.

I can turn pages in a book.

I can paint with my feet.

I can identify my cereal box

I can hide.

I can follow bear tracks.

Concepts Learned in Sounds

Concepts Learned

Many things make sounds.

Some sounds are loud.

Some sounds are soft.

Some sounds are high.

Some sounds are low.

Some sounds are fast.

Some sounds are slow.

I can make sounds with my body.

I can clap my hands.

I can listen to music.

I can find things that are hidden.

Animals make sounds.

I can move to music.

Toys can make sounds.

Songs, Poems, Rhymes, and Fingerplays

Ants Go Marching

　　The ants go marching one by one,
　　Hurrah, hurrah.
　　The ants go marching one by one,
　　Hurrah, hurrah.
　　The ants go marching one by one,
　　The little one stops to suck his thumb,
　　And they all go marching down
　　Into ground to get out of the rain,
　　BOOM! BOOM! BOOM!

Animal Fair

　　I went to the animal fair.
　　The birds and the beasts were there.
　　The big baboon by the light of the moon
　　Was combing his auburn hair.
　　You should have seen the monk;
　　He sat on the elephant's trunk.
　　The elephant sneezed and fell on his knees,
　　And what became of the monk,
　　The monk, the monk, the monk?

Are You Sleeping?

　　Are you sleeping,
　　Are you sleeping,
　　Brother John, Brother John?
　　Morning bells are ringing,
　　Morning bells are ringing.
　　Ding, ding, dong!
　　Ding, ding, dong!

Baby Bumblebee

　　I'm bringing home a baby bumblebee,
　　Won't my mommy be so proud of me?
　　I'm bringing home a baby bumblebee,
　　"Ouch! It stung me!"

Baa, Baa, Black Sheep

　　Baa, baa, black sheep,
　　Have you any wool?
　　Yes, sir, yes, sir,
　　Three bags full.
　　One for my master,
　　One for my dame,
　　And one for the little boy
　　Who lives in the lane.

The Bear Went Over the Mountain

　　The bear went over the mountain,
　　The bear went over the mountain,
　　The bear went over the mountain,
　　To see what he could see.

　　To see what he could see,
　　To see what he could see,
　　The bear went over the mountain,
　　To see what he could see.

B-I-N-G-O

　　There was a farmer had a dog,
　　And Bingo was his name-o.
　　B-I-N-G-O,
　　B-I-N-G-O,
　　B-I-N-G-O,
　　And Bingo was his name-o.

Bumping Up and Down in My Little Red Wagon

　　Bumping up and down in my little red
　　　　wagon,
　　Bumping up and down in my little red
　　　　wagon,
　　Bumping up and down in my little red
　　　　wagon,
　　Won't you be my darlin'?

Bus Song

　　The wheels on the bus go round and round,
　　Round and round, round and round.
　　The wheels on the bus go round and round,
　　All around the town.

Clap, Clap, Clap Your Hands

　　Clap, clap, clap your hands
　　Clap your hands together.
　　Clap, clap, clap your hands
　　Clap your hands together.

Down by the Bay

　　Down by the bay
　　Where the watermelons grow
　　Back to my home
　　I dare not go.

For if I do
My mother will say,
"Did you ever see a bear combing his hair?"
Down by the bay.

Eensy Weensy Spider
The eensy weensy spider
Climbed up the water spout.
Down came the rain
And washed the spider out.

Out came the sun
And dried up all the rain,
And the eensy weensy spider
Climbed up the spout again.

Eye Winker, Tom Tinker
Eye Winker,
Tom tinker
Nose smeller,
Mouth eater
Chin chopper,
Gully, gully, gully!

Farmer in the Dell
The farmer in the dell,
The farmer in the dell,
Hi, ho, the derry-o,
The farmer in the dell.

Five Little Ducks
Five little ducks went out to play,
Over the hill and far away.
Mama Duck called with a quack, quack,
quack.
And four little ducks came swimming back.

Four little ducks went out to play,
Over the hill and far away.
Mama Duck called with a quack, quack,
quack.
And three little ducks came swimming back.

Three little ducks went out to play,
Over the hill and far away.
Mama Duck called with a quack, quack,
quack.
And two little ducks came swimming back.

Two little ducks went out to play,
Over the hill and far away.
Mama Duck called with a quack, quack,
quack.
And one little ducks came swimming back.

One little duck went out to play,
Over the hill and far away.
Mama Duck called with a quack, quack,
quack.
And five little ducks came swimming back!

Go In and Out the Window
Go in and out the window,
Go in and out the window,
Go in and out the window,
As we have gone before.

Good Morning to You
Good morning to you.
Good morning to you.
We're all in our places
With bright, shining faces.
Good morning to you.

The Hammer Song
Johnny works with one hammer, (move one
hand)
One hammer, one hammer.
Johnny works with one hammer.
Then he works with two.

Johnny works with two hammers, (move two
hands)
Two hammers, two hammers.
Johnny works with two hammers.
Then he works with three.

Johnny works with three hammers, (move
two hands and one foot)
Three hammers, three hammers.
Johnny works with three hammers.
Then he works with four.

Johnny works with four hammers, (move
two hands and two feet)
Four hammers, four hammers.
Johnny works with four hammers.
Then he works with five.

Johnny works with five hammers, (move two
   hands, two feet and head)
Five hammers, five hammers.
Johnny works with five hammers.
Then he goes to sleep!

Heads, Shoulders, Knees, and Toes
Head, shoulders, knees, and toes,
Head, shoulders, knees, and toes,
And eyes and ears and mouth and nose.
Head, shoulders, knees and toes, knees and
   toes.

Hokey Pokey
You put your right hand in.
You put your right hand out.
You put your right hand in,
And you shake it all about.
Then you do the hokey pokey,
And you turn yourself around.
That's what it's all about!

You put your left hand in…
You put your right foot in…
You put your left foot in…
You put your right elbow in…
You put your left elbow in…
You put your backside in…
You put your head in…
You put your whole self in…

How Many Cars Do You See?
How many cars do you see?
Vroom, vroom, vroom,
One, two, three!

Humpty Dumpty
Humpty Dumpty sat on a wall,
Humpty Dumpty had a great fall;
All the King's horses and all the King's men
Couldn't put Humpty together again.

Jack and Jill
Jack and Jill went up the hill,
To fetch a pail of water;
Jack fell down and broke his crown,
And Jill came tumbling after.

If You're Happy and You Know It
If you're happy and you know it,
Clap your hands. (clap, clap)

If you're happy and you know it,
Clap your hands. (clap, clap)
If you're happy and you know it,
Then your face will surely show it.
If you're happy and you know it,
Clap your hands. (clap, clap)

I See the Moon
I see the moon.
The moon sees me.
God bless the moon,
And god bless me.

Little Boy Blue
Little Boy Blue,
Come blow your horn.
The sheep's in the meadow.
The cow's in the corn.
Where is the boy
Who looks after the sheep?
He's under the haystack,
Fast asleep.

Little Miss Muffett
Little Miss Muffett
Sat on a tuffet,
Eating her curds and whey;
Along came a spider,
And sat down beside her,
And frightened Miss Muffett away.

Mary Had a Little Lamb
Mary had a little lamb,
Little lamb, little lamb.
Mary had a little lamb.
Its fleece was white as snow.

And everywhere that Mary went,
Mary went, Mary went,
And everywhere that Mary went,
The lamb was sure to go.

It followed her to school one day,
School one day, school one day.
It followed her to school one day,
Which was against the rule.

It made the children laugh and play,
Laugh and play, laugh and play.
It made the children laugh and play
To see a lamb at school.

The More We Get Together (tune: "Did You Ever See a Lassie?")

 The more we get together,
 Together, together,
 The more we get together,
 The happier are we.

 For your friends are my friends,
 And my friends are your friends,
 The more we get together,
 The happier we'll be.

My Turtle

 This is my turtle
 He lives in a shell.
 He likes his home very well.
 He pokes his head out
 When he wants to eat,
 And he pulls it back
 When he wants to sleep.

Old MacDonald Had a Farm

 Old MacDonald had a farm,
  E-I-E-I-O.
 And on his farm he had some cows,
  E-I-E-I-O.
 With a moo-moo here and a moo-moo there,
 Here a moo, there a moo, everywhere a moo-
  moo.
 Old MacDonald had a farm,
  E-I-E-I-O.

 Continue with other animals:

 Sheep...baa-baa....
 Pigs...oink-oink....
 Ducks...quack-quack....
 Chickens...chick-chick....

Open, Shut Them

 Open, shut them, open, shut them,
 Give a little clap.
 Open, shut them, open, shut them,
 Put them in your lap.

 Creep them, creep them, creep them, creep
  them,
 Right up to your chin.
 Open wide your smiling mouth,
 But do not let them in.

 Creep them, creep them, creep them, creep
  them,
 Past your cheeks and chin.
 Open wide your smiling eyes,
 Peeking in-BOO.

Pat-a-Cake

 Pat-a-cake, pat-a-cake, baker's man,
 Bake me cake as fast as you can.
 Pat and roll and mark it with "B."
 Put it in the oven for baby and me.

Rain, Rain Go Away

 Rain, rain, go away,
 Come again another day;

 Rain, rain, go away,
 Little (Abbey) wants to play.

Ring Around the Rosie

 Ring around the rosie,
 A pocket full of posies.
 Ashes, ashes,
 We all fall down!

Rock-a-Bye, Baby

 Rock-a-bye, baby,
 On the tree top.
 When the wind blows,
 The cradle will rock.
 When the bough breaks,
 The cradle will fall,
 And down will come baby,
 Cradle and all.

Row, Row, Row Your Boat

 Row, row, row your boat
 Gently down the stream.
 Merrily, merrily, merrily, merrily
 Life is but a dream.

A Tisket, a Tasket

 A tisket, a tasket,
 A green and yellow basket.
 I wrote a letter to my love,
 And on the way I lost it.
 I lost it; I lost it.
 And on the way I lost it.
 A little boy picked it up,
 And put it in his pocket.

There Was a Little Turtle Who Lived in a Box

The was a little turtle who lived in a box,
He swam in the water and climbed on the
    rocks.
He snapped at a mosquito; he snapped at a
    flea;
He snapped at a minnow; and he snapped at
    me.
He caught the mosquito; he caught the flea;
He caught the minnow, but he didn't catch
    me!

Three Men in a Tub

Rub a dub, dub,
Three men in a tub,
The butcher,
The baker,
And the candlestick maker.

Twinkle, Twinkle, Little Star

Twinkle, twinkle, little star,
How I wonder what you are.
Up above the world so high,
Like a diamond in the sky.
Twinkle, twinkle little star,
How I wonder what you are.

Where Is Thumbkin?

Where is thumbkin?
Where is thumbkin?
Here I am; here I am.
How are you today, sir?
Very well, I thank you.
Fly away: fly away.

Where is pointer?
Where is pointer?
Here I am; here I am.
How are you today, sir?
Very well, I thank you.
Fly away; fly away.

Where is tall one?

Where is ring finger?

Where is pinky?

References and Resources

Adams, C.E. & Fruge, E. (1996). *Why children misbehave.* Oakland, CA: New Harbinger.

Ainsworth, M.D.S., M.C. Blehar, E. Waters, & S. Wall. (1978). *Patterns of attachment: A psychological study of the strange situation.* Hillsdale, NJ: Erlbaum.

Ainsworth, M.D.S., S.M. Bell, & D. Stayton. (1974). Infant-mother attachment and social development. In *The introduction of the child in a social world,* ed. M.P. Richards, 197-213. London: Cambridge University Press.

Albrecht, K. (1997). Conferencing with parents of infants and toddlers. *Child Care Information Exchange.* 116, 51-53.

Albrecht, K. (1997). *Welcome to Learning: More about babies and toddlers.* KinderCare Learning Centers.

Albrecht, K.M., & Ward, M. (1989). Growing pains. *Pre-K Today,* 36, 54-55.

Allen, K.E., & L.R. Marotz. (1999). *Developmental profiles: Pre-birth through eight.* New York: Delmar.

American Public Health Association/American Academy of Pediatrics. (1992). *Caring for our children: National health and safety performance standards: Guidelines for out-of-home child care programs.* Washington, D.C.: American Public Health Association/American Academy of Pediatrics.

Ames, L.B., C. Gillespie, J. Haines, & F.L. Ilg. (1979). *The Gesell Institute's child from one to six: Evaluating behavior of the preschool child.* New York: HarperCollins.

Aronson, S.S. (1998). Breastfed babies in child care. *Child Care Information Exchange,* 120, 22-23.

Ball, J, & A. Pence. (1999). Beyond developmentally appropriate practice: Developing community and culturally appropriate practice. *Young Children,* 54 (2), 46-62.

Barclay, K., C. Benelli, & A. Curtis. (1995). Literacy begins at birth: What caregivers can learn from parents of children who read early. *Young Children,* 50 (4), 24-28.

Bailey, Becky. (1998). *10 principles of positive discipline.* Oviedo, FL: Loving Guidance.

Bailey, Becky. (1997). *I love you rituals.* Oviedo, FL: Loving Guidance.

Baumrind, D. (1972). Socialization and instrumental competence in young children. In E. Hartup (Ed.), *Research on young children.* Washington, DC: National Association for the Education of Young Children (NAEYC).

Bell, S.M. & M.D.S. Ainsworth. (1972). Infant crying and maternal responsiveness. *Child Development,* 43, 1171-1190.

Bellis, M. (1999). Look before you loop. *Young Children,* 54 (3), 80-83.

Belsky, J. (1988). The "effects" of infant day care reconsidered. *Early Childhood Research Quarterly,* 3, 235-272.

Berk, L.E. (1994). Vygotsky's Theory: The importance of make-believe play. *Young Children,* 50 (1), 30-39.

Berk, L.E. & A. Winsler. (1995). *Scaffolding children's learning.* Washington, DC: National Association for the Education of Young Children (NAEYC).

Blakey, N. (1996). *Lotions, potions, and slime mudpies and more!* Berkeley, CA: Tricycle Press.

Blecher-Sass, H. (1997). Good-byes can build trust. *Young Children,* 52(7), 12-15.

Bodrova, E. & D.J. Leong. (1996). *Tools of the mind: The Vygotskyian approach to early childhood education.* Englewood Cliffs, NJ: Merrill/Prentice Hall.

Bove, C. (1999). L'inserimento del bambino al nido (Welcoming the child into child care): Perspectives from Italy. *Young Children,* 54 (2), 32-34.

Brazelton, T. B. (1992). *Touchpoints: The essential reference.* Reading, MA: Addison-Wesley.

Brazelton, T.B. & B. Cramer. (1990). *The first relationship.* New York: Addison-Wesley.

Bredekamp, S. (1987). *Developmentally appropriate practice in early childhood programs serving children from birth to age 8 (exp. ed.).* Washington, DC: National Association for the Education of Young Children (NAEYC).

Bredekamp, S. & C. Copple. (1997). *Developmentally appropriate practice in early childhood programs,* Revised edition. Washington, DC: National Association for the Education of Young Children (NAEYC).

Brezel, F., M.F. Kalinowski & T. Drummond. (1985) Lights! camera! action! *Child Care Information Exchange,* 42, 18-21.

California Department of Education. (1990). *Flexible, fearful, or fiesty: The different temperaments of infants and toddlers* {videotape}. Sacramento, CA.

California Department of Education. (1990). A *guide to social-emotional growth and socialization.* Ed. J.R. Lally. Sacramento, CA: Department of Education.

Carnegie Corporation of New York. (1994). *Starting points: Meeting the needs of our youngest children.* New York: Carnegie Corporation of New York.

Carnegie Task Force on Learning in the Primary Grades. (1996). *Years of promise: A comprehensive learning strategy for America's children.* New York: Carnegie Corporation of New York.

Cataldo, C. (1983). *Infant and toddler programs.* Menlo Park, CA: Addison-Wesley.

Catlin, C. (1996). *More toddlers together: The complete planning guide for a toddler curriculum, volume II.* Beltsville, MD: Gryphon House.

Catlin, C. (1994). *Toddlers together: The complete planning guide for toddler curriculum.* Beltsville, MD: Gryphon House.

Cherry, C. (1976). *Creative play for the developing child: Early lifehood education through play.* Belmont, CA: Fearon.

Chess, S. & A. Thomas. (1987). *Know your child.* New York: Basic Books.

Chey, E. (1999). Study: Kids learn better with windows and skylights. *Houston Chronicle,* 7/5/99.

Clarke-Stewart, K.A. (1993). *Daycare.* Cambridge, MA: Harvard Press.

Clarke-Stewart, K.A. (1988). Evolving issues in early childhood education: A personal perspective. *Early Childhood Research Quarterly,* 3, 139-149.

Clarke-Stewart, K.A. (1998). Infant day care: Maligned or malignant? *American Psychologist,* 44, 266-273.

Cost, quality, and outcomes study team. (1995). Cost, quality, and child outcomes in child care centers: Key findings and recommendations. *Young Children,* 50 (4), 40-44.

Council for Professional Recognition. (1992). *The child development associate: Assessment system and competency standards for infant/toddler caregivers.* Washington, DC: Council for Early Childhood Professional Recognition.

Cryer, D. & L. Phillipsen. (1997). Quality details: a close up look at child care program strengths and weaknesses. *Young Children,* 52(2), 51-61.

Curry, N.E. & C.N. Johnson. (1990). *Beyond self-esteem: Developing a genuine sense of human value.* Washington, DC: National Association for the Education of Young Children (NAEYC).

Daniels, J.E. (1998). A modern mother's place is wherever her children are: Facilitating infant and toddler mothers' transitions in child care. *Young Children,* 53 (6), 4-14.

Dibble, C.H. & K.H. Lee. (2000). *101 Easy, wacky, crazy activities for young children.* Beltsville, MD: Gryphon House.

Dreikurs, R. (1964). *Children: The challenge.* New York: Hawthorne/Dutton.

Dunn, J. (1993). *Young children's close relationships: Beyond attachment.* Newbury Park, CA: Sage.

Early Childhood Committee of the Pennsylvania Chapter of the American Academy of Pediatrics. *Preparing for illness: A joint responsibility of parents and caregivers.* Bryn Mawr, PA: American Academy of Pediatrics.

Edwards, C., L. Gandini & Forman, G. (1994). *The one hundred languages of children: The Reggio Emilia approach to early childhood education.* Norwood, NJ: Ablex.

Edwards, C., Gandini, L., & Forman, G. (1998). *The one hundred languages of children: The Reggio Emilia approach to early childhood education—Advanced Reflections.* Norwood, NJ: Ablex.

Eisenberg, A. (1996). *What to expect in the first year.* New York: Workman.

Elicker, J. & C. Fortner-Wood. (1995). Adult-child relationships in early childhood programs, *Young Children,* 51 (1), 69-79.

Erickson, E.H. (1963). *Childhood and society.* New York: Norton.

Fein, G.G., A. Gariboldi & R. Boni. (1993). The adjustment of infants and toddlers to group care: The first six months. *Early Childhood Research Quarterly,* 8, 1-14.

Fox, N. & G.G. Fein. (Eds.). (1988). Infant day care (Special issue). *Early Childhood Research Journal,* 3.

Gandini, L. (1993). Fundamentals of the Reggio-Emilia approach to early childhood education, *Young Children,* 49(1), 4-8.

Gardner, H. (1983). *Frames of mind: The theory of multiple intelligences.* New York: Basic Books.

Gerber, M. (1979). *Resources for infant educarers: A manual for parents and professionals.* Los Angeles: Resources for Infant Educarers.

Gerber, M. & A. Johnson. (1997). *Your self-confident baby.* New York: Wiley.

Goleman, D. (1995). *Emotional intelligence.* New York: Bantam Books.

Goleman, D. (1998) *Working with emotional intelligence.* New York: Bantam Doubleday Dell.

Gonzales-Mena, J. & D.W. Eyer. (1997). *Infants, toddlers, and caregivers.* Mountain View, CO: Mayfield.

Gordon, I. (1970). *Baby learning through baby play.* New York: St. Martin's.

Gowen, J.W. (1995). Research in review: The early development of symbolic play, *Young Children,* 50 (3), 75-84.

Granovetter, R. & J. James. (1989). *Sift and shout: Sand play activities for children ages 1-6,* Lewisville, NC: Kaplan Press.

Greenman, J. (1988). *Caring spaces, learning places: Children's environments that work.* Redmond, WA: Exchange Press.

Greenman, J. & A. Stonehouse. (1996). *Prime times: A handbook for excellence in infant and toddler programs.* St. Paul, MN: Redleaf Press.

Greenspan, S. & N.T. Greenspan. (1989). *The essential partnership.* New York: Penguin.

Greenspan, S. & N.T. Greenspan. (1994). *First feelings: Milestones in the emotional development of your baby and child.* New York: Penguin.

Hayes, C.D., F.L. Palmer, & M. Zaslow. (1990). *Who cares for America's children: Child care policy for the 1990's.* Washington, DC: National Academy Press.

Herr, J. & T. Swim. (1999). *Creative resources for infants and toddlers.* Albany, NY: Delmar.

Highberger, R. & C. Schramm. (1976). *Child development for day care workers.* Boston: Houghton-Miflin.

Hofferth, S.L. & D.A. Phillips. (1987). Child care in the United States, 1970-1995. *Journal of Marriage and Family,* 49(3), 559-571.

Honig, A. (1982). *Playtime learning games for young children.* Syracuse, NY: Syracuse University Press.

Honig, A. (1989). *Love and learn: Discipline for young children.* Washington, DC: National Association for the Education of Young Children (NAEYC).

Honig, A. (1995). Singing with infants and toddlers. *Young Children,* 50 (5), 72-78.

Honig, A. & H.E. Brody. (1996). *Talking with your baby: Family as the first school.* Syracuse, NY: Syracuse University Press.

Howes, C. & C.E. Hamilton. (1992). Children's relationships with caregivers: Mothers and child care teachers. *Child Development* 64, 859-866.

Howes, C. & C.E. Hamilton. (1993). The changing experience of child care: Changes in teachers and in teacher-child relationships and children's social competence with peers. *Early Childhood Research Quarterly,* 8, 15-32.

Howes, C., D.A. Phillips & M. Whitebrook. (1992). Thresholds of quality: Implications for the social development of children in center-based care. *Child Development,* 63, 449-460.

Hughes, F.P., J. Eliker & L.C. Veen. (1995). A program of play for infants and their caregivers. *Young Children,* 50 (2), 52-58.

Ilg, L.B. & F.L. Ames. (1976). *Your two year old.* New York: Delacorte Press.

Jones, E. (1993). *Growing teachers: Partners in staff development.* Washington, DC: National Association for the Education of Young Children (NAEYC).

Jones, S. (1992). *Crying baby, sleepless night.* New York: Warner.

Jorde-Bloom, P. (1993). *A great place to work: Improving conditions for staff in young children's programs.* Washington, DC: National Association for the Education of Young Children (NAEYC).

Katz, L.G. (1977). *Talks with teachers: Reflections on early childhood education.* Washington, DC: National Association for the Education of Young Children (NAEYC).

Katz, L.G. (1998). Benefits of the mix. *Child Care Information Exchange,* 124, 46-49.

Katz, L.G., D. Evangelou & J.A. Hartman. (1990). *The case for mixed-age grouping in early education.* Washington, DC: National Association for the Education of Young Children.

Katz, L. & P. McClellan. (1997). *Fostering social competence: The teacher's role.* Washington, DC; National Association for the Education of Young Children (NAEYC).

Kendrick, A.S., R. Kaufman & K.P. Messinger. (1988). *Healthy young children: A manual for programs.* Washington, DC: National Association for the Education of Young Children (NAEYC).

Kohl, M. F. (1999). *Making make-believe.* Beltsville, MD: Gryphon House.

Kontos, S. & A. Wilcoz-Herzog. (1997). Teachers' interactions with children: Why are they so important? *Young Children,* 52(2), 4-12.

Korner, A.F. & E.B. Thoman. (1972). Visual alertness in neonates as evoked by maternal care. *Journal of Experimental Psychology,* 10, 67-68.

Kovach, B.A. & D.A. Da Ros. (1998). Respectful, individual, and responsive caregiving for infants: The key to successful care in group settings. *Young Children,* 53 (3), 61-64.

La Leche League International. (1990). *Breastfeeding fact sheet.* Franklin Park, IL: Center for Breastfeeding.

Lally, J.R. (1995). The impact of child care policies and practices on infant/toddler identity formation. *Young Children,* 51 (1), 58-67.

Leach, P. (1997). *Your baby and child: From birth to five.* New York: Knopf.

Leavitt, R.L. (1994). *Power and emotion in infant-toddler day care.* Albany, NY: State University of New York Press.

Legg, J. (1989). All parents are not alike: Focusing on the developmental needs of parents. *Child Care Information Exchange,* 69, 43-44.

Lickona, T. (1994). *Raising good children.* New York: Bantam Doubleday Dell.

Mann, M.B. & K.R. Thornburg. (1998). Maternal guilt: Helping mothers of infants and toddlers in child care. *Child Care Information Exchange,* 122, 26-29.

Marion, M. (1998). *Guidance of young children.* New York: Prentice Hall.

McBride, S.L. (1999). Family centered practices. *Young Children,* 54 (3), 62-68.

McMullen, M.B. (1999). Achieving best practices in infant and toddler care and education. *Young Children,* 54 (4), 69-75.

Melmed, M. (1997). Parents speak: Zero to three's findings from research on parents' views of early child development. *Young Children* 52 (2), 46-49.

Meyerhoff, M.K. (1992). Infant/toddler day care versus reality. *Young Children,* 47 (6), p. 44-45.

Miller, K. (2001). *Ages and stages.* Glen Burnie, MD: TelShare.

Mitchell, G. (1998). *A Very Practical Guide to Discipline with Young Children.* Glen Burnie, MD: Telshare.

Morris, S.L. (1995). Supporting the breastfeeding relationship during child care: Why is it important. *Young Children,* 50 (2), 59-62.

National Academy of Early Childhood Programs. *Accreditation criteria and procedures.* (1991). Washington, DC: National Academy of Early Childhood Programs.

National Association for the Education of Young Children. (1988). NAEYC position statement on standardized testing of young children 3 through 8 years of age. *Young Children,* 43, 42-47.

National Association for the Education of Young Children. (1996). NAEYC position statement: Responding to linguistic and cultural diversity— Recommendations for effective early childhood education. *Young Children,* 51, 4-12.

National Association for the Education of Young Children. (1998). *Helping children gain self-control.* Washington, DC: National Association for the Education of Young Children (NAEYC).

National Center for Clinical Infant Programs. (no date). *Heart start: The emotional foundations of school readiness.* National Center for Clinical Infant Programs.

Neugebauer, B. (1992). *Alike and different: Exploring our humanity with children.* Washington, DC: National Association for the Education of Young Children (NAEYC).

New, R.S. (1999). Here, we call it "Drop off and pickup": Transition to child care American-style. *Young Children,* 54 (2), 32-34.

Parten, M.B. (1932). Social participation among preschool children. *Journal of Abnormal Psychology,* 27, 243-269.

Phillips, D.A. (1987). *Quality in child care: What does the research tell us?* Washington, DC: National Association for the Education of Young Children (NAEYC).

Piaget, J. (1962). *Play, dreams, and imitation in childhood* (C. Gattegno & F.M. Hodgson, Trans.) New York: Norton.

Piaget, J. (1977). *The origins of intelligence in children.* New York: International Universities Press.

Pike, R.W. (1994). *Creative training techniques handbook: Tips, tactics, and how-to's for delivering effective training.* Minneapolis, MN: Lakewood Publications.

Powell, D.R. (1998). Reweaving parents into the fabric of early childhood programs. *Young Children,* 53(5), 60-67.

Pratt, M.W. (1999). The importance of infant/toddler interactions. *Young Children,* 54 (4), 26-30.

Raikes, H. (1993). Relationship duration in infant care: Time with high-ability teacher and infant-teacher attachment. *Early Childhood Research Quarterly,* 8, 309-325.

Redleaf, R. & A. Robertson. (1999). *Learn and play the recycle way: Homemade toys that teach.* St. Paul, MN: Redleaf Press.

Reisenberg, J. (1995). Reflections on quality infant care. *Young Children,* 50 (6), 23-25.

Rockwell, R., D. Hoge & B. Searcy. (1999). *Linking language and literacy: Simple language and literacy activities throughout the curriculum.* Beltsville, MD: Gryphon House

Rogers, C.S. & J.K. Sawyer. (1988). *Play in the lives of children.* Washington, D.C.: National Association for the Education of Young Children (NAEYC).

Roskos, K.A. & S.B. Neuman. (1994). Of scribbles, schemas, and storybooks: Using literacy albums to document young children's literacy growth. *Young Children,* 49 (2), 78-85.

Rubenstein, J.L. & C. Howes. (1979). Caregiver and infant behavior in day care and in homes. *Developmental Psychology,* 15, 14.

Scallan, P.C. (1987). Teachers coaching teachers: Development from within. *Child Care Information Exchange,* 58, 3-6.

Scallan, P.N. (1988). How to implement a coaching program in your center. *Child Care Information Exchange,* 59, 35-37.

Schiller, P. (1999). *Start smart: Building brain power in the early years.* Beltsville, MD: Gryphon House.

Schweinhart, L. & D.P. Weikart. (1996). *Lasting differences: The High/Scope preschool curriculum comparison study through age 23.* Monographs of the High/Scope Educational Research Foundation, #12, Ypsilanti, MI: High/Scope Press.

Shelov (AAP). (1998). *Caring for your baby and child.* New York: Bantam, Doubleday, Dell.

Shepard, LA, S.L. Kagan & E. Wurtz. (1998). Goal 1 early childhood assessments resource group recommendations. *Young Children,* 53 (3), 52-54.

Shore, R. (1997). *Rethinking the brain: New insights into early development.* New York: Families and Work.

Silberg, J. (1999). *125 Brain games for babies.* Beltsville, MD: Gryphon House.

Silberg, J. (2000). *125 Brain games for toddlers and twos.* Beltsville, MD: Gryphon House.

Silberg, J. (1993). *Games to play with babies.* Beltsville, MD: Gryphon House.

Silberg, J. (1993). *Games to play with toddlers.* Beltsville, MD: Gryphon House.

Sroufe, L. A., & J. Fleeson. (1986). Attachment and the construction of relationships. In W.W. Hartup & A. Rubin (Eds.) *Relationships and Development* (pp. 51-71). Hillsdale, NJ: Erlbaum.

Sroufe, L. E. (1988). A developmental perspective on day care. *Early Childhood Research Quarterly,* 3, 283-291.

Stonehouse, A. (1995). *How does it feel?: Child care from a parent's perspective.* Redmond, WA: Exchange Press.

Stremmel, A.J., M.J. Benson & D.R. Powell. (1993). Communication, satisfaction, and emotional exhaustion among child care center staff, directors, and assistant teachers. *Early Childhood Research Quarterly,* 8, 221-233.

Tabors, P.O. (1998). What early childhood educators need to know: Developing programs for linguistically and culturally diverse children and families. *Young Children,* 53(6), 20-26.

Teaching Tolerance Project. (1997). *Starting small: Teaching tolerance in preschool and the early grades.* Montgomery, AL: Southern Poverty Law Center.

Texas Workforce Commission. (1999). Saying goodbye: Making hard transitions easier. *Texas Child Care.* Austin, TX: Texas Workforce Commission.

Thompson, R.A. (1988). The effects of infant day care through the prism of attachment theory: A critical approach. *Early Childhood Research Quarterly,* 3, 273-282.

Whitehead, L.C. & S.I. Ginsberg. (1999). Creating a family-like atmosphere in child care settings: All the more difficult in large child care centers. *Young Children,* 54 (2), 4-10.

Wilmes, L. & D. Wilmes. (1996). *Play with big boxes.* Elgin, IL: Building Blocks.

Wilmes, L. & D. Wilmes. (1996). *Play with small boxes.* Elgin, IL: Building Blocks.

Wittmer, D. & Honig. A.S. (1994). Encouraging positive social development in young children. *Young Children,* 49(5), 4-12.

Wong, D.L., M. Hockenberry-Eaton, M.L. Winkelstein, D. Wilson & E. Ahmann. (1999). *Nursing care of infants and children.* New York: Mosby.

Index

0 to 6 months

curiosity possibilities, 64, 83, 127, 148, 195, 212–213, 265, 284–285, 332–333, 353, 395–396, 414–415

dramatic possibilities, 62, 80, 124, 146, 191–192, 262, 282, 350, 392, 412

food guide, 303

language development, 227, 230, 232, 438

literacy possibilities, 65–67, 84–85, 129–131, 150–151, 197–199, 213–214, 267–269, 286–287, 334–335, 354–355, 397–398, 415–417

motor skills, 300, 302, 439

movement play, 86, 132, 153, 270, 290–291, 336, 356, 419

music possibilities, 85, 131–132, 151, 215–216, 269–270, 287–290, 335, 355–356, 399–400, 417–418

outdoor possibilities, 70, 88, 133, 154, 272, 292–293, 338, 358, 402

project possibilities, 134–135, 273, 359–360, 402–403

sensory/art possibilities, 63, 82, 125, 147, 263–264, 283–284, 331, 352, 394

6 to 12 months

curiosity possibilities, 64–65, 83–84, 127–128, 148–149, 195–196, 212–213, 265–266, 284–285, 333, 353, 396, 415

dramatic possibilities, 62–63, 80–82, 124, 124, 191–192, 210, 262, 282–283, 330, 350–351, 392–393, 412

food guide, 303

language development, 227, 230, 232, 438

literacy possibilities, 66–67, 84–85, 129–131, 150–151, 198–199, 213–214, 267–269, 286–287, 334–335, 354–355, 397–398, 415–417

motor skills, 300, 302, 439

movement possibilities, 69–70, 86–87, 132–133, 153, 200, 270, 291, 337–338, 356–356, 401, 419

music possibilities, 85–86, 131–132, 151–152, 215–216, 269–270, 288–290, 335–336,

355–356, 399–400, 417–418

outdoor possibilities, 70, 88, 133–134, 154, 216, 272, 292–293, 338–339, 358, 402, 420

project possibilities, 71, 88–89, 134–135, 154–155, 202, 217–218, 273, 293, 339–340, 359–360, 402–403, 421

sensory/art possibilities, 63–64, 82, 126, 147–148, 211, 263–265, 283–284, 331–332, 394–395, 412–413

10 Principles of Positive Discipline by Becky Bailey, 55

12 to 18 months

curiosity possibilities, 64–65, 83–84, 127–128, 148–150, 195–196, 212–213, 265–266, 285, 333, 353, 396–397, 415

dramatic possibilities, 62–63, 80–82, 124, 146, 191–192, 210, 262–263, 282–283, 330, 350–351, 392–393, 412

food guide, 303

language development, 227, 230, 232, 438

literacy possibilities, 66–67, 84–85, 129–131, 150–151, 198–199, 213–214, 267–269, 286–287, 334–335, 354–355, 397–398, 415–417

motor skills, 300, 302, 439

movement possibilities, 86–87, 132–133, 153, 200, 216, 270–271, 290–291, 337–338, 357, 401, 419

music possibilities, 85–86, 131–132, 151–152, 215–216, 269–270, 288–290, 335–336, 355–356, 399–400, 417–418

outdoor possibilities, 70, 88, 133–134, 154, 201, 216–217, 272, 292–293, 338–339, 358–359, 402, 420

project possibilities, 71, 88–89, 134–135, 154–155, 202, 217–218, 273, 293, 339–340, 359–360, 402–403, 421

sensory/art possibilities, 63–64, 82, 126, 147–148, 193–195, 211, 263–265, 283–284, 331–332, 352, 394–395, 412–414

125 Brain Games for Babies by J. Silberg, 257

125 Brain Games for Toddlers by J. Silberg, 118

A

A Very Practical Guide to Discipline with Young Children by G. Mitchell, 243, 318

Accident/incident report, 432–433

Activity bars, 56, 141

Activity gyms. *See* Play gyms

Adjustment

facilitating, 105–106

postcards, 118–119

Ages and Stages by Karen Miller, 47, 55

Aggression, 374–375

postcard, 384–385

Ainsworth, M. D. S., 42, 98

Alike and Different by B. Neugebauer, 47

All Aboard Trucks by Lynn Conrad, 209, 213, 223

All My Little Ducklings by Monica Wellington, 191, 198, 205

American Academy of Pediatrics, 302

Pennsylvania chapter, 305–306

Anecdotal record forms, 428

Animal Sounds by Aurelina Battaglia, 281, 287, 297

Animals (*See also* Puppets; Teddy bears)

caterpillars, 262

farm, 282, 288

fish, 420, 426

plastic, 82, 94, 298, 333, 420, 426

rubber ducks, 418, 426

spiders, 262

stuffed, 25, 55, 63, 125, 130–131, 141, 193, 206, 262–263, 265, 268–269, 271–272, 277–278, 298, 319, 357

turtles, 123, 130, 140, 206, 278

Appliance boxes, 350, 360, 395

Are You My Mother? by P. D. Eastman, 79, 84, 93

Art possibilities. *See* Project possibilities; Sensory/art possibilities

Art knives, 127, 195, 262, 350, 358

Art paper, 345, 421

Arthur's Eyes by Marc T. Brown, 145, 150, 159

Arthur's Nose by Marc T. Brown, 145, 150, 159

Assessment, 13–14, 18–21
    communicating, 226–227, 438
    connecting, 96–97, 436
    expressing feelings, 366–367, 440
    instrument, 32–33, 163
    moving around, 300, 439
    nonstandardized, 18–19
    overview, 446
    relating, 162–163, 437
    separating, 32–33, 435
    using, 21

Attachment
    and language development, 238
    development, 98
    discriminate, 167, 179
    object permanence, 100
    postcard, 111
    stages of, 98–100

Autonomy, 308–309
    postcards, 341–342

B

Baby at Home by Monica Wellington, 61, 67, 75

Baby bouncers. *See* Bouncy seats

Baby Faces by Margaret Miller, 61, 67, 75

Baby Goes Shopping by Monica Wellington, 61, 67, 75

Baby in a Buggy by Monica Wellington, 61, 67, 75

Baby in a Car by Monica Wellington, 61, 67, 75

Baby lotion, 118
    containers, 125, 135, 141, 392, 407

Baby powder, 118, 331, 346, 394, 426
    containers, 125, 135, 141, 392, 407

Baby's Bath by Judy Nayer, 411, 425

Bags, 146, 158, 216, 222, 276, 282
    freezer, 129
    paper, 87, 139, 139, 171, 216, 244, 337
    resealable plastic, 130, 159, 198, 206, 214,

    224, 360, 412–413, 426
    shopping, 330, 346
    trash, 311

Balls
    beach, 357, 364
    tennis, 395

Baskets, 62, 200, 216, 337, 346, 351, 386
    laundry, 338
    picnic, 87, 93, 146, 159–160, 277
    shopping, 125

Bathing suits, 210

Beach balls, 357, 364

Bear cave, 262, 268–269

Bell necklaces, 284, 298

Bell, S. M., 42, 98

Bells, 170, 212, 224, 282–284, 291, 296

Berk, L. E., 128

Big and Little by Margaret Miller, 191, 197, 205

The Big Book of Things That Go by Caroline Bingham, 209, 223

Big Dog, Little Dog by P. D. Eastman, 191, 198, 205

Big Sister and Little Sister by Charlotte Zolotow, 191, 198, 205

Big Truck, Big Wheels by Bobbie Kalman & Petrina Gentile, 209, 213, 223

Binoculars, 93, 159, 277, 393

Biographies, 108–109

Biting, 107
    anticipating, 174–175
    handling, 173–174, 374–375
    postcards, 115–117, 182–184
    preventing, 174
    responding, 175–176
    supervising, 175

Blankets, 43, 55, 57, 63, 70, 76, 81, 125, 141, 153, 155, 158–159, 218, 272, 277–278, 292, 326, 339, 350, 358, 364, 402, 407

Bleach, 119, 315

Blocks, 26, 93, 169–170, 216, 330, 344–345
    picture, 334
    plastic, 335
    soft, 56

texture, 170
Boni, R., 104
Books read list, 431
Books, 27, 29, 76
    accordion, 267
    cereal box, 267–268
    cookbooks, 80
    for babies, 242–243, 249
    logo, 268
    on communicating, 243, 261, 268, 272,
        277–278, 281
    on connecting, 108, 118, 123, 129–131, 135,
        140, 141, 145, 150–151, 158–160
    on expressing feelings, 391, 407, 425–426
    on moving around, 326, 329, 334–335,
        344–345, 349, 364
    on relating, 170, 176, 186, 191, 209, 213, 223,
        224
    on separating, 47, 55, 61, 75, 79, 84–85, 93
    open/close, 154
    overview, 447
    parent pictures, 65, 72
    picture files, 129
    picture, 160
    self-concept, 75
    sound, 286, 298
    teacher-made, 147, 197, 214, 217
    telephone, 337
    wallpaper, 170
Boots, 74, 405, 412, 421
Bottles
    plastic, 155, 169, 244, 283, 314–315, 418–419,
        422
    soda, 195, 206, 276, 293, 298, 415
    spray, 81, 133, 201, 330, 403
    squirt, 344, 359, 360, 403, 413, 426
    sunscreen, 222
    water, 276, 293, 298
Bouncy seats, 25, 57, 88, 94, 125, 283, 314, 331,
    338, 345, 426
Bows, 74, 81, 405
Boxes, 29, 119, 140, 146, 153, 155, 169, 171, 196,

200, 205–206, 244, 262, 264, 271, 278,
    283, 292–293, 298, 330, 333–334, 337, 351
    appliance, 350, 360, 395
    Boo! 149
    busy, 26, 213, 224
    cardboard, 133, 160
    cereal, 267, 278
    food, 80–81, 83, 139, 330, 407
    oatmeal, 128, 140, 205, 298, 407
    shoe, 149, 153, 160, 169
    slide, 128
    texture, 178
Bracelets, 24, 74, 405
Brain growth, 228
    postcards, 252–253
Brain-based care, 234–235
Brazelton, T. B., 102–103
Breastfeeding, 302–304
Bredekamp, S., 19–20
Bridges Are to Cross by Philemon Sturges, 349,
    355, 363
Bright Eyes, Brown Skin by Cheryl Willis Hudson,
    145, 150, 159, 391, 398, 406
Brown Bear, Brown Bear by Bill Martin, Jr.,
    261–262, 273, 277
Bubble solution, 421–422, 426
Bubble wands, 421–422, 426
Bubble wrap, 57, 284
Buckets, 359, 420
Building a House by Byron Barton, 349, 354–355,
    363
Burlap, 118, 170
Busy boxes, 26, 213, 224
Butcher paper, 194, 202, 278, 293, 298
Buttons, 335
By the Seashore by Maurice Pledger, 411, 415,
    425

C

Calendars, 29
California State Department of Education, 37, 47

Cameras, 65, 71, 202, 264
  disposable, 109
  Polaroid, 360, 364
Camping props, 79, 93
Camping props, 81, 87–88, 93
Can You Hop? by Lisa Lawston, 329, 334, 344
Cans, 81, 83, 128, 140, 149, 170, 333
  coffee, 128, 170, 339–340, 346
  formula
  watering, 217, 224
Car seats, 124, 135, 141, 210, 218, 224
  safety postcard, 138
Card stock, 197, 214, 217
Cardboard, 65, 127, 195, 197, 214, 217, 266–268, 351
  boxes, 133, 160
  tubes, 244, 393, 407, 422
Caring for Your Baby and Child by S. Shelov, 325
Carnegie Task Force, 105
Carpets, 55
  samples, 401, 407
Carrots, 358, 360, 364
Cars, 211, 224, 333
Cassette tapes, 27, 278, 282, 288–289, 292–293, 298, 401, 407, 412
Catalogs, 80, 267, 344, 346
Catch Me If You Can by Bernard Most, 329, 334, 344
CD players, 288–289, 401
CDs, 27, 288–289, 401
Cereal boxes, 267, 278
Cereals, 148, 155, 169, 170, 303
Chart paper, 202
Chess, C., 37
Chew toys, 119
Child abuse
  documenting, 381–382
  preventing, 381
Child development
  attachment stages, 98–100, 238
  communicating, 228–232
  connecting, 98–100

discipline, 315–317
emotional development, 367–369
expressing feelings, 367–369
health, 305–307, 310–314
innovations in, 22
intellectual development, 231–232
language development, 229–231, 237–238
moving around, 301–307
multiple intelligences, 240–241
nutrition, 302–304
object permanence, 100
Parten on, 165
physical development, 301–302
Piaget on, 164–165, 239–240
play, 164
principles, 73
relating, 164–166
safety issues, 314–315
separating, 34–35, 238–239
social, 164
Vygotsky on, 165–166
Children: The Challenge by R. Dreikurs, 318
Chime balls, 290, 298
Chime rattles, 417, 426
Chocolate Covered Cookie Tantrum by Deborah Blumenthal, 391, 397, 406
Choke tubes, 307, 361
Chugga Chugga Choo Choo by Kevin Lewis, 209, 213, 223
Clap Your Hands by Lorinda Bryan Cauley, 61, 75, 281, 286, 297, 391, 398, 406, 411, 419, 425
Classroom cloths, 393
Cleaning props, 79, 93, 343–344, 362, 425
Clifford Counts Bubbles by Norman Bridwell, 411, 416, 425
Clifford the Big Red Dog by Norman Bridwell, 261, 269, 277
Clifford's Bath by Norman Bridwell, 411, 416, 425
Close Your Eyes by Jean Marzollo, 145, 150, 159
Coats, 135, 146, 210
Coffee cans, 128, 170, 339–340, 346
Collages, 211, 332, 359

Communicating, 225–298
    activity centers, 258
    attachment, 238
    child development, 228–232
    concepts learned, 276, 296, 458–459
    curiosity possibilities, 265–266, 284–285
    curriculum webs, 259, 279
    developmental challenges, 236–237
    developmental growth, 235–236
    dramatic possibilities, 262–263, 282–283
    environments, 257–258
    intellectual development, 231–232
    interactive experiences, 233–234
    language development, 229–231, 237–238
    literacy possibilities, 267–269, 286–287
    movement possibilities, 270–271, 290–291
    multiple intelligences, 240–241
    music possibilities, 269–270, 287–290
    observation/assessment, 226–227, 438
    outdoor possibilities, 272, 292–293
    parent participation, 273–274, 293–295
    parent partnerships, 244–256
    Piaget on, 239–240
    possibilities plans, 259–298
    project possibilities, 273, 293
    resources, 242–243, 257, 261 276–278,
        296–298
    sensory/art possibilities, 263–265, 283–284
    separation anxiety, 238–239
    teacher competencies, 243
    teaching, 234–243
Communication sheets, 36
Concepts learned, 28–29
    communicating, 276, 296, 458–459
    connecting, 139, 158, 452–453
    expressing feelings, 405, 424, 460–461
    moving around, 343, 362, 456–457
    overview, 450–451
    relating, 204, 222, 454–455
    separating, 74, 92, 450–451
Conferencing, 375–381
    as parent education, 376–377

    formal oral, 379–380
    formal/written, 377–378
    informal oral, 380–381
    informal/written, 378–379
    open-ended questions, 377
Connecting, 18, 95–160
    child development, 98–100
    concepts learned, 139, 158, 452–453
    curiosity possibilities, 127–128, 148–150
    curriculum webs, 121, 143
    dramatic possibilities, 124–125, 146
    environments, 118–120
    interactive experiences, 101
    literacy possibilities, 129–131, 150–151
    movement possibilities, 132–133, 153
    music possibilities, 131–132, 151–152
    observation/assessment, 96–97, 436
    outdoor possibilities, 133–134, 154
    parent participation, 135–138, 155–157
    parent partnerships, 108–118
    possibilities plans, 121–160
    project possibilities, 134–135, 154–155
    resources, 108, 119, 139–141, 158–160
    sensory/art possibilities, 125–128, 147–150
    teacher competencies, 108
    teaching, 102–108
Construction paper, 127, 132, 170, 395
Construction props, 79, 93, 210, 222, 344–345
Construction Zone by Tana Hoban, 209, 213, 223
Contact paper, 29, 56, 71, 127, 134, 141, 147,
        170, 206, 211, 214, 224, 267, 271, 332, 334,
        339–340, 346, 383
Containers, 62, 76, 125, 170, 211, 344, 346, 351,
        362, 364, 392, 412, 414, 420, 425–426
    clear, 386
    food, 79–81, 83, 86–87, 92–94, 128, 139, 140,
        155, 159–160, 276, 293, 298, 335, 340, 343,
        346, 407, 426
Contemplating Your Bellybutton by Jun Nanao, 61,
        66, 75
Content knowledge, 28–29
Continuity of care, 104–105

Cookbooks, 80–81

Cooking, 404

props, 79, 92

Copple, C., 19

Corduroy by Don Freeman, 261–262, 277

Corduroy, 118, 170, 263

Corn, 338, 352, 360, 364

husks, 352, 360, 364

Cornmeal, 211

Cotton, 118

balls, 65, 118

Coupon exchange, 244

The Cow That Went Oink by Bernard Most, 281, 287, 297

Cradle gyms, 26

Crayons, 25, 63, 195, 264, 293, 332, 339

Creativity, 373–374

Crying, 42–44, 164

Cubbies, 55

Cuddle toys, 55, 63, 76, 158, 160, 407 (*See also* Animals, stuffed; Teddy bears)

Cupcake tins, 169

Cups, 170

Curiosity possibilities, 25–28

communicating, 265–266, 284–285

connecting, 127–128, 148–150

expressing feelings, 395–397, 414–415

moving around, 332–333, 353

relating, 195–196, 212–213

separating, 58, 64–65, 83–84

Curriculum webs, 14, 29

communicating, 259, 279

connecting, 121, 143

expressing feelings, 389, 409

moving around, 327, 347

overview, 446

relating, 189, 207

separating, 59, 77

Curry, N. E., 19

Curtains, 55, 149, 155, 160, 351, 360, 364

D

Da Ros, D. A., 103–105

Daddy Makes the Best Spaghetti by Anna Grossnickle Hines, 79, 85, 93

Daddy, Daddy, Be There by Candy D. Boyd, 79, 84–85, 93

Developmental challenges, 236–237

Developmental tasks

assessing, 18–19

continuum, 20–21

Diaper bags, 125, 135

Diapering, 36, 41–42, 306, 310–311

Diapers, 125, 171

Diarrhea, 305

Dirt, 80, 202, 426

Discipline, 44–45

biting, 108, 173–176

calling for help, 171–172

connecting, 107–108

distraction, 44

expressing feelings, 374–375

managing aggression, 374–375

moving around, 315–317

natural consequences, 315

planning, 173

postcard, 384–385

problem-solving, 171

redirection, 45

relating, 171–176, 187

setting limits, 315–317

taking turns, 172

trading, 172

walking away, 172–173

Discriminate attachment, 98–99, 167

postcard, 179

Dishcloths, 92, 343

Distraction, 44–45

Dolls, 25, 55, 62, 70, 76, 125, 206, 350, 358

The Doorbell Book by Jan Pienkowski, 281, 286, 297, 349, 355, 363

Doorbells, 296

Doughnuts, 383

Dramatic possibilities, 25
  communicating, 262–263, 282–283
  connecting, 124–125, 146
  expressing feelings, 392–393, 412
  moving around, 330, 350–351
  relating, 192–193, 210
  separating, 58, 62–63, 80–82
Dressing by Helen Oxenbury, 329, 334, 344
Dress-up clothes, 25, 61–62, 74–75, 124, 126,
    140, 169, 338, 346, 405
Drums, 291, 298, 401
Duck Song by Kenneth Grahame, 411, 416, 425
Dustbuster toys, 362, 425

E

Ear infections, 294
  postcard, 324
Edwards, C., 26, 105, 119, 373
Egg cartons, 169
Elastic pulls, 127
Emotional development, 367–369
  stimulating, 370–372
Emotional Intelligence by D. Goleman, 243, 383,
    386
The Enormous Turnip by Kathy Parkenson, 191,
    198, 205
Environments, 13, 23, 29
  centers vs. experiences, 57–58, 120, 188, 326,
    387
  communicating, 257–258
  connecting, 118–120
  discipline, 187
  expressing feelings, 386–387
  minimalism, 386
  moving around, 325–326
  multiple intelligences, 257–258
  outdoors, 325–326
  overview, 446
  play props, 186–187
  relating, 186–188
  sanitation, 324

separating, 55–58
windows, 386
Erikson, E. H., 32, 43, 102
The Essential Partnership by S. Greenspan & N. T.
    Greenspan, 47
Exer-saucers, 57, 69, 76, 364
Expressing feelings, 365–426
  child development, 367–369
  concepts learned, 405, 424, 460–461
  curiosity possibilities, 395–397, 414–415
  curriculum webs, 389, 409
  dramatic possibilities, 392–393, 412
  environments, 386–387
  interactive experiences, 369–370
  literacy possibilities, 397–398, 415–417
  movement possibilities, 401, 419
  music possibilities, 399–400, 417–418
  observation/assessment, 366–367, 440
  outdoor possibilities, 402, 420
  parent participation, 403–404, 421–424
  parent partnerships, 383–386
  possibilities plans, 389–426
  project possibilities, 402–403, 421
  resources, 383, 391, 405–407, 411, 425–426
  sensory/art possibilities, 394–395, 412–414
  teacher competencies, 382
  teaching, 370–383
Expressive language, 231
Eyer, 128
Eyes, Nose, Ears and Toes by Jane Conteh-
    Morgan, 145, 150, 159
Eyes, Nose, Fingers, Toes by Judy Hindley, 61, 66,
    75

F

Fabric, 118, 155, 160, 170, 178, 395
  scraps, 332
Families. *See also* Parent participation; Parent
    partnerships; Parent postcards; Parents
Family by Helen Oxenbury, 79, 85, 93
Feather dusters, 362, 414, 425–426

Feedback, 21–22

Feeding, 36, 41–42

Fein, G. G., 104

Fiber fill, 319

File folders, 29, 107

Film, 264, 360, 364

Finger paints, 25, 71, 76, 160, 345, 364, 395, 407

Fingerplays, 27, 29, 123, 130–131, 145, 152, 159, 191, 199, 205, 209, 214, 223, 261, 277, 281, 329, 336, 344, 349, 398, 411, 425, 462–466

    overview, 447

First Feelings by S. Greenspan & N. T. Greenspan, 118, 383, 386

Fish, plastic, 420, 426

Fleeson, 100

Flexible, Fearful, or Fiesty by the California Dept. of Education, 47

Floor time, 372–373

Flour, 56, 63, 82, 94, 331, 346, 394, 426

Foods, 63

    containers, 79–81, 83, 86–87, 92–94, 128, 139, 140, 155, 159–160, 276, 293, 298, 335, 340, 343, 346, 407, 426

    introducing solids, 309–310

Forman, G., 26, 105, 119, 373

Forms, 428–440

    accident/incident report, 432–433

    anecdotal records, 428

    assessment instruments, 435–440

    books read list, 431

    communication sheet, 429–430

    parent visit log, 434

    planning, 445-451

Formula, 302–304

    cans, 128

    feeding issues, 304

    heating, 314

Foster Social Competence by L. Katz & P. McClellan, 176

Freezer bags, 129

Freight Train by Donald Crews, 209, 213, 223

From Head to Toe by Eric Carle, 61, 67, 75

Fruits, 303

    plastic, 159, 277

Full-day programs, 20

Furniture, 351

G

Games to Play with Babies by J. Silberg, 118

Gandini, L., 26, 105, 119, 373

Gardening props, 79–80, 86, 88, 92

Gardner, 240–241

Gariboldi, A., 104

Gelatin, 148

    blocks, 394

    unflavored, 407

Gender roles

    postcard, 220

Gerber, Magda, 42, 57, 102–104, 118, 237, 309

Gift wrap, 397

    homemade, 421

Glitter, 195, 415, 426

Gloves, 74, 222, 265, 405

    disposable, 306

    gardening, 92

Glue, 65, 88, 127, 130, 149, 154, 160, 169, 178, 195, 197, 217, 263, 266–268, 283, 298, 392, 395, 415, 418–419

Going places props, 146, 158, 222

Goleman, D., 240–241, 243

Gonzalez-Mena, 128

Good-Byes Can Build Trust by H. Blecher-Sass, 47

Goodnight Moon by Margaret Wise Brown, 123, 129, 140, 145, 150, 159

Good-night props, 158

Gordon, Ira, 42, 103, 371

Gradual enrollment, 39–40

Greenman, J., 20, 102, 104

Greenspan, Stanley, 57, 368

Greg and Steve's Body Rock Dance, 319

Guidance of Young Children by M. Marion, 318

Guidance

    connecting, 107–108

expressing feelings, 374–375

moving around, 315–317

natural consequences, 315

relating, 171–176, 187

separating, 44–45

setting limits, 315–317

Gym mats, 27–28, 133, 272

H

Hamilton, C. E., 100, 103

Hammers, 81, 210, 222, 330

Hand brooms, 81, 93, 330, 344

Handkerchiefs, 109, 403

Handwashing, 310–311

Happy Birthday, Moon by Fred Asch, 145, 150, 159

Hard hats, 93, 210, 222, 330, 344–345

Harold and the Purple Crayon by Crockett Johnson, 349, 355, 363

Hats, 25, 139, 158, 169, 192, 205, 222, 405

construction, 93, 210, 222, 330, 344–345

sun, 92

Healthy Young Children by A. S. Kendrick et al., 318

Heart Start by National Center for Clinical Infant Programs, 108

Helping Children Gain Self-Control by National Association for the Education of Young Children, 325

Hole punches, 65, 88, 197, 217, 267–268, 273

Honig, A., 96, 102, 104, 239

Houses by Claude Delafosse, 349, 355, 363

Houston Chronicle, 386

How Does It Feel? by A. Stonehouse, 47

Howes, C., 100, 102–103

Humpty Dumpty and Other Rhymes by Iona Opie, 349, 355, 363

I

I Don't Want to Take a Bath by Julia Sykes, 411, 416, 425

I Hear by Helen Oxenbury, 281, 286, 297

I Love You Rituals by Becky Bailey, 55

I See by Rachel Isadora, 61, 67, 75

I Touch by Rachel Isadora, 61, 67, 75

If You Give a Mouse a Cookie by Laura J. Numeroff, 261, 277

Ignoring, 107

In & out props, 140

Independence, 308–309

postcards, 341–342

Index cards, 339, 346

Indiscriminate attachment, 98

postcard, 111

Individualized scheduling, 40–41

Infant health

choke tubes, 307

conversations, 311–312

diapering, 310–311

handwashing, 310–311

illness, 305–306, 312–314

policies, 305

Infant personalities, 22

fearful, 37

feisty, 38

flexible, 37

separating, 37–38

Information exchange forms, 429–430

Inside, Outside, Upside Down by Stan & Jan Berenstein, 123, 130, 140

Intellectual development (*See also* Child development)

multiple intelligences, 240–241

Piaget's theory, 231–232, 239–240

Interactive experiences

communicating, 233–234

connecting, 100

expressive feelings, 369–370

innovations in, 22

moving around, 307–308

overview, 446

relating, 166–167

separating, 35–36

Ivory soap, 413, 426

J

Jackets, 124, 139, 158, 222

Jack-in-the-boxes, 26, 148–149, 160, 285, 298

Jars, 26, 65, 118, 135, 418

Jewelry, 25, 74, 284, 340, 405

Johnny Jumpers, 57, 69, 76, 94, 331, 356–357, 364, 401, 407

Johnson, A., 47, 57, 103–104, 118

Johnson, C. N., 19

Jones, E., 43

Jumbo-Shaped Board Books: Tugboat by Wilfred Wood, 411, 416, 425

Junk mail, 267, 278

Just Like Daddy by Frank Asch, 79, 85, 93

K

Kaufman, R., 306

Kendrick, A. S., 306

Key rings, 25

Keys, 124, 139, 146, 158, 160, 210, 222, 224

Kitchen tools, 80, 92, 330, 343

Korner, A. F., 42–43

Kovach, B. A., 103–105

L

La Leche League International, 303

Lally, J. R., 102

Laminate, 29, 141

Language development, 229–231 (*See also* Communicating)

and attachment, 238

expressive, 231

fostering, 238–238

receptive, 231

Laundry baskets, 338

Lavender, 118

Lazy Susan, 357

Leavitt, R. L., 102

Lemon scent, 118, 395

Lighting, 119, 413

Linking Language and Literacy by R. Rockwell, D.

Hoge, & B. Searcy, 243

Literacy possibilities, 22, 27

communicating, 267–269, 286–287

connecting, 129–131, 150–151

expressing feelings, 397–398, 415–417

moving around, 334–335, 354–355

relating, 197–199, 213–214

separating, 58, 65–67, 84–85

using pictures, 29

The Little Engine That Could by Watty Piper, 261, 269, 277

The Little Red Hen by Byron Barton, 191, 198, 205

Logos, 268

Love and Learn by A. Honig, 325

M

Magazines, 29, 80, 130, 154, 170, 211, 214, 218, 244, 267, 344, 346, 360, 364, 383

Making Make-Believe by M. Kohl, 186

Manipulatives, 26, 330, 345

Maps, 222, 344

Marion, M., 315

Markers, 71, 134, 202, 214, 218, 264, 267, 273, 293, 319, 332, 338–339, 345, 350, 360, 421

permanent, 402, 414

washable, 195

Masking tape, 63, 353, 364

Max's Bath by Rosemary Wells, 61, 67, 75, 411, 416, 425

Max's Bedtime by Rosemary Wells, 61, 67, 75

McMullen, M. B., 96, 103

Measuring tapes, 81, 93, 222, 330, 344

Meats, 303

sticks, 155

Messinger, K. P., 306

Metal rings, 129, 197, 206, 224, 267–268, 273, 278, 360

Mid-day reunions, 109

Milk cartons, 170

Milk, 303–304

Mirrors, 26, 56, 64, 76, 119–120, 149, 169, 332–333, 351, 353, 356, 364, 396, 401, 407

Mittens, 74, 265, 405

Mobiles, 26, 56, 134

Moving around, 299–364
    child development, 301–307
    concepts learned, 343, 362, 456–457
    curiosity possibilities, 332–333, 353
    curriculum webs, 327, 347
    dramatic possibilities, 330, 350–351
    environments, 325–326
    interactive experiences, 307–308
    literacy possibilities, 334–335, 354–355
    movement possibilities, 336–338, 356–357
    music possibilities, 335–336, 355–356
    observations/assessment, 300, 439
    outdoor possibilities, 338–339, 358–359
    parent participation, 340–342, 360–361
    parent partnerships, 319–324
    possibilities plans, 327–364
    project possibilities, 339–340, 359–360
    resources, 318, 325, 343–346, 362–364
    sensory/art possibilities, 331–332, 352
    teacher competencies, 318
    teaching, 308–318

Modeling, 171

Moo, Baa, La La La by Sandra Boynton, 281, 287, 297

Moore, Thomas, 289

Mops, 81, 93, 344

More, More, More Said the Baby by Vera Williams, 61, 67, 75

Morris, S. L., 303

Motor skills, 26, 299–364 (*See also* Moving around; Movement possibilities)

The Mouse Party by Bridgette Beguino, 145, 150, 159

Movement possibilities, 27–28
    communicating, 270–271, 290–291
    connecting, 132–133, 153
    expressing feelings, 401, 419
    moving around, 336–338, 356–357
    relating, 200, 216
    separating, 58, 69–70, 86–87

Mud, 86, 419

Muffins, 383

Multiple intelligences, 240–241 (*See also* Child development)
    fostering, 257–258

Music possibilities
    communicating, 269–270, 287–290
    connecting, 123, 131–132, 145, 151–152, 159
    expressing feelings, 399–400, 417–418
    moving around, 335–336, 355–356
    relating, 199, 215–216
    separating, 56, 58, 61, 68–69, 79, 85–86, 93

Music
    ballads, 293
    blues, 293
    classical, 27, 55
    contrast, 288
    instrumental, 288
    jazz, 293
    nature, 412
    opera, 293
    soft, 63, 119, 158
    tapes, 298
    Thomas Moore, 289
    toys, 212

My Five Senses by Aliki, 391, 398, 406

My Five Senses by Jan Belk Monclure, 391, 398, 406

My Home by Bill Thomas & Brian Miller, 61, 67, 75

My Very First Mother Goose Book by Iona Archibald Opie, 261, 268, 277

N

National Academy of Early Childhood Programs, 20

National Association for the Education of Young Children, 18

Natural consequences, 315

postcard, 321

Newspapers, 214, 310, 334, 337, 346

No! No! Jo! by Kate McMullen, 329, 334, 344, 391, 406

No! No! No! by Anne Rockwell, 329, 334, 344, 391, 397–398, 406

Noisemakers, 79, 85, 93–94, 345

Nonverbal cues, 36

Notebooks, 36, 107, 170

Nutrition, 302–304
    solid foods, 309–310
    teaching, 309–310

O

Oatmeal boxes, 128, 140, 205, 298, 407

Object permanence, 100
    postcard, 157

Office materials, 93

On the Day I Was Born by Debbi Chocolate, 61, 66, 75

On the Day You Were Born by Debra Frazer, 261, 269, 277

Oral stimulation, 119

Orange juice cans, 149

Outdoor possibilities, 28, 64, 325–326
    communicating, 272, 292–293
    connecting, 133–134, 154
    expressing feelings, 402, 420
    moving around, 338–339, 358–359
    relating, 201, 216–217
    separating, 58, 70, 88

Outside Inside by Carolyn Crimi, 123, 130, 140

P

Pacifiers, 53

Paintbrushes, 193, 264, 273, 332, 402–403, 420–421, 426

Paints, 56, 64, 147, 193, 211, 264, 273, 332, 352, 358, 402, 414, 421
    finger, 25, 71, 76, 160, 345, 364, 395, 407
    tempera, 76, 345, 364, 403, 407, 413

washable, 202, 402

Palmer, Hap, 85

Pans, 67, 81, 87, 92, 94, 146, 330, 343, 346

Paper bags, 87, 139, 337

Paper plates, 352, 358, 414

Paper, 25, 63–64, 71, 88, 130, 135, 147, 154, 160, 195, 197, 201, 211, 264, 266, 271, 273, 331–333, 337, 339, 350, 352, 358–359, 364, 393, 395–396, 401–403, 413–414
    art, 345, 421
    butcher, 194, 202, 278, 293, 298
    chart, 202
    construction, 127, 132, 170, 395
    disposable, 310
    sandwiches, 276
    scraps, 332, 346
    self-adhesive, 170
    shredded, 394, 407
    strips, 360
    toilet tissue, 413, 426
    wrapping, 397

Parent participation
    communicating, 273–274, 293–295
    connecting, 135–138, 155–157
    expressing feelings, 403–404, 421–424
    moving around, 340–342, 360–361
    relating, 203–204, 218–221
    separating, 48, 58, 72–73, 89–91

Parent partnerships, 13, 23, 28
    communicating, 244–256
    connecting, 108–118
    expressing feelings, 383–386
    moving around, 319–324
    relating, 177–185
    separating, 47–55

Parent postcards, 23, 28
    communicating, 245–256, 275, 294–295, 443
    connecting, 136–138, 156–157, 442
    dissemination schedule, 441–444
    expressing feelings, 384, 404, 423–424
    moving around, 320–324, 341–342, 361, 443, 444

relating, 179–185, 203–204, 219–221, 442–443

separating, 49–54, 72–73, 90–91, 110–117, 441–442

Parents

    communication sheets, 428–430, 432–433

    conferencing, 375–381

    educating, 13

    teas, 198

    validating, 106–107

    visit log, 434

Parten, M. B., 165

Pat the Bunny by Dorothy Kunhardt, 261, 269, 277, 391, 397, 406

Patterning, 171

Peek a Boo by Janet Ahlberg, 61, 67, 75

Peek a Moo by Bernard Most, 281, 287, 297

Peer play. *See* Play; Parten

Pens, 135, 197, 331, 333, 339, 350, 393, 396, 401

Perro Grande, Perro Pequeno by P. D. Eastman, 191, 198, 205

Personality, 37-38

Pete's Puddles by Harriet Roche, 411, 416, 425

Peter's Trucks by Sallie Wolf, 209, 213, 223

Phillips, D. A., 102

Photographs, 29, 38, 48, 56, 61, 65, 88, 134, 149, 154, 334, 340, 346, 359, 383

Physical development, 301–302

Piaget, Jean, 164–165

    intellectual development theory, 231–232, 239–240

Picnic props, 87, 93, 146, 155, 159, 262–263, 276–277

    baskets, 87, 93, 146, 159–160, 277

Picture files

    communicating, 277, 296–297

    connecting, 140, 159

    expressing feelings, 406, 425

    moving around, 344, 363

    relating, 205, 222–223

    separating, 75, 93

Picture necklaces, 340

Pictures, 38, 154, 170, 211, 217, 224, 267, 351, 359, 364, 383

Pillows, 55, 63, 76, 109, 158, 350

Plan making, 173

Plants, 197, 206

Plastic

    bags, 129–130, 159, 198, 206, 214, 224, 311, 360, 412–413, 426

    bottles, 169, 283, 415, 418, 419, 422

    cylinders, 395

    fish, 82, 94

    fruits, 159, 277

    jars, 26, 65, 118, 418

    pipes, 170

    soda bottles, 155, 159–160, 195, 206, 293

    tools, 81, 210, 330

Play gyms, 133, 141, 272, 278, 326, 339, 345

Play, 164–166

    cues, 186–187

    Parten on, 165

    Piaget on, 164–165

    postcard, 203

    props, 186–187

    Vygotsky on, 165–166

Pliers, 81, 330

Pockets, 282, 340, 346

Polar Bear, Polar Bear, What Do You Hear? by Bill Martin, Jr., 281, 287, 297

Popcorn poppers, 291, 298

Pop-up toys, 149, 160, 212, 224, 285, 298

Portfolios, 107, 135

Possibilities plans, 14, 24–29

    Big & Little, 189–206, 454

    Bubbles, Mud & Puddles, 409–426, 459

    Cars, Trucks & Trains, 207–224, 455

    communicating, 259–298

    Competent Me, 327–346, 456

    connecting, 121–160

    expressing feelings, 389–426

    Inside & Outside, 121–141, 452

    Me! 59–76, 450

    moving around, 327–364

Mommies & Daddies, 77–94, 451
Open & Close, 143–160, 453
overview, 445–461
relating, 189–224
resources, 29
Senses, 389–407, 458
separating, 59–94
Sounds, 279–298, 461
Storybook Classics, 259–278, 460
Windows, Walls, Doors, & Hallways, 347–364, 457
Poster board, 197, 206, 214, 217, 263, 278, 340
Pots and Pans by Patricia Hubbell, 61, 67, 75
Pots, 67, 81, 87, 92, 94, 146, 330, 343, 346
	gardening, 202
Powell, D. R., 102
Pre-enrollment visit, 47
Primary teaching, 22
	components, 103
	connecting, 102–103
Problem-solving, 171, 173 (*See also* Curiosity possibilities)
	postcard, 185
Process knowledge, 28–29
Project possibilities, 28
	communicating, 273, 293
	connecting, 134–135, 154–155
	expressing feelings, 402–403, 421
	moving around, 339–340, 359–360
	relating, 202, 217–218
	separating, 58, 71, 88–89
Prop boxes, 29
	boxes, 205
	camping, 79, 93
	cleaning, 79, 93, 343–344, 362, 425
	construction, 79, 93, 222, 344
	cooking, 79, 92
	dress-up, 61–62, 74–75, 405
	gardening, 79, 92
	going places, 146, 158, 222
	good-night, 158
	hats, 205
	in & out, 140
	overview, 447
	picnic, 146, 159, 276–277
	shoes, 205
	shopping, 125, 139
	sounds, 296
	storybooks, 277
	work, 79, 93
Puddles by Jonathan London, 411, 416, 425
Pumpkins, 193, 338
Puppets, 169, 265–266, 277–278, 298, 350, 414–415
Purses, 25, 124–125, 127, 139, 146, 158, 169, 210, 222, 282
Puzzles, 127, 195–196, 266

Q ~ R

Quilts, 55, 133, 153, 155, 159, 170, 218, 272, 277, 292, 339, 407
Rags, 93, 344
Raikes, H., 102
Rain gear, 412, 421
Rain Song by Lezlie Evans, 411, 416, 425
Rain sticks, 296
Raising Good Children by T. Lickona, 186
Raising Self-Reliant Children in a Self-Indulgent World by H. Glenn & J. Nelsen, 186
Rattles, 25, 62, 74, 76, 85, 119, 124, 127, 153, 160, 192, 206, 212, 224, 282, 287, 291, 296, 298, 332, 335, 345, 392, 401, 405, 407, 426
	chime, 417, 426
	food containers, 79, 86, 93
	hammer, 80
	keys, 83, 94
	phone, 83
Reading skills. *See* Literacy possibilities, 27
Receptive language, 231
Recipe cards, 92, 343
Reciprocity, 42, 103–104
	and language development, 229–230
Redirection, 45

Refrigerator, 412

Reisenberg, J., 102

Relating, 18, 161–224

    child development, 164–166

    concepts learned, 204, 222, 454–455

    curiosity possibilities, 195–196, 212–213

    curriculum webs, 189, 207

    dramatic possibilities, 192–193, 210

    environments, 186–188

    interactive experiences, 166–167

    literacy possibilities, 197–199, 213–214

    movement possibilities, 200, 216

    music possibilities, 199, 215–216

    observation/assessment, 162–163, 437

    outdoor possibilities, 201, 216–217

    parent participation, 203–204, 218–221

    parent partnerships, 177–185

    possibilities plans, 190–224

    project possibilities, 202, 217–218

    resources, 176, 186, 205–206, 222–224

    sensory/art possibilities, 193–195, 211

    teacher competencies, 176

    teaching, 167–176

Resources, 23, 29

    communicating, 242–243, 257, 261 276–278, 296–298

    connecting, 108, 118, 139–140, 140–141, 145, 158–160

    expressing feelings, 383, 391, 405–407, 411, 425–426

    moving around, 318, 325, 343–346, 362–364

    relating, 176, 186, 191, 205–206, 209, 222–224

    separating, 47, 55, 74–76, 92–94

Responding to Linguistic and Cultural Diversity by National Association for the Education of Young Children, 243

Rethinking the Brain by R. Shore, 108, 243

Rhymes, 27, 464-468

    "Clap, Clap, Clap Your Hands," 391, 398, 406, 464

    "Eensy Weensy Spider," 191, 199, 205, 263, 465

    "Eye Winker, Tom Thinker," 61, 66, 75, 391, 398, 406, 465

    "How Many Cars Do You See?" 209, 214, 223, 466

    "Humpty Dumpty," 466

    "I See the Moon," 123, 130, 140, 349, 354, 363, 466

    "Jack and Jill," 349, 354, 363, 411, 416, 425, 466

    "Little Boy Blue," 466

    "Little Miss Muffett," 191, 198, 205, 165, 261, 277, 466

    "My Turtle," 467

    "Open, Shut Them," 123, 131, 140, 281, 289, 297, 467

    overview, 447

    "Pat-a-Cake," 79, 86, 93, 261, 270, 277, 329, 344, 349, 356, 363, 467

    "Rub-a-Dub-Dub," 411, 417, 425, 468

    "There Was a Little Turtle," 219, 468

    "This Is My Turtle," 123, 130, 140

    "Where Is Thumbkin?" 145, 152, 159, 468

Rhythm instruments, 291

Ribbon, 197, 206, 224, 421, 426

Riding toys, 201, 206, 216

Rituals

    postcard, 49

    separating, 47

Rocks, 420

Rogers, C. S., 164

Room arrangement. *See* Environments

Routines, 50, 91

Rubber ducks, 418, 426

The Runaway Bunny by Margaret Wise Brown, 261, 269, 277

S

Safety. *See also* Environments; Infant health

    glasses, 222

    postcard, 361

Salt shakers, 414, 422

Sand, 80, 194, 211

Sandals, 74, 405

Sandboxes, 194

Sandpaper, 133, 195–196, 395

Sawyer, J. K., 164

Scarves, 74, 139, 158, 201, 222, 405

Scents, 65, 118, 393, 395

Scheduling

    individualized, 40–41

School bells, 296

Schweinhart, L., 100, 106

Scissors, 127, 130, 154, 194, 195, 201, 214, 262, 266–267, 271, 350, 395, 414

Scooting toys, 216

Scrubbers, 201, 362, 425

Security items, 54

Seeds, 197–198, 202

Self-concept, 59–76

Self-control, 320

Sensory table, 194, 211, 394, 414, 426

Sensory/art possibilities, 25

    communicating, 263–265, 283–284

    connecting, 125–126, 147–148

    expressing feelings, 394–395, 412–414

    moving around, 331–332, 352

    relating, 193–195, 211

    separating, 58, 63–65, 82

Separating, 18, 31–94

    child development, 34–35

    concepts learned, 74, 92, 450–451

    curiosity possibilities, 64–65, 83–84

    curriculum webs, 59, 77

    dramatic possibilities, 62–63, 80–82

    environments, 55–58

    interactive experiences, 35–36

    literacy possibilities, 65–67, 84–85

    movement possibilities, 69–70, 86–87

    music possibilities, 68–69, 85–86

    observation/assessment, 32–33, 435

    outdoor possibilities, 70, 88

    parent participation, 72–73, 89–91

    parent partnerships, 47–55

    possibilities plans, 59–94

    project possibilities, 71, 88–89

    resources, 47, 74–76, 92–94

    sensory possibilities, 63–64, 82

    teaching competencies, 46

    teaching, 37–47

Separation anxiety, 22, 99

    helping, 238–239

    postcard, 250

Shaker bottles, 169, 291

Sheep in a Jeep by Nancy Shaw, 209, 213, 223

Sheets, 76, 81, 93, 141, 159, 277

Shelves, 155, 386

Shoeboxes, 149, 153, 160, 169

Shoes, 74, 140, 146, 158, 192–193, 202, 205, 222, 405

Shopping

    bags, 330, 346

    carts, 87

    lists, 139

    prop boxes, 125, 139

Shore, R., 100, 102, 119, 228

Shovels, 80, 86, 419

Sleeping bags, 81, 93

Slide boxes, 128

Soap, 64, 310–311

    containers, 81, 364, 407

    Ivory, 413, 426

Social development, 22, 164

    postcards, 180–181

Socks, 140, 149, 169, 200, 350, 360, 364, 405, 414

Soda bottles, 155, 159–160, 195, 206, 276, 293, 298, 415

Songs, 29, 464-468

    "A Tisket, a Tasket," 145, 152, 159, 467

    "Animal Fair," 464

    "Ants Go Marching," 464

    "Are You Sleeping?" 61, 68–69, 75, 349, 356, 363, 464

    "Baa, Baa, Black Sheep," 464

    "Baby Bumblebee," 391, 400, 406, 464

    "The Bear Went Over the Mountain," 464

    "B-I-N-G-O," 464

    "Brown Bear," 261, 269, 277

"Bumping Up and Down," 261, 269–271, 277, 464

"Clap, Clap, Clap Your Hands," 464

"Down by the Bay," 464-465

"Drive, Drive, Drive Your Car," 209, 214, 223

"The Eensy Weensy Spider," 261, 269–270, 277, 465

"The Farmer in the Dell," 465

"Five Little Ducks," 411, 418, 425, 465

"Go In and Out the Car," 209, 215, 223

"Go In and Out the Window," 123, 131, 140, 349, 355, 363, 465

"Good Morning to You," 145, 151, 159, 465

"Head, Shoulders, Knees, and Toes," 329, 336, 344, 466

"The Hokey Pokey," 123, 132, 140, 466

"I Went to the Store," 79, 85, 93

"If You're Happy and You Know It," 145, 151, 159, 281, 291, 297, 329, 335–336, 344, 466

"Johnny Works with One Hammer," 61, 68, 75, 465-466

"Mary Had a Little Lamb," 466

"The More We Get Together," 467

"Old MacDonald Had a Farm," 281, 288, 297, 391, 400, 406, 467

"Open, Shut Them," 281, 289, 467

"Rain, Rain, Go Away," 467

"Ring Around the Rosie," 261, 269–270, 277, 467

"Rock-a-Bye, Baby," 467

"Row, Row, Row Your Boat," 281, 292, 297, 411, 417, 425, 467

"Shake It All Around," 319

"Twinkle, Twinkle Little Star," 191, 199, 205, 468

"The Wheels on the Bus," 209, 215–216, 223, 464

"Where Is Baby?" 391, 399, 406

"Where Is Thumbkin?" 281, 289–290, 297, 391, 399, 406, 468

Sorting toys, 26, 169

Sound props, 296

Sound toys, 224

Spitting up, 305

Sponges, 359, 360, 364, 420, 426

Spools, 169–170

Spray bottles, 81, 133, 201, 330

Squeak toys, 282, 296, 298

Squeegees, 359, 360, 364

Squirt bottles, 344, 359–360, 403, 412, 426

Start Smart by P. Schiller, 257

Starting Small by Teaching Tolerance Project, 47

Sticky dots, 194

Stimulation, 119
    intellectual development, 234–243
    oral, 119

Stonehouse, A., 102, 104

Stools, 28

Stranger anxiety, 99–100

Streamers, 134

String, 26, 65, 88, 170, 212, 283, 357, 412

Strollers, 70, 272, 358, 364

Stroufe, L. E., 100

Sun hats, 92

Sunglasses, 74, 92, 222, 405

Sunscreen bottles, 222

Symbolic play. See Dramatic possibilities

T

Taking turns, 172

Talking With Your Baby by A. Honig & H. E. Brody, 243

Tape players, 278, 282, 288–289, 292–293, 401

Tape, 64–65, 86, 88, 130, 132, 147, 149, 153–154, 169–170, 194–196, 198–199, 201–202, 212, 217, 264, 271, 283, 284, 334–335, 351–352, 357–358, 360, 392–393, 395, 397, 401–403, 412–413, 415, 418–419, 421
    duct, 360
    masking, 63, 353, 364
    packing, 337
    poster, 359

Tapestry, 118

Teacher competencies, 23
  communicating, 243
  connecting, 108
  expressing feelings, 382
  moving around, 318
  relating, 176
  separating, 46
Teacher observation, 13–14, 18–21
  communicating, 226–227, 438
  connecting, 96–97, 436
  expressing feelings, 366–367, 440
  for assessment, 18–19
  instrument, 32–33
  moving around, 300, 439
  overview, 446
  relating, 162–163, 437
  separation anxiety, 32–33, 435
  using, 21
Teaching innovations, 23
  communicating, 234–243
  conferencing, 375–381
  connecting, 102–108
  crying, 42–44
  developmental challenges, 236–237
  developmental growth, 235–236
  discipline, 44–45, 171–176, 374–375
  discriminate attachment, 167
  expressing feelings, 370–383
  families, 38–39
  floor time, 372–373
  gradual enrollment, 39–40
  independence, 308–309
  individual scheduling, 40–41
  infant temperament, 37–38
  making toys, 168–171
  maximizing interactions, 41–42
  moving around, 308–318
  nutrition, 309–310
  preventing child abuse, 381–382
  prosocial behavior, 168
  relating, 167–176
  separating, 37–47

  stimulating emotional development, 370–372
  supporting creativity, 373–374
Teddy bears, 262–263, 265, 268–269, 271–272, 277, 278
Teething biscuits, 155
Telephones, 83, 94, 282, 333, 345
Temperament, 37-38
Tempera paints, 76, 345, 364, 403, 407, 413
Texture blocks, 170
Thank-you notes, 383
Thoman, E. B., 42–43
Thomas the Tank Engine by Wilbur & Vera Awdry, 209, 213, 223
Thomas the Tank Engine Coming and Going by Wilbur & Vera Awdry, 209, 213, 223
Thomas, A., 37
Thumb-sucking, 308
  postcard, 51
Thundercake by Patricia Polacco, 281, 286, 297
The Tiny Seed by Eric Carle, 191, 198, 205
Toilet paper, 413, 426
Tool belts, 210
Tools of the Mind by E. Bodrova & D. J. Leong, 243
Tools
  gardening, 92
  plastic, 81, 210, 330, 344, 345
Toothpaste, 412–413, 426
Touch Me by Eve Witte & Pat Witte, 391, 397, 406
Touchpoints by T. B. Brazelton, 55, 386
Towels, 62, 64, 81, 92–93, 109, 126, 330, 343–344
  paper, 310–311
Toy bars, 25, 56
Toys, 29, 125, 126, 149, 192, 206, 224, 277, 386, 397
  hanging, 170
  making, 168–171
  swap, 177
  teacher made, 168-171
Tracking tubes, 396
Trading, 172

Training, 13

Trains by Byron Barton, 209, 213, 223

Transition, 36

    postcards, 50, 136–137

Triangulation, 186–187

Trucks by Byron Barton, 209, 213, 223

Trucks by Mallory Loehr, 209, 213, 223

Trucks, 93, 194, 200–201, 206, 211, 224, 330, 344–345

Tub toys, 62

Tubs, 25, 62–63, 70, 76, 80, 82, 86, 92, 125–126, 141, 201, 206, 292, 331, 394, 407, 419–420, 426

Turntables, 357, 364

U ~ V

Vacuum toys, 362, 425

Values, 204

Vegetables, 303, 343

The Very Busy Spider by Eric Carle, 261, 277

The Very Hungry Caterpillar by Eric Carle, 261, 266, 277

Visit logs, 109

Vocabulary files, 29

    communicating, 277, 296–297

    connecting, 140, 159

    expressing feelings, 406, 425

    moving around, 344, 363

    relating, 205, 222–223

    separating, 75, 93

Vygotsky, 165–166

W

Wading pools, 25, 82, 126, 331

Wagons, 216, 262, 271, 338

Walking away, 172–173

Walking charts, 340

Wallets, 125, 158

Wallpaper, 339, 346

    sample books, 170

Washcloths, 62, 70, 81, 201, 311, 330, 362, 420, 425–426

Water bottles, 159, 203, 276, 298

Water toys, 25, 292

Water, 25, 57, 62, 64, 70, 81–82, 119, 125–126, 133, 155, 160, 193, 195, 201, 263, 292, 303, 311, 315, 330, 359, 393, 402–403, 413–415, 419–420

Watering cans, 217, 224, 263

Webs. *See* Curriculum webs

Weikert, D. P., 100, 106

What Daddies Do Best by Laura Numeroff, 79, 85, 93

What Do Babies Do? by Debby Slier, 61, 67, 75

What Mommies Do Best by Laura Numeroff, 79, 85, 93

What to Expect in the First Year by A. Eisenberg, 55

Whitebrook, M., 102

Who Says "Quack"? by Jerry Smith, 281, 287, 297

Why Children Misbehave by C. Adams & E. Fruge, 318, 325

Will I Have a Friend? by Miriam Cohen, 123, 129, 140

Wind chimes, 292, 298

Windows, 350, 386, 413

Wong, D. L., 303

Work props, 79, 93

Working with Emotional Intelligence by D. Goleman, 383

Written documentation, 36, 109, 273

    anecdotal record forms, 428

    books read list, 431

    formal conferences, 377–378

    informal conferences, 378–379

    information exchange forms, 429–430

    note calendar, 177

    suspected abuse, 382–382

Y

Yarn, 65, 88, 129, 197, 206, 217, 224, 267–268, 273, 278, 340, 360

You Can't Catch Me by Rosanne Litzinger, 329, 334, 344

You Go Away by Dorothy Corey, 79, 84, 93

Your Baby and Child by P. Leach, 55

Your Self-Confident Baby by M. Gerber & A. Johnson, 47